MUSICALITY IN THEATRE

ASHGATE INTERDISCIPLINARY STUDIES IN OPERA

The *Ashgate Interdisciplinary Studies in Opera* series provides a centralized and prominent forum for the presentation of cutting-edge scholarship that draws on numerous disciplinary approaches to a wide range of subjects associated with the creation, performance, and reception of opera (and related genres) in various historical and social contexts. There is great need for a broader approach to scholarship about opera. In recent years, the course of study has developed significantly, going beyond traditional musicological approaches to reflect new perspectives from literary criticism and comparative literature, cultural history, philosophy, art history, theatre history, gender studies, film studies, political science, philology, psycho-analysis, and medicine. The new brands of scholarship have allowed a more comprehensive interrogation of the complex nexus of means of artistic expression operative in opera, one that has meaningfully challenged prevalent historicist and formalist musical approaches. The *Ashgate Interdisciplinary Studies in Opera* series continues to move this important trend forward by including essay collections and monographs that reflect the ever-increasing interest in opera in non-musical contexts. Books in the series will be linked by their emphasis on the study of a single genre—opera—yet will be distinguished by their individualized and novel approaches by scholars from various disciplines/fields of inquiry. The remit of the series welcomes studies of seventeenth century to contemporary opera from all geographical locations, including non-Western topics.

Musicality in Theatre
Music as Model, Method and Metaphor in Theatre-Making

DAVID ROESNER

Routledge
Taylor & Francis Group

LONDON AND NEW YORK

First Published 2014 by Ashgate Publisher

Published 2016 by Routledge
2 Park Square, Milton Park, Abingdon, Oxfordshire OX14 4RN
711 Third Avenue, New York, NY 10017, USA

First issued in paperback 2016

Routledge is an imprint of the Taylor & Francis Group, an informa business

British Library Cataloguing in Publication Data
A catalogue record for this book is available from the British Library

The Library of Congress has cataloged the printed edition as follows:
Roesner, David.
  Musicality in theatre: music as model, method and metaphor in theatre-making / by David Roesner.
    pages cm. -- (Ashgate interdisciplinary studies in opera)
  Includes bibliographical references and index.
  ISBN 978-1-4094-6101-2 (hardcover: alk. paper)
1. Music in the theater. 2. Theater -- Production and
direction. I. Title.

  MT960.R37 2014
  782.1--dc23

                                                          2013051048

ISBN 13: 978-1-138-24838-0 (pbk)
ISBN 13: 978-1-4094-6101-2 (hbk)

For Christina, Vincent and Laurenz

Contents

List of Figures

Series Editor's Preface

Ashgate Interdisciplinary Studies in Opera provides a centralized and prominent forum for the presentation of cutting-edge scholarship that draws on numerous disciplinary approaches on a wide range of subjects associated with the creation, performance, dissemination, and reception of opera and related genres in various historical and social contexts. The series includes topics from the seventeenth century to the present and from all geographical locations, including non-Western traditions.

In recent years, the field of opera studies has not only come into its own but has developed significantly, going beyond traditional musicological approaches to reflect new perspectives from literary criticism and comparative literature, cultural history, philosophy, art history, theater history, gender studies, film studies, political science, philology, psychoanalysis, and even medicine. The new brands of scholarship have allowed a more comprehensive and intensive interrogation of the complex nexus of means of artistic expression operative in opera, one that has meaningfully challenged prevalent historicist and formalist musical approaches. Today, interdisciplinary, or as some prefer cross-disciplinary, opera studies are receiving increasingly widespread attention, and the ways in which scholars, practitioners, and the public think about the artform known as opera continue to change and expand. *Ashgate Interdisciplinary Studies in Opera* seeks to move this important trend forward by including essay collections and monographs that reflect the ever-increasing interest in opera in various contexts.

However, *Musicality in Theatre: Music as Model, Method and Metaphor in Theatre-Making* branches out beyond this conception of opera studies to deal with dramatic theater as a concept writ large. Opera is, of course, one of the manifestations of the concept, but the volume does not focus on opera as it is commonly recognized. Rather, the author more generally addresses musicality as an aesthetic *dispositif* through which to understand the processes of various genres of theatrical drama. The idea of 'opera' is never far below the surface here; it remains a point of reference throughout the volume with the 'operatic' underlying much of the discussion and serving as a model for investigating how the aural and the visual, as well as the theoretical and the practical, intersect. Challenging interdisciplinary boundaries, Roesner explores the fluid relationships between opera, musical theater, and theater *tout court* to demonstrate the ways in which music has continued to be influential in developments of theatrical forms. By tracing these relationships from the perspective of theater history in the modern and post-modern period, the author has produced a timely project that contributes new views and opens the way for further enquiry about music and the stage.

Roberta Montemorra Marvin

Acknowledgements

All books even if 'single-authored', are always also the result of constellations of collective creativity and support. Great thanks are therefore due to all those who formed the specific constellation for this book. An initial survey of my research topic through SCUDD – the Standing Conference of Drama Departments UK – provided very helpful responses and starting points. At the University of Exeter I was supported wonderfully by my drama colleagues, in particular Prof. Mick Mangan, Prof. Graham Ley, Dr Jane Milling and Dr Rebecca Loukes, and inspired by my students and PhD supervisees. My new drama department at the University of Kent provided a very welcoming and interested environment, which helped me to finish the book despite the normal turmoil of changing location.

While writing the book I was also able to share preliminary ideas in a range of encounters all of which have helped to question and refocus my thinking and have added interesting angles. In particular, these were workshops I gave at the University of Agder, Kristiansand; the Deutsches Theater Berlin; Exeter Performers Playground; Körber Studio Junge Regie, Hamburg; and conference papers at University of the Arts, Zurich; Birmingham Conservatoire; TAPRA 2012 at University of Kent; the Conference of the German Society for Theatre Studies 2012 at Bayreuth; and the colloquium of CNRS/ARIAS at the University of Montreal.

In preparing the final manuscript Dr Lynne Kendrick's proofing and feedback, Solomon Lennox's assistance with illustration rights, and Katherine Murray's assistance with indexing were of great help, as was the editorial team at Ashgate, all of whom I owe thanks. I am also much indebted to the Arts and Humanities Research Council (AHRC), which generously funded a significant part of my writing time and travel costs with a fellowship grant. And finally I am immensely thankful to my family and friends for enriching my life in a wonderful wide range of ways and for all the loving support they provide.

Introduction
Premises and Promises

Setting the Scene

When telling people about this book project, I was often asked: so, is this a book about opera, music-theatre or musicals? For the sake of clarity, then, I should say that it is not. It is a book about dramatic theatre, or what the German-speaking world curiously calls Sprechtheater (literally 'speaking theatre', as opposed to kinds of theatre where singing or dancing dominate). In order to maintain focus and coherence, I will concentrate mostly on European theatre from the historic avant-garde until today, and while I cover a range of theatrical forms, from text-based, character-driven drama to surreal, anti-psychological or postdramatic theatre as well as improvised and/or devised forms of theatrical performance, there is a uniting element in the experimental, reformatory, sometimes revolutionary nature of the practices under investigation. Specifically, I set out to trace the central role that music has had until today in innovating theatre: to demonstrate how music as model, method and metaphor in theatre-making has made a vital and lasting impact.[1] I call this the 'musicality dispositif' and will come back to this notion shortly. Before I do, it is worth setting the scene by establishing the context for this dispositif between conflicting tendencies of separation vs. amalgamation of art forms, as well as carefully stripping the idea of 'musicality' of some of its less helpful layers.

While the focus of the book is on dramatic theatre, the idea of 'opera' remains a constant if sometimes unspoken reference point throughout this book: the discourses and practices discussed here touch on core questions of the operatic, reflecting the relationship of music and dramatic representation, suggesting models for the interplay of sonic and visual elements of the stage as well as the relationship of acting and directing with musicianship. The theatrical practices in question have often been informed by opera and vice versa. Most of the practitioners I am going to discuss in this book have continuously engaged with both theatre and opera. Appia's engagement with Wagner is an obvious case in point, but we can also look to Meyerhold's opera direction, Beckett's or Jelinek's libretti for operatic works or the tendency of contemporary actors or directors whom we may associate strongly with 'musicality' (Katie Mitchell, Christoph Marthaler, Robert Wilson, Joseph Bierbichler, Graham F. Valentine, to name but a few) to travel back and forth between theatre and opera productions or deliberately attempt to

---

[1] That said, I do, however, think – as I will explain in the conclusion – that the idea of musicality I suggest here can offer a valuable perspective to all kinds of theatrical genres and even further to other artforms or disciplines in the humanities.

dissolve their all too rigid distinction. Still, the *discourses* of musical qualities and their value in theatre-making rarely refer to opera directly: the notion of music serving as a model is most often instrumental music (from baroque, classical and romantic music to popular styles such as jazz and rock). Paraphrasing Nick Till, one could say that quite a few of the practices analyzed here can be described as operatic, as long as they are not called opera.[2]

This book, then, also stretches the idea of what 'opera' is: many of its case studies *implicitly* call the clear distinction between genres or art forms such as theatre, opera, concert or dance into question, and the differences are more often than not contextual rather than intrinsic. In an ontological sense opera might then simply mean 'work' (Robert Wilson, for example, has used the term in that way based on its etymology). The practices discussed in this book have, however, traditionally been characterized and categorized as 'theatre'. And while it is within this context that musicality is particularly extensively investigated and experimented with, I suggest that this concept would equally benefit the canon of thought on opera and the operatic from which it is largely absent.

Two Paradigms, Both Alike in Dignity

Theatre has always been a hybrid art form. From its beginnings in ancient Greece, which combined speech, song, music and dance, to today's multimedial and multimodal spectacles, theatre history is, amongst many other things, a history of ever-changing relationships and interplays of different artistic practices, aesthetic materials and influences, modes of creation, reception and semiosis.

Historically and culturally, different theatrical conventions and hierarchies have developed, privileging at times the visual and spectacular aspects of performance (as in medieval religious plays), the poetry of the spoken word (as in Jean Racine's tragedies), the physical and even visceral immediacy of performance (for example in Antonin Artaud's, Jerzy Grotowski's or Eugenio Barba's theatrical experiments) or the aural and temporal aspects of theatre, which explore its analogy to music (as in Christoph Marthaler's or Gardzienice's stage creations).

But while theatre has always had the tendency and capacity to encompass, interact with and be influenced by other, 'purer' art forms, such as music, literature, poetry, painting, sculpture, architecture and photography, there seems to have been a continuous tension between two paradigms: the notion of separate, distinct art forms on the one hand, and the thrust towards close relations, cross-fertilization, synthesis and even amalgamation of different artistic practices and techniques on the other, which reoccur under different names and ideological and aesthetic premises throughout history. For the relationship between music and theatre, for

---

    [2]   Nicholas Till, '"I don't mind if something's operatic, just as long it's not opera". A Critical Practice for New Opera and Music Theatre', *Contemporary Theatre Review*, 14/1 (2004), pp. 15–24.

example, Claudio Monteverdi's 'dramma per musica' (1607), Richard Wagner's 'Gesamtkunstwerk' (1849) or Mauricio Kagel's 'Instrumentales Theater' (1960) are but a few examples. Opera in general has, of course, always been by definition one of the key art forms to steer against the purist tendencies and promote a truly interdisciplinary form, but ironically the conventional *practice* of opera-making has often perpetuated the segregation by establishing clearly defined and demarcated roles which deal exclusively with either the one or the other aspect (theatre being the domain of librettist and director; music that of the composer and conductor).

The paradigm of the separation of the arts, I would argue, has been particularly successful and influential on an *institutional* level: theatres, conservatories and drama schools, college and university departments, newspaper, radio and internet critics and ticket subscription schemes (like the popular *abonnements* in German, French or Swiss theatre, which usually are specifically for theatre, ballet/dance or opera performances). All these are very often characterized by clear distinctions between practical and theoretical disciplines, job divisions and/ or marketing strategies relating to a sustained notion of separate art forms with distinct requirements, with regard to training, production, reception, and critical and academic evaluation and analysis. The separation in arts education dates back to the sixteenth century with the foundation of academies for the arts and has had a strong impact on founding separate institutions and erecting separate buildings for theatre, opera, ballet/dance, visual arts and concerts. The driving forces behind this are well known: securing the authority that comes with specialisms, an acute awareness of different materialities and ontologies,[3] an interest in measurable excellence in specialized modes of artistic performance and, finally, the notion of marketability and distinct consumer behaviour: here, the diversification of culture as a product has thus gone hand in hand with the individualism of a capitalist society.

Despite these compelling reasons and forces towards the paradigm of separation, there has been a continuous stream of discursive contributions in artistic practices and theoretical discourse that has in many different ways amounted to a synthetic paradigm. (Daniel Albright's book *Untwisting the Serpent* [2000] is a particularly interesting and far-reaching collection and analysis of this discourse.) In the case of the relationship of music and theatre, these propositions start with Plato, who according to music historian Wayne Bowman did not distinguish music very clearly from other art forms like dance, visual arts, speech or rhetoric. Instead, boundaries between these art forms were conceived to be very fluid

---

[3] This discussion culminated in Gotthold Ephraim Lessing's seminal *Laokoon* essay (1766). See Erika Fischer-Lichte's introduction in Fischer-Lichte/Kristiane Hasselmann/ Markus Rautzenberg (eds.), *Ausweitung der Kunstzone* (Bielefeld, 2010), pp. 7–29, and Daniel Albright's chapter 'Laocoön Revisited' in his book *Untwisting the Serpent: Modernism in Music, Literature, and Other Arts* (Chicago, IL/London, 2000), pp. 5–33, for more detailed discussions of Lessing's essay.

or non-existent.[4] Similarly, scholars agree that what constitutes the birth of theatre was not the logocentric, text-based drama we have later accepted as prototypical, but a 'unity of speech, music and dance'.[5] When tracing the history of theatre further, it becomes evident, as Erika Fischer-Lichte has pointed out, that at least in Europe 'certain hierarchies between the arts have most often been in place, but rarely to the extent of excluding arts such as music altogether'.[6] On turning thus from theatre's beginnings to its most recent developments, it becomes apparent that, again, we are faced with a wide and vibrant range of interplays of the arts and correspondingly quite a strong academic interest in these, despite the continuing separation on institutional levels. Theatre scholars have increasingly focused on the breaking of artistic boundaries, on interart relationships, and on inter-, trans- and intradisciplinary methods of analysis.[7] All these, however, would not have been notable or noteworthy without the backdrop of a shared understanding of clear differences and boundaries between art forms and their related educational and academic disciplines and institutions.

---

[4]   See Wayne D. Bowman, *Philosophical Perspectives on Music* (Oxford, 1998), p. 21.

[5]   Karl-Heinz Göttert, *Geschichte der Stimme* (München, 1998), p. 44. (All translations are mine unless noted otherwise.) See also Siegfried Melchinger, *Die Welt als Tragödie. Bd. 1: Aischylos, Sophokles* (München, 1979) and Graham Ley, *The Theatricality of Greek Tragedy: Playing Space and Chorus* (Chicago, 2007).

[6]   Erika Fischer-Lichte, *Theaterwissenschaft* (Tübingen, 2010), p. 195.

[7]   See, for example, Gabriele Brandstetter/Helga Finter/Markus Weßendorf (eds.), *Grenzgänge. Das Theater und die anderen Künste* (Tübingen, 1998); David Cecchetto et al., *Collision: Interarts Practice and Research* (Newcastle, 2008); Freda Chapple/ Chiel Kattenbelt, *Intermediality in Theatre and Performance* (Amsterdam, 2006); Erika Fischer-Lichte/Kristiane Hasselmann/Markus Rautzenberg, *Ausweitung der Kunstzone* (Bielefeld 2010); Guido Hiß, *Synthetische Visionen* (München, 2005); Marianne Kesting, 'Musikalisierung des Theaters – Theatralisierung der Musik', *Melos – Zeitschrift für neue Musik*, 3 (1969): 101–9; Ulla Britta Lagerroth/Hans Lund/Erik Hedling (eds.), *Interart Poetics: Essays on the Interrelations of the Arts and Media* (Amsterdam, 1997); Eckart Liebau/Jörg Zirfas, *Die Sinne und die Künste: Perspektiven ästhetischer Bildung* (Bielefeld, 2008); Petra Maria Meyer, Intermedialität des Theaters. Entwurf einer Semiotik der Überraschung (Düsseldorf, 2001); Alison Oddey, *Re-Framing the Theatrical. Interdisciplinary Landscapes for Performance* (Basingstoke, 2007); Stephen Pierson, 'Cognitive Science and the Comparative Arts: Implications for Theory and Pedagogy' (2001), http://www.cognitivecircle.org/ct&lit/CogCircleResearch/CogLit_Pedag.html   [10.01.10]; Irina Rajewsky, *Intermedialität* (Tübingen, 2002); Matthias Rebstock/David Roesner (eds.), *Composed Theatre* (Bristol, 2012); David Roesner, *Theater als Musik* (Tübingen, 2003); David Roesner, 'Musikalisches Theater – Szenische Musik', in Anno Mungen (ed.), *Mitten im Leben. Musiktheater von der Oper bis zur Everyday-Performance mit Musik* (Würzburg, 2011): 193–211; Reinhard Josef Sacher, *Musik als Theater. Tendenzen zur Grenzüberschreitung in der Musik von 1958–1968* (Regensburg, 1985); Günther Schnitzler/ Edelgard Spaude (eds.), *Intermedialität. Studien zur Wechselwirkung zwischen den Künsten* (Freiburg im Breisgau, 2004).

This book sits somewhere between those two 'master narratives' or paradigms: it explores how the theatre, while being for the most part acknowledged by its creators and recipients as a distinct art form, sought to reinvigorate, reform and revolutionize itself by invoking a sense of 'musicality'[8] as a vital component and aspect of its creation. Paradoxically, I will thus investigate how practitioners – across very different cultural and historical contexts – sought to 're-theatricalize'[9] the theatre by using ideas, 'frames'[10] and techniques from another art form: music.[11] Michael Chekhov, for example, uses the following motto for one of the chapters of his seminal work *To the Actor* (1953): 'Each art constantly strives to resemble music (W. Paret).'[12] This has strong echoes of the perhaps better-known dictum by art historian Walter Pater from 1873: 'All art constantly aspires towards the condition of music',[13] and of course Friedrich Nietzsche's influential idea of the birth of tragedy out of the spirit of music in his eponymous book *Die Geburt der Tragödie aus dem Geiste der Musik* from 1872.[14]

Taking this last date as a starting point,[15] I will investigate how reformers and revolutionists of the theatre have integrated a sense of musicality into process and performance, how they have idealized and functionalized *their* ideas and ideals of music for their visions of theatre, both towards utopian designs as well as concrete practices. The period between approximately 1870 and today is particularly – but not exclusively – suited to this approach. The orientation towards music was one of the important drivers for the avant-garde, but also for post-modern or postdramatic theatre developments from the 1960s until today. As Brauneck remarks, one of the

---

8   I will explore this term in detail below.

9   As Manfred Brauneck reminds us, 'the central idea of Copeau's theatre reform was the "re-theatricalization" of theatre, a term taken from Georg Fuchs's reformatory programmatic' (Manfred Brauneck, *Theater im 20. Jahrhundert* [Reinbeck bei Hamburg, 1998 (1982)], p. 83).

10   Erving Goffman, *Frame Analysis: An Essay on the Organization of Experience* (London, 1974).

11   A similar study could of course be written with a focus on visual arts or film as key reference points and drivers for theatrical innovation. There have already been attempts in this direction, such as: Peter Simhandl (ed.), *Bildertheater. Bildende Künstler des 20. Jahrhunderts als Theaterreformer* (Berlin, 1993); and Robert Knopf (ed.), *Theatre and Film. A Comparative Anthology* (New Haven and London, 2005).

12   Michael Chekhov, *To the Actor. On the Technique of Acting* (London, 2002 [1953]), p. 95. Not having found a 'W. Paret', I assume this is a typographical error and the quotation is actually a version of Walter Pater's dictum.

13   Walter Pater, *The Renaissance. Studies in Art and Poetry* (Oxford/New York, 1986 [1873]), p. 87.

14   See also Mario Frendo, 'Embodied Musicality: Nietzsche, Grotowski, and Musicalized Processes in Theatre Making', *Studies in Musical Theatre*, 7/2 (2013), pp. 207–19.

15   Christopher Balme makes the same choice for his anthology of reformatory theatre writings *Das Theater von Morgen* (Würzburg, 1988), looking at modernism in theatre between 1870 and 1920.

common characteristics of the theatre reformers of the late nineteenth and early twentieth centuries was their 'orientation towards Friedrich Nietzsche's outline of a new aesthetic':

> Nietzsche's formula of a theatre from 'the spirit of music' indicated the direction of this development. Music became a new aesthetic paradigm, in which the programmatic anti-rationalism of this movement manifested itself.[16]

This makes the avant-garde a good point of departure for this study, even though the influence of music on other art forms was already very strong in earlier periods. Here, however, theatre was less strongly the site where notions of musicality took hold; rather it was architecture in the Renaissance (Alberti, Palladio,[17] for example), or literature and poetry in the classical and romantic period (Goethe, Kleist, Hoffmann, for example) that 'aspired to the condition of music'.

Three aspects of this study of musicality in theatre[18] will be the through-lines of this book in terms of perspective, methodology and focus.

a. The concentration on theatre *processes*: I will investigate the interplay of musicality and theatre, particularly at the stage of conception, creation, composition and rehearsal; this forms the 'genetic' aspect of how I approach the material.[19]

b. A dual understanding of music as model/method and metaphor. One could also speak, with reference to Ferdinand de Saussure, of the *parole* and the *langue* of music:[20] the actual manifestation of music as a concrete idiom (model, method) and the abstract idea of music and its potentiality (metaphor). 'Metaphor' in this context is just shorthand for a wider range of 'non-literal' relations to musical aesthetics – these may well also take the form of a simile, analogy or correspondence:[21] I will thus analyze the actual music or musical practices that theatre practitioners have used, incorporated and interacted with, but also how their *ideas* of music – i.e. music as an aesthetic principle and notion – have influenced their theatre work; here, I focus on the musicological and music aesthetic aspects of the material.

---

[16]   Brauneck, *Theater im 20. Jahrhundert*, p. 63.

[17]   See for example Robin Maconie, *The Concept of Music* (Oxford, 1990), pp. 158–66 for a detailed discussion of the musicality in Palladio's architecture.

[18]   When speaking of 'musicality in theatre', I refer both to musicality for theatre as an art form as well as for *the* theatre as a concrete, if ephemeral, event, as well as an institution and/or edifice.

[19]   See Josette Féral, 'Introduction: Towards a Genetic Study of Performance – Take 2', *Theatre Research International*, 33 (2008): 223-33; Gay McAuley, *Not Magic But Work: An Ethnographic Account of a Rehearsal Process* (Manchester, 2012) or Annemarie Matzke, *Arbeit am Theater: Eine Diskursgeschichte der Probe* (Bielefeld, 2012) for a genetic approach to performance, or, as I would call it, a process analysis approach.

[20]   See Ferdinand de Saussure, *Cours de linguistique générale* (Paris, 1922).

[21]   I will discuss these in more detail later in this introduction.

It is worth noting here that despite this kind of contextualization of theatre-makers' endeavours within the musical aesthetics and musical developments of their time, it is one of my contentions that the directors, actors and writers in question draw on quite an eclectic pool of musical ideas across styles and epochs rather than always relating to the latest musical developments of their contemporary composers or theorists. You frequently find, for example, references to 'symphonies' and 'sonatas'[22] long after these forms were most influential in music.

c. A discussion of the artists' intentions, manifestos and proclamations: how are music and theatre integrated at the level of what the artists say about their work, their programmatic writings? I ask, in other words, how music impacts on the reflection and vocabulary of theatre-making. This is where I concentrate on analyzing discourse in relation to the material.

Before I start my investigation, I need to evaluate the critical term that underpins this whole study and that I deliberately employ in a somewhat contrary manner to its everyday use: musicality. I will try to make this term productive, for the context of theatre, beyond its use in music or music education, and will suggest an even wider potential in the conclusion.

Musicality – From a Normatively Descriptive to a Heuristic Concept

For a long time, practitioners and theorists of the theatre have employed a range of concepts derived literally or metaphorically from music as an art form. They have, for example, claimed that the theatre lighting 'should touch the spectator as does music. Light must have its own rhythm, the score of light can be composed on the same principle as that of the sonata'.[23] They have approached acting like a jazz improvisation (Joseph Chaikin[24]) or directing a theatre ensemble like a conductor would work with an orchestra (J.W. Goethe, according to Pius Alexander Wolff[25]).

---

[22] Kurt Schwitters's *Ur-Sonate* or Jean Tardieu's *La Sonate*, for example.

[23] Meyerhold in Anatoly Antohin, 'Meyerhold Biomechanics' (2005), http://biomechanics.vtheatre.net/meyer.html [17.08.2011].

[24] See Joseph Chaikin, *The Presence of the Actor* (New York, 1972).

[25] Dieter Borchmeyer writes: 'Pius Alexander Wolff says in his writings "Über den Vortrag im Trauerspiel" ["On declamation in tragedy"]: "The way in which Goethe staged a piece of dramatic writing was quite like that of a director of music, and he loved to use music as a model for all the rules he prescribed and to speak of it as a parable in all his instructions. The declamation was directed by him during rehearsals just like you would rehearse an opera. The tempi, the fortes and pianos, the crescendo and diminuendo, etc. would be determined by him and supervised with the most conscientious strictness." In actual fact it says in Goethe's rules [for actors, DR], that one could call "the art of declaiming a prosaic tonal art", which generally had a lot of "analogies" with music' (Dieter Borchmeyer, 'Saat von Göthe gesäet ... Die "Regeln für Schauspieler" – ein theatergeschichtliches Gerücht', in Wolfgang F. Bender [ed.], *Schauspielkunst im 18. Jahrhundert* [Stuttgart, 1992], pp. 261–87, p. 275). See also Beate A. Schmidt/Detlef Altenburg (eds.), *Musik und Theater um 1800* (Sinzig/Rhein, 2012).

They have at times sought to instil the theatre with a sense of musicality from the outside, or to evoke or 'excavate' what T. Nikki Cesare calls the 'inherent musicality of theatrical performance'.[26]

In order to make the term 'musicality' productive for a discussion and analysis of theatre processes and qualities of performance, it is important to redefine it and disentangle it from its more common use as a descriptor of individual musical ability. This is what Mary Louise Serafine in her cognitive theory of music refers to as 'music as "trait"'.[27] She elaborates:

> Some proclivity called musicality or musical talent, aptitude, ability, or intelligence is held to exist inside a person as a central core or germ and to be responsible for the person's activity in music.[28]

This developmental aspect of an individual's musical ability is not only unhelpful for the following study, but also in itself problematical. Musicality is often ascertained according to a very limited set of measurable factors, such as the 'discrimination of pitch and timing differences',[29] an approach which, in my view, fails to encompass a more holistic view of music as an art form. But even with those limited tests for musicality as an ability, it seems that 'experts in the field have historically been unable to agree on what musicality is, what its components are, and how it should be measured'.[30] In addition, there is a considerable strand of musicologists, pedagogues and ethnographers who convincingly claim that musicality is a *universal* human trait, and that the 'human capacity for musicality is integral to the human capacity for culture'.[31] The music pedagogue Heinrich Jacoby, for example, criticized as early as the 1920s the judgmental notion of a sense of 'musicality' that was primarily derived from striving towards the benchmarks of high art. He put forward a notion of musicality as being a general expressive capacity of all human beings, comparable to their mother tongue.[32] More recently, Oliver Sacks has supported this view from

---

26   T. Nikki Cesare, '"Like a chained man's bruise": The Mediated Body in Eight Songs for a Mad King and Anatomy Theater', *Theatre Journal*, 58 (2006), pp. 437–57, p. 439.

27   Mary Louise Serafine, *Music as Cognition* (New York, 1988), pp. 7–12.

28   Serafine, *Music as Cognition*, pp. 7–8

29   Susan E. Trehub, 'The Developmental Origins of Musicality', *Nature Neuroscience*, 6/7 (2003), pp. 669–73, p. 669.

30   Serafine, *Music as Cognition*, p. 10.

31   Ian Cross, 'Musicality and the human capacity for culture' [preprint], published in: *Musicae Scientiae, Special Issue: Narrative in music and interaction* (2008), pp. 147–67, http://www.mus.cam.ac.uk/~ic108/PDF/IRMC_MS07_2.pdf [29.12.2009]. In addition to Cross, Heinrich Jacoby, *Jenseits von 'Musikalisch' und 'Unmusikalisch': Die Befreiung der schöpferischen Kräfte dargestellt am Beispiele der Musik* (Hamburg, 1984 [1921–1927]) and John Blacking, *How Musical is Man?* (Seattle, 1973) provide some examples for a discussion of musicality beyond being an individual, distinguishing characteristic.

32   See Jacoby, *Jenseits von 'Musikalisch' und 'Unmusikalisch'*, pp. 35–6. More recently, Henkjan Honing has put forward similar arguments in his study *Musical Cognition:*

a neurosciences point of view: 'There is clearly a wide range of musical talent, but there is much to suggest there is an innate musicality in virtually everyone.'[33] Consequently, the notion of a 'musicality of theatre' would then refer to the intrinsic affinity of the stage to music, with which it was, so to speak, issued at birth.[34] Striving towards a musicality in theatre should thus be seen, I suggest, perhaps less as a case of learning and training an externally defined set of requirements, but as an act of excavating and 'liberating'[35] an intrinsic quality of this art form.

Instead of understanding musicality as a normative category, then, to describe a presence or lack of a native or learnt ability,[36] I will use it heuristically to analyze a varied set of interart movements – in this case between theatre and music.[37] Different practitioners refer to different aspects of music, some using the terms 'musical' or 'musicality', others only implying them. The notion of musicality in theatre that I seek to develop here does not, therefore, consist of a normative set of criteria, but functions as an umbrella term which covers a range of aspirations of one art form (theatre) towards another (music), which is contingent on changing historical contexts, aesthetic discourses and artistic aims and purposes.[38] This is

---

A Science of Listening (Piscataway, NJ, 2009).

[33] Oliver Sacks, *Musicophilia: Tales of Music and the Brain* (New York, 2007), p. 101.

[34] I am using this term here both as an anthropomorphism but also as a theatre historical reference to the beginnings of theatre as a decidedly musical art form in ancient Greece. Nietzsche's notion of the 'Birth of Tragedy out of the Spirit of Music' (1872) is an unavoidable reference in this context.

[35] Here I refer to Jacoby's eponymous concept of the 'Befreiung der schöpferischen Kräfte' [liberation of the creative forces] (*Jenseits von 'Musikalisch' und 'Unmusikalisch'*).

[36] See Eva Alerby/Cecilia Ferm, 'Learning Music. Embodied Experience in the Life-World', *Philosophy of Music Education Review*, 13/2 (Fall 2005), pp. 177–85, with regard to their distinction of these as 'absolute contra relativistic musicality' (p. 178).

[37] The current debate on 'interarts' is of some interest here – see Lagerroth/Lund/Hedling, *Interart Poetics*; Cecchetto et al., *Collision*, or Fischer-Lichte/Hasselmann/Rautzenberg, *Ausweitung der Kunstzone*. Fischer-Lichte distinguishes two main tendencies of interarts with reference to Lessing and Wagner (as mentioned earlier). For musicality in theatre, it is particularly Lessing's model that provides an early example of interart reflection: it 'compares the individual arts with regard to their specific powers and queries the possibilities and limits of transferring the potential of one art form onto others and thus transgressing the boundaries between them' (p. 8).

[38] This has in principle already been proposed for the field of literature, for example by Northrop Frye, who says that 'by "musical"', he means 'a quality in literature denoting a substantial analogy to, and in many cases an actual influence from, the art of music' (Frye 1957 in Steven Paul Scher [ed.], *Literatur und Musik* [Berlin, 1984], p. 170). More recently, in his introduction to an edition of the journal *Die Zeitschrift für Literaturwissenschaft und Linguistik (Lili)* dedicated to 'Musikalität' (musicality), Ralf Schnell suggested: 'Deviating from common parlance we will in the following understand "musicality" not in its usual sense of "musical talent" or "musical abilities", but as a factor of aesthetic productivity' (Ralf Schnell, 'Einleitung', *Die Zeitschrift für Literaturwissenschaft und Linguistik*, 141/1 [Online] [2006], http://www.uni-siegen.de/lili/ausgaben/2006/lili141.html?lang=de [11.07.2011]).

based, consequently, on a concept of music that is equally fluid and acknowledges historical, social, geographical, economic and other influences on what we understand to *be* music and how we interpret what it *means*:

> [...] music is whatever people choose to recognize as such, and its meanings are constituted by an open-ended interpretive process constrained only by sounds and the live experiences of those engaged with them. [...] Music is thus plural and dynamic, and its meanings are relative to a potentially infinite range of interpretive variables.[39]

Music semiologist Jean-Jacques Nattiez, whose position is paraphrased in this quotation, further pinpoints this thought: 'There is never a single, culturally dominant conception of music; rather, we see a whole spectrum of conceptions.'[40] This widened, non-normative notion of music and musicality forms the basis for thinking of musicality as an aesthetic *dispositif*.

Musicality as an Aesthetic *Dispositif*

I have initially used the word 'paradigm' when juxtaposing ideas and practices of segregation and synthesis in relation to theatre and the other arts. What I would like to suggest for the discussion of musicality in theatre, however, is to see it in the Foucauldian sense as an aesthetic *dispositif*. While on the one hand the notion of a 'paradigm' is more fundamental and transformative than that of a *dispositif*, the latter is more far-reaching. A paradigm, according to Thomas Kuhn, whose book *The Structure of Scientific Revolutions* (1992 [1970]) established the notion of 'paradigm shifts', 'is what members of a scientific community, and they alone, share'.[41] Michel Foucault, in contrast, casts the net of what a *dispositif* entails much wider:

> What I'm seeking to characterize with this name is, first of all, an absolutely heterogeneous assembly which involves discourses, institutions, architectural structures, regulatory decisions, laws, administrative measures, scientific enunciations, philosophical, moral, and philanthropic propositions; in short: as much the said as the un-said, these are the elements of the dispositive.[42]

---

[39]　Bowman, *Philosophical Perspectives*, p. 201.

[40]　In Bowman, *Philosophical Perspectives*, p. 245.

[41]　Thomas Kuhn, *The Essential Tension* (Chicago, 1977), p. 294.

[42]　Jeffrey Bussolini, 'What is a Dispositive?', *Foucault Studies*, 10 (2010), pp. 85–107, p. 91. I will stick to the French spelling, *dispositif*, as many scholars do, to indicate the origin of the concept.

Siegfried Jäger paraphrases this definition and interestingly connects it to the Wagnerian ideas of a *Gesamtkunstwerk*. A *dispositif* is then,

> the interaction of discursive behaviour (i.e. speech and thoughts based upon a shared knowledge pool), non-discursive behaviour (i.e. acts based upon knowledge), and manifestations of knowledge by means of acts or behaviours [...]. *Dispositifs* can thus be imagined as a kind of Gesamtkunstwerk, the complexly interwoven and integrated *dispositifs* add up in their entirety to a *dispositif* of all society.[43]

I would argue that approaching musicality as an aesthetic *dispositif* has a number of epistemological advantages. Firstly, it is non-exclusive: it embraces any number of discourses, processes and arrangements of knowledge and power. It allows us, in relation to the topic of this book, to look at a wide range of aspects, from practices and creation processes to pamphlets, manifestos or accounts, which precede, succeed or accompany these; from systems of belief to strategies of their dissemination, from edifices of thought to the architecture and set-up of institutions.

Secondly, *dispositifs* are not world-views, like paradigms. They can coexist, overlap and interact, where paradigms always suggest a full and irreversible shift. (One cannot go back to a heliocentric worldview, for example.) This better reflects the role of the notion of musicality in theatre as I see it, since I am not suggesting it as a comprehensive or all-encompassing approach to any form of theatre, but as one significant light amongst many to be shed on the 'opaque sphere' that is theatre.[44] What I am trying to illuminate is that there have always been other aesthetic *dispositifs*, such as that of a musicality of theatre, despite the predominance of the *dispositif* of the *separate* art forms. This predominant *dispositif* has led to a widely established and pervasive system of distinct educational disciplines, methods and institutions, individual aesthetics, politics and processes of creativity and distinguishable modes and professions of reception, as well as audiences and stake-holders. There have, however, also always been artists, teachers, institutions and audiences who chose to challenge this dominant mindset.

---

[43] Siegfried Jäger, 'Theoretische und methodische Aspekte einer Kritischen Diskurs- und Dispositivanalyse' (2000), http://www.diss-duisburg.de/Internetbibliothek/Artikel/Aspekte_einer_Kritischen_Diskursanalyse.htm [08.07.2011] (English translation taken from Wikipedia entry 'Dispositif').

[44] 'Theatre remains an opaque sphere for which – fortunately – we have a name and thus a place in society, even if both the name and the place in society are subjected to historical dynamics. No-one is able to penetrate this sphere as each approach happens subject to concrete historical circumstances and also by means of the most unsuited medium we can think of: language. The descriptive, linguistic attempts are like spotlights, directed at the sphere. Each one of them, whether it is purely empirical or semiotic, following theories of interaction or character performance, will only ever shed light on part of the sphere' (Andreas Kotte, *Theaterwissenschaft* [Köln/Weimar/Berlin, 2005], pp. 62–3).

Addressing musicality as an aesthetic *dispositif* emphasizes, thirdly, its non-ontological nature. I am not trying to establish an essentialist view that aims to add another *intrinsic* feature to the list of aspects and criteria for the theatre, or that provides a number of boxes to tick in order to establish whether some theatre is more musical than others. It is about analyzing a discursive formation and the range of claims and emphases made within it, explicitly or implicitly, through statements, actions, structures or otherwise. The *dispositif* is not a factual reality but an epistemological model, a mode of describing, understanding and analyzing, which manifests itself in its effects. In this sense, I should also highlight that I am not suggesting a musical *dispositif* based on *one* definition of what music *is* but as a framework to analyze how music – as historically and culturally contingent – is being understood and put forward in each context.[45]

Finally, the idea of the *dispositif*, by having 'an eminently strategic function',[46] draws attention to the *purposeful* use of an idea, which supports a central question for this book, namely what strategic function musicality as a *dispositif* has in theatre-making and theatrical innovation. What greater aesthetic and artistic aims and purposes does it serve? This inevitably also raises questions of power, which are strongly embedded in Foucault's idea of a *dispositif*. If, for example, we look back to see the paradigm of the separation of the arts as a *dispositif*, it fosters a way of understanding this as a discursive formation that involves currents and vectors of power. Establishing specialisms and devolving and disaggregating artistic practice, knowledge and organization means channelling power to fewer people, thus creating areas of what Max Scheler calls 'Herrschaftswissen'[47] [control knowledge]. In theatre this may mean that if actors only know how to act, musicians how to play their instruments, designers how to model and build a set, create costumes or devise the lighting, etc., the director accumulates all the integrative power and retains the interpretative sovereignty.

As Ian Hacking reminds us, the notion of discipline (both as a virtue and as a field of artistic activity or a scholarly territory) also carries this notion of power:

> But then there is the verb, to discipline: the master chastises to ensure that the disciples toe the line … Many who object to disciplines do so because they sense that they have been flogged by the institutional structures that determine the disciplines. There is no freedom to live other lives, or to create other kinds of knowledge.[48]

---

[45]   See also David Roesner, 'Musikalität als ästhetisches Dispositiv: Analogien und Transfers', in Jörg Huber/Roberto Nigro/Elke Bippus (eds.), *Ästhetik x Dispositiv. Die Erprobung von Erfahrungsfeldern*, *T:G/09* (Zürich/Wien/New York, 2012), pp. 195–206.

[46]   Foucault in Bussolini 'What is a Dispositive?', p. 91.

[47]   See Alfons Deeken, *Process and Permanence in Ethics: Max Scheler's Moral Philosophy* (New York, 1974), p. 225.

[48]   Ian Hacking in Benjamin Evans, 'Five Problems for Interdisciplinary Art', in Cecchetto et al., *Collision*, pp. 19–33, p. 20.

We will find that the notion of power, sometimes in the form of hierarchy, is never far from the aesthetic *dispositif* of musicality: musicality is at times invoked to reverse or disperse concentrations of power, but equally at times as another way of justifying or reinforcing hierarchical structures, such as a system of dependency of the actor from the director.

In addition to these larger epistemological aspects of the musicality *dispositif*, there are some quite concrete analytical focal points it affords in relation to theatre, both as process and performance, such as musicality as a perceptive quality, an embodied quality, or a cognitive and communicative quality.

Perceptive Quality

In order to be a 'factor of aesthetic productivity',[49] musicality needs to be also understood as a factor of a particular kind of aesthetic *perception*;[50] a frame[51] in which attention and emphasis is, for example, given to sonoric aspects of language, or rhythmic structures of movements. Paul Hegarty describes an aspect of this when he says, referring to John Cage's theories: 'The world, then, is revealed as infinitely musical: musicality is about our attentiveness to the sounds of the world.'[52] Douglas Kahn (1999), Petra Maria Meyer (2008) or Lynne Kendrick and myself (2011)[53] have explored this shift of attention, this 'acoustic turn', as Meyer calls it in her eponymous book, and have drawn attention to the (re-)engagement of the arts with aurality, sonification, musicalization or noise. This provides an important and rich context for this investigation. I am, however, not suggesting that a rediscovery of and concentration on the aural sphere of theatre, the acoustic stage so to speak, is equivalent to a focus on theatre's musicality even though both aspects are strongly related.

---

[49] Schnell, 'Einleitung'.

[50] See also film scholar James Tobias's point: 'I aim to understand musicality – not strictly music – across multiple media, not film alone. [...] Musicality may drive the narrative, but it is also a mode of reception' (James Tobias, 'Cinema, Scored. Toward a comparative methodology for music in media', *Film Quarterly*, 57/2 [2003], pp. 26–36, p. 29).

[51] With reference to Goffman's original definition of frames, Todd Gitlin adds: 'Frames are principles of selection, emphasis and presentation composed of little tacit theories about what exists, what happens, and what matters' (Gitlin, *The Whole World Is Watching: Mass Media in the Making and Unmaking of the New Left* [Berkeley/Los Angeles, CA/London, 1980], p. 6). Oliver Seibt calls them even more succinctly 'culturally acquired schemata of interpretation' [kulturell erlernte Interpretationsschemata] (Oliver Seibt, *Der Sinn des Augenblicks. Überlegungen zu einer Musikwissenschaft im Alltäglichen* [Bielefeld, 2010], p. 185).

[52] Paul Hegarty, *Noise/Music: A History* (London, 2007), p. 6.

[53] See also Christa Brüstle et al. (eds.), *Aus dem Takt. Rhythmus in Kunst, Kultur und Natur* (Bielefeld, 2005), Ross Brown, *Sound: A Reader in Theatre Practice* (Basingtoke, 2010), Bruce R. Smith, *The Acoustic World of Early Modern England* (Chicago, 1999), or Salomé Voegelin, *Listening to Noise and Silence. Towards a Philosophy of Sound Art* (New York/London, 2010).

On the one hand, I would limit the field: while all sound can be made into and/or perceived as music or appreciated in similar ways as we would with music (a distinction I will come back to), not all sound is musical and not all attention to acoustic aspects a thrust towards a musicality of theatre. It needs, I would argue, an intention either of the producing or receiving parties of the theatre to direct their attention towards what they understand to be 'musical' aspects of theatre process and/or performance. This idea is summed up neatly in Luciano Berio's definition: 'music is everything that one listens to with the intention of listening to music',[54] and is expressed more scientifically in Daniel Levitin's definition of music as 'a type of perceptual illusion in which our brain imposes structure and order on a sequence of sounds'.[55]

On the other hand, I also want to *extend* the idea of musicality as a perceptive quality that goes beyond the aural sphere. Musicality, then, exceeds appreciating all *sounds* as (potentially) musical – it also warrants an attention to musical qualities or relationships of *non-auditory* events, such as silent movement, gesture, lighting or even colour schemes:

> Music has become an independent structure of theatre. This is not a matter of the evident role of music and of music theatre, but rather of a more profound idea of theatre *as* music. Both of these definitions describe musicality and musicalization as theatre which behaves like music.[56]

For all of this, there is again no normative way of looking at it (or listening to it); practitioners propose or imply different things for what it means to perceive musically, and unpacking this will be an important aspect of my analysis.

Embodied Quality

Eva Alerby and Cecilia Ferm (2005), Tia deNora (2000) and many others remind us that music is an embodied art. Paolo Chagas writes, 'sounds affect the whole body, and embodiment is shaped by our aural history and by multiple levels of interaction with the sonic environment'.[57] Consequently, music is neither

---

[54]   Berio in Mary Bryden (ed.), *Samuel Beckett and Music* (Oxford, 1998), p. 24.

[55]   Daniel J. Levitin, *This Is Your Brain On Music: Understanding a Human Obsession* (London, 2008), p. 109.

[56]   Markee Rambo-Hood, 'Postdramatic Musicality in The Black Rider', *Networking Knowledge: Journal of the MeCCSA Postgraduate Network*, 3/2 (2010), pp. 1–11, pp. 2–3.

[57]   Paulo C. Chagas, 'Polyphony and Embodiment: A Critical Approach to the Theory of Autopoiesis', *TRANS. Revista Transcultural de Música*, 9 [Online] (2005), http://www.sibetrans.com/trans/a179/polyphony-and-embodiment-a-critical-approach-to-the-theory-of-autopoiesis [16.08.2011].

a 'kind of physical feat where the body mechanically executes the musical directives of mind' nor 'a simple interpretive act in which players seek to discover and reproduce the music encoded in a score.' Both ideas fundamentally neglect the formative role the body plays in making music.[58]

Musicality in theatre, I would argue, is equally closely related to the body as an ephemeral semiotic sign and phenomenal site of musical expression and perception. The rhythmicality of movement and gesture is one example of this, the musical aspects of vocal expression that are conditional on the individual physique and vocal apparatus is another. Questions of rhythm and timing that reappear time and time again in the discourses about actor training (Stanislavski's 'tempo-rhythm'[59] is a famous example) are often rehearsed and trained across the fluid borders of the analytical, cerebral appreciation of organized time and a more intuitive, physical feeling for timing.

Musicality as *dispositif*, then, also highlights the embodied, pre-linguistic aspects of theatre. Ramón Pelinski writes 'that many musical practices have primary significations without any need for the linguistic vehicle of rational thought'.[60] Musicality, as we will see, is often cited or instrumentalized as a vehicle of immediacy, as a pre-rational stimulus, which theatre practitioners like Artaud or Grotowski were keen to (re-)introduce to the theatre, and possibly a way of transcending the long-dismissed but still highly influential Cartesian dualism of mind and body.[61] As Pelinski puts it,

> the immediacy, the phenomenal reality and spatiotemporal situatedness of embodied perception are traits of a musical experience whose privilege it is to precede and found a musical knowledge in its rationality as well as in its functionality.[62]

The perception of actor, director, spectator and others involved in performance processes is thus potentially more embodied when theatre's musicality is embraced or emphasized.

The impact of music on embodiment, however, goes further than modifying our perception. Following music sociologist Tia DeNora's seminal observations that physiological states, behaviour, mood and feeling as well as social role and action

---

[58] Bowman, *Philosophical Perspectives*, p. 293. Bowman cites a paper by Eleanor Stubley from 1966.

[59] See Bella Merlin, *Acting – The Basics* (London/New York, 2010), p. 216.

[60] Ramón Pelinski, 'Embodiment and Musical Experience', *TRANS. Revista Transcultural de Música*, 9 [Online] (2005), http://redalyc.uaemex.mx/pdf/822/82200914.pdf [16.08.2011].

[61] See Frendo, 'Embodied Musicality'.

[62] Pelinski, 'Embodiment and Musical Experience'.

style can be regularized and/or modified by music,[63] I would argue that part of the strategic use of music and musicality that DeNora sees shaping social identities can also be applied to the creation of dramatic characters, stage personae and performative presence. DeNora's formulation of 'musically composed identities'[64] could thus also refer to fictional on-stage identities: we will see that, not unlike respondents to her ethnographic case studies, who '"find themselves" in musical structures',[65] theatre practitioners have similarly used musical structures to find characters or non-fictional performative qualities, both in order to create these, but also to make them repeatable.

One of the ways in which this connection between musicality and embodiment works is by what DeNora calls 'musical entrainment'.[66] This is an important feature in training, shaping or synchronizing bodily movements, used for example in music therapy, neonatal care, but also in aerobic classes and exercise regimes, and can equally be found, as we will see in more detail, in Meyerhold's biomechanical exercises. DeNora elaborates:

> In much the same way that bodily movements can be produced – consciously or semi-consciously – in relation to musical properties, so, too, a range of bodily processes can be entrained in relation to other temporally organized environmental media.[67]

DeNora even calls music a 'prosthetic technology of the body':[68]

> Music can be seen to function as a prosthetic device, to provide organizing properties for a range of other embodied experiences and in ways that involve varying degrees of deliberation and conscious awareness on the part of music's conscripts.[69]

One of the continuous debates in acting theories until today, has been precisely about those 'varying degrees of deliberation', the level of rationality and conscious control during the act of acting, and musicality has frequently been invoked – sometimes as a means of abandonment of reflection, sometimes as an aid to a stronger rational awareness – to exercise influence over these varying degrees.

---

[63]   See Tia DeNora, *Music in Everyday Life* (Cambridge, 2000), p. 79.
[64]   DeNora, *Music in Everyday Life*, p. 68.
[65]   DeNora, *Music in Everyday Life*.
[66]   DeNora, *Music in Everyday Life*, p. 78.
[67]   DeNora, *Music in Everyday Life*, p. 79.
[68]   DeNora, *Music in Everyday Life*, p. 102.
[69]   DeNora, *Music in Everyday Life*, p. 103.

Cognitive and Communicative Quality

As well as being seen to change our perception and our physical engagement with theatre, the musical dispositif also foregrounds musicality as a cognitive quality,[70] as a way of thinking and understanding. Honing puts it very succinctly: 'Music is cognition'[71] – but what characterizes the 'listener's overall perception, expectation, and memory'[72] when he/she 'transforms [the components of music] into a pleasurable listening experience – into music'?[73] According to Serafine, 'musical thought may be defined as human aural-cognitive activity that results in the posing of artworks embodying finite and organized sets of temporal events described in sound'.[74] While Serafine thus emphasizes the productive, propositional aspects of musical thinking, Pelinski highlights a notion of non-linguistic thought in musical perception: 'the content of musical perception is simultaneous and identical with its meaning. As an intentional object of perceptual experience, music doesn't symbolize; it doesn't reflect reality: it is reality'.[75] Bowman further explores a contrasting approach with reference to musicologist Susanne Langer who did see music as symbolic, but would have agreed with Pelinski to understand music as a form of knowing (rather than a mere representation of it) and as a 'special kind of intelligence'.[76]

> Like discourse, Langer argues, art is intelligent; like language, works of art are vehicles for understanding: they are symbols. Humans use symbols to wrest images from the world of the ongoing flow of perceptual presence, in effect making it hold still so it can be comprehended. Because music no less than language is a vehicle for the conception of reality, musical experiences are important instances of knowing.[77]

I think that both aspects – thinking productively and perceptively 'in music' – can apply to areas outside of music and are characteristic of the modes of transference I would describe as the musicality *dispositif*. Theatre practitioners are often

---

[70] See for example Mary Louise Serafine, *Music as Cognition* (New York, 1988); Alerby/Ferm, 'Learning Music'; Cross, 'Musicality'; Honing, *Musical Cognition*; Jerrold Levinson, 'Musical Thinking', *JMM*, 1 [Online] (2003), http://www.musicandmeaning. net/issues/showArticle.php?artID=1.2 [18.01.10]; Levitin, *This Is Your Brain On Music*; or Bruno Nettl, '"Musical Thinking" and "Thinking about Music" in Ethnomusicology: An Essay of Personal Interpretation', *The Journal of Aesthetics and Art Criticism*, 52/1 (1994), pp. 139–48.

[71] Honing, *Musical Cognition*, p. 87.

[72] Honing, *Musical Cognition*.

[73] Honing, *Musical Cognition*.

[74] Serafine, *Music as Cognition*, p. 69.

[75] Pelinski, 'Embodiment and Musical Experience', p. 31.

[76] Bowman, *Philosophical Perspectives*, p. 199.

[77] Bowman, *Philosophical Perspectives*, p. 202.

quite interested in translating the kinds of 'pre-conceptual and pre-linguistic'[78] perceptual and cognitive experiences music affords into the rehearsal room and onto the stage.[79] They face, however, the dilemma that in order to share these ideas, in order to communicate the musical *dispositif* inter-subjectively, they inevitably have to resort to language. Pelinski argues that there are two ways to resolve this contradiction: 'to appeal to "non-linguistic thought", or to use a language based upon conceptual metaphors'.[80] My interest in this book is in analyzing the second strategy: the discursive use of metaphors of music in the world of theatre. I am also, while acknowledging musical cognition as an important aspect of a musicality *dispositif*, not attempting to measure, test or 'prove' musical cognition in theatre-making. What I am interested in is how practitioners metaphorically talk about and concretely functionalize music, what claims they make about, for example, rhythm in performance or musical form in directing, and what that tells us about their processes and aesthetics.

Before turning to my first case study, Adolphe Appia, I should pause briefly on this aspect of the 'metaphor'[81] that has come into play already occasionally. Is metaphor really the right term for what the musicality *dispositif* affords?

A Range of Possible Relationships and Interplays

> Perhaps a thing is valid only by its metaphoric power; perhaps that is the value
> of music, then: to be a good metaphor.[82]

When looking at comparative studies of influences of one art form on another, whether the focus is on intermediality, ekphrasis, visual music or wider interart

---

[78]   Pelinski, 'Embodiment and Musical Experience', p. 32.

[79]   There has of course been a well-documented parallel development in the fine arts towards 'visual music' or 'colour music' spearheaded by artists such as Paul Klee and Wassily Kandinsky (see Kerry Brougher et al., *Visual Music: Synaesthesia in Art and Music Since 1900* [London, 2005]).

[80]   Pelinski, 'Embodiment and Musical Experience', p. 32.

[81]   At the risk of stating the obvious, any discourse about music or musicality is of course also inevitably metaphorical – we describe sounds spatially as 'high' or 'low', as texture ('dull', 'sharp', 'soft', 'silky') and attribute moods and psychological states to them ('happy', 'sad'). Sometimes these metaphors even work reciprocally: we can describe someone as 'upbeat', which refers to a kind of music with fast tempo, which we would then metaphorically describe as 'happy' or 'positive'. So when music becomes a metaphor for theatre, its description is likely to be a metaphor of the second order, much like, as Petr Bogatyrev has pointed out, signs on stage which are often signs of signs: a cardboard crown signifying a real crown signifying a king or queen (see Roland Posner/Klaus Robering/Thomas Albert Sebeok [eds.], *Semiotik: Ein Handbuch zu den zeichentheoretischen Grundlagen von Natur und Kultur, Volume 3* [Berlin/New York, 2003], p. 3105).

[82]   Roland Barthes in Stephen Benson, 'For Want of a Better Term? Polyphony and the Value of Music in Bakhtin and Kundera', *Narrative*, 11/3 (2003), pp. 292–311, p. 292.

relationships, scholars have used and promoted different terms and concepts for how to describe the relationship between, for example, literature and music, painting and poetry, or film and theatre. Among the kinds of relations that have been put forward, are, for example: 'combination',[83] 'replacement',[84] 'influence',[85] 'correspondence',[86] 'analogy',[87] 'transposition',[88] 'translation',[89] 'mutual implication',[90] 'quotation',[91] 're-presentation',[92] 'simile'[93] and, of course, 'metaphor'.[94]

So which of these best describes the kind of interart transfer that is aimed for by those promoting musicality in theatre? My answer is: potentially all of the above. In contrast to studies of art *works*, for which the analysis seeks to provide an answer to what the relationship between different art forms, modes of representation and performance and modes of perception *is*,[95] my study looks at

---

[83] See Calvin S. Brown, 'Theoretische Grundlagen zum Studium der Wechselverhältnisse zwischen Literatur und Musik', in Steven Paul Scher (ed.), *Literatur und Musik* (Berlin, 1984), pp. 28–39.

[84] Brown, 'Theoretische Grundlagen'.

[85] See Northrop Frye in Brown, 'Theoretische Grundlagen'.

[86] See Guido Hiß, *Der theatralische Blick* (Berlin, 1993); Hiß, *Synthetische Visionen*; or Siglind Bruhn, 'A Concert of Paintings: "Musical Ekphrasis" in the Twentieth Century', *Poetics Today*, 22/3 (2001), pp. 551–605.

[87] See Brown, 'Theoretische Grundlagen'; Monika Schwarz, *Musikanaloge Ideen und Struktur im französischen Theater: Untersuchungen zu Jean Tardieu und Eugene Ionesco* (München, 1981); or Troy Thomas, 'Interart Analogy: Practice and Theory in Comparing the Arts', *Journal of Aesthetic Education*, 25/2 (1991), pp. 17–36.

[88] See Bruhn, 'A Concert of Paintings'; or Rajewsky, *Intermedialität*.

[89] See Rajewsky, *Intermedialität*.

[90] Claudia Gorbman in Nicholas Cook, *Analysing Musical Multimedia* (Oxford, 1998), p. 21.

[91] See Tamar Yacobi, 'Interart Narrative: (Un)Reliability and Ekphrasis', *Poetics Today*, 21/4 (2000), pp. 711–49.

[92] Yacobi, 'Interart Narrative'.

[93] See Jane Milling/Graham Ley, *Modern Theories of Performance* (Basingstoke, 2001).

[94] See Benson, 'For Want of'; Sven Bjerstedt, *Att agera musikaliskt. Musikalitet som norm och utbildningsmål i västerländsk talteater* [*Musicality in Acting: Musicality as a Standard and an Educational Goal for Western Spoken Theatre*] (Master Thesis, Lunds Universitet, Musikhögskolan i Malmö, 2010).

[95] Troy Thomas for example claims that 'analogy is almost the only usable method for making interart comparisons and that the so-called "structural" modes of analysis are in fact only safe (and usually predictable) forms of analogizing' (Thomas, 'Interart Analogy', p. 17). Here we find the assumption that comparisons between the arts can only be based on 'corresponding structural features' (ibid.). I will argue that, at least on the level of the *productive* references theatre practitioners make to music, this is not the case – structural features are an important *tertium comparationis* in the musical aspirations, but certainly not the only one.

what relationship the practitioners envisage and describe as an *aspiration*: do they use a notion from music as a simile, for example – like Michael Chekhov, who asks his students to 'listen' to daily life atmospheres 'as you listen to music'[96] – or a transformative method – a more literal template for specific musical techniques or formal principles in areas of improvisation, composition or performance, such as counterpoint, permutation, parametrical thinking, polyphony, orchestration or theme and variation?

When I said earlier that all sound can be made into and/or perceived as music, or appreciated in similar ways as we would with music, I pre-empted these kinds of distinctions: separating between musicality as a frame of mind, a particular mode of reception that approaches certain phenomena *as if* they were music, or conscious attempts to treat different materials – sonic or otherwise – *as* music. Either way, in doing so it is still a wide open question, what 'musicality' as a mode of perception or production stands for and what the individual associates with it or attributes to it. Is 'music' about immersion, pre-linguistic contemplation, raw emotion or sophisticated construction and architecture of time?[97] Does it apply to the overall shaping of time, to sonic qualities of speech, to specific qualities of movement, to structural relationships between distinct elements of production? Again, it is potentially all of the above. Distinguishing these kinds of different relations between music and theatre and their strategic function in the *dispositif* is a central aim of this book, without, however, trying to invent or establish a taxonomy or systematic categorization. This would, in my view, lead to unnecessary simplifications – I am much more interested in investigating and discussing 'what it is' rather than 'which category it belongs to'. The aim of this book is also not to verify or falsify discourses on musicality. As Carl Dahlhaus attests,

> There is no need to state the obvious: that the poetological use of musical termini – from counterpoint and thorough bass to the fugue and sonata form – is almost always skewed and bent. Essential to musical comparison is, however, not the answer that it gives – an answer, which tends to be vague and intangible –, but the question, that it demarcates. The metaphor fulfils an unlocking role, a first approach to a problem.[98]

In the following chapters I shall investigate what problems and questions theatre-makers seek to address by invoking musicality and how each manifestation plays out in defining and redefining their notions of theatre and music alike.

---

[96]   Chekhov, *To the Actor*, p. 55.

[97]   Derek Bailey has described this paradox as follows: 'For most people, it seems, music is either sensual, a matter of the emotions and feelings, or a type of aural jig-saw puzzle – Leibniz's "counting without knowing that it is counting"' (Derek Bailey, *Improvisation. Its Nature and Practice in Music* [Ashbourne, Derbyshire, 1980], p. 148).

[98]   Carl Dahlhaus, 'Kleists Wort über den Generalbass', in Joachim Kreutzer (ed.), *Kleist-Jahrbuch 1984* (Berlin, 1984), pp. 13–24, p. 13.

While the first three chapters follow a more chronological approach and focus on the development of the musicality *dispositif* in some of the most influential theatre visionaries of the late nineteenth and early twentieth centuries, the fourth and fifth chapter each explores a central aspect of the *dispositif* across a wider historical period: the fourth chapter focuses on musicality and dramatic *writing* from Gertrude Stein through to Elfriede Jelinek, and Chapter 5 explores traces of 'jazz musicality' from its early roots in the 1920s to more contemporary manifestations in the 1970s and the early twenty-first century. The last chapter then investigates how these many legacies of musicality in directing, acting, training, writing and dramaturgy are continued, developed and reoriented in contemporary forms of theatre, from the so-called 'Regietheater' to devised and postdramatic practices.

Chapter 1
Appia – Musicality and the 'Inner Essence'

For any discussion of musicality in the theatre of modernism and after, the writings of Swiss designer and theatre practitioner Adolphe Appia (1862–1928) are an obvious and inevitable place to start. Not only has he discussed the relationship of music and theatrical performance in great detail, but he has also had an astonishingly broad influence on theatre-makers to this day. One of his biographers, Richard Beacham, credits him with 'fundamentally advanc[ing] the art of theatre'.[1]

My interest in Appia is a selective one: as with all of the practitioners I will discuss in this book, I do not attempt to represent their work, thoughts and achievements fully and completely, but concentrate on the questions at hand: what role, judging by their processes and/or theoretical suggestions, does musicality play in their theatre practice? What notions of music do they employ? What impact does the aesthetic *dispositif* of musicality have on the theatre and its development in each case?

Many of the key analogies, aims and claims employed and invoked towards a musicality of theatre have roots in Appia's thinking, even though his theoretical edifice, which is strongly influenced by Richard Wagner's word-tone drama, seems to focus on the development of what we might now call music-theatre.[2] As I will argue towards the end of this chapter, however, many of his key ideas about the relationship of music, musicality and theatre have also influenced the *dramatic* theatre in particular, advancing theatre design, playing a seminal role in the development of the director and leaving a strong mark on aspects of actor training.

I avoid approaching Appia (or any other of the theatre-makers in this book) from the *Gesamtkunstwerk* angle – the (problematic) one-word summary of Wagner's most influential legacy. Apart from the fact that Appia disliked the term, as his very highly developed sense of a hierarchy of the arts in the theatre did not

---

[1]   Richard C. Beacham, *Adolphe Appia: Texts on Theatre* (London/New York, 1993), p. 1.

[2]   Appia's influence on developments in the staging of music-theatre has been demonstrably significant as well, and has, as Patrick Carnegy argues and analyzes in great detail, strongly influenced directors such as Wieland Wagner, who has been credited with introducing the notion of 'Regietheater' (I will come back to this term in Chapter 6), to opera. See Patrick Carnegy, *Wagner and the Art of the Theatre* (New Haven/London, 2006); Gerhard R. Koch et al. (eds.), *Wagnerspektrum 2/2005: Schwerpunkt / focussing on Regietheater* (Würzburg, 2005) and Robert Sollich et al. (eds.), *Angst vor der Zerstörung: Der Meister Künste zwischen Archiv und Erneuerung* (Berlin, 2008).

sit well with the synthetic ambitions associated with Wagner's thrust, my focus in the study is very different: while the idea of the total work of art promotes the amalgamation of the arts, the 'integration of all arts in one work' or the 'universal-poetic fusion of all genres',[3] my interest is more specifically in the development (often the reform) of theatre as a distinct art form and a selective cluster of genres within the performing arts in general through analogies, metaphors or actual techniques from music.

I will thus look at Appia's writings in two sections, first exploring the philosophical, aesthetic and transcendental[4] claims he makes for the role of music in the 'theatre of the future'[5] and second the role of musicality in the concrete reforms he suggested. In a third step I will discuss the impact of both on the actor and director and conclude with a discussion on how and why Appia's theories can be and have been applied to dramatic theatre. It is worth pausing briefly on the distinction between 'music' and 'musicality', since Appia, in contrast to other, later theoretical stances, does almost always mean 'actual'[6] music in a more conventional sense and only occasionally hints at the wider use of music not as a sonic actuality but as an idea and aesthetic potential. I distinguish the two pragmatically and heuristically: using 'music' where an intentionally created and crafted sound event is concerned, and 'musicality' when entering the realm of the analogy, the transference of musical principles, aesthetics or effects onto other aspects of theatrical performance and process.

Philosophical and Ideological Aspects

Appia published his first major treatise *Die Musik und die Inscenierung* [*Music and the Art of Theatre*] in 1899, precisely and significantly on the brink between the two centuries. As we will see, his thinking is still clearly rooted in the nineteenth century and the influence music had for the arts then. Music historian Hans Merian wrote in 1902 that music was not only the 'leading art of the nineteenth century, but some of its essence penetrated other artistic genres as well. We could, therefore, call the nineteenth century the musical century'.[7] A hundred years later, Uta Grund

---

    [3] Guido Hiß, *Synthetische Visionen: Theater als Gesamtkunstwerk von 1800 bis 2000* (München, 2005), pp. 7–8.

    [4] Balme asserts that the 'symbolist notion of theatre was based on a transcendental component, which was incompatible with the "rough" materiality and sensuality of theatre and seemed only realizable, strictly speaking, through poetry or music' (Christopher Balme [ed.], *Das Theater von Morgen. Texte zur deutschen Theaterreform* [Würzburg, 1988], p. 18).

    [5] See Adolphe Appia, 'Theatrical Production and its Prospects for the Future (1921)', in Beacham, *Adolphe Appia: Texts on Theatre*, pp. 124–34.

    [6] I am aware that speaking of 'actual' music is problematical, not only since John Cage's radical erosion of boundaries between, for example, music and everyday sound.

    [7] Merian in Christian Kaden/Volker Kalisch, 'Musik', in Karl-Heinz Brack (ed.), *Ästhetische Grundbegriffe* (Stuttgart/Weimar, 2005), pp. 256–308, p. 288.

still calls 'musicalization [...] a further paradigm [...] which decidedly influenced the aesthetics around 1900'.[8] From within this context, however, Appia laid the ground for many consequential developments of the theatre of the twentieth and even twenty-first centuries.

Inner Essence [Das innere Wesen]

One of the key claims Appia makes is indebted to the German philosopher Arthur Schopenhauer – Appia uses a quotation from him as a motto for *Music and the Art of Theatre* and refers to it again later in his essay 'Theatrical Production and its Prospects for the Future' (1921):

> Schopenhauer writes that music does not express the phenomenon, but only the inner essence of the phenomenon; therefore it expresses nothing related to the story, geography, social conditions, and customs; no actual objects of any sort.[9]

Music, in other words, is the means by which the dramatist presents

> not just the external effects of emotions, the outward appearance of dramatic life; but, using these emotions themselves, the dramatic life in its fullest reality, as we can know it only at the most profound level of our being.[10]

Appia talks symbolically about the 'hidden world of our inner life',[11] which needs to be expressed in art: 'this life *cannot be expressed* except through music, and music can express only that life'.[12] Appia combines these metaphysical claims with quite concrete assertions that music allows the playwright/composer to control the theatrical form, the *mise en scene*,[13] and does so essentially by shaping time and rhythm. Music, then, solves Appia's problem of finding 'a principle, deriving directly from the drama's original conception [...] to prescribe the *mise-en-scène*'.[14]

This proves to be a recurring motif for Appia: music as a vehicle or guarantor for something transcendental, something that cannot be put into words.

---

[8]   Uta Grund, *Zwischen den Künsten. Edward Gordon Craig und das Bildertheater um 1900* (Berlin, 2002), p. 159.

[9]   Appia, 'Theatrical Production', p. 130.

[10]   Adolphe Appia, 'Music and the Art of the Theatre (1899) [Excerpts]', in Beacham, *Adolphe Appia: Texts on Theatre*, pp. 29–58, p. 31.

[11]   Appia in Jane Milling/Graham Ley, *Modern Theories of Performance* (Basingstoke, 2001), p. 34.

[12]   Appia in Milling/Ley, *Modern Theories*, p. 34, original emphasis.

[13]   See Adolphe Appia, 'Theatrical Experiences and Personal Investigations (1921)', in Beacham, *Adolphe Appia: Texts on Theatre*, pp. 22–8 and 161–6, pp. 25–6.

[14]   Adolphe Appia, *Music and the Art of the Theatre* (Coral Gables, FL, 1962), p. 13, original emphasis.

As Bowman puts it, paraphrasing Schopenhauer: 'Music thus has the power to communicate the incommunicable, to penetrate the rational veil of representation and appearances – to give us insight into truths more profound than reason can ever grasp.'[15] Again, this applies on two levels: metaphysically, music captures what Appia calls an 'inner life' and unlocks theatre's potential to express this, but it also communicates, more pragmatically, essential aspects of staging, which seem to be incommunicable by conventional, linguistic means. If reaching for and conveying an 'inner essence' through music is Appia's philosophical credo, the aesthetic 'mantra' and one of the central artistic aims associated with music in his writings is that of the unity of the artwork.

Unity and Order

The idea of unity and order is inherently connected to his suggestion to make music the predominant expressive force of the word-tone drama. He credits music with providing a sense of unity in a number of ways. First, by controlling the translation of the playwright's intentions onto the stage much more reliably than mere words could do. Since words are not prescriptive enough with regard to timing and rhythm, music unifies the various means of expression under the will of the individual artist: the playwright and composer. It thus helps to transcend the 'division of labour'[16] and the individualism of the actor and welds together the different layers and aspects of the work. Music facilitates what all art needs, according to Appia: 'a harmonious relationship between feeling and form, an ideal balance between the ideas which the artist desires to express, and the means he has for expressing them … .'[17] Appia is acutely aware that this harmony is more difficult to achieve in drama than in any other art form: 'The more types of media required for the realization of any work of art, the more elusive is this harmony.'[18] Music, for Appia, is not only uniquely suitable for bringing the many disparate elements of theatre together harmoniously; its unifying effect also extends, secondly, to the audience's reception, he argues. Music 'joins them together as a single entity'[19] and facilitates their need to 'escape from themselves in order to rediscover themselves'.[20]

Appia clearly makes a strong case that music renders the sum of all theatrical expression greater than its parts. His claim that music is the 'foundation', on which theatre can be expressive to all of our senses, is a particular take on the *perceptive* qualities that the musicality *dispositif* affords:[21] providing access to a higher reality

---

[15]   Wayne D. Bowman, *Philosophical Perspectives on Music* (Oxford, 1998), p. 72.
[16]   Appia, 'Theatrical Experiences', p. 25.
[17]   Appia, 'Music and the Art', p. 29.
[18]   Appia, 'Music and the Art', p. 29.
[19]   Appia, 'Music and the Art', p. 40.
[20]   Appia, 'Music and the Art', p. 40.
[21]   See the section on musicality and perception in the Introduction.

of the artwork, an essence of it. Appia is indebted here to the music aesthetical topos of romanticism, according to which music 'while not allowing us to grasp, to appropriate the eternal which transcends [our] sensual perception, lets [us] glimpse it, experience and feel it'.[22] The reference to Schopenhauer, the romantic period's foremost philosopher when it comes to music, is thus unsurprising.

It is worth noting this understanding of music, since subsequent practitioners have pursued very different strategies when calling for a musicality of theatre and have at times worked precisely *against* the unity and harmony that Appia associates so strongly with music. His musicality strategy not only concerns the aesthetics of the overall theatrical event, the harmony of design, lighting, blocking and timing, but is also his maxim for the actor: to achieve a holistically expressive performance, which harmonically unites movement, gesture and vocal expression. Although the rhythm and quality of the movement are stylized musically, the actor's performance is meant to be natural, allowing access to a deeper psychological 'authenticity'. In contrast, subsequent practitioners have often used musicality as a vehicle for defamiliarization and anti-psychological performance.

Hierarchy

In order to achieve the unity and order just mentioned, theatre-makers have to, according to Appia, fundamentally revise the hierarchy of the expressive means of theatrical staging. Appia places music at the very top in his graph of theatrical hierarchy,[23] even though at the time of the origins of opera it was confined to being a *servant* to the words of the libretto according to Monteverdi's famous 'seconda prattica'.[24]

As we will see, Appia is once again ahead of his time in thematizing hierarchy in theatre: the importance and dominance of certain elements, most notably the notion of logocentrism, which the avant-garde theatre artists question or reject, has since then become a recurring topos in writings from Antonin Artaud to Heiner Goebbels. Musicality is one of the answers to the perceived problem, one of the means by which to topple traditional hierarchies – with consequences for both the aesthetic interplays in performance and the interpersonal working relations in making theatre.

Musicalization in the context of Appia's writing as a way of reversing existing hierarchies is not accompanied by the revolutionary or anarchical 'gestus' employed later by the Futurists or Dadaists; his aim is not novelty, but a recalling of and reorientation towards an expressive 'essence' that he claims to have been lost in decades of accumulating theatrical conventions. By making the original

---

22 Kaden/Kalisch, 'Musik', p. 290.
23 See Appia, 'Music and the Art', p. 38.
24 Monteverdi, against the trend of his time, decided to give the words preference over the music; the composition should 'serve' the meaning of the text. This became a key step toward the musical theatricality that enabled the birth of opera.

artistic and expressive intentions of the author paramount, and calling (ideally) for author, composer and director to be one person as well as by implementing music as the main tool of preserving and communicating their intentions, Appia seeks to guarantee a true and immediate artistic experience. The ideal of this experience for the artist and audience is an emphatic vision of 'life'.

Art and Life: Music's Role as (a) Key

For Appia, music – more than any other art – encompasses 'life'[25] and therefore facilitates the kind of theatre he envisions: theatre as a 'living art'.[26] Particularly in his later years, this becomes his mantra and summarizes his artistic goal. 'Life' as Appia sees it, is about depth, it is not about a 'lively' surface; and music's role is not centrally to animate the aesthetic surface of the theatre experience, but to grant access to deeper-seated levels of expression and experience. It serves as an entry point:

> The poet-musician, by virtue of the music, presents us not just the external effects of emotions, the outward appearance of dramatic life; but, using these emotions themselves, the dramatic life in its fullest reality, as we can know it only at the most profound level of our being.[27]

Appia, it seems, sees music as a kind of key that allows the artist to unlock a profound aesthetic experience for the audience, an insight into the human condition as an emotional reality, emphasizing the potential beauty of this experience. His writing is thus emphatic and associates music with freedom of expression, of communality, with joint experience, with purity and beauty.[28]

Music (and I would argue also musicality) has a second function in Appia's quest for a 'living art': it not only unlocks the audience's inner life, but also serves as a kind of artistic awakening: 'As musical rhythm enters into us, it tells us: "*You* are the work of art."'[29] As we will see in more detail in the section on the actor, music(ality) thus becomes an important vehicle in actor training for Appia, unearthing or rekindling expressive qualities in the performer, which he felt that dramatic conventions threatened to bury.

Given all this rather emphatic and at times quasi-religious or messianic philosophy, it is surprising that Appia, as a writer and practitioner, actually engaged with theatre quite pragmatically, putting his theories into action.

---

[25]   Appia, 'Music and the Art', p. 32.
[26]   Appia, 'The Work of Living Art (1919)', in Beacham, *Adolphe Appia: Texts on Theatre*, pp. 167–78.
[27]   Appia, 'Music and the Art', p. 31.
[28]   See Appia, 'The Work of Living Art', p. 174.
[29]   Appia in Denis Bablet/Marie-Louise Bablet, *Adolphe Appia 1882–1928. Actor – Space – Light* (London/New York, 1982), p. 55, original emphasis.

Pragmatic Aspects – The 'Realästhetik' of Appia

In politics, we are familiar with the idea of 'Realpolitik', which takes account of what's actually achievable beyond the manifestos, party programmes and election speeches, and how one might reach these revised aims. In the arts, I suggest, there is something similar – a 'Realästhetik', which emerges when aesthetic credos and concepts meet the realities of production and the momentum of collaborations and artistic creation in the moment. This is by no means necessarily negative; while Realästhetik might be seen as (foul) compromise and a sell-out of the integrity of artistic ideologies by some, it can also be a way of 'grounding' a theoretical approach and allowing the evidence of actualities (of working conditions, of people, of a time and place) to make the work empirically the best it can be in a given context. The circumstantial limitations and constraints can even inspire work that transcends that which lofty theories and declamations of intentions were unable to imagine.

Appia's influence – not only on theatre theory, but more importantly on how theatre (and music-theatre) are *made* – has been described elsewhere;[30] my interest here is to investigate how Appia actually paved the way towards concepts of musicality in theatre, such as the idea of musicality as a transferable principle (particularly with respect to light), the widened notion of a score (with its implications for practices of notation and creation) and his identification of rhythm as a core principle of dramatic performance.

Musicality as a Transferable Principle

When Appia demands that theatrical lighting be designed and used 'according to its musical qualities',[31] he spearheads one of the most important aesthetic drives in the arts of the twentieth and early twenty-first centuries: intermediality. The notion that art forms can be designed and/or perceived along conventions of other art forms has become an important recognition in redefining boundaries between genres, art forms, between art and life. As Grund asserts, Appia's 'new, symbolically essentialist aesthetic was the result of [...] an intimate knowledge of musical structure and a pronounced synaesthetic grasp for visual effects on stage'.[32]

---

[30] See, for example, Walther R. Volbach, *Adolphe Appia. Prophet of the Modern Theatre. A Profile* (Middletown, 1968); Bablet/Bablet, *Adolphe Appia 1882–1928*; Beacham, *Adolphe Appia: Texts on Theatre* and Beacham, *Adolphe Appia. Artist and Visionary of the Modern Theatre* (Reading, 1994); Peter Simhandl, *Bildertheater. Bildende Künstler des 20. Jahrhunderts als Theaterreformer* (Berlin, 1993); Milling/Ley, *Modern Theories of Performance*; Carnegy, *Wagner and the Art of the Theatre*.

[31] Appia in Manfred Brauneck, *Theater im 20. Jahrhundert* (Reinbeck bei Hamburg, 1998 [1982]), p. 68.

[32] Grund, *Zwischen den Künsten*, p. 155.

This advance into interart poetics has also led to a profound questioning of the ontology and materiality of art forms.[33] Musicality is one of the main strands of this development and has been applied to language (e.g. Dadaism, sound poetry[34]), film (e.g. Ruttman, Vertov[35]), visual art (e.g. Kandinsky, Klee[36]) and theatre; – a series of developments for which Appia deserves a great amount of credit. He realized and insisted on theatre as an art, which shapes and controls time and thus makes it a close relative of music. Consequently, Appia aimed 'at a global *musicalization of scenic expression*',[37] claiming that music may be translated 'not just into the gestures and actions of the actor but into the entire inanimate setting as well'.[38]

This transference works on different levels for Appia. There is a more general, less tangible way in which he sees music influence all scenic elements through its expressiveness:

> Music is discovered to be closely linked not just to the word, but also to that part of the drama to which the scenic elements of production give visible form. It ought therefore to be possible to examine the expressive quality of music and consider how it relates to the *mise en scène*.[39]

More concretely, music(ality) for Appia has a direct impact on how to approach the actor's movements and the spatial design.[40] If we look at the actor first, Appia claims that music becomes an intermediary between them and any props or small design elements:

> If music did not so profoundly alter the natural time-durations of life, it could not force the actor to renounce his ordinary activity in order to become a means of expression. [...] But this very transformation, which deprives the actor of his personal, arbitrary life, brings him closer to the inanimate elements of the

---

[33]   See also Matthias Rebstock/David Roesner (eds.), *Composed Theatre. Aesthetics, Practices, Processes* (Bristol, 2012).

[34]   See Mladen Ovadija, *Dramaturgy of Sound in the Avant-Garde and Postdramatic Theatre* (Montreal, 2013).

[35]   See Hans Emons, *Für Auge und Ohr: Musik als Film – oder die Verwandlung von Kompositionen in Licht-Spiel* (Berlin, 2005).

[36]   See Kerry Brougher/Jeremy Strick/Ari Wiseman/Judith Zilczer, *Visual Music: Synaesthesia in Art and Music Since 1900* (London, 2005).

[37]   Hiß, *Synthetische Visionen*, p. 101, original emphasis.

[38]   Appia, 'Music and the Art', p. 35.

[39]   Appia, 'Music and the Art', p. 31.

[40]   This thinking has proven to be highly influential until today as the recently published volume *Theater ohne Fluchtpunkt: Das Erbe Adolphe Appias: Szenographie und Choreographie im zeitgenössischen Theater* [*Theatre Without Vanishing Points: The Legacy of Adolphe Appia: Scenography and Choreography in Contemporary Theatre*], ed. by Gabriele Brandstetter and Birgit Wiens (Berlin, 2010), documents.

production, and those elements are forced by the music to furnish a degree of expression proper to their close relationship with the living actor.[41]

Music is a multi-functional 'shifter'[42] for Appia: while it objectifies, reifies and controls the animate (the actors), making their performance less volatile and contingent on individual fluctuation of concentration, etc., it simultaneously animates and enlivens the inanimate of performance, charging them with expressivity. Although Appia does not provide a lot of detail on *how* music achieves this, judging from the context of his writings and practice it is probable that aspiring to the harmonic proportions of much classical and romantic music in the quality and timing of gestures, as well as the 'motivic' use of gesture and or objects (and colours) over the course of a production, are the key.

Motivic composition is one of the prevalent principles of the Western classical tradition: referring to the introduction and compositional development of small meaningful melodic parts (such as the famous four-note motif g, g, g, e♭, which opens Beethoven's Fifth Symphony). A motif 'is a short and distinctive pattern, usually of simple rhythmic and pitch design. Because of its brevity, the motif is easily recognized and frequently plays an important role in melodic organization'.[43] Composing with motifs is concerned with discovering a wealth of permutations and procedures with which to continuously mould the motivic material into a variety of shapes and forms and extract more and more musical meaning from it by presenting it in different ways and contexts. The key difference from, say, the recurrence of a catch phrase in a sitcom (Joey's 'How you doin'?' in *Friends* [1994–2004], for example), is that motivic composition (and also the use of leitmotifs for that matter) does not mean merely repeating fixed expressions in different contexts but actively transforming the motif, and also requires that this is worked on *musically*, for example by putting it in retrograde (backwards) or inversion (backwards and upside down).[44]

---

[41] Appia, *Music and the Art*, p. 36.

[42] I mean this in the linguistic sense, where shifters are pronouns such as 'I' or 'you', which take on different meanings/referents according to who the speaker is.

[43] William Christ et al., *Materials and Structure of Music. Third Edition* (Englewood Cliffs, NJ, 1980), p. 68.

[44] Looking at German-speaking theatre, three practitioners come to mind, Thomas Bernhard (Austria), René Pollesch (Germany) or Christoph Marthaler (Switzerland) for whom a motivic approach is quite central in shaping the evolving dramatic text (Bernhard), post-modern performance (Pollesch), or music-theatrical collage (Marthaler). While Appia uses music-compositional thinking as a *constructivist* activity to get to a deep-seated core of expression and meaning, later practitioners (such as the three just mentioned), however, often *deconstruct* their material (language, gesture, sound, etc.) and implicitly question the existence of that one holistic 'inner life' Appia so desires to bring to the fore.

When applied to spatial design, musicality has a name for Appia: 'rhythmic spaces'.[45] Here, the musicality lies to a degree in the design of space itself by using architectural proportions inspired by music,[46] but perhaps more importantly, Appia's rhythmic spaces are designed to facilitate, if not provoke, a musicality in their envisioned *use* – the interaction of space, light, performer and the audience's gaze:

> In the spring of 1909 Appia created about twenty designs which he termed 'Rhythmic Space'. [...] Because of the qualities of architectural harmony and proportion with which Appia imbued them, though lacking any element of time or movement themselves, as the eye surveyed them they could nevertheless visually provide a strong sense of rhythm.[47]

The use of columns, steps and levels creates distinctive rhythmic patterns and movement qualities for the light and the actors, both of which will animate the set and shape the passing time in it (see Figure 1.1). Actors and lights can be, or even *must* be, composed on this three-dimensional canvas in time and space. Again, this practice has resonated strongly amongst theatre practitioners up to today, from Einar Schleef to Robert Wilson, from Heiner Goebbels to Robert Lepage.

Light
A particularly innovative application of musicality to the 'non-musical' aspects of performance was Appia's treatment of light. He speaks of a 'mysterious affinity between music and light'[48] and uses this argument to advance lighting from a predominantly illustrative and subservient design element to 'a fully expressive medium in its own right'.[49] It is interesting to note that this significant reevaluation of a *visual* design element is motivated and justified *musically*. Appia's understanding of light is similar to his concept of music, particularly light's analogous ability to express the 'inner essence' and its potential to animate the stage visually and shape theatrical action temporally:[50] 'Light has an almost

---

[45]   See Beacham, *Adolphe Appia: Texts on Theatre*, p. 11; Beacham, *Adolphe Appia. Artist and Visionary*, pp. 76–9.

[46]   This tradition was established, as I have mentioned in the Introduction, in the Renaissance by Alberti, Palladio and others, continuing to have currency from Daniel Libeskind to David Byrne. The latter turns the idea around by creating music that is strongly influenced by architecture (see http://www.ted.com/talks/david_byrne_how_architecture_helped_music_evolve.html [11.10.2011]).

[47]   Beacham, *Adolphe Appia: Artist and Visionary*, p. 79.

[48]   Appia, 'Music and the Art', p. 51.

[49]   Beacham, *Texts on Theatre*, p. 5.

[50]   See Appia, 'Music and the Art', p. 51.

Figure 1.1   Adolphe Appia, 'Rhythmic Space'

miraculous flexibility … it can create shadows, make them living, and spread the harmony of their vibrations in space, just as music does.'[51]

I would argue that it is precisely through this analogy that Appia realizes light's formal potential and rhythmic quality. By applying musical thinking, Appia liberates light from its mere pragmatic and narrative/atmospheric functions: light no longer only just helps us to see the actor and the painted scenery better or identify the location, general atmosphere or time of day by imitating realistic light settings. Like music, it is a time-based art, which is characterized by parameters within which contrasting ends of spectra can be compositionally designed and exploited. Light can be dark and bright, soft or hard, wide or focused, red, blue, yellow, green or any other colour. It can change abruptly, gradually or imperceptibly.

[51]   Adolphe Appia, 'Actor, Space, Light, Painting (1919)', in Beacham, *Texts on Theatre*, pp. 114–15, p. 114.

We can be aware of its source (a candle on a table) or aware of the absence of a visible source – a phenomenon that in (film-)music theory has been discussed as acousmatic[52]. And finally – and this leads us to another important Appian impulse for the musicality *dispositif* – light is, like music, a potentially polyphonic medium: a multitude of lights can coexist, interact, merge, contrast and be perceived both in their totality and individuality, quite different from one of drama's more traditional ingredients: the spoken word, which, when not presented linear and solo, very quickly becomes cacophonic and – in a discursive sense – meaningless.

Score

Organizing simultaneity is a central aspect of music as an art form and thus also of interest for the musicality *dispositif*. One of its expressions, symbols and tools is the score or 'Partitur'. While Appia may not be the first to suggest this metaphor and method for organizing theatrical performance, he is particularly vocal about it. Appia starts his thinking, unlike some later practitioners (to which we will turn in the following chapters), with an *actual* musical score, such as an operatic composition by Wagner, but then urges theatre-makers to translate its properties to the *mise en scène* as a whole: the score, he says, must be the 'inspiration, regulator, guide and balance; it alone has the last word to which we must listen and obediently respond ... If the director does this, unity is assured ... .'[53] His approach touches on a few highly influential topoi: using and translating a *musical* practice of notation and creation for the theatre evokes thinking in simultaneous 'voices' or 'parts', in musical parameters (such as volume, duration or timbre) and promotes metaphors/similes such as the stage as an orchestra, the actor as an instrument and the director as a conductor – ideas we will reencounter frequently in this book.

What are Appia's perceived strategic benefits of the score as both master plan and main reference point for the theatrical creation? One benefit is the pragmatic answer to his philosophical call for the unity of the artwork and access to an unadulterated version of the playwright's expression. The score allows them to record and control the transition from page to stage in much more detail and depth:

> Imagine a dramatist with an incredible talent for music-poetic expression, using it freely, and simultaneously setting down in great detail every minute detail of staging in his score! His work contains by definition its theatrical form [...].[54]

Appia explains why the score is preferable to a mere play, when comparing both – and points most strongly at the obvious difference: the much more immediate and precise control over *time* a score affords its author, which is something Appia

---

[52]   See Pierre Schaeffer, *Traité des objets musicaux: Essai interdisciplines* (Paris, 1966); Michel Chion, *Audio-Vision. Sounds on Screen* (New York, 1994).

[53]   Appia, 'Theatrical Experiences', p. 25.

[54]   Appia, 'Theatrical Experiences', pp. 25–6.

emphatically desires: 'Time! Yes! Time is determined by the score but not by the playtext ... .'[55]

Appia is so convinced about the necessity of an absolute control over the creation and performance process in theatre that he even speaks affirmatively about the 'tyrannical influence'[56] of the score! He responds, it seems, to theatrical conventions of his time that placed overwhelming power into the hands of the performer/star and their deliberation and often arbitrary taste, which demonstrated their concern for perpetuating their fame rather than communicating the words and ideas of the particular play. Nonetheless, the unashamed call for a quasi-dictatorial artistic mastermind rings a bit odd for today's reader, most of all in the context of Appia's striving for a holistic, harmonious and humane approach to the theatre and its performers, as particularly his collaboration with Émile Jaques-Dalcroze and the development of eurhythmics would suggest.

Why, then, is Appia so concerned about the jurisdiction over time in the artistic process? He seems to suggest that only through an art form that controls time – music via the score – can we fully express and experience the 'intensity of [our] inner life',[57] which is pre-linguistic and pre-rational. He argues:

> If music controls time, it must have valid reason and sufficient justification for doing so ... We ourselves are this justification ... We happily admit that music expresses what our words and gestures are unable to express ... Music has nothing to enlarge, or prolong; it simply expresses ... Music reveals to the listener the form and intensity of his inner life in proportions that he accepts because he understands their origin ... .[58]

Music, Appia argues, is an art form whose materiality, shape and form are similar to that which he calls the 'inner life' (our idea or sensation of the world). It is thus able, unlike words, to allow us immediate access to our inner life without taking the detour of translating it into language. This is strikingly similar to what musicologist and philosopher Susanne Langer outlines more than fifty years later in her symbolist theory of music. She also credits music with the ability to capture things that escape words. Music historian Wayne Bowman explains that Langer distinguishes 'two ways of symbolization' calling them '"discursive" (after "discourse") and "presentational"':

> The former, obviously, is what language employs, while the latter is exemplified by music and the arts. [...] Langer claims variously that music makes change perceivable, makes time audible, and creates a 'sonorous image of passage'; but it is music's special relationship to feeling that is its most significant value.

---

55 Appia, 'Theatrical Production', p. 126.
56 Appia, 'Theatrical Production', p. 126.
57 Appia, 'Theatrical Production', p. 126.
58 Appia, 'Theatrical Production', p. 126.

Music should be regarded neither as a symptom nor as the cause of feeling, she urges, but rather as the logical symbolic expression of the inner, felt life. [...] Music does for feeling what language does for thought.[59]

This means, as Bowman summarizes, that 'the limits of what we can express linguistically or discursively, are not, she argues, the limits of what we can know';[60] or in other words: 'If words could convey what music does, we would not need music.'[61] Langer's conviction that 'music is a symbolic representation of the *form* of feeling' [my emphasis] rather than about 'exposing, discharging, or expressing feeling'[62] echoes Appia's theories on music and the 'inner life' strongly, even if perhaps unconsciously. Like Schopenhauer, Appia believes that music is the closest approximation to representing the idea or objectified 'will' of the world.

With respect to contemporary theatre, there is a key realization that Appia captures with his notion of the score, which has then further developed and continued to influence theatre-makers until today. I refer to the constant *simultaneity* of events on the theatre stage, its potential polyphony and the many possibilities of interplays and relations, order and disorder, resonances or dissonances between all these events and the crucial role the director plays in shaping these relationships. The musicality *dispositif* focused amongst other things on the 'harmony' of theatrical media (harmony understood here in a musical, not psychological or atmospheric sense), i.e. exploring the full range of formal and semantic relations, which go beyond a simple dichotomy of consonance and dissonance.

Since the discovery and invention of polyphony around the ninth century (AD), music of all genres and categories has been decidedly occupied with researching and experimenting with forms of interplay and harmony of different voices and levels. The development of an understanding of the interaction of *theatrical* voices, layers and expressive means, however, has been quite limited so far. Means and signs are generally reduced to their *semantic* meanings, and the correspondences of these meanings have been essentially reduced to two basic models: they are seen to be either in accordance or in contrast.[63] This is obviously too limited a view, as theatre scholar Guido Hiß confirms:

> The joining up, the *composition* of the multimedia form [in theatre, DR] does not evolve as a simple equalization of different expressive elements [...]. The multimedial code constitutes a realm of meaning, in which the involved partial systems react to each other in such a way that they mutually interpret each other.[64]

---

[59]   Bowman, *Philosophical Perspectives*, p. 200.
[60]   Bowman, *Philosophical Perspectives*, p. 206.
[61]   Bowman, *Philosophical Perspectives*, p. 210.
[62]   Bowman, *Philosophical Perspectives*, p. 210.
[63]   See Hiß's critique on Erika Fischer-Lichte's *Semiotik des Theaters* in Guido Hiß, *Der theatralische Blick* (Berlin, 1993), pp. 50–53.
[64]   Hiß, *Der theatralische Blick*, p. 51, original emphasis.

Even if the material nature of theatre and music is, of course, different – we can appreciate, for example, a motet in 40 voices by Thomas Tallis as pure canorousness, while 40 different simultaneously spoken texts will be regarded as a cacophony – the notion of musicality in theatre provides us with richer, more multi-faceted and accurate ways of dealing with the consonances and interplays of the wide range of theatrical 'voices'.

If we look at composer and director Heiner Goebbels's works, for example – especially *Black on White* (Frankfurt 1996), *Eraritjaritjaka* (Lausanne 2004) and *Stifter's Things* (Lausanne 2007) – which take Appia's notion of the theatre as score into the twenty-first century while being diametrically opposed to other premises of Appia,[65] we can see prime examples of how text, music, lighting, set and movement at times entangle in complementary rhythms, provide sonic punctuation for each other, concentrate or disperse the atmosphere, flirt with changing causal connections,[66] remain mutually foreign, develop anthropomorphic autonomy, become co-performers and so on.[67]

In short, an awareness of the interplay of scenic elements and theatrical means, which makes use of the wealth of models available in musical voicing and composition techniques, expands the scope for staging theatre far beyond the homologue/antithetic dichotomy and enriches the theatre with differentiated, engaging and imaginative interplays between the theatrical voices. The models may be borrowed and adapted from classical music, forms of improvisation and arrangement-practices in jazz, or from methods of sampling, sound editing and track-work in pop or hip-hop.

Notation

Both the simultaneity and increasing level of abstraction in Appia's anti-naturalist theatre bring about the necessity of different forms of notation beyond the established modes of the playtext or the musical score. Appia calls for a notation in a 'language accessible to all'[68] to help the actors fulfil their task. He reasons that while the 'poetic-music notation of his role is conveyed through the conventional signs of music and language, so an equivalent method for the visual expression must be found [...]. A system of hieroglyphs seems appropriate to this purpose ...'.[69]

---

[65]   Goebbels is a vocal advocate for the separation of elements on stage, rather than seeking their unity or harmony. See for example his lecture 'Aesthetics of Absence: Questioning Basic Assumptions in Performing Arts', Cornell Lectures on Contemporary Aesthetics, at http://www.heinergoebbels. com/en/archive/texts/texts_by_heiner_goebbels/read/450 [10.10.2011].

[66]   For example: does André Wilms accompany Ravel's string quartet with his rhythmical onion chopping in *Eraritjaritjaka*, or vice versa? See the videos of a lecture by Heiner Goebbels, published by the European Graduate School, for an in-depth discussion of *Eraritjaritjaka*, http://www.egs.edu/faculty/heiner-goebbels/videos [18.03.2010].

[67]   See H. Goebbels, *Aesthetic of Absence* (London, 2014) (forthcoming).

[68]   Appia, 'Music and the Art', p. 39.

[69]   Appia, 'Music and the Art', p. 39.

Beacham asserts that this idea pre-empts Rudolf Laban's dance/movement notation (which he first published in 1928), but I would also see it as a precursor of graphic notation in music and the kind of scored instructions you find, for example, in Mauricio Kagel's instrumental theatre scores (e.g. *Staatstheater* 1967–1970, see Figure 1.2).[70]

The introduction of the idea of notation changes the 'form of intellectual and social organization',[71] as musicologist Robin Maconie says with reference to musical notation. Forms of notation relying on musical models may actually be introduced into the process of theatre-making or lurk in the back of people's minds as a metaphor and a way of visualizing and temporalizing one's thinking – either way, notational practices, particularly in the form of scores, change the creative process.

Maconie reminds us that notation naturalizes certain ways of expression and resists others – some things are better confined to memory (by repetition and a kind of oral/visual culture of handing down) than others. Notation in contrast creates 'the possibility of musical speculation of an abstract kind'[72] – it enables a different type of artistic endeavour, while steering away from another. It is thus an aspect of the musicality *dispositif* that effects a transition: theatre used to be an art form of physically trying out something, looking at the embodied evidence of rehearsal results to see whether something works or not; with the turn towards notation other kinds of theatre-making become possible, with different aesthetic results.[73]

Rhythm
In connection with the idea of the transferability of musicality and the notion of the score, Appia explores another topos that has proven highly consequential for theatre-making in the twentieth/twenty-first centuries: rhythm. Where the notion of the score reflects how Appia was concerned with simultaneity (or vertical relation) of events, his emphasis on rhythm shifts the attention towards the 'horizontal' unfolding of performance in time and the relation of its parts, be it the larger segments of time or the pace and succession of smaller units from individual scenes to the briefest exchanges.

---

[70]   From Mauricio Kagel 'Staatstheater | Szenische Komposition'. © 1967 by Universal Edition A.G., Wien/UE 15197. Instructions read, for example, 'Tin shoes, Plexiglas or tins, fixed to the soles, several steel balls within' (21), 'Tray shoes, e.g. half of a film canister attached with clasps to bare feet' (32).

[71]   Robin Maconie, *The Concept of Music* (Oxford, 1990), p. 121.

[72]   Maconie, *The Concept of Music*, p. 115.

[73]   Again, this has found particular influential expression in Robert Wilson's work – see for example John Rockwell, *Robert Wilson: The Theater of Images* (New York, 1984); Simhandl, *Bildertheater*; Arthur Holmberg/Christopher Innes, *The Theatre of Robert Wilson* (Cambridge, 1996); Holm Keller, *Robert Wilson* (Frankfurt am Main, 1997); David Roesner, *Theater als Musik. Verfahren der Musikalisierung in chorischen Theaterformen bei Christoph Marthaler, Einar Schleef und Robert Wilson* (Tübingen, 2003); Maria Shevtsova, *Robert Wilson* (London, 2007).

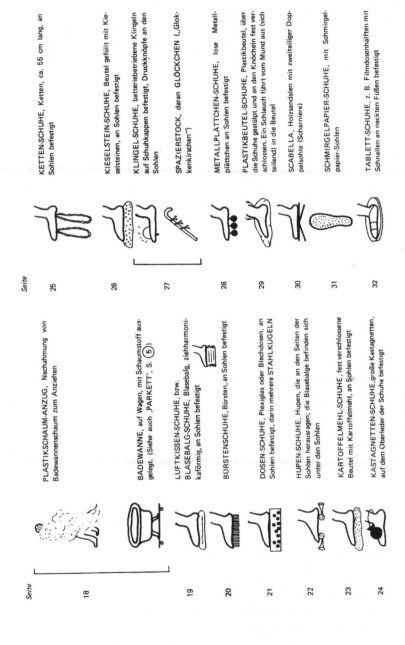

Figure 1.2 Excerpt from the notational instructions for Mauricio Kagel's *Staatstheater*, 1967–1970

Theatre-makers have always considered rhythm with regard to vocal delivery in acting but have applied and developed mostly *rhetorical* models from Corax of Syracuse, Aristotle and Cicero rather than *musical* principles. Here, the main purpose of using and mastering rhythmical devices – the use of pauses, accentuation, changes of tempo, establishing and breaking metre, repetitions and variations – is a *semantic* one, rendering an argument convincing and persuasive. Appia, however, calls for an *aesthetic* use of rhythm: all the arguments he presents for the need to control and shape time, both on a micro- and macro-rhythmical level of the performance, have the purpose of maximizing the expressive qualities and reach both of the performers and the other elements of the performance.

While rhythmical considerations usually follow semantic ones on stage in naturalist theatre – a pause in a speech may signify a moment of change in the character's mind-set, a 'pause' in lighting (a moment of darkness for example) may signify the passing of time, perhaps the advent of a new day – Appia breaks the mould for more abstract and musical uses of rhythm, putting considerations about durational balance and proportion, unity and variety of tempi, repetition and contrast in rhythmical movement or text delivery at the forefront of his theatrical manifesto. Rhythm for Appia, as Simhandl points out, formally regulates the temporal proportion between the different arts contributing to the theatre event.[74]

Both 'horizontally' and 'vertically', rhythm and rhythmic relations help to create *form*. Form (or structure) in theatre can also be called 'dramaturgy' and has often and traditionally been developed semantically: organizing the relaying of information, the development of characters and their relations, of the succession of comic, tragic, suspenseful, romantic or other episodes.[75] For Appia, form in theatre is a *musical* phenomenon, emerging from rhythms, motif or timbre relationships, repetition and variation. Goebbels echoes this a century later and also points out that the two (semantic and musical form) are not mutually exclusive:

> The best way to define a musical approach on theatre is to be conscious about form, to undertake research on forms. It doesn't mean it is formal – forms always mean something, forms always have a very strong impact on our perception, more perhaps than the perspective reduced to semantics and topics. The idea of a 'form' can be very rich and open and does not have to be reduced to 'symmetry', 'repetition' or 'rhythm'.[76]

To give a brief example: in a very 'Appian' production, Robert Wilson's *Oedipus Rex* (Paris 1996) was set on stage-filling steps. The various complex rhythms

---

[74]   See Simhandl, *Bildertheater*, p. 14.

[75]   See Cathy Turner/Synne K. Behrndt, *Dramaturgy and Performance* (Basingstoke, 2007) for a much more detailed discussion of the term 'dramaturgy'.

[76]   Heiner Goebbels, '"It's all part of one concern": A "Keynote" to Composition as Staging', in Rebstock/Roesner, *Composed Theatre*, pp. 111–20, p. 114.

of the music aside, the production contrasted the individual movement of the singers with the collective, barely perceptible rhythm of the entire chorus moving downwards and sideways over the steps, crossing them once during the one-hour performance. This was broken down within itself into several individual rhythms, as members of the chorus did not move in unison, but were instructed individually when to move a step sideways or downwards, causing a rippling effect, however slowed down.[77]

It is worth noting that Appia's notion of rhythm is one of measure, metre and unity. It is the *normative* understanding of rhythm as a regulating, flowing and unifying principle, which was prevalent in music aesthetics until Hugo Riemann (1905). Since rhythm reappears regularly in practitioners' writings until the present day, it is worth taking a closer look at the history of the term and concept in music.

'Rhythm' is one of the most frequently used musical notions in theatre-making and has lost considerable traction and definition in the process. Already in 1988 sociologist Hans Ulrich Gumbrecht noted that the 'phenomenon "rhythm" has become an arbitrary (and thus worthless) offer to solve an (almost) arbitrary range of questions'.[78]

It is not my intention to offer a general definition of rhythm, but to differentiate between varying understandings and instrumentalizations of this term in the context of theatre-making. Firstly, though, I suggest going back to *musical* definitions of rhythm to narrow the focus. Secondly I suggest looking at rhythm as a *productive* category that influences training, acting, directing, designing and devising processes. Several authors have discussed rhythm as a *perceptive* category in depth elsewhere[79] but my interest here is a different one.

From an etymological perspective,[80] 'rhythmos' is already an equivocal term. Wilhelm Seidel, musicologist and one of the foremost researchers on musical rhythm, explains:

---

[77] See the film documentation *Oedipus Rex. A Robert Wilson Workshop* by Elisabeth Bühler and Thomas Wollenberger from 1995, available at the New York Public Library.

[78] Hans Ulrich Gumbrecht, 'Rhythmus und Sinn', in Hans Ulrich Gumbrecht/K. Ludwig Pfeiffer (eds.), *Materialität der Kommunikation* (Frankfurt am Main, 1988), pp. 714–29, p. 714.

[79] See for example Helga de la Motte-Haber/Hans-Peter Reinecke, *Ein Beitrag zur Klassifikation musikalischer Rhythmen. Experimentalpsychologische Untersuchungen* (Köln, 1968); André-Pierre Benguerel/Janet D'Arcy, 'Time-warping and the perception of rhythm in speech', *Journal of Phonetics*, 14 (1986): 231–46; Christa Brüstle et al. (eds.), *Aus dem Takt. Rhythmus in Kunst, Kultur und Natur* (Bielefed, 2005); and the section on rhythm by the research group *Theatre as a paradigm of modernity*, University of Mainz 1992–2001, http://www.uni-mainz.de/Organisationen/GradkoTheater/themen-ss99.html [28.09.2011].

[80] See Émile Benveniste, 'Der Begriff des "Rythmus" und sein sprachlicher Ausdruck', in his *Probleme der allgemeinen Sprachwissenschaft* (München, 1974), pp. 363–74, for an extensive etymological discussion of the term.

What does rhythm mean? The answers of musicologists differ: some say flow, 'homogenous stream', wave, others say measure, order, number and all refer back to the ancient meaning of the word. [...] In the process described by the term originally, both components, flow and measure, are contained.[81]

With respect to a notion such as Appia's 'rhythmic spaces', it is worth noting that, musically speaking, 'only movements, not states [...] can be the object of rhythmical order'.[82] This is why I suggested that the rhythmicality of his designs lies in the implications they have for the movement of actors and lights within them – only then the constitutive aspects of rhythm, temporality and movement, are introduced.

The normative notion of order, which Appia bases his sense of rhythm on, can be found in writings from Plato (fourth century BC) to Hanno Helbling;[83] but *which* norms and rules were applied and which recommendations composers or theoreticians made for a 'correct' or 'balanced' use of rhythm has always been subject to music historical developments, one might even say trends and fashions of rhythm.

It remains unclear to me what the implicit rhythmic norms are that Appia refers to, but his insistence on unity, order and discipline as rhythmic qualities suggests that he is referring to balanced proportions and a clear sense of metre that is still a prevalent understanding of rhythm today, even though the twentieth century in particular has explored rhythm in a much wider sense. Often *all* rhythm is being reduced to a sense of *regular*, meter-based rhythms. It is a misunderstanding to think rhythm only refers to repetitive patterns. Even just two successive beats or words or sounds are immediately in a rhythmic relationship. We will thus encounter different, non-regular, non-normative notions of rhythm in the works and writings of other theatre practitioners, where the rhythmic dispositive may be used not for balance, order and harmony, but perhaps instead for sharp contrast, friction, disorder. Christa Brüstle et al. explain:

> The notion of rhythm does not only imply regularity, but also interruption, breaking, pause, difference and discontinuity, namely in the interplay, the mutual reference. In this sense rhythm is described as subjective interplay between expectation and surprise by Paul Valéry and demonstrates, according to Helmuth Plessner, 'instability in its stability, regularity in the irregular'.[84]

Appia, however, is still strongly indebted to the classical tradition (and through it to ancient Greek musical and rhetorical ideals) that foregrounds measure and order. He is a strong advocate for theatre as a rhythmic art form and not only

---

[81]   Wilhelm Seidel, *Über Rhythmustheorien der Neuzeit* (Bern/München, 1975), p. 29.
[82]   Wilhelm Seidel, *Rhythmus – eine Begriffsbestimmung* (Darmstadt, 1976), p. 2.
[83]   Hanno Helbling, *Rhythmus. Ein Versuch* (Frankfurt am Main, 1999).
[84]   Brüstle et al., *Aus dem Takt*, p. 10.

introduces a more abstract and musical understanding of theatre rhythm to the field, but also explores in detail how to apply it to the most obvious rhythmic 'device' on stage – the actor – but also to lighting, décor and space.

After analyzing some of the key characteristics of Appia's sense of musicality in the theatre, I shall now look at the consequences his suggestions and convictions have for the director and the actor.

Consequences for the Director and Actor

The Director's Task

Appia's writing firmly established the notion of the director in European theatre, in conjunction with the ideas and practices of the like-minded Edward Gordon Craig and based on Richard Wagner's towering cultural presence. While the title 'director' was 'first seen as a job description in theatre as late as 1771 in Vienna',[85] it ranked very low in the theatrical pecking order until the end of the nineteenth century: even at the beginning of the twentieth century a director would still be described as 'book-keeper, sign-post, school-master, copyist'.[86] Appia was instrumental in toppling this hierarchy and began, like Craig, to 'radically question the bourgeois-illusionistic theatre'[87] not only 'retaining the function of the director'[88] but extending it in the process.

The role of the director and its definition by Appia are intimately connected with, if not born out of, the musicality *dispositif*:[89] more precisely, indebted to the idea of music as a means of transporting the true poetic intentions of the playwright-composer through to production. We find here already, at the dawn of the 'director', the analogy between this role and that of a *conductor* and therefore the assumption that their role is an inherently *musical* one. We will reencounter this simile in the course of this book, but it is worth pausing on this, not least since Appia has quite a specific kind of conductor in mind as a model for his director: 'His influence must be magnetic, rather like that of a genial conductor.'[90]

---

[85]   Jens Roselt, 'Vom Diener zum Despoten. Zur Vorgeschichte der modernen Theaterregie im 19. Jahrhundert', in Nicole Gronemeyer/Bernd Stegemann (eds.), *Lektionen: Regie* (Berlin, 2009), pp. 23–37, p. 25.

[86]   Ludwig Barnay in Roselt, 'Vom Diener zum Despoten', p. 27.

[87]   Roselt, 'Vom Diener zum Despoten', p. 36.

[88]   Roselt, 'Vom Diener zum Despoten', p. 36.

[89]   Lawrence Switzky calls this 'the birth of the director out of the spirit of music' in his article 'Hearing Double: "Accousmatic" Authority and the Rise of the Theatre Director', *Modern Drama* 54/2 (Summer 2011), pp. 216–43, p. 219.

[90]   Appia in Milling/Ley, *Modern Theories*, p. 33.

In music history, there is a wide range of models for conductors[91] – from the gentle *primus inter pares* to the draconian dictator – just as the idea of the orchestra, the conductor's typical workplace, has undergone continuous changes. Maconie goes so far as to call the orchestra a 'compendium of civilizations',[92] based on the following observation:

> The symphony orchestra is a hybrid. Some instruments are old, some are relatively new. Some are for melody, some for noise; some are loud and some are soft; some are played with hands and some with breath; some are for singing and others for rhythm. There are instruments from the East and instruments from the West, some virtually unchanged from ancient times and others embracing the most up-to-date technology.[93]

In addition to the changes to its texture and its composition, there are also social and organizational aspects to be considered. Maconie:

> An orchestra is also a social microcosm. [...] We have been discussing an orchestra as an entity, a performing body. The achievement of unity under the conductor's baton is the normally overriding impression conveyed of orchestral organization. Certainly up to the mid-eighteenth century, we are conscious of the orchestra being used as a grand ensemble and demonstrating the organizational skill necessary to co-ordinate large numbers of players and to integrate a number of different musical processes simultaneously.[94]

The orchestra has undergone a transition from a 'vertically organized social hierarchy'[95] of the ensemble led from the piano to the complex, more 'industrial social model in which a production and its timetable are broken down into smaller units'.[96]

As with practically all musical analogies that theatre-makers employ, the conductor-orchestra setting they envision is an historically contingent analogy, an instrumentalization of an implicit or explicit *interpretation* of what a conductor or orchestra stand for in their original context. Appia clearly refers to the development of conducting in the nineteenth century when the conductor by and large ceased to be an instrumentalist coordinating an ensemble from their harpsichord, lute or

---

[91]   Anecdotally and quite entertainingly, Itay Talgam has pointed this out, when suggesting certain conducting styles as models for organizational leadership. See http://www.ted.com/talks/itay_talgam_lead_like_the_great_conductors.html [30.09.2011].

[92]   Maconie, *The Concept of Music*, p. 57.

[93]   Maconie, *The Concept of Music*, p. 57.

[94]   Maconie, *The Concept of Music*, pp. 59–60.

[95]   Maconie, *The Concept of Music*, p. 60.

[96]   Maconie, *The Concept of Music*, p. 60.

violin, and became the physically elevated and hierarchically dominant figure and interpretative sovereign.

Appia's director/conductor would be able to 'co-ordinate large numbers of actors and to integrate a number of different theatrical processes',[97] to borrow Maconie's wording. This is a logical extension of the theatre-as-score metaphor: with Appia begins a strong consciousness of theatre as a multi-medial and multi-modal art form, whose different means of expression need artistic coordination. Ideally for Appia, all the expressive channels would be routed through one person, but with his theatre-practical sense of reality he is quite aware of the limits:

> Under proper conditions, the playwright might be his own leading actor, designer and stage director; if he is a composer, he ought to be a singer and a conductor ... Of course, this asks too much of him![98]

At any rate, the director should no longer follow 'long-established and fixed conventions',[99] namely of being a mere arranger of scenic action at the mercy of and in subservience to the dominating actor and star. Appia emphasizes a different hierarchy: his director very authoritatively 'presides over the elementary preparation for the staging' like a 'despotic school-master' and 'artificially enforces the synthesis of the representative elements'.[100] The image of the conductor whom all contributing artists face and follow in the service of a higher objective provides Appia with the justification for the absolute levels of control he wants to grant the director. He borrows this from the developing notion of the conductor at his time, which is characterized by musicologist Christopher Small like this:

> For the modern conception of conducting to take hold – the conductor in charge of every detail of the performance and the sounds blended into a unified texture that is directed toward outside listeners – it was necessary that the players' musical autonomy and power of independent action be abolished.[101]

In comparison to later strategies of musicality and the advent of *Regietheater* (director's theatre),[102] it is interesting to note that despite the absolute control Appia seeks to give the director (even if guided and controlled by the drama

---

[97]   See Maconie, *The Concept of Music*, p. 60.

[98]   Appia, 'Theatrical Experiences', p. 25.

[99]   Appia, 'Music and the Art', p. 41.

[100]   Appia, 'Music and the Art', p. 41. It is interesting to read that despite all of Appia's insistence on the essence and the natural, he does call the synthesis of elements the theatre director enables 'artificial' (*künstlich*), which takes account of the crafted, deliberate and abstract nature of this union.

[101]   Christopher Small, *Musicking: The Meanings of Performing and Listening* (Hanover, 1998), p. 83.

[102]   See Chapters 5 and 6 and footnote 2 in this chapter.

in its musically defined temporal and expressive shape), he also wanted the director's task to be unnoticed by the audience:[103] 'The director's preparation of the feast should not be noticed by an audience that is to be offered only hot and well-prepared dishes.'[104] The cooking metaphor here overrides the conducting metaphor. Although having their back to the audience, the conductor still often is a major attraction and visual focus of the concert-goer and can, depending on the level of grandeur and self-promotion, get in the way of what Schopenhauer would call the 'immediate aesthetic experience'[105] of the musical work; an immediacy which, for Appia, any artistic encounter should aspire to.[106] The cook, however, usually remains entirely unseen, and also a good waiter (actor/musician) is best when *virtually* invisible; present only as a transparent provider and medium for the food (work of art). This idea has a history in the classical music world: the musician's task or function has long been seen as striving towards 'transparency, invisibility or personality negation'.[107] Small adds that 'the convention of the concert hall denies them [the musicians] any expressive use of bodily gesture, confining them to gestures in sound that are made through their instruments'.[108]

In theatre, however, the outgoing nineteenth century was dominated by the star system, placing the actor quite literally centre stage. Appia, alongside Craig, sought to radically change this, as we know. He asks: 'How can we kindle the life which sparks [...] the actor into subservience [...]?'[109] Again, the answer is: musicality.

The Actor's Task

I should start with a caveat: when Appia refers to what has been translated as 'the actor' he actually speaks of the *Darsteller*,[110] not the *Schauspieler* (actor; literally: 'show-player'), nor the *Sänger* (singer), as one might suspect given the operatic tendencies of the word-tone drama. This activity, *darstellen*, comprises a wider notion than 'acting' and can refer to activities such as describing, explaining, presenting, depicting and showing. Appia's use of the term is significant as he seeks to redefine the actor's role in the context of a new art form, but also

---

[103] In contrast, later theatre practitioners frequently use musicality as a device towards tangible abstraction, de-familiarization or self-reflexivity.

[104] Appia, 'Theatrical Experiences', p. 161.

[105] See http://plato.stanford.edu/entries/schopenhauer-aesthetics/ [09.08.2012].

[106] Concepts like immediacy, authenticity, truth, etc., while ubiquitous in theatre manifestos, are of course hugely problematical: in this book I am not using these terms as factual or ontological descriptions, rather I refer to the practitioners' short-hand as elements of discourse, in order to understand the practices, aesthetics or ethics of performance they seek to communicate.

[107] Lydia Goehr, *The Quest for Voice: On Music, Politics, and the Limits of Philosophy* (Oxford, 1998), p. 145.

[108] Small, *Musicking*, p. 155.

[109] Appia, 'Music and the Art', p. 43.

[110] Adolphe Appia, *Die Musik und die Inscenierung* (München, 1899), p. 34.

because the meaning of the term is situated somewhere between presenting and representing. So it already signifies a moving away from a naturalist notion of acting as the amalgamation of actor and character or even a disappearance of the actor behind the character.

I want to emphasize three aspects of this revision, which Appia justifies qua musicality and seeks to put in place with the help of musical means: objectifying the actors' task, music's role in their processes of expression, and the concrete impact this has on the training of actors.

'Objectifying' the Actor's Tasks Through Musical Instructions

Theatre historian Marvin Carlson summarizes the change in attitude towards the actor that is expressed in Appia's writings:

> The symbolist vision of the ideal actor, what Craig called the Über-marionette, is clearly required in Appia's theatre. By means of music 'the living human body throws off the accident of personality and becomes purely an instrument for human expression.' […] Clearly the actor as an original artist is demoted in this system, subordinated to the artistic ensemble expressed in the master score (the partitur), and controlled by music.[111]

Appia asks that the actor's actions be precisely set and scored in the music and claims the consequence of this to be that 'the living body discards its arbitrary veil of individuality and becomes an instrument consecrated to universal human expression'.[112] The choice of the word 'instrument' (also in the German original) should be noted – it places the actor firmly in the overall analogy of the director as conductor, the performance as scored and the theatre as an orchestra. It does, however, stand in contrast to other instrument analogies, which credit the actor with being both the instrument *and* the instrumentalist.[113] In Appia's version it is rather the poet-composer and then the director who 'play' the instruments, a category to which the actors but also inanimate theatrical objects belong:

> But for the author of a word-tone drama, the actor is not the only nor even the most important interpreter of his intention. He is instead only one medium, neither more nor less important than others, available to the poet … [The actor] becomes part of an organic unity and must submit to the rules governing the harmony of this organic entity.[114]

---

[111] Marvin Carlson, *Theories of the Theatre: A Historical and Critical Survey, From the Greeks to the Present. Expanded Edition* (Ithaca, NY/London, 1993), p. 295.

[112] Appia, 'Music and the Art', p. 40.

[113] See Bella Merlin, *Acting – The Basics* (London/New York, 2010), p. 27. According to Robert Gordon this idea goes back to the French actor Constant Coquelin (see Robert Gordon, *The Purpose of Playing: Modern Acting Theories in Perspective* [Ann Arbor, 2006], p. 102).

[114] Appia, 'Music and the Art', p. 32.

This is, explicitly, a move against the 'disproportionate importance'[115] that the actor has gained in Appia's view. But the objectification is not primarily trying to deny the actors their personality; in fact, the actor, according to Appia, needs a high level of 'versatility'[116] and the ability to privilege the execution of 'precise and direct instructions'[117] over exhibiting their virtuosity. This is in order for the actor not to become the central focus but an '*intermediary* between the music and the inanimate part of the stage production'.[118]

While this does effectively mean a clear change in hierarchy for the actor's standing in the production and its creation process, it is, I would argue, an attempt by Appia to restore some of the reputation, skill and sincerity of acting by reintegrating actors into the stage production as a whole and using music to guarantee the artistic excellence of their performance. Music, in Appia's vision, supports this in a variety of ways: it acts as a kind of rhythmic 'guardrail', a form of validation and a 'filter' for the actor's work. As mentioned earlier, it firstly helps to prevent their acting from becoming arbitrary and imprecise by 'dictating' their 'facial expressions and gestures'.[119] Secondly, by giving the acting *form* – both in itself and within the more abstract shape and rhythm of the production – it adds nobility to their craft. Appia consciously places a quotation by Friedrich Schiller at the beginning of his book *Music und die Inscenierung* as a motto: 'When music reaches its noblest power, it becomes form.'[120] And finally Appia suggests that like a water filter the musicality *dispositif* somehow 'purifies' what the actors are doing, cleansing the actor of murky self-promotion and self-centred indulgence. Music, then, is not only a symbolic language with a unique ability to express the inner world and an organizing and synthesizing principle. It is also a kind of filter preventing actors from acting randomly, privately, uncontrolledly, etc., in order to maintain and guarantee quality, as Beacham argues: 'Appia's insistence on the depersonalization of the actor, and the necessity of integrating him with the other elements of production, anticipates Gordon Craig's call for actors without egos ... .'[121] For Appia, however, 'far from weakening the indispensible spontaneity of the actor, [this] bestows that quality on him in the highest degree. Just as music allows only the purest expression of the dramatist's personal conception to emerge, so it allows only the noblest aspects of the actor's personality'.[122]

In Appia's sense of a musicality of theatre, then, the actor's role may seem diminished, subordinated and disempowered, but Appia's aim is to bring out the best in the actor, seeking to 'chisel away' their personal idiosyncrasies

---

[115] Appia, 'Music and the Art', p. 32.
[116] Appia, 'Music and the Art', p. 32.
[117] Appia, 'Music and the Art', p. 32.
[118] Appia, 'Music and the Art', p. 32, original emphasis.
[119] Appia, 'Music and the Art', p. 32.
[120] Schiller in Appia, *Music and the Art*, p. xxi.
[121] Beacham, *Adolphe Appia: Texts on Theatre*, p. 234.
[122] Appia in Beacham, *Adolphe Appia: Texts on Theatre*, p. 234.

and mannerisms in order to integrate them harmoniously into the theatrical production as a whole.

Music Shapes Both Expression and Perception

In the following quotation, which repeats and summarizes how Appia sees the impact of musicality on the actor, there is yet another aspect to note.

> Let us move to the actor! We have observed that musical expression fundamentally modifies the external form of our gestures, i.e. their successive durations in time, and that therefore the actor need no longer interpret his part, but rather clearly present it as it has been entrusted to him. The value of the actor will be his cooperation; music transfigures him, making him unable to resist. The bearer of an inner action obviously behaves in a different manner to one interpreting an action dictated by external circumstances … . Our final problem is to enliven space through music using the actor who is himself transformed and transfigured by musical qualities … .[123]

Music, according to Appia, not only organizes and shapes what actors *do*; it also changes how we *perceive* what they do, 'charging' (or 'enlivening') their actions with expression and meaning. Music creates a 'milieu in which the living body takes on artistic significance'.[124] There is a telling anecdote that pinpoints this statement: Prince Serge Wolkonski on visiting rehearsals of Appia and Dalcroze[125] in Hellerau recounts the story of a man who happened to cross the stage during rehearsals and, by virtue of the accompanying music, 'without suspecting it, […] became the presenter of a eurhythmic pantomime'.[126] The music here seems to have 'elevated' a largely unconscious and unassuming everyday action on a stage to a moment of artistic expression, a theatrical action. One aspect of performance where this becomes particularly manifest, according to Appia, is with regard to emotion. Guided and 'lifted' by musicality, the actor no longer needs to 'evoke' any emotion that is 'divorced from the music'.[127] As I understand Appia here, he maintains that the actor does not need to *fill* his role with emotion, but *merely* convey the emotion or be a medium for the emotion already contained in the music providing the '*extraordinary forms imposed on him*'.[128]

---

[123] Appia, 'Theatrical Production', p. 130.

[124] Appia, 'Music and the Art', p. 40.

[125] 'Independently of Appia Dalcroze had pursued the aim – in summary – to educate the human body as a visual pendant of musical structures. To this end he developed before the turn of the century a system of exercises, in which each note value was allocated to a particular movement of the body' (Grund, *Zwischen den Künsten*, p. 156).

[126] Wolkonski in Beacham, *Adolphe Appia. Artist and Visionary*, p. 91.

[127] Appia, 'Music and the Art', p. 41.

[128] Appia, 'Music and the Art', p. 41, original emphasis.

Characteristically, Appia extends this capacity of music even to the inanimate elements of performance and the interaction of the actor with these. Music provides, creates and modifies scenery and atmosphere:

> [...] if we place a character with that setting, and for five minutes allow the music to suggest a mood, or some activity – no matter what – or merely to allow the music to flow over his body, the atmosphere will suddenly acquire life, the setting will become *expressive*, and the walls of the room *because they are not part of this expression, will cease to exist.*[129]

This last aspect seems to allow or even require a certain amount of passivity on the part of the actor ('merely allow[ing] the music to flow over his body'), but even this and certainly all previous descriptions of their task clearly require a different kind of training for the new type of actor Appia envisions.

Actor Training

Appia does give specific instructions for actor training and, unsurprisingly, emphasizes musicality as a key requirement and area of development. His ideal is a 'musicalized body' and actors who have sensitized their bodies to respond to and produce an 'esthetic harmony' in gesture, speech and movement. In order to achieve this, Appia calls for a 'system of musically based "gymnastics" as vital to the training of the actor'.[130] He explains:

> [...] we may well wonder what use rhythmic gymnastics will be for our actors, since they find so little direct application for it on stage. It goes without saying that if we inculcate rhythm into actors through some normal method and at the same time make them aware of the purely esthetic harmony of their bodies, that discipline will have a highly beneficial influence on their musical sense and musical qualities, as well as on the purity and appropriateness of their performance; it will, moreover, bring them closer to a kind of moderation that borders on style. But this is a general consequence – one that has to do especially with restraint and a sense of music. [...] The discipline of rhythm will have made him particularly aware of the dimensions in space that correspond to the countless varieties of musical sequences. Instinctively he will seek to make those dimensions apparent on stage [...].[131]

This statement again contains the key coordinates by which Appia locates music and its role in the relations of the arts: for him it is the art form that provides a sense of discipline, formal variety and at the same time consistency and 'moderation'

---

[129] Appia, 'Music and the Art', pp. 46–7, original emphasis.
[130] Beacham, *Adolphe Appia: Texts on Theatre*, p. 233.
[131] Appia in Bablet/Bablet, *Adolphe Appia*, p. 53.

(amounting to 'style'[132]) and, as I would read his comment on space and dimension, a strong awareness of form. He stresses this elsewhere when calling for a *'formal education'*[133] for the actor. As I have discussed earlier, this is not *per se* a call for order, balance, proportion, but in Appia's understanding of musicality these are the desiderata and only a musicalized body can meet them.

Training actors to move rhythmically and to let music shape and guide their movements is beneficial, says Appia, well beyond the margins of the word-tone drama with a fully composed score. The acquired skills are basic essentials, which translate to other forms of drama. While the first attempt should be 'to [introduce music] into the play [whenever possible] so that, though unable to exercise its primary expressive function, it might nevertheless serve to support and round out the action, ennobling the drama by forging, if only in passing, that unity between itself and poetry which Appia considered the basis for true dramatic art',[134] Appia saw benefits even when that proved impractical. Beacham describes how Appia envisioned how musical training could pay off even in performances with little or no actual music:

> The art of acting should be refined by engaging the performer in rigorous training in musically coordinated movement; in fact, in eurhythmics. Through such training the body itself could be conditioned by music to exercise a more genuinely expressive role in place of purely imitative technique. In time such thoroughgoing training would result in 'an organism so saturated with music that it can free itself from music's tutelage', to perform expressively in non-musical drama.[135]

Appia did approach dramatic texts as well, directing, for example, Shakespeare's *Hamlet* in 1922: 'Appia's basic approach to the play was similar to that used with music dramas.'[136] The composed music of the word-tone drama is here replaced by internalized 'scores' – musically arranged patterns of speech, gestures and movements in space – strictly overseen and rehearsed by the director-conductor in a space which aesthetically and practically supports and encourages rhythmic abstraction and form.

---

[132] It is highly likely that Appia knew of Goethe's famous distinction between nature, manner, style in his essay 'Einfache Nachahmung der Natur, Manier, Styl' (1788), in which he rates style the highest and, ahead of Schopenhauer, points at the inner essence (here: 'Wesen der Dinge') of things: 'Just as simple imitation depends on a quiet regime and comfortable surroundings, and manner has a facility for grouping superficial appearances, so style is based on the profoundest knowledge, on the essence of things insofar as we can recognise it in visible and tangible forms' (Johann Wolfgang Goethe, 'Simple Imitation of Nature, Manner, Style', in John Gage [ed.], *Goethe on Art* [London, 1980 (1788)], pp. 21–4, p. 22).

[133] Appia, 'Music and the Art', p. 43, original emphasis.

[134] See Beacham, *Adolphe Appia: Artist and Visionary*, p. 150.

[135] Beacham, *Adolphe Appia: Artist and Visionary*, p. 150.

[136] Beacham, *Adolphe Appia: Artist and Visionary*, p. 151.

In Performance

One of the astonishing things about Appia's musical approach to theatre is how his often idealistic and at times even romantically exorbitant claims seem to have successfully borne fruit in the creation of the performances. In particular, his collaboration with Dalcroze was met with enthusiastic reactions, which, surprisingly, stress how *natural* the results came across. Prince Wolkonski, who saw Dalcroze and Appia's *Orpheus and Eurydice* production of 1912–1913, gives his impressions as follows:

> Through all three acts one never had the feeling that one was at a presentation: we had before us real life, translated into music, magnificent music, which became living. It could not be otherwise, since all the performers were possessed by music; it possesses them both physically and emotionally; the music was for them a principle of life like the act of breathing … the radiating inner beauty was indescribable. Most impressive of all was the naturalness – one forgot that it was an opera – the most conventional and unbelievable of all arts.[137]

Even if we put this praise into the context of a period of theatre when acting styles were largely dominated by the melodramatic and the operatic, it is still remarkable that firmly imposing musical form and rhythm seemed to result in effacing the artificiality of operatic performance.[138] Where musicalization today often provides a means of abstraction or defamiliarization in opposition to a film-realistic naturalism and uses a more explicit sense of form and temporal architecture against any attempts to disguise the constructedness of the theatre situation, Appia – in the context of his time – appears to have achieved the opposite: using musicalization as a means to a more natural, seamless and immediate performance, that made the audience forget they were watching a performance.

It would seem to me that there are two overarching themes of his theatrical credo: firstly, that musicality acts as a guarantor of coordination and unity[139] – musicality can control time and shape of performance in a balanced, unifying way – much like classical composers from Mozart to Gluck have masterfully crafted the 'architecture' of their compositions and produced what we now consider pure, elegant music. The second theme is that musicality provides the key to inner dimensions of expression, a true nature and spirit. In Appia's transfiguration of the self and the absolutism with which the poet-composer-director is put in place, there are strong resonances of the music aesthetics of the romantic period: the

---

[137] Wolkonski in Beacham, *Adolphe Appia: Artist and Visionary*, p. 105.

[138] Recordings of dramatic speeches of the period such as those from Alexander Moissi sound exaggerated, larger-than-life and operatic to our contemporary ears. Hear, for example, Moissi's Faust at http://www.youtube.com/watch?v=i66lgFux9jc [10.10.2011]. Moissi was one of the most celebrated actors of his time, the early twentieth century.

[139] See Beacham, *Adolphe Appia: Texts on Theatre*, p. 111.

genius cult of the nineteenth century, Wagner's idea of an 'eternal melody' (which deliberately meant to oppose the periodization of the classical era) and that famous notion of the German romantic poet Joseph von Eichendorff:

> There slumbers a song in all things
> As they dream on and on
> And the world commences to sing
> If only you find the magic word.[140]

This is the darker, more mystical, more soul-searching aspect of Appia's musicality – his 'magic word', however, is not a word, but music itself. Appia taps into the romantic idea(l)s of the numinous, the longing, the subconscious as well as, paradoxically, the self-referential and ironic. As we will see in the following chapters many of these themes and strategies reoccur in different forms and contexts, while others, new ones, are introduced. Musicality as a *dispositif*, as will become evident, does not imply *one* aesthetic or *one process* – the survey through a range of historical and contemporary positions will demonstrate the range and variety at least as much as the similarities and continuations of approaches.

Conclusion: Appia's Relevance for the Dramatic Arts

Even though Appia's theories were triggered by and developed with a strong reference to Richard Wagner's operas, there is plenty of reason and evidence to support his relevance for a study of the role of musicality in the *dramatic* theatre.

On the one hand, history has already made up its mind about Appia's influence: a wide range of *theatre* practitioners have claimed his influence and have explicitly referred to Appia's work as an inspiration. More than that, the influence is also evidenced by the productions themselves, from the stage designs of Erich Wonder, Anthony Gormley or Olaf Altmann to the acting and directorial styles of Max Reinhardt, Jacques Copeau, Einar Schleef or Michael Thalheimer.

In other words, Appia's legacy puts him at least as strongly at the beginning of a *theatrical* reform movement, as it has initiated change in the conventions of *operatic* production. Appia's work gives ample reason to explore the musicality of theatre as it does to trace the developments in staging music-theatre.[141] With regard to opera itself, Appia was actually openly dismissive of this art form at times, claiming that 'modern opera is an extraordinary art, but it is already passé',[142] later calling it 'only a discordant juxtaposition'.[143] On the other hand, and perhaps more

---

[140] In Angela Esterhammer (ed.), *Romantic Poetry, Vol. 7* (Amsterdam, 2002), p. 34.
[141] See also Hiß, *Synthetische Visionen*, p. 98.
[142] Appia in Bablet/Bablet, *Adolphe Appia*, p. 53.
[143] Appia in Bablet/Bablet, *Adolphe Appia*, p. 54.

importantly, Appia himself has indicated that his thinking was not restricted to the word-tone drama of Wagnerian coinage. He says:

> Let us return briefly to the literary play! It tries to supply what only music could give it, and with true instinct grants sovereignty to the actor. [...] But the remarkable thing is that music has entered into the realm of the spoken drama! [...] Pure, unadulterated truth seemed then to appear gently and free the actor of the tinsel that obscured him, of the inessentials that thwarted him. [...] During the brief period when the incidental music is heard, [the actor's] gestures are modified, he perceived the divine element penetrating his body, and he would be unfeeling not to be affected by it.[144]

The (comparatively less significant) presence of just some incidental music and an actor with an open ear for musical structures of the language and dramaturgy of the play seem to enable a similar access to the 'divine' and the 'unadulterated truth' as did a through-composed score for Appia. It does not even need the musicality of the dramatic language to stand in for the score; the principles of music can be applied even to the actors' pre-linguistic expression: 'There is another way of integrating the human into the expression, which is, to transfer the basic principles of music onto him, without the necessity of involving words.'[145] So even though Appia reiterates in the same chapter that the 'art of stage production can be a true art only when its source is music',[146] he goes on to explain: 'To take music as the source of drama does not suggest that musical sound must itself be the origin of the dramatic idea, but rather that the object of the music should also be the object of that idea.'[147]

The musicality *dispositif*, as I have indicated earlier, is in many ways exactly this: one art form taking another as its source, without necessarily incorporating it in a direct or manifest way. A novel can be 'theatrical' without including dramatic dialogue or stage directions as such; music can be filmic, without including actual footage when performed, etc. In a more recent theoretical framework, this phenomenon has been called a 'trans-medial intermediality' based on 'the assumption that methods and modes of representation (aesthetic conventions) operate in several media'.[148] This brings certain fundamental aesthetic principles into play as *tertia comparationis* such as rhythm, narrative, perspective, metaphor, etc.[149] For Appia, this tertium is 'the object of music':[150] the 'inner life'. Beacham explains:

---

[144] Appia, 'Theatrical Production', p. 128.

[145] Appia, *Die Musik*, p. 37.

[146] Appia, 'Theatrical Production', p. 128.

[147] Appia, 'Theatrical Production', pp. 128–9.

[148] Freda Chapple/Chiel Kattenbelt (eds.), *Intermediality in Theatre and Performance* (Amsterdam/New York, 2006), p. 13.

[149] Cf. Jens Schröter, 'Intermedialität', http://www.theorie-der-medien.de/text_detail.php?nr=12 [20.02.2006].

[150] Appia, 'Theatrical Production', p. 129.

Thus, by carefully investigating the meaning which a given work could have for its audience, and using staging to refine and express that meaning, one might create dramatic works that – even in the absence of music – could aspire to be the controlled, coordinated and unified condition that Appia insisted must be the basis for any autonomous theatrical art.[151]

The fundamental principles, ways of working, hierarchies and reforms, which Appia initially derived from staging essentially *operatic* work, were later extended and cross-transferred to *dramatic* works, and the manifest composed score at the top of the process and hierarchical chain replaced by a (shared or imposed) notion of musicality. This emerged either from a dramatic text (such as a Chekhov or Beckett play), an individual's strongly developed sense for musicality of theatrical action (such as Christoph Marthaler's or Ruedi Häusermann's) or a *shared* sense of the 'right' timing, timbre and musical form, cultivated and carefully trained by groups and ensembles (such as Gardzienice, Song of the Goat or Bred in the Bone).

I will now look at a particularly prominent and influential cross-section of theatre artists who embedded the musicality discourse firmly in dramatic theatre and anchored it in a wider European context, in England, France and particularly in Russia.

---

[151] Beacham, *Adolphe Appia: Texts on Theatre*, p. 111.

Chapter 2

Meyerhold – Theatre 'Organized According to The Music's Laws'[1]

Introduction

There is a clear sense of continuity and legacy in the immensely rich period of theatre between 1900 and the beginning of the Second World War. Many of the most influential theatre-makers of this time knew each other, saw each other's work or at least read each other's manifestos, writings or training manuals. One of several connecting factors in this still-quite-diverse field is that many of the theatre reforms we have become accustomed to subsuming under the label 'the avant-garde' are strongly fuelled – amongst other things – by a sense of musicality. Musicality, here, was not seen as garnish on the aesthetic surface of the theatrical event or merely a useful addition to the actor-training curriculum as part of a kind of 'liberal arts' ideology, but was placed at the centre of the avant-garde's quest for a rediscovery of the theatrical:

> Music obtained a relatively dominant position within the theatrical code of the avant-garde. For the generation which set out to recreate theatre as thoroughly anti-illusionist, this recreation seemed only possible 'out of the spirit of music'; not only Appia and Craig, but also Meyerhold and Tairov were convinced to have rediscovered in music the foundation for everything theatrical and to have found the condition for the possibility of a truly 'theatrical' theatre.[2]

One of the strongest expressions of musicality as both an inherent principle of theatre and a vehicle towards recovering its essence can be found in Vsevolod Emilevich Meyerhold's (1874–1940) work and writings, to which I will add some aspects of other theatre-makers' discourses and processes for complementing and comparison. It was, according to Edward Braun, 'the concept of "musicality" that characterized Meyerhold's style and set him apart from every other stage-director of his time'.[3] Harlow Robinson adds the following differentiation:

---

[1]   Meyerhold in Aleksandr Gladkov, *Meyerhold speaks. Meyerhold rehearses* (London/New York, 1997), p. 115.

[2]   Erika Fischer-Lichte, *Semiotik des Theaters. Band 1* (Tübingen, 1994 [1983]), p. 179.

[3]   In Harlow Robinson, 'Love for Three Operas: The Collaboration of Vsevolod Meyerhold and Sergei Prokofiev', *The Russian Review*, 45/3 (1986), pp. 287–304, p. 289.

This 'musicality' was both literal and figurative: an important part of Meyerhold's
theory of biomechanics was rhythm, finding a technical musical foundation for
the movements of actors on stage and the movement of a whole production.
Meyerhold also used musical terminology to describe more exactly the pace,
movement and gestures of any staged work, and even referred to his schema for
a production as a 'partitura' (score).[4]

This is only one of the many ways in which Meyerhold's musicality gets mentioned
and discussed in various places.[5] There is, however, a lack of a more comprehensive
analysis, which carefully distinguishes the various musical aspects Robinson and
others refer to. I will thus try to tie together the most important findings from
this perspective and contextualize the specific shape or coinage of Meyerhold's
musicality *dispositif*, investigating how it sits in relation to Appia (Chapter 1) and
the theatre-makers and theatre practices yet to be discussed (Chapters 3–6).

One recurrent theme – even though diverse in detail in its various definitions
and forms of realization – is the project of the 're-theatricalization of theatre',
already coined by Georg Fuchs in his 1904 manifesto *Die Schaubühne der Zukunft*
[*The Stage of the Future*].[6] This was generally associated with a two-pronged
movement: on the one hand, there was a keen interest in past theatre forms,
particularly of the popular vernacular, ranging from the *commedia dell'arte* via
puppet theatre, Punch and Judy, to forms of cabaret, musical and vaudeville. On
the other hand there was a thrust forward away from the *status quo* of a naturalistic
and mimetic theatre aesthetic towards a more stylized, symbolic, or 'artful'
theatrical language. Both movements, as I will explore, are strongly connected to
notions of musicality.

By orientating themselves towards past theatre forms, in particular the
commedia dell'arte, theatre-makers took particular interest in the physical
virtuosity, the grotesque humour and playfulness, the capacity for improvisation
and the general liveliness of the form and the interaction with its audiences. I will
come back to these aspects when discussing the training philosophy and practices
of Meyerhold and his contemporaries.

Moving towards a more stylized, more explicitly *theatrical* theatre made
use, I would argue, of two aspects of music that have often been at the forefront
of treatises or debates on music aesthetics: music's perceived *immediacy* as an
artistic language, and, paradoxically, its simultaneous tendency to strict form and
abstraction. Musicologist Robin Maconie highlights the universal appeal of music
due to this paradox:

---

[4]   Robinson, 'Love for Three Operas', pp. 289–90.

[5]   I will refer to all the relevant sources in the course of this chapter.

[6]   See also Christopher Balme (ed.), *Das Theater von Morgen. Texte zur deutschen
Theaterreform* (Würzburg, 1988), p. 12.

The advantages of music over other forms of non-verbal communication lie in its universality as a medium of expression and the fact that it employs a centuries-old written language of considerable range and subtlety. It therefore meets the requirements of subjective immediacy and documentary precision.[7]

With regard to music's formal strength and tendency to develop strict and coherent sets of rules, Friedrich Schiller had already called for a reform of drama, arguing that the 'simple imitation of nature' should be replaced by 'introducing symbolic devices, which stand in for the subject matter' and thus create 'air and light for the arts'.[8] Following Schiller's reasoning, I argue that for Meyerhold two of the most powerful 'symbolic devices' to transform the theatre were indeed music and musicality.

This has concrete consequences for the role of the actor and director and the nature of the training and rehearsal processes, which I will discuss in the next section. I will then look more closely at the understanding of music and the notion of musicality present in Meyerhold's work and writings, with some comparisons to his contemporaries in the second section. Finally, I will come back to the notion of 'theatricality' and its connection to 'musicality' in this particular period of theatre, investigating more closely why the attempt to reorient the theatre towards its 'essence' seems to take the route through another art form: music.

Directing, Actor Training and Rehearsing

An important premise in Meyerhold's theatre aesthetics lies in his evaluation of the roles of the author, director, actor and spectator. He de-emphasizes the role of the author (he was known for restructuring and rearranging plays quite liberally), but also redefines the role of the director. For Meyerhold there are two main 'types' of theatre: 'theatre-triangle' and 'straight-line theatre', which he distinguishes particularly with regard to the communication flow between author, director, actor and audience. The triangular theatre allows the audience to 'see the work of the author and actor through the *work of the director*'.[9] Meyerhold, however, clearly prefers the 'Theatre of the Straight Line': here, 'the actor freely reveals his soul to the spectator after having incorporated the work of the director, just as the director had incorporated the work of the author'.[10] It is a chain of processes of appropriation, transformation and reinterpretation of work, and – at least on paper – a move away from Appia's

---

[7]   Robin Maconie, *The Concept of Music* (Oxford, 1990), pp. 3–4.

[8]   Schiller in Balme, *Das Theater*, p. 14.

[9]   Vsevolod Meyerhold, 'From "On the Theatre". Translated by Nora Beeson', *The Tulane Drama Review*, 4/4 (1960), pp. 134–48, p. 142, original emphasis.

[10]   Meyerhold, 'From "On the Theatre"', p. 142.

director as 'despotic school-master'.[11] 'The actor's work', Meyerhold insists, 'must do *more* than acquaint the audience with a director's conception. An actor can inspire an audience only if he transforms himself into the author and director'.[12] The actor Meyerhold has in mind becomes a freer, more contributing part of the collaboration; a highly trained individual who co-authors and *interprets* (within boundaries set by the director's concept) the performance. Even though Meyerhold also employs the actor-as-musician metaphor frequently, his idea of a 'straight-line theatre' deviates clearly from Appia's idea of the actor as an orchestra musician following 'accurately the dictates of a conductor'.[13] This would fall under Meyerhold's concept of a triangular theatre which requires the actor/musician to surrender part of their '*individualistic* virtuoso technique'[14] to achieve symphonic unity.

The kind of musical education that Meyerhold puts forward for the training and rehearsal practices in his 'straight theatre' is based on a musically inspired notion of both improvisation and structure and a highly developed autonomous sense of musicality both as an individual and as part of an ensemble – but without the strict hierarchies of a symphony orchestra.[15] How is a notion of musicality utilized in the redefinition of the actor and director's tasks? First of all, Meyerhold claims that the director needs to be a musician:

> If you asked me today where the difficulty lies in the art of the director, I would say: 'It lies in the fact that he needs to contain the uncontainable.' The challenge of the art of directing is that the director needs to be a musician most of all. He in particular has to deal with one of the most difficult aspects of the art of music, he develops the scenic movements always contrapuntally.[16]

Meyerhold not only emphasizes the importance of a musical approach towards theatre to provide a form or coherence to something that cannot easily be captured ('uncontainable'), but importantly he already introduces a notion here, which we will see to gain more and more currency in the musicality *dispositif* in the

---

[11] Adolphe Appia, 'Music and the Art of the Theatre (1899) [Excerpts]', in Richard C. Beacham (ed.) *Texts on Theatre* (London/New York, 1993), pp. 29–58, p. 41.

[12] Meyerhold, 'From "On the Theatre"', p. 143, my emphasis.

[13] Meyerhold, 'From "On the Theatre"', p. 143.

[14] Meyerhold, 'From "On the Theatre"', p. 143, my emphasis.

[15] Meyerhold's contemporary Max Reinhardt echoes this idea emphatically when writing in a letter to Friedrich Graf Ledebour in July 1940: 'The theatre is by its nature an orchestral art. The exquisite quality of all individual instruments, but most of all how they play together, how they sound together, remains pivotal for the essence of theatre' (cit. in Panja Mücke, *Musikalischer Film – Musikalisches Theater* [Münster, 2011], pp. 124–5). For Reinhardt, then, musicality is also not an additional feature, but core element of theatre; a defining factor of what is 'theatrical' in and of itself.

[16] Vsevolod Meyerhold, *Vsevolod Meyerhold: Theaterarbeit 1917–1930*. Edited by Rosemarie Tietze (München, 1974), p. 175.

twentieth and twenty-first centuries: the idea of a contrapuntal or polyphonic relationship of the different elements of theatre.[17] Meyerhold, himself a trained musician and violinist who even considered a musical career, therefore insists on musical training for theatre-makers. Based on his own experience he claimed that he considered his 'musical education the basis of [his] work as a director'[18] and went on to say:

> If you'd ask me: 'Which core course in a faculty of a future theatre-university, which core course should form part of its curriculum?' – I would say: 'Naturally music'. If a director isn't a musician, then he isn't capable of developing a real production. Because a real production (I don't mean the opera, the theatre of the music-drama and the musical comedy –, I even mean such dramatic theatre, where the whole performance proceeds without any musical accompaniment) can only be devised by a musician as a director.[19]

As we will see in more detail, music (as material) and musicality (as a principle of working and creating) play central roles in Meyerhold's process of conceptualizing and rehearsing production *and* have implications for his training philosophy. With this emphasis on process, Meyerhold taps into a music aesthetical concept that in contrast to modernity's focus on the *result* and the *musical work* leans towards an understanding of music as an educational and creative process.[20] Musicality, Meyerhold argues, is a powerful device for the actor, and helps the collaboration with the director enormously:

> It is ten times easier for me to work with an actor who loves music. Actors should be trained in music, while they are still in school. All actors like music 'for setting the mood', but very few understand that music is the best organiser of time in a production. Figuratively speaking, the actor's acting is in single combat with time. And here, music is his best helper. It doesn't even need to be heard, but it must be felt.[21]

First of all, this had immediate impact on the various drafts for curricula at Meyerhold's Studio. In his 'studio programme for 1916–1917', 'musical recitation

---

[17] See also 'Musicality of the grotesque' in this chapter and Chapter 6.
[18] In Robinson, 'Love for Three Operas', p. 287.
[19] Meyerhold, *Vsevolod Meyerhold*, pp. 176–7.
[20] This concept goes far back into antiquity and the Middle Ages and was captured succinctly by Augustine of Hippo's definition of music as a 'scientia bene modulandis' (the ability to create/design well) (cit. in Christian Kaden, 'Musik', in Karl-Heinz Brack [ed.], *Ästhetische Grundbegriffe. Historisches Wörterbuch in sieben Bänden* [Stuttgart/Weimar, 2005], pp. 256–308, p. 257).
[21] Meyerhold in Gladkov, *Meyerhold speaks*, p. 115.

in drama'[22] is one of five elements of the basic course of study. At an advanced stage, music seems to become more and more important and 'musical proficiency (as instrumentalist or singer)' is listed first out of seven criteria for achieving certification as a 'studio comedian'.[23] Meyerhold emphasizes the importance of musicality as both an intellectual capacity, a knowledge of music, a familiarity with its laws and terminology (to which we will come back), but also as an embodied and cognitive phenomenon.[24] 'By employing principles of music', Dragasevic argues, 'Meyerhold professionalized theatre as an art form, as a discipline that needs to be studied and interpreted with its unique spatial and temporal rules'.[25]

I would argue that some of the qualities and abilities Meyerhold hopes to instil in the budding actor, specifically the awareness and mastery of temporal processes, are comparable to what musicologist Serafine lists as elements of musical cognition. Biomechanics as a central element of Meyerhold's training consists of stylized, highly rhythmical movement sequences, often rehearsed to music to aid the accuracy and help internalize musical proportions of duration and dynamics.[26] This trains what Serafine calls 'succession' in temporal processes, which includes the ability for 'idiomatic construction', 'motivic chaining', 'patterning' and 'phrasing'.[27] Musical-rhythmical cognition for the actor becomes an integral aspect for creating and mastering movement in the production processes.

By making several of the biomechanical exercises *partner* exercises, Meyerhold trains another aspect of the actor's musical cognition: 'simultaneity'.[28] Serafine explains that 'the critical issue here is whether and how two events may be superimposed and retain their identities intact, or whether and under what conditions they form a new whole which is perceived as an integrated event'.[29]

---

[22]   Vsevolod Meyerhold, *Meyerhold on Theatre* (London, 1998), p. 153.

[23]   Meyerhold, *Meyerhold on Theatre*, p. 155.

[24]   Rudlin reports similar curricular tendencies for Copeau. See John Rudlin, 'Jacques Copeau: The Quest for Sincerity', in Alison Hodge (ed.), *Twentieth Century Actor Training* (London, 2000), pp. 43–62, p. 69.

[25]   Dolja Dragasevic, *Meyerhold, Director of Opera. Cultural Change and Artistic Genres* (PhD Doctoral Dissertation, Goldsmith College, 2005), p. 347.

[26]   See Kelli Melson, *The Practice and Pedagogy of Vsevolod Meyerhold's Living Legacy of Actor Training: Theatrical Biomechanics* (PhD, Exeter, 2009), which also contains a DVD with footage of biomechanical exercises to music as demonstrated by Meyerhold's disciple Gennadi Bogdanov.

[27]   Mary Louise Serafine, *Music as Cognition. The Development of Thought in Sound* (New York, 1988), pp. 74–7.

[28]   Serafine, *Music as Cognition*, p. 77. Musicality and in particular rhythmic sensibility are of course not the only aims of biomechanical training, but a significant aspect, I would argue. Pitches lists the basic skills to be acquired through biomechanical training as: precision, balance, coordination, efficiency, rhythm, expressiveness, responsiveness, playfulness and discipline (see Jonathan Pitches, *Vsevolod Meyerhold* [London, 2003], pp. 112–16).

[29]   Serafine, *Music as Cognition*, p. 77.

In a nutshell, the exercises train the actors to coordinate their movements, both when they are in 'unison' (i.e. both actors doing the same thing at the same time), but also when they are 'contrapuntal' (i.e. when they differ, but are precisely interlinked). This heightens their awareness of simultaneous events in rehearsals and later in performance, particularly when these are not coordinated by narrative or a logical 'cause-and-effect' relationship, but juxtaposed on a more abstract, compositional or rhythmical level. Jonathan Pitches exemplifies this using an example from Meyerhold's work on *The Government Inspector* (1926):

> The rigid discipline of the ensemble testifies to the collective training of biomechanics, slowly building up an unspoken understanding between actors which is underpinned by a strong sense of rhythm. Here, there are two rhythms at work – the individual bumbling of the Postmaster, set against the collective rhythm of the mass as they respond to the new focus and pan round to take in the letter.[30]

For the Meyerholdian *director* the same awareness of different kinds of simultaneity is crucial to be able to construct, conceptualize and direct the performance as a polyphonic event. Serafine's definition of 'composing' sits well with how Meyerhold characterizes the task of the director, if we assume that the 'material' of theatre encompasses more than just 'sounds':

> The term composing refers to all deliberate acts of combining sounds within a specified time frame for the purposes of creating interesting temporal events. Composing may or may not involve the fixing of an aural organization of events (as through visual notation or electronic recording), but it always involves sound events that are to some degree intentional and planned.[31]

The way in which Meyerhold conceives of training also supports the idea that musicality – in combination with physical dexterity, a high level of dramaturgical reflection and the ability to improvise – needs to become second nature to the actor, in other words, part of his or her embodied knowledge, amounting to what Pitches calls 'physical musicality'.[32]

Meyerhold thus often compares actor training to professionally learning to master an instrument: 'An actor must study as a violinist does, for seven to nine years. You can't make yourself into an actor in three to four years.'[33] It takes longer, according to Meyerhold, to master the physical and technical demands of the actor's 'instrument' – him/herself – and to 'emulate the integration of music

---

30   Pitches, *Vsevolod Meyerhold*, p. 106.
31   Serafine, *Music as Cognition*, p. 71.
32   Pitches, *Vsevolod Meyerhold*, p. 97.
33   Meyerhold in Gladkov, *Meyerhold speaks*, p. 108.

and movement achieved naturally by a great musician'.[34] Béatrice Picon-Vallin concludes that for Meyerhold 'the musical model, regarding both directing and acting, is based on an ideal technical understanding, controlled and progressive training, a single set of laws and a single vocabulary'.[35]

When I now explore further how this training and the musicality *dispositif* translate into Meyerhold's rehearsal studio, there are a number of aspects worth commenting on. First of all, one of the consequences of his direct comparison of actor and musical training is a rather demystified view of the art of acting, particularly when seen in contrast to some of his contemporaries such as Stanislavski but also Vakhtangov, who at times spoke in much more obfuscatory terms about training.[36] Meyerhold emphasizes craftsmanship in both the musician and the actor and betrays a 'dislike for artistic shamanism'[37] as one of his musical collaborators, the composer Mikhail Gnesin, reports. The essayist Aleksandr Gladkov adds that Meyerhold 'rarely mentioned the word "creativity", preferring to it the more modest substitutes: "craft", "work", "mastery". However, Meyerhold considered even this last word too grand'.[38]

This relatively sober view of the creative process is underpinned by Meyerhold's fascination with the theories of efficiency and productivity, developed around the emerging class of factory workers, in particular the writings of Frederick Winslow Taylor. Meyerhold explicitly refers to the factory worker as a model, since his work, he argues, 'borders on art'.[39] And again it is a musical quality – rhythm – that among other aspects, according to Meyerhold, characterizes the skilled worker. What the actor can learn from the factory worker is '1) an absence of superfluous, unproductive movements; 2) rhythm; 3) the correct positioning of the body centre of gravity; 4) stability'.[40]

Meyerhold sought to apply the idea of 'Taylorization' to the theatre by streamlining rehearsal processes and making performances more efficient. The musical question of 'rhythm' is thus not a mere aesthetic question for Meyerhold, a means of controlling a balanced and graceful timing, as we have also seen in Appia's writing, but part of a modern ambition for efficiency and fluidity of work.[41] One drastic example of how Taylorization manifested itself in Meyerhold's studio was the technique of asking the actors to condense a whole

---

[34]   Pitches, *Vsevolod Meyerhold*, p. 97.

[35]   Béatrice Picon-Vallin, 'Meyerhold's Laboratories', in Mirella Schino (ed.), *Alchemists of the Stage. Theatre Laboratories in Europe* (Holstebro/Malta/Wroclaw, 2009), pp. 119–39, p. 135.

[36]   Vakhtangov, for example, claims that 'the essence of creativity lies in "the richness of an actor's soul and his ability to reveal this richness" before the audience' (cit. in Andrei Malaev-Babel, *The Vakhtangov Sourcebook* [London, 2011], p. 21).

[37]   Gnesin in Gladkov, *Meyerhold speaks*, p. 65.

[38]   Gladkov, *Meyerhold speaks*, p. 63.

[39]   Pitches, *Vsevolod Meyerhold*, p. 71.

[40]   Pitches, *Vsevolod Meyerhold*, p. 71.

[41]   See also Braun in Meyerhold, *Meyerhold on Theatre*, p. 183.

play into 'a three-minute résumé';[42] an extreme rhythmical approach, an exercise in 'diminution'[43] of material, one could say. I will come back to these kinds of structural-compositional aspects of Meyerhold's musicality shortly, but I want to tease out three more actor-related themes of using musicality in rehearsals: music's contribution to character creation, a musical approach to diction and Meyerhold's notion of improvisation.

Creating Characters Supported by Music

One of Meyerhold's unique methods of developing characters with his actors was to provide them with a piece of music that he felt encapsulated the rhythm, movement and mood of the character at that point, sometimes for each individual entrance or scene. Samuel L. Leiter explains this in more detail for the production *Teacher Bubus* (1925):

> This rather unsuccessful political satire made extensive use of musical complement to provide rhythmic backing to the performance. Seated on a high perch at the rear of the stage, a pianist in tails played forty-six selections, mainly chosen from Chopin and Liszt, to underscore each character and element in the comedy. Meyerhold was extremely fond of accentuating characters by individual rhythmic leitmotifs.[44]

This way of using musical accompaniment and incidental music transcended its conventional function to set a general mood for the scene or a transition between acts. Meyerhold tailored the excerpts (or commissioned new pieces) to provide both a kind of subtext for the actor *and* a rhythmic manifestation of that subtext and thus a form to use as guidance for speech, movement and gesture. Cast member Erast Garin describes this as 'acting to music' which in consequence 'turned the verbal material into an original recitative':[45] 'The rhythm of the Chopin étude provides each character with possibilities for a completely different free arrangement of movement and speech.'[46] This technique of using music for character creation and as a dramatic dialogue partner was certainly inspired by Wagner's use of the orchestra, which Meyerhold was very familiar with, not least

---

[42] Meyerhold, *Meyerhold on Theatre*, p. 146.

[43] Diminution is a musical term originally used 'in the context of improvised embellishment during the Renaissance and Baroque periods to describe a melodic figure that replaces a long note with notes of shorter value' (Grove Music Online, entry 'diminution' at http://www.oxfordmusiconline.com/sub-scriber/article/grove/music/42071?goto=dimi&_start=1&pos=16 [09.12.2011]).

[44] Samuel L. Leiter, *From Stanislavsky to Barrault. Representative Directors of the European Stage* (New York, 1991), p. 61.

[45] In Paul Schmidt (ed.), *Meyerhold at Work* (Manchester, 1981), p. 151.

[46] In Schmidt, *Meyerhold at Work*, p. 152.

due to staging *Tristan and Isolde* in 1909. Describing a moment in *Teacher Bubus* Meyerhold writes: 'Suddenly the actress pauses, and the orchestra speaks for her. Just like with Wagner.'[47]

But again, Meyerhold's engagement with Wagner is not limited to a literal appropriation of ideas or techniques, but a metaphorical transformation of them: Meyerhold speaks of the 'orchestration' of movement for his productions and thus compares the function of Wagnerian orchestra to his own 'scores' of movement and gesture:

> Richard Wagner with his orchestra provided inner tension; the music sung by the singers seemed insufficiently powerful to convey the inner experiences of his heroes. Wagner called on his orchestra for help, feeling that only an orchestra could reveal Mystery to the audience. In 'drama', likewise, the word is not sufficiently strong to bring out the inner meaning. Pronunciation, even good pronunciation, does not mean speaking. It is necessary to seek new ways of expressing the inexpressible, and to reveal what is concealed. As Wagner makes his orchestra speak about the spiritual experiences of his heroes, so I make plastic movements express inner feelings. [...] And if the director, absorbed in the author's theme, hears the inner music, then he will propose to the actors plastic movements which will enable the spectator to hear this inner music.[48]

At the time, and within the given conventions in dramatic theatre, both Meyerhold's *use* of music and his sense of *musicality* were seen as innovative and unprecedented: Boris Pasternak, who was an admirer of Meyerhold's work, describes how theatre music at the time was seen by the public as 'only lulling background or an annoying accompaniment that gets in the way of "what the words mean"' and how Meyerhold's visionary achievement was to use it 'as a living impulse, [...] as an integral element in the dialogue, [...] as an organic part of the performance'.[49] Paul Schmidt summarizes (also based on Pasternak's letter to Meyerhold, after he saw his production *Woe to Wit* from 1928):

> [...] music was used in a way entirely unheard-of in the theatre. No longer accompaniment, no longer simply mood music, melodramatic background, music became an integral part of the drama, making it into an opera – a dramatic spectacle where emotion and action are both expressed by music.[50]

This observation casts light on Meyerhold's creative use of music, written from the perspective of the audience and describing the effect on the spectator. I would add that it is particularly the *productive* use of music in the *working process* that

---

[47]   Meyerhold, *Vsevolod Meyerhold*, p. 93.
[48]   Meyerhold, 'From "On the Theatre"', p. 145.
[49]   Pasternak in Schmidt, *Meyerhold at Work*, p. 149.
[50]   Schmidt, *Meyerhold at Work*, p. 141.

forms part of Meyerhold's musicality. Besides the inevitable influence of Wagner, there is another interesting stimulus for this approach – the work of the silent film comedians. Meyerhold was an outspoken fan of the films of Charlie Chaplin, Buster Keaton and Harold Lloyd, who 'encapsulated the physical clarity and economy of craft Meyerhold was seeking his production'.[51] I would argue that this sympathy for their work was not limited to the mastery of acting but also extended to the use of music in the creation process. Chaplin and others used live music on the set while developing, improvising and performing in front of the camera – music that was played only to support the performer since it could not yet be captured on film. Silent film expert Richard Koszarski explains:

> Nothing better illustrates the idiosyncratic nature of silent-film performance than the use of sideline musicians on the set to inspire the cast during filming, a practice that Kevin Brownlow dates to 1913. As in a Victorian theater piece, this underscoring of drama with music enhanced the essential melodramatic nature of the performance, but here it was for the benefit of the actors, not the audience. 'During the making of a picture music has become essential', wrote one accompanist in 1923. [...] Musicians needed to command a repertoire of sad, dramatic and joyous arrangements and to be capable of flitting in an instant from the *Moonlight* Sonata to 'Yes, We Have No Bananas'. Gounod's 'Ave Maria' and the intermezzo from *Cavalleria Rusticana* were judged most successful for tears, while dramatic action might call for Tchaikovsky's Fourth Symphony, the Massenet *Élégie*, or a Chopin prelude.[52]

Dan Kamin elaborates on this practice with respect to Chaplin, stressing the importance of rhythm for his work:

> He had two aids on the set: the loud clicking of the silent camera, imposing a steady beat and also telling him how much the film was undercranked; and the constant presence of musicians, often a trio, who played to help establish the mood. Virginia Cherrill, co-star of *City Lights*, said that the musicians were in constant attendance during the two-year period of filming, playing 'whatever Chaplin felt like that day'.[53]

As in Meyerhold's rehearsal practice, music helped the performer to develop a clear form and rhythm for their portrayal, but also enabled them to transcend the naturalistic mimetic acting style in favour of a heightened and stylized expression and movement. In the case of the silent comedians, this was a vital aspect for developing the desired *comedic* effect (as the musicalization supported comic

---

[51] Pitches, *Vsevolod Meyerhold*, p. 102.

[52] Richard Koszarski, *An Evening's Entertainment. The Age of the Silent Feature Picture, 1915–1928* (New York, 1990), p. 131.

[53] Dan Kamin, *Charlie Chaplin, One-man Show* (London, 1984), p. 79.

strategies of exaggeration of action and creating the necessary distance from the audience[54]); for Meyerhold this was an important part of achieving his aesthetic of the grotesque, which I will come back to. Meyerhold uses music to aid precision[55] in his actors, particularly for the often swift and abrupt changes in tempo and mood that Meyerhold was known to use in his productions. What does precision mean here? One aspect is certainly finding the right pace for a particular speech or movement sequence, which music may help to establish; another, to support transitions between distinct 'acting fragments', which may vary in direction, mood, style, energy and tempo, and for which a musical cue may provide a clear stimulus or jumping-off point:

> A character pronounces a phrase that marks the end of a given fragment of acting, and during this time a certain music begins to be heard. This musical piece defines the start of another fragment, thus, based on this musical track, you construct another acting fragment, which does not resemble the previous one.[56]

Meyerhold's musicality is, however, not limited to a particularly compositional use of music to create the macro- and microstructure of his productions, but is also a conscious attempt to transfer certain laws and properties of music onto theatre in a wider sense: 'He did not substitute music for theatre, he turned theatre into music.'[57] One area where this analogy applies is his approach to speech and diction.

Working on Diction

Meyerhold had strong views about diction and lamented the decline of the actor's ability to work with language in statements like the following:

> He has reduced his art to the most alarming chaos. As if that were not enough, he considers it his bounden duty to introduce chaos into all the other art forms as soon as he lays hands on them. He takes music and violates its fundamental principles by inventing 'melodeclamation'. When he reads poetry from the stage he heeds the content of the verse, rearranging the logical stresses and ignoring completely every consideration of metre, rhythm, caesura, pause and musical notation.[58]

---

[54] Henri Bergson, for example, stresses the 'absence of feeling which usually accompanies laughter' and explains: 'To produce the whole of this effect, then, the comic demands something like a momentary anesthesia of the heart. Its appeal is to intelligence, pure and simple' (Henri Bergson, *Laughter. An Essay on the Meaning of the Comic* [Rockville, MD, 2008 (1900)], pp. 10–11).

[55] See Meyerhold in Schmidt, *Meyerhold at Work*, p. 155.

[56] In Picon-Vallin, 'Meyerhold's Laboratories', p. 135.

[57] Boris Pokrovsky in Patrick Carnegy, *Wagner and the Art of the Theatre* (New Haven/London, 2006), p. 212.

[58] Meyerhold, *Meyerhold on Theatre*, p. 130.

What is very clear from this depiction is the emphasis Meyerhold placed on the *musical* qualities of speech on stage.[59] Already in his Studio in Zhukovski Street, opened in 1908, Meyerhold collaborated with a composer, Mikhail Gnesin, to train and develop the actors' musical sensibility for speech and to train 'choral and musical declamation in drama'[60] or the 'music of the diction'.[61] Gnesin also 'attempted to give actors a musical score to manage the pitch of the voice separately from the emotions, which disturb diction. For Sophocles's Antigone he composed a "half-spoken, half-sung" score, played at the Studio'.[62]

It seems to me that, at least for Meyerhold, one could describe this musical approach to character development and diction as working from the outside inwards rather than vice versa. This applies, on the one hand, to the individual, who, aided by external musical structures, develops a code of gestures and movement patterns to establish a character; and later fills this outward appearance with an inner core of attitude and emotion. On the other hand, it applies to the relationship of form and content; here, Meyerhold concentrates on the formal and structural qualities of performance, which then inevitably have an effect on the emerging contents, rather than the other way around. Finally, even on the level of preparing and constructing a production, Meyerhold starts with the overall outward shape, the rhythmic structure of the performance and the musical character of its parts rather than starting from a nucleus, or a central narrative aspect and then seeing the production gradually take shape in an emergent process.

A good example of this last aspect can be found in Norris Houghton's description of Meyerhold's work on *La Dame aux Camélias* (1934): 'The laws

---

[59] It should be noted that employing a musical approach to diction had been proposed long before Meyerhold – particularly vocally by the German classicists and Johann Wolfgang Goethe. Hedwig Walwei-Wiegelmann's collection *Goethes Gedanken über Musik* (Frankfurt am Main, 1985) documents Goethe's idea that 'each and every artistry should be accompanied by a sense of music' (Goethe in Walwei-Wiegelmann, *Goethes Gedanken*, p. 65) and that the actor should 'quasi musically compose even his prosaic parts in his mind in order not to botch them monotonously following his individual habits, but to treat them with appropriate variety in metre and measure' (ibid.). Consequently, as Pius Alexander Wolff reports, rehearsals for dramatic texts were often conducted by Goethe 'like rehearsing an opera: "the tempi, the fortes and pianos, the crescendo and diminuendo were determined by him and supervised with the most meticulous precision"' (cit. in Philipp Stein, *Goethe als Theaterleiter* [Berlin/Leipzig, 1904], p. 66). For more detail see also Ulrich Kühn, *Sprech-Ton-Kunst. Musikalisches Sprechen und Formen des Melodrams im Schauspiel- und Musiktheater (1770–1933)* (Tübingen, 2001) and Dieter Borchmeyer, 'Saat von Göthe gesäet ... Die "Regeln für Schauspieler" – ein theatergeschichtliches Gerücht', in Wolfgang F. Bender (ed.), *Schauspielkunst im 18. Jahrhundert. Grundlagen, Praxis, Autoren* (Stuttgart, 1992), pp. 261–87.

[60] Picon-Vallin, 'Meyerhold's Laboratories', p. 122.

[61] Konstantin Rudnitsky, *Meyerhold the Director* (Ann Arbor, 1981), p. 70.

[62] Picon-Vallin, 'Meyerhold's Laboratories', p. 122. See also Dragasevic, *Meyerhold, Director of Opera*.

of musical construction and of musical contrast, the effects of sound and tempo, are all applied by him in working out the play. [...] *La Dame aux Camélias* was composed as follows [...]'[63] – here, Houghton provides Meyerhold's full list of all the scenes, with the name of the scene on the left hand and the musical character and tempo on the right, described in the conventional Italian terms developed in classical music, such as Andante, Allegro grazioso, Lento, Scherzando, Adagio, or Tempo di Valse. Houghton continues:

> The right-hand column was not taken from a musical score played behind the scenes or an orchestra pit as an accompaniment to the action. Indeed, there is little music played in the whole production. It is rather a key to the movement, to the timbre and pitch of voices, to the tempo of action, and, of course, when there is music, to its quality.[64]

In this way, Meyerhold developed a clear sense of the overall composition, the general musical and rhythmical shape of the performance, which provided the framework for developing the individual scenes, actions and characters. He stressed that 'an actor must know the composition of the entire production, must understand and feel it with his whole body. Only then does he make himself a component of it and begin to sound in harmony with it'.[65] With this in mind, it may surprise at first that Meyerhold was equally adamant about the actor's ability to improvise as an essential condition for a meaningful collaboration. How do improvisational freedom and a thoroughly premeditated compositional structure go together?

Meyerhold and Improvisation

Meyerhold's notion of improvisation was highly influenced by two main sources: the theatre tradition of the *commedia dell'arte* and a *musical* notion of improvisation, which follows certain rules and is still highly structured.[66] This kind of improvisation is very common in various musical styles Meyerhold was familiar with, from Renaissance dance music to the practices of jazz improvisation over an established harmonic scheme of a jazz standard or new composition.[67] While improvisation in music, even if we confine our view to Western classical and

---

[63]   Norris Houghton, *Moscow rehearsals. An account of methods of production in the Soviet Theatre* (London, 1938), p. 120.

[64]   Houghton, *Moscow rehearsals*, p. 122.

[65]   Meyerhold in Gladkov, *Meyerhold speaks*, p. 105.

[66]   See also Chapter 5, Theatre and Jazz.

[67]   Meyerhold already used some jazz music for his performances; he did, for example, invite the Sidney Bechet's Quintet to play for a few weeks in his production of *D.E.* (1924) when it was touring the USSR (see Robert Leach, *Vsevolod Meyerhold* [Cambridge, 1989], p. 118).

popular music, knows many different forms, there is an underlying sense in which improvisation is part of a dialectic relationship between premeditated composition and different degrees of deviation from a given template or model. The *New Grove Dictionary of Music and Musicians* gives a few examples:

> While risk is always present, its character varies greatly. In the improvisation of a fugue the difficulty is in adhering to the predetermined form; in the *kalpana svara* of Karnatak music it is the juxtaposition of rhythmic patterns that depart from but return to the *tāla*; in Iranian music it is the maintenance of a balance between quoting memorised material and moving too far beyond it; in South Slavonic epics it is of keeping to the textual line structure while alternating memorised scenes with commentary. In most instances audiences evaluate improvisations by their balancing of obligatory features against imaginative departures from them.[68]

In other words, the tendency in musical improvisational practice is that it relies on 'the existence of well-known, implied conventions of performance (such improvisation may therefore be recognized by the composer – perhaps within limits – as well as the performer as essential to the complete performance of the work)'.[69] According to Pitches, the 'implied conventions' Meyerhold introduced as a 'controlling influence among the playfulness'[70] were indeed provided by music. This is also confirmed by Braun: 'The actor ... is free to act *ex improvisio*. However the actor's freedom is only relative because he is subject to the discipline of the musical score.'[71] Meyerhold even makes an explicit reference to a musical practice as a template for his idea of improvisation:

> Aside from the great works of dramatic literature, there are plays which in themselves are nothing remarkable, but which grandly bear the traces of great performances. They are like a canvas for stunning improvisations by the actor, just as many of Anton Rubinstein's piano pieces are outlines for a virtuoso performer to fill in.[72]

---

[68]   Bruno Nettl et al., 'Improvisation', in Stanley Sadie (ed.), *New Grove Dictionary of Music and Musicians, 2nd edition, Vol. 12* (London, 2001), pp. 94–133, p. 95.

[69]   Wegman in Nettl et al., 'Improvisation', p. 98.

[70]   Pitches, *Vsevolod Meyerhold*, p. 26.

[71]   In Pitches, *Vsevolod Meyerhold*, p. 26. For a different, but also musical approach to improvisation in theatre see George Rodosthenous's chapter 'Improvisation as the Beginning of the Compositional Process' (in Matthias Rebstock/David Roesner [eds.], *Composed Theatre* [Bristol, 2012], pp. 169–82), in which he discusses Eugenio Barba's notion of 'directorial improvisation' and improvisation within the limits of a performance score or graph.

[72]   Meyerhold in Gladkov, *Meyerhold speaks*, p. 107.

Often, when talking about improvisation in theatre we associate it with a practice of emergence and creative serendipity, where something unplanned and unforeseeable happens from the nucleus and stimulus of a simple situation, location, character or opening line. If there are any rules,[73] they are meant to *unleash* theatrical action and ensure that the improvisation is not stifled or blocked easily. Meyerhold, in contrast, emphasizes discipline and an avid awareness of the *boundaries* of improvisation within a compositional structure in his writings:

> Often what seems to be a sudden improvisation is in reality the result of a broad plan worked out in its entirety. The general composition worked out before a rehearsal sets up firm points of stability, solid posts which determine the ideas arising along the way. In the heart of directing, improvisation is obligatory, just as in acting, but always within the limits of the general composition. All possible improvisational variations must be self-limited by the feeling for the composition. People possessing that ability have the right to improvise.[74]

Meyerhold specifies what this means in the following example:

> Take any episode where there is an alternation: dialogue 12 minutes, monologue 1 minute, trio 6 minutes, ensemble 'tutti' 5 minutes, and so forth. You get a relationship: 12:1:6:5, and that defines the composition of the scene. One must watch that the relationship is strictly observed, but this doesn't limit the opportunity for improvisation in the work of the actor. It is precisely that stability in time which enables the good actor to enjoy what is fundamental to his art. [...] The relationship between composition and improvised play is the new production formula of our school.[75]

In rehearsal, this also meant that there was a clear sense of a 'score' for the production, not dissimilar to a musical score as a very detailed set of instructions for performance, which provided the framework within which the actor's freedom could develop. According to Leiter, Meyerhold had 'eight to fifteen assistants',

---

[73]   Keith Johnstone, author of *Improvisation and the Theatre* (London, 1981), provides a long list of such rules and games but these are predominantly motivated by character and narrative development.

[74]   Meyerhold in Edward Braun, *Meyerhold. A Revolution in Theatre* (London, 1979), p. 77. For further evidence of Meyerhold promoting improvisation strictly within compositional boundaries I cite Gladkov, who writes about Meyerhold that 'he gave the actor the right within certain compositional limits to select freely out of this reserve [...]' (Gladkov, *Meyerhold speaks*, p. 180) and Meyerhold himself, who explains that 'an actor's joy isn't in repeating what was successful, but in variations and improvisations within the limits of the composition as a whole' (Meyerhold in ibid., p. 108).

[75]   Meyerhold in Gladkov, *Meyerhold speaks*, pp. 135–6.

Figure 2.1   Meyerhold and Mayakovsky rehearsing *The Bath House*, 1930

who 'noted down his every word including every correction and adjustment he made in the course of rehearsals'[76] (See Figure 2.1). He elaborates:

> [...] one being in charge of all matters related to the dialogue; another to record all the physical action; and another to deal with the wealth of miscellanea developing during rehearsals. The notes were organised and collated daily to provide what Houghton said was 'probably the most elaborate and detailed prompt book' in the world.[77]

In many ways, this stratification and recording/notating of activity resembles a kind of musical score, albeit a score that is developed alongside the rehearsal process, rather than preceding it.[78] When developed, this score, however explicitly notated, became binding:

---

[76]   Leiter, *From Stanislavsky*, p. 73.

[77]   Leiter, *From Stanislavsky*, pp. 73–4.

[78]   Meyerhold himself however used no notes. Leiter captures the specific dialectic between planning and spontaneity in his work like this: 'A magnificent combination of inspiration and careful preparation give many the false impression that everything was being made up at the spur of the moment' (Leiter, *From Stanislavsky*, p. 74).

Meyerhold's actors had to *consciously* embody a very precisely prescribed physical score [...] and had little room for any deviations from that score. [...] In Meyerhold's own words: 'the actor must know how to act "with the music" and not "to the music"'.[79]

There is another aspect of Meyerhold's notion of improvisation, which connects it to the influence from the *commedia dell'arte* as well as the jazz idiom. The similarity between these two improvisational practices has already been pointed out by theatre scholar and *commedia* expert Cesare Molinari:

> A *compagnia dell'arte* probably behaved like a New Orleans jazz band when putting together a performance: on the basis of given rhythmical structure, every instrument intervenes either as an accompaniment or in soloist function occupying the spaces and the pauses which open up in the orchestral texture, or responding to thematic suggestions stemming from someone else's initiative.[80]

But the allusion to jazz practices is not confined to the idea of a collective improvisation to a 'given rhythmical structure', but also highlights that improvisation did not mean pure invention from scratch, but often – like in the *commedia* and like in jazz – a 'free combination of previously prepared elements'.[81]

Meyerhold's Musicality

For Meyerhold musicality is both the *aim* and the *means* of his new theatre aesthetic. Morris defines it as 'a quality of action and sensibility aspired to and realized by the actor'[82] and as we have seen, it provides him with a vehicle for giving actor training a clear purpose and shape, and prepares them for what he then sees as the key qualities of an actor: precision, a highly developed sense of timing, physical ability and a sense of improvisational inventiveness combined

---

[79]   Pitches, *Vsevolod Meyerhold*, p. 97.

[80]   Cesare Molinari, *La Commedia dell'Arte* (Milano, 1985), pp. 39–40. The *comici dell'arte* had a stock of verbal and physical routines, often written down in their notebooks or *zibaldoni*, in response to certain themes and situations, not unlike jazz musicians, particularly in the traditional jazz genres, who keep a stock of melodic phrases, 'licks' and 'riffs' ready for application to recurrent chord progressions. Improvisation in all these cases is quite literally a com-position, a putting together or on-the-spot montage, of memorized 'business'.

[81]   Meyerhold in Gladkov, *Meyerhold speaks*, p. 180. His contemporaries, notably Vakhtangov and Tairov, as well as Copeau in France, all had improvisation high on their respective theatrical agendas, but arguably none of them emphasized a dialectic relationship with a (musical) sense of composition as strongly as Meyerhold did.

[82]   Eilon Morris, *Via Rythmós. An Investigation of Rhythm in Psychophysical Actor Training* (PhD thesis, University of Huddersfield, 2012), p. 70.

with a strong structural awareness. As Pitches puts it, 'ultimately the use of "real music", live or recorded, was subordinate in his mind to the actors internalizing the *concept* of musicality'.[83] Working with this approach, then, allows him to pursue his aim: a theatre aesthetic that follows what he calls the 'laws' of music:

> I dream of a production rehearsed to music, but performed without music. Without it, and yet with it, because the rhythm of the production will be organized according to the music's laws and each performer will carry it within himself.[84]

It is not, however, at all clear what 'music's laws' *are*, according to Meyerhold. His sense of musicality is complex, just as the range of his musical references is quite eclectic: he relates to classical forms, like the sonata or the symphony, which privilege structure and motivic and thematic development; but he also uses the protagonists of romantic piano music, from Chopin and Liszt, sharing an interests in atmospheric depth and dextrous virtuosity with them; he takes inspiration from Russian opera (from Glinka and Dargomyzhsky to Prokofiev and Shostakovich); and he adapts the popularity and improvisational freedom of folk songs and jazz music to his approach to the theatre. The musical influences are far-reaching and Meyerhold could be described as a musical omnivore.

The principles of montage and collage (the former was developed most prominently with and by his student Sergei Eisenstein), with their characteristic contrasts, clashes of genres and styles, and stark rhythmic juxtapositions, seem to most aptly describe his use and sense of musicality. In evaluating Meyerhold's musicality further, I will focus on four aspects that I found particularly prominent in his discourse: his use of musicality as a constructivist method; his interest in musical terminology; a strong focus on rhythm as the most transferable aspect of musicality; and a musicality of contrast and counterpoint in pursuit of a grotesque theatre aesthetic.

Musicality as a Constructivist Method

As we have seen, Meyerhold's musicality is expressed both in the way he used music as a 'vital component'[85] of his theatre and in transferring its principles to the training and creation processes.

His use of music was not an illustrative one, merely seeking to enhance the atmosphere or underline a certain mood, but a constructive part of the creative, compositional process: he either selected and 'montaged' pre-existing music or commissioned it in order for it to become not a sound-track for his productions, but a time-structure, a commentary, counterpoint and sub-text for the scenes and the actors. Leach exemplifies this process in describing Meyerhold's work on

---

[83]   Pitches, *Vsevolod Meyerhold*, p. 98, original emphasis.
[84]   Meyerhold in Gladkov, *Meyerhold speaks*, p. 115.
[85]   Braun in Meyerhold, *Meyerhold on Theatre*, p. 195.

Teacher Bubus (1925), for which Meyerhold chose over forty pieces by Chopin and Liszt:

> For two months, he and Arnshtam, the pianist, worked together, Meyerhold 'composing' the production while Arnshtam played over the pieces. [...] Meyerhold's use of music was central to his organization of rhythm. Music was a constant feature virtually throughout every production – there was hardly a Meyerhold production without a vast amount of 'incidental music'.[86]

It is interesting to see that the notion of 'composing', which for Appia was firmly attributed to the poet, who ideally was also the composer of the word-tone drama, shifts to the director in Meyerhold's case.[87] Another contrast to Appia lies in the liberty Meyerhold took in restructuring the text he was working with, consciously incorporating contrast and interruptions. Meyerhold's use of musicality is both 'responsible in large measure for weaving the disparate elements of the piece[s] together'[88] and also to introduce discontinuities and contradictions. Whereas Appia emphasized unity, Meyerhold introduced a scenic rhythm that disrupted the former act and scene structure of a play, creating a new theatrical rhythm of fragmented, episodic scenes, which were 'related by theme and to some extent by story, but not by the conventional means of continuing characters running through the plot'.[89] In the case of *The Forest* (1924), Meyerhold broke it down into 'thirty-three episodes, arranged on the principles of Eisenstein's "collision montage", "each one conflicting with the next"'.[90]

Braun underlines the structural importance of Meyerhold's musical selections, and also points us to the close relationship between the 'complex musical score which accompanied the production[s]' and the 'overall musical structure',[91] which transcended this. Working on Chekhov's *The Cherry Orchard*,

> Meyerhold defined its musical structure in which the actual music was *one element* in an over-all rhythmical harmony designed to reveal the 'subtext' of the drama. [...] More than anything, it was this concept of 'musicality' that set Meyerhold apart from every other stage-director of his time.[92]

---

[86]   Leach, *Vsevolod Meyerhold*, pp. 117–18.

[87]   Emmanuil Kaplan gives a vivid account of this by describing in detail the opening of the performance of Gogol's *The Government Inspector* and the precise musical and rhythmical decisions made in the direction (see Kaplan in Meyerhold, *Meyerhold on Theatre*, pp. 217–18).

[88]   Leach, *Vsevolod Meyerhold*, p. 118.

[89]   Leach, *Vsevolod Meyerhold*, p. 118.

[90]   Leach, *Vsevolod Meyerhold*, pp. 119–20. The references within this quotation are from a lecture by Meyerhold entitled 'Chaplin and Chaplinism', in which he discussed Eisenstein's and Chaplin's techniques of montage.

[91]   Braun in Meyerhold, *Meyerhold on Theatre*, p. 217.

[92]   Braun in Meyerhold, *Meyerhold on Theatre*, p. 217, my emphasis.

Dragasevic summarizes:

> In his theatre directing was an art that depended on rhythm and music to
> harmonise and unite the visual, audio and spatial elements of performance. The
> multi-layering of musical lines and rhythms in his performances, represented
> in sounds, actions, events, speech, acting, light, visual lines and patterns,
> demonstrated in detail how his score was composed. Rather than traditionally
> following the dramatic plot or development of character, Meyerhold elaborated
> upon the construction of musical lines, tempi and rhythms, and in this way,
> treated the staging of both opera and drama as a symphonic piece.[93]

In comparison to Appia, then, musicality becomes a much more explicitly
constructive element of theatre performance. Appia sought to control a faithful
transition from page to stage by means of music or musicality; Meyerhold uses his
sense of musicality to deconstruct, reassemble and build the performance; from
the 'overall composition' to the minutest detail.[94]

There is certainly a strong sense of musicality expressed both through
conscious compositional construction *and* the performers' awareness of it in
process and performance. Meyerhold even speaks of a 'compositional sense of
well-being'[95] as if musicality was a symptom of a 'healthy' theatre. Meyerhold
often chooses musical metaphors or similes to explain and exemplify an 'outward
in' approach:

> We saw that we would have to piece together this performance according to
> all of the rules of orchestral composition. Every actor, taken individually, isn't
> singing yet; they need to be embedded in groups of instruments or roles; these
> groups again need to be interwoven in a highly complicated orchestration; the
> lines of the leitmotifs have to be raised up in this complicated structure, and
> actors, light, movement, even objects – similar to an orchestra – everything has
> to be conducted together.[96]

Musical Terminology in Pursuit of a Precise Language for Rehearsal

For Meyerhold, musical notions and their terminology are more than evocative
metaphors – they form part of his pursuit of a more exact and more effective
language for the training and rehearsal process. As Robinson put it, Meyerhold
attempted 'to develop a precise musical vocabulary for the productions he

---

[93] Dragasevic, *Meyerhold, Director of Opera*, p. 348.

[94] Cf. Schmidt, *Meyerhold at Work*, p. 93.

[95] Meyerhold in Schmidt, *Meyerhold at Work*, p. 136.

[96] In Matthias Rebstock, 'Composed Theatre: Mapping the Field', in Matthias
Rebstock/David Roesner (eds.), *Composed Theatre. Aesthetics, Practices & Processes*
(Bristol, 2012), pp. 17–51, p. 25.

directed, involving the concepts of rhythm, meter, and even "harmonic" movement'.[97] Making musical terminology operational in directing takes the musicality *dispositif* a step further than merely using it to describe one's practice. What appealed to Meyerhold, I would argue, is its (at least, perceived) clarity and objectivity. He says: 'Musical terminology helps us a great deal. I love it because it possesses an almost mathematical exactness.'[98] Instructions for actors can be quite opaque, highly individual and heavily metaphorical,[99] and a lot of time is often spent between actors and directors figuring out what each of them means by the words and images they use.[100] In comparison, musical instructions such as 'allegro', 'accelerando', 'legato', 'brighter timbre' or 'higher pitch' – while still in need of interpretation – provide a narrower margin for misunderstanding. Meyerhold thus insists on the necessity for the actor to be familiar with musical terminology, just as much as they need to be in control of their physical skills:

> I still have to deal with actors, who use the word 'rhythm' where one should speak of 'metre' and *vice versa*. An actor needs to have knowledge in this area. – In the area of mimesis he needs to learn how to move his muscles, has to pay attention to the vectors of power triggered by movement, and know the effect of weight, gravitation, path, velocity. What does a 'natural' mean on stage? What does movement-tempo mean? What is the difference of legato and staccato? If the actor doesn't distinguish between metre and rhythm, then he doesn't know the difference between legato and staccato either.[101]

A century later, a director like Heiner Goebbels echoes this sentiment when saying that

> although he had overheard a visiting director at the theatre department in Giessen warn his students never to give actors instructions like 'faster/slower

---

[97] Robinson, 'Love for Three Operas', p. 287.

[98] Robinson, 'Love for Three Operas', p. 290.

[99] Vakhtangov, for examples, speaks of developing the 'character's embryo', and invokes 'the richness of an actor's soul and his ability to reveal this richness' (cit. in Malaev-Babel, *The Vakhtangov Sourcebook*, pp. 23, 21) before the audience.

[100] See Thorsten Mundi's extensive study of rehearsal language(s), *Benno, fieps Dich rein! Die Probensprache des Theaters als Medium der Bedeutungsproduktion* (München, 2005). He defines 'theatre jargon' (*Theaterslang*) as 'the language of the rehearsal. [...] The object of theatre-slang is the artistic transformation of a fictional text with technical craftsmanship and moral intention for the eyes of a public audience. Characteristic of theatre-slang is the simultaneity of influences from technical terminology, idiomatic language, colloquialism and metaphorical speech. It is determined by the personal relationship of the speakers, is exclusively attributable to the inner-institutional communication of the theatre and is characterized in its micro-structure by its functional polyvalence' (p. 138).

[101] Meyerhold, *Vsevolod Meyerhold*, p. 171.

or louder/softer', this was something he, Goebbels, precisely practiced, not least because he trusted his actors to translate these musical instructions into their respective languages effectively and relate them to whatever level of interior imagery, subtext, energy direction etc. they might need.[102]

Again, the director refers to an external musical effect, rather than a motivation, inner image or emotional state in his instruction, and in addition to providing a level of clarity and precision trusts the actor to find their own way of achieving this effect and making it repeatable.

It is not only the communicative aspect of the musical *dispositif*, however, that prompts Meyerhold's use of musical terminology, it is also the cognitive aspect[103] – a shift in how to *think* about theatre. He is often quoted saying: 'I understood what the art of the stage director was when I learned to provide harmony for the melodic line of the performance – which is what acting is.'[104] Here, it is a metaphoric use of the notions of melody and harmony that prompts Meyerhold to conceptualize the relationship between acting and directing in a particular way. Thinking of acting as the melody of a theatre performance, and the *mise en scène* as the harmony to be composed or arranged by the director opens the director's attention to the wide range of *musical* relationships between theatre elements; their structural coherence, rhythmical correlation, and homophonic or polyphonic nature, and de-emphasizes their merely or predominantly semiotic function of telling the tale.

The use of musical terminology for Meyerhold is thus also an important part of how he reads a play, how he determines the dramaturgy and conceptualizes his production. See, for example, his analysis of Chekhov's *The Cherry Orchard*; talking about Act Three of the play, he writes:

> Translated into musical terms, this is one movement of the symphony. It contains the basic elegiac melody with alternating moods in pianissimo, outbursts in forte (the suffering of Ranevskaya), and the dissonant accompaniment of the monotonous cacophony of the distant band and the dance of the living corpses (the philistines). This is the musical harmony of the act, and the conjuring scene

---

[102] David Roesner, '"It is not about labelling, it's about understanding what we do" – Composed theatre as discourse', in Rebstock/Roesner, *Composed Theatre*, pp. 319–62, p. 327. See also Heiner Goebbels, 'Wenn ich möchte, dass ein Schauspieler weint, geb' ich ihm eine Zwiebel', in Anton Rey/Hajo Kurzenberger/Stephan Müller (eds.), *Wirkungsmaschine Schauspieler* (Berlin/Köln, 2011), pp. 64–70, p. 67, where he recounts the same anecdote in the context of a reflection on the actor's work on form.

[103] See the Introduction for a discussion of these and other aspects of the musicality *dispositif*.

[104] In Robinson, 'Love for Three Operas', p. 290. Gladkov provides a slightly different version of this quotation: 'Using a different type of comparison, I can also say that if acting is the melody, then the mises en scène are the harmony' (Meyerhold in Gladkov, *Meyerhold speaks*, p. 124).

is only one of the harsh sounds which together comprise the dissonant tune of
the stupid dance. Hence it should blend with the dancing and appear only for a
moment before merging with it once more. On the other hand, the dance should
be heard constantly as a muffled accompaniment, but only in the background.[105]

This is a remarkable approach, since it addresses the atmospheric and emotional
qualities of Chekhov's text almost exclusively through a complex virtual
orchestration and translation into musical parameters of pitch and melody
('elegiac', 'dissonant'), volume ('pianissimo'), duration ('only for a moment')
and timbre ('harsh', 'muffled'). Meyerhold thus provides both an interpretation
and a precise template for its staging. Parametrical thinking as *one* possible
characteristic of a musical-compositional *dispositif* here becomes a productive
method of dramaturgical analysis.

One cluster of terms that features particularly prominently in Meyerhold's
writing focuses on aspects of rhythm, and it is worth looking at how he defines
and instrumentalizes rhythm in more detail.

'Rhythm, rhythm and again rhythm'[106]

'Meyerhold attached primary significance to the question of rhythm in
performance', actor Zakhava reports[107] and gives an example: on planning a
production of *Boris Godunov* in 1936, he remembers Meyerhold saying that
'the rhythm in this production should be "rapid and impetuous"', and that 'the
only way to master Pushkin's material is by seeking out its tempi'.[108] Leach also
attests that 'attention to rhythm was perhaps Meyerhold's chief guiding principle
throughout his career',[109] and Meyerhold marks the importance of rhythm with
the following anecdote about the production of *The Forest* (1924) more than a
decade earlier:

> Once I had to post an order that if the scene between Pyotr and Aksyusha, which
> was to last two minutes, ran a minute longer, I would impose a penalty on the
> actors. Actors must be taught to be aware of time on the stage, as musicians are
> aware of it. A musically organized production isn't a production where music is
> being played or sung all the time behind the scenes, but rather a production with
> a precise rhythmic score, with precisely organized time.[110]

---

[105] Meyerhold, *Meyerhold on Theatre*, p. 28.
[106] Meyerhold in Leach, *Vsevolod Meyerhold*, p. 113.
[107] In Schmidt, *Meyerhold at Work*, p. 93.
[108] Zakhava in Schmidt, *Meyerhold at Work*, p. 93.
[109] Leach, *Vsevolod Meyerhold*, p. 112.
[110] Meyerhold in Gladkov, *Meyerhold speaks*, pp. 117–18.

Rhythm for Meyerhold is about gaining control over time, achieving efficiency of movement and striking an aesthetic balance: 'A performance of a play is an alternation of dynamic and static moments, as well as dynamic moments of different kinds.'[111] But rhythm is also an interpretive tool: finding the 'right' rhythm for a scene unlocks a certain interpretation of it: 'That is why the gift of rhythm seems to me one of the most important a director can have. Dragging out or speeding up an act can completely change the character of a performance.'[112]

In aiming to unlock his notion of rhythm in more detail, based on the discursive evidence and Meyerhold's preoccupation with it, I find it helpful to use the following distinction of five main aspects of rhythm in the realm of performance and performativity, as proposed by Brüstle, Ghattas, Risi and Schouten. These are:

(a) the relationship of order and movement, (b) the processuality of rhythm, (c) the intermodality of rhythmical perception, particularly in the sense of the mutual strengthening and weakening of individual sensory perceptions, (d) the physiological and cognitive conditions of rhythmical perception and subjective rhythmization and (e) the physical effect as affective participation or distancing to rhythmical experience.[113]

I will look at these in relation to Meyerhold's rhythmical *dispositif* one by one, even though there are clearly overlaps between the five aspects and, equally, most phenomena will be interesting to look at under more than one of the aspects. The following is thus not a taxonomy of rhythmical aspects, but a heuristic differentiation in order to cover an appropriate range of viewpoints.

Order and Movement

Particularly when we examine Meyerhold's biomechanical exercises, it is hard not to note how central the interplay between rhythmical order and acrobatic movement is here: movement is not only organized rhythmically, in the sense that it happens in time and is structured in recognizable patterns, but also with regard to degrees of physical strength (tension – relaxation), succession of different forms (bending, stretching, rotation, etc.) and spatial aspects (extension and direction of movement). On all these levels, however, 'the plastic form was subordinated to the musical rhythm of the motion, not to its real-life logic'.[114] For Meyerhold, an important rhythmical paradigm was the three-way structure of preparation, action and end-point, which he used as a basic structure throughout:

---

[111] Meyerhold in Schmidt, *Meyerhold at Work*, p. 155.

[112] Meyerhold in Schmidt, *Meyerhold at Work*, p. 155.

[113] Christa Brüstle/Nadia Ghattas/Clemens Risi/Sabine Schouten (eds.), *Aus dem Takt. Rhythmus in Kunst, Kultur und Natur* (Bielefeld, 2005), p. 14.

[114] Rudnitsky, *Meyerhold the Director*, p. 67.

He broke everything down (from the tiniest gesture to the overall structure of the play) into a tripartite rhythm. [...] These three parts are the very building blocks of biomechanical theatre. From the work of an individual actor to the orchestration of large ensembles, from a line in a small scene to the formal analysis of the whole play, *otkaz, posil'* and *tochka* determine everything.[115]

What this also suggests is that Meyerhold's notion of rhythm was less indebted to what we usually associate with the term – even measure, regularity and repetition[116] – than to what music philosopher Susanne Langer later described as the 'essence of rhythm', namely: 'the preparation of a new event by the ending of a previous one'.[117] Exploring the flexible relationship between preparation, action and ending constitutes the freedom of the actor and director and is also, I would argue, the basis for Meyerhold's emphatic distinction of rhythm and metre:

> He wanted 'not metre, but rhythm, rhythm and again rhythm', he told the pianist, Arnshtam, and by way of explanation contrasted the circus performer with the actor. Where the circus artist needs music of a strict metre, based on a metronome, perhaps, the actor should learn to work rhythmically within musical phrases.[118]

From a musicological point of view, the relationship of rhythm and metre is complex and has undergone significant changes in the course of history. 'Metre' could, however, be summarized as a *terminus technicus* as follows: metre signifies the 'recurrence of a basic beat of definite duration' which could also be called a 'steady pulse in the background'.[119] Cooper and Meyer put it this way:

> The pulse is one of a series of regularly recurring, precisely equivalent stimuli. Like the ticks of a metronome or a watch, pulses mark off equal units in the temporal continuum. Though generally established and supported by objective stimuli (sounds), the sense of pulse may exist subjectively.[120]

Rhythm, is it worth noting, is not necessarily linked to a regular pulse or metre: even though we are accustomed to expect or seek for a metre in most music, many forms of music either play with this perceptive habit, by overlaying or alternating metres in quick succession, or resist recognizable metrical organization altogether. Conversely, where there *is* a metre – whether it is our flashing indicator, a ticking

---

[115] Pitches, *Vsevolod Meyerhold*, p. 115.
[116] See Brüstle et al., *Aus dem Takt*, p. 9.
[117] Brüstle et al., *Aus dem Takt*, p. 9.
[118] Leach, *Vsevolod Meyerhold*, p. 113.
[119] Clemens Kühn, *Musiklehre* (Laaber, 1981), p. 128.
[120] Grosvenor W. Cooper/Leonard B. Meyer, *The Rhythmic Structure of Music* (Chicago/London, 1960), p. 3.

clock or our own pulse – we tend to organize it rhythmically into groups of two or three in our perception, sometimes even into larger periodic patterns.[121]

While Meyerhold acknowledged that a steady beat can help with developing precision in the 'rhythmical organisation of the actor',[122] Meyerhold ultimately wanted to grant the actor freedom from a rigid adherence to a metronomic metre – an agogic[123] creativity, one might call it. His actor Garin describes that 'on a canvas of metre, [the actors] mastered free rhythmical movement' and that they 'apprehended without difficulty the tempi and character of movement through music: legato, staccato, etc'.[124]

It is not only with reference to metre that Meyerhold's rhythmical aesthetic promotes a musically expressive rather than clockwork-mechanistic approach; Garin's mention of 'legato' and 'staccato' as a phrasing instruction, rather than a metrical device, point to the importance Meyerhold attributes to phrasing as much as metre and tempo. Before I give a more detailed example of how Meyerhold discusses this, I feel the term 'tempo' needs some further reflection, since it has – like 'rhythm' – 'worn out' a bit due to widespread and not always discriminate use. In music, when there is a stable metre, tempo can be determined in absolute terms as 'beats per minute', and both classical and popular music make use of this quantification frequently. Where tempo is given more loosely as part of the characterization of a piece ('allegro', 'lively', 'getragen', 'sostenuto', etc.), it is musical convention and performance history that give an indication of how fast or slow to play the relevant piece.

In theatre, the premise is a different one, as Pfister explains: 'The wide range of variations in tempo in different productions of a textual substrate in comparison to the smaller range of variations in tempo in performances of a musical piece goes back to the fact that the plurimedial text [i.e. the theatrical performance, DR] is not fully determined by the textual substrate and that the performance tempo is one of the quantities, which – in contrast to the more precisely fixed tempi in music – evades notation.'[125]

I would add that tempo in theatrical performances is always a *relative* phenomenon: whether a scene, a gesture or a speech are perceived as fast or slow, depends on similar scenes, gestures or speeches we have witnessed either outside of the theatre, i.e. in everyday life, or in the form of certain conventions established within the given theatrical genre or the specific performance in question. For this comparative view on tempo, different criteria come into play from an audience's

---

[121] See also Eilon Morris's chapter 'Defining Rhythm' in his *Via Rythmós*, pp. 17–36.

[122] Chuzhak in Leach, *Vsevolod Meyerhold*, p. 114. Actor Garin described this as 'an absolute feeling for time, and precise calculation – to count in fractions of seconds' (cit. in ibid.).

[123] In music, 'agogic' refers to 'slight fluctuations in tempo aiding an expressive interpretation' (Kühn, *Musiklehre*, p. 27).

[124] In Leach, *Vsevolod Meyerhold*, p. 114.

[125] Manfred Pfister, *Das Drama. Theorie und Analyse* (München, 1988 [1982]), pp. 378–9.

perspective. Peter Pütz, for example, bases his theory on tempo on the narrative (in film this would be called the 'story') and its dramaturgical structure, the way in which information is released ('the plot'). The impression of different tempi, he claims, is based on different kinds of dramatic succession, and the tension between anticipation and realization.[126] This approach, however, is limited and fails whenever theatre is not predominantly narrative – from medieval religious plays to Dada, from the Theatre of the Absurd to Postdramatic Theatre.

I would thus argue that many theatre forms, independently of the existence of a dramatic substrate, create a *musical* sense of expectation and realization or surprise and do this on three levels: they establish an *immanent* tempo-relation (for example, a gesture seems slow or fast compared to a similar gesture occurring earlier in the same performance), a *connotative* or *external* tempo-relation (a gesture is slow compared to how it is normally executed in daily life) or, with reference to Pfister, a *progressive* tempo-relation, which is determined by the density, intensity and quantity of events within a given time-span.

Meyerhold discusses the relationship of metre, tempo and rhythm as a fluid one, a productive tension between discipline and deviation:

> Contemporary conductors know that music is made up not only of notes but also those almost imperceptible *luft-pauses* between the notes. In the theatre, this is called the sub-text, or one might also say, the between-text. Stiedry[127] once told me that the poor conductor performs what is indicated in the score, whereas the good one performs what the score offers him for his free interpretation as an artist. That is, you can play: one, two-three, or also another way: one-two, three. The time segment is the same, the structure is different: it gives a different rhythm to the meter. Rhythm is what overcomes the meter, what disputes meter. Rhythm is knowing how to leap off the meter and back again. The art of such a conductor allows for rhythmical freedom in a measured segment. The art of the conductor lies in mastering the empty moments between rhythmic beats. It is essential that the theatre director also be aware of this.[128]

Meyerhold describes here vividly how to negotiate metric precision with interpretive rhythmical freedom. Internalizing the former through rigorous training allows the actor and director to then deviate and play with rhythm creatively. This is an interplay which is unique to the musicality *dispositif* and which he renders productive if not paradigmatic here: he short-circuits the *creative-productive* and the *interpretive* aspects of text-based theatre-making, using music-making as a model for striking the balance between them. Whereas Appia tended toward the interpretive – the efforts of the director, designer and actor were all in service of the play or score –

---

[126] Peter Pütz, *Die Zeit im Drama* (Göttingen, 1977 [1970]), p. 54.

[127] Fritz Stiedry (1883–1968) was an Austrian conductor and composer who emigrated to Russia in 1933.

[128] Meyerhold in Gladkov, *Meyerhold speaks*, p. 135.

and while later theatre generations often focus on the creative-productive force of musicality, as we will see, Meyerhold seeks to combine musical discipline with musical inventiveness, control with freedom, based on musical models he was familiar with. Finding a middle ground between these poles also means focusing closely on musicality (and here: rhythmicality) as a continuous *process* rather than an achievable end-point, which brings us to the second of Brüstle et al.'s aspects.

Processuality

Rhythm is not something that is directed at '*reaching a point in time*', but characterized by its 'use of repetition of structural similarities and its *processuality*'.[129] Rhythm is a continuously evolving process in time for both the musician and the listener, who engage in what Wolfgang Iser calls a 'dialectic of protention and retention':[130] an oscillating activity of reviewing and interpreting rhythmically what we have just experienced against the expectations we are continuously forming and renewing based on the former. 'In every instant of perception we extrapolate what we have seen with respect to its further development and relate those parts already realized to the expected whole.'[131]

It is a different kind of attention afforded by both the actor and spectator: the rhythmic *dispositif* takes away some of the teleological pressure of reaching a destination, a result, a final interpretation. Here, as Brüstle et al. put it, the 'perception of rhythms is characterized by shifting the attention from the end point of temporal processes to their course'.[132] This is also what distinguishes a biomechanical exercise from athletic training; the latter is a step towards an envisioned result – jumping as high as x, running as fast as y – whereas in the biomechanical exercise the attention of physical balance, strength and rhythmical precision in the *process* is an end in itself. Even when transferring the skills acquired onto the stage, the aim is not a perfected gesture, poise or posture, but a continuous and sharpened awareness of the *course* of movements that benefit the actors and enable them to perform in Meyerhold's theatre.

The attention to rhythm that the actor and the spectator are afforded, it should be added then, is clearly not limited to acoustic events,[133] but involves different

---

[129] Brüstle et al., *Aus dem Takt*, p. 16, original emphases.

[130] In Guido Hiß, Der theatralische Blick (Berlin, 1993), p. 66. This dichotomy is based on Edmund Husserl's On the Phenomenology of the Consciousness of Internal Time (Dordrecht, 1990 [1928]), p. 41.

[131] Hiß, *Der theatralische Blick*, p. 66.

[132] Brüstle et al., *Aus dem Takt*, p. 16.

[133] Rhythm is not an exclusively acoustic phenomenon in music either, where baton-waving conductors, foot-tapping musicians, head-banging rock stars, jumpy-montaged music videos, flashing disco lights and much more link the *visual* experience of rhythm inseparably to our *aural* perception; but it is more common than in theatre to at least theoretically conceive of rhythm in music as a predominantly acoustic phenomenon. It is not unheard of for listeners (and musicians) to close their eyes while playing/listening, but certainly more unusual amongst theatre audiences or actors.

senses or modes of perception, which we synthesize (or try to process separately) into an overall rhythmical experience.

Intermodality

While musical parameters such as pitch, melody, timbre and volume are almost exclusively *aural* phenomena,[134] rhythm is experienced also through vision and touch; potentially even through smell and taste.[135] In Meyerhold's theatre there is a particular emphasis on the intermodal interplay of rhythms of speech, movement, music and *mise en scène*. A close attention to rhythm pervades *all* elements of the staging ('There was no production by Meyerhold which did not reaffirm his conception of rhythm as the basis of all dramatic expression'[136]), but also synthesizes the different aspects of the actor's craft: 'For Meyerhold rhythm is the glue which binds all the other skills of the actor together.'[137] Visual, architectural, spatial and material aspects of stage design all contribute to and co-determine the overall rhythmic experience. According to Leach, 'the stage set itself was thus a factor in the creation of the dramatic rhythm',[138] and Pitches underlines this point by saying, 'the keystone in realising this musical vision of the play was production's design'.[139] As might be expected, there are thus strong similarities in how Meyerhold and Appia see lighting as an important *rhythmic* element of the production. Scholar and director Anatoly Antohin attests,

> Meyerhold elevated the role of light and lighting to a level equal to the role of music and rhythm in the performance. 'The light should touch the spectator as does music. Light must have its own rhythm, the score of light can be composed on the same principle as that of the sonata.'[140]

---

[134] I am aware that we also experience all of these phenomena in a physical way beyond our hearing as they are sound waves hitting our body, but for most people the experience of a melody or the distinction between different speaking voices are going to be predominantly *aural* experiences. The world-renowned deaf percussionist Evelyn Glennie is an impressive but rare exception to this rule (see Thomas Riedelheimer's documentary *Touching the Sound*, Filmquadrat / Skyline Productions 2004).

[135] Think of sommeliers and their descriptions of wines, which often include temporal aspects of how the experience of smell and taste evolves in time. The duration and intensity of the aftertaste, also described as 'length', or the development of the flavours in the glass according to exposure to oxygen, are just two examples.

[136] Braun in Meyerhold, *Meyerhold on Theatre*, p. 194.

[137] Pitches, *Vsevolod Meyerhold*, p. 115.

[138] Leach, *Vsevolod Meyerhold*, p. 112.

[139] Pitches, *Vsevolod Meyerhold*, p. 99.

[140] Anatoly Antohin, 'Meyerhold Biomechanics' (2005), http://biomechanics.vtheatre.net/meyer.html [17.08.2011].

With regard to stage design, however, he goes a step further: the often multi-layered stages with a complex system of stairs and levels do create 'rhythmic spaces' in Appia's sense, facilitating specific movements for the actors on stage, but Meyerhold also often introduced mobile set pieces such as turning wheels or moving screens, which contributed independently to the rhythmicity of the performance. For his production of *D.E. (Give us Europe!)* (1924), for example, he used 'a series of eight to ten red wooden screens, about 12 feet long and 9 feet high, which were moved on wheels by stage-hands concealed behind each one'.[141] Pitches describes in detail how this 'kinetic staging', as Meyerhold calls it, created a distinct rhythm, a constantly moving performance, that exposed certain scenes due to the uniqueness of their location, and placing others in a 'theme with variations' relationship.[142]

There is another side to the intermodality of rhythm in Meyerhold's theatre-making. As he describes it, not only does the experience of rhythm(s) occur through all of our senses, but rhythmical experience through *one* sense can also radiate to our other senses, evoking sonic, visual and visceral impressions. This is, at least, what he credits the rhythm in Chekhov's language with:

> The secret of Chekhov's mood lies in the *rhythm* of his language. It was the rhythm which was captured by the actors of the Art Theatre during the rehearsals of that first production of Chekhov [*The Seagull*] [...]. The atmosphere was created, not by the *mise en scène*, not by the crickets, not by the thunder of horses' hooves on the bridge, but by the sheer musicality of the actors who grasped the rhythm of Chekhov's poetry and succeeded in casting a sheen of moonlight over their creations.[143]

Musicality here is associated with being a key to theatrical *imagination*. It is the evocative quality of rhythm in particular that 'sets the scene'. I will come back to this shortly but first want to address two basic levels of rhythmical impact, which are crucial to Meyerhold's theatre-making: the physiological and the cognitive.

Physiology and Cognition

Meyerhold's training and theatre-making seeks to bring together the way the actor and director *think* and cognitively *structure and conceptualize* theatrical action with a highly developed 'body-knowledge'. I would argue that in contrast to Appia, whose notion of rhythm was strongly influenced by a 'biological' idea of 'natural' flux, reoccurrence and temporal balance – a kind of 'organic' rhythm that was then captured and sublimated by art (in particular, music) – Meyerhold promotes a more artificial (in the sense of 'man-made') and thus constructivist rhythmical paradigm. This is inspired by industrialization, by mechanization and

141 Braun in Meyerhold, *Meyerhold on Theatre*, p. 193.
142 See Pitches, *Vsevolod Meyerhold*, p. 98.
143 Meyerhold, *Meyerhold on Theatre*, p. 32.

ideas of efficiency: it is less about expression, or 'inner essence', than a vital part of the *craft* of the actor. Meyerhold, as we have seen, explicitly likens acting to other hands-on professions ('the blacksmith, the foundry-worker'[144]) as they all 'must have rhythm, must be familiar with the laws of balance'.[145]

The biomechanical training and the insistence on a tripartite rhythm trains the 'productive mental (individual) effort'[146] that rhythmical perception requires: what is needed in order to perceive rhythm as rhythm is the active review, anticipation and patternization of events by the actor. Biomechanical training thus helps to shape the cognitive activity of 'thinking in rhythm'. Since this cognitive activity is always embodied and tied closely to very distinct physical movement patterns, it also becomes part of the body-knowledge of actors and their 'instinctive' motional vocabulary. Thus one might describe Meyerhold's notion of rhythm also as more muscular, more athletic than that of Appia, who in his collaboration with Dalcroze emphasized the more fluent dance qualities of actors' movements, in contrast to Meyerhold's contention that it is 'only via the sports arena' that we can 'approach the theatrical arena'.[147] The sports metaphor also points to the dialectic of individual and group, and rhythm, as Eilon Morris has pointed out, is a potent factor in this respect: 'the capacity of rhythmic attending to bring about social cohesion and group bonding is an essential aspect of an ensemble training process'.[148]

While Meyerhold certainly employs the cognitive and physiological aspects of rhythm, he also has clear strategic aims towards the wider effects of rhythmization in service of his theatre aesthetics and the dialectic of affection and distance.

Affection and Distance

The experience of rhythm and its co-construction as a sensory and cognitive act can trigger a wide range of responses, depending on personal and cultural dispositions. We can find rhythms energizing, intoxicating and feel stimulated to move and dance to them, but equally we can find them particularly enervating, grinding or nerve-wracking; or simply boring and numbing. In turn, these experiences may affect us, draw us nearer to a phenomenon and make us literally 'tap along' or conversely create distance or rejection, which can be visceral, emotional, but also critical and reflective.

Theatre-maker and activist Augusto Boal, for example, suggests for his 'newspaper theatre' (or 'living newspaper'), a political theatre technique that Meyerhold also made use of in *D.E.*,[149] to use 'rhythmical reading'. He explains: 'as a musical commentary, the news is read to the rhythm of the samba, tango,

---

[144]   Braun in Meyerhold, *Meyerhold on Theatre*, p. 200.
[145]   Braun in Meyerhold, *Meyerhold on Theatre*, p. 200.
[146]   Brüstle et al., *Aus dem Takt*, p. 18.
[147]   Meyerhold, *Meyerhold on Theatre*, p. 200, original emphasis.
[148]   Morris, *Via Rythmós*, p. 114.
[149]   See Richard Stourac/Kathleen McCreery, *Theatre As a Weapon: Workers' Theatre in the Soviet Union, Germany and Britain, 1917–1934* (London, 1986), p. 16.

Gregorian chant, etc., so that the rhythm functions as a critical "filter" of the news, revealing its true content, which is obscured in the newspaper'.[150]

The friction or incongruence between the news story and the musical rhythms of South American dance music or Western sacred vocal music creates a moment of distance and defamiliarization – an aesthetic and political aim Meyerhold also pursued ardently. Rhythmization provided Meyerhold with a tool for stylization, which he argued was an important first step toward analysis: 'Stylisation involves a certain degree of verisimilitude. In consequence, the stylizer remains an analyst *par excellence.*'[151] The emphasis here, I would argue, lies on 'a certain degree'; Meyerhold insisted that theatre was not to provide a simple imitation of life (we will come back to this) and argued that rhythmization and musicalization were 'not true to life, but theatrically true'.[152] Art, he argues, cannot convey the 'sum of reality' but instead 'dismantles reality'.[153] For the actors this meant that rhythm was clearly introduced as a device of defamiliarization, a tool to prevent an overly emotional or emphatic approach: actress Vera Verigina attests that it was 'essential to keep that rhythm all the time so as not to be seized by personal emotion'.[154] And Leach elaborates:

> Rhythm was seen at this period as an expressive element in its own right. [...] Meyerhold came to think of rhythm in the theatre rather as the Formalist critics thought of it in poetry: a major means by which the artist 'deforms' his subject matter. Each component is subjected to the rhythm, which is thus not really an organising agent but has a direct impact upon the meaning as well.[155]

An important rhythmical strategy for Meyerhold was to exploit extensively the 'subjective interplay between expectation and surprise'[156] – Paul Valéry's characterization of rhythm. Meyerhold used drastic and abrupt changes in rhythm as a trademark of his musicality. Pitches recounts how one of the actors in *The Government Inspector*, Erast Garin, 'embodie[d] this concept of musicality'[157] and that in a particular moment of the production 'the entire scene was dictated by the rhythmic shifts of Garin'.[158] Grotowski echoes this rhythmical aesthetic later when

---

[150] In George W. Brandt (ed.), *Modern Theories of Drama* (Oxford, 1998), p. 255.

[151] Meyerhold in Brandt, *Modern Theories of Drama*, p. 135, original emphasis.

[152] Meyerhold, *Meyerhold on Theatre*, p. 82. Howard Barker captures this idea succinctly when demanding that theatre search for a 'higher truth than mere authenticity' (*Arguments for a Theatre* [London, 1989], p. 26). This strikes me as a good characterization of what Meyerhold was after: truth, yes, but not a mimetic truth, rather an abstraction, concentration, sublimation of truth.

[153] Meyerhold in Brandt, *Modern Theories*, p. 135.

[154] Verigina in Leach, *Vsevolod Meyerhold*, p. 112.

[155] Leach, *Vsevolod Meyerhold*, p. 112.

[156] Valéry in Brüstle et al., *Aus dem Takt*, p. 10.

[157] Pitches, *Vsevolod Meyerhold*, p. 97.

[158] Pitches, *Vsevolod Meyerhold*, pp. 97–8.

saying: 'rhythm is not synonymous with monotony or uniform prosody, but with pulsation, variation, sudden change'.[159]

As we will see, Meyerhold's concept of musicality, his 'rhythmic orchestration of the activities of his cast',[160] was guided by his fondness for the grotesque, while at the same time his musical approach to theatre enabled and shaped his aesthetics of the grotesque. It is worth developing this point further, since it exemplifies aptly how different theatre-makers may employ a similar *dispositif* (e.g. rhythmization) in pursuit of contrasting performative strategies and aesthetic aims. Directors like Appia, Tairov or Stanislavski had different visions of the impact of rhythm on the theatre of the future: we have seen that for Appia, for example, the use of rhythm – while clearly seen as a *musical* and not merely a rhetorical device – supported an aesthetic of flow, beauty, 'style'[161] and 'naturalness', where the 'simple imitation' of life was seen to be deficient in capturing the 'inner essence' of life. Tairov, in contrast to both Appia and Meyerhold, developed the notion of a theatrical rhythm that would emancipate itself from music in pursuit of a 'theatrical mystery', which would emphasize and celebrate a wide range of *emotions*, creating a fantastical, surreal world:

> In the future this work [on rhythm] will expose exceptionally exciting possibilities to the theatre. [...] Then perhaps will appear the wonderful possibility for the construction of genuine theatrical mystery, when triumph and despair, happiness and grief are woven into a single circle of alternating action when their uncoordinated rhythms will give birth to a new and startling harmony.[162]

Stanislavski's notion of rhythm was, unsurprisingly, more closely connected to the psychology of the character and a way of approaching narrative and embodiment for the actor. Houghton describes the function of rhythm in Stanislavski's rehearsals:

> Stanislavski used to use ten rhythms in a fractional arrangement. In rehearsing every movement was marked. The normal rhythm was 5. Rhythm 1 was that of a man almost dead, 2 that of a man weak with illness, and so on progressively to rhythm 9 which might be that of a person seeing a burning house, and to 10 when he is on the point of jumping out of the window.[163]

---

[159] Grotowski in Sven Bjerstedt, *Att agera musiklaiskt* (Master Thesis, Lunds Universitet, Musikhögskolan i Malmö, 2010), p. 69.

[160] Pitches, *Vsevolod Meyerhold*, p. 98.

[161] Again, I refer here to the way in which Goethe uses and distinguishes simple imitation, manner and style in his influential essay 'Einfache Nachahmung der Natur, Manier, Styl' (1788) (see Goethe, 'Simple Imitation of Nature, Manner, Style', in John Gage [ed.], *Goethe on Art* [London, 1980], pp. 21–4).

[162] Alexander Tairov, *Notes of a Director* (Coral Gables, FL, 1969), pp. 104–5.

[163] Houghton, *Moscow rehearsals*, p. 75.

Rhythm was thus clearly a measure of *psychological* states (of anxiety, energy, motivation, etc.) and intimately associated with narrative. Stanislavski's distinction between tempo and rhythm (and the creation of the term 'tempo-rhythm') also pay testimony to the fact that he was not so interested in the *musical* analogy. For Stanislavski, 'tempo and rhythm must not be confused, for tempo comes from outside whereas rhythm comes from within'.[164] This is a distinction that, musically speaking, does not hold up: what Houghton describes above are different tempi, not rhythms, and the distinction between tempo and rhythm is also a relatively arbitrary psychological allocation not backed up by musical theory. Tempo is an *effect* of specific rhythmical choices – the succession and nature of musical events in time – and is often associated closely with the implicit or explicit establishing of 'metre'. Stanislavski, however, creates a psychological analogy, which helps the actor distinguish between an inner, felt 'tempo' in contrast to the pace of external events and/or his or her visible gesture and movements. The aim, as we know, was to achieve the most convincing, subtle and differentiated portrayal of a character.[165] For Meyerhold, though, rhythm created an opportunity and tool for stylization, as well as an aesthetic of contrasts, of a montage of clashes and grotesque contradictions.

Musicality of the Grotesque

What is the 'grotesque' for Meyerhold? In one of his most influential pieces of writing, 'The Fairground Booth', which is present in various anthologies of theatre manifestos, Meyerhold defines and praises the grotesque as follows:

> Grotesque usually implies something hideous and strange, a humorous work which with no apparent logic combines the most dissimilar elements by *ignoring their details and relying on its own originality, borrowing from every source anything which satisfies its joie de vivre and its capricious, mocking attitude to life*. […] The grotesque deepens life's outward appearance to the point where it ceases to appear merely natural. […] The art of the grotesque is based on the conflict between form and content.[166]

There are a few aspects to tease out from this: to begin with, the grotesque, according to Meyerhold, transcends the 'merely' natural; it does not seek to imitate ordinary life like a mirror, but rather distorts and exaggerates. The paradoxical *bon mot*, that something is 'distorted into being recognizable',[167] is an apt description

---

[164] Houghton, *Moscow rehearsals*, p. 75.

[165] See the chapter 'Tapping emotions' in Morris, *Via Rythmós*, pp. 55–69.

[166] Meyerhold in Brandt, *Modern Theories*, pp. 135–7, original emphasis.

[167] This originally German phrase, 'bis zur Kenntlichkeit entstellt', has been attributed to various sources, among them Ernst Bloch and Bertolt Brecht and is now an often used expression.

of Meyerhold's grotesque aesthetic. Much like in the grotesque aesthetic of the *commedia dell'arte* or Jacques Callot's etchings of it, there is an amplification and distortion of proportions – both visually and rhythmically – which is meant, however, to *reveal* something about life and society rather than disguise it. Craig expressed a similar programmatic vision for his theatre, when claiming, 'the stage should never attempt to imitate nature, but create its own forms and visions never yet seen in nature. [...] Verse, ritual, music and dance, the mask, stylized gesture, and nonrealistic decor must all unite to hold the door against a "pushing world"'.[168]

This distance or separating 'door' safeguards, according to Craig, the imagination of the audience: 'Music and others keep us from the unimaginative ways of representing "the real world" by merely putting a frame around it.'[169] For Meyerhold it not only provides a critical perspective for the audience, but also creates incongruence, which is one of the key ingredients of humour and laughter, which Meyerhold embraced as much as the *commedia dell'arte* did. For the audience this was intended to be both entertaining and disorienting: Meyerhold claimed that the grotesque supports or creates ambivalence in the spectator[170] and Pitches argues that 'the grotesque [...] borrows from a range of sources and combines them in unusual and thought-provoking ways. It does this with the aim of shifting an audience's perspective, surprising them into new discoveries'.[171]

This 'unusual combination' or incongruence operates on several levels. On the 'vertical' axis,[172] there is incongruence between elements present on stage at a given moment in time (for example, the small size of the stage element clashed with the large ensemble of *The Government Inspector* assembled on it); but there is even, as Meyerhold indicates, incongruence *within* certain elements, a conflict 'between form and content'. The rhythmical delivery of newspaper articles, for example, creates such a contrast for the element of language. On a 'horizontal' axis, incongruence dominates the succession of events, which are deliberately juxtaposed and characterized by sudden shifts in tone, rhythm, visual composition, which is where the notion of 'montage' comes in.

Seen as aesthetic principles, both the grotesque and montage are usually described predominantly as *visual* phenomena. From visual artists Callot and Goya to the vivid imagery of writers such as E.T.A. Hoffmann, from the masks of *commedia* to the 'montage of attractions' in Eisenstein's or Kuleshov's filmic experiments, the focus is on *visual* manifestations of the strange, ugly, *animalesque*, disgusting, contrasting and incompatible. Meyerhold certainly makes use of all of this, but extends the notion of the grotesque into the realm

---

[168] Craig in Marvin Carlson, *Theories of the Theatre* (Ithaca, NY/London, 1993), pp. 304–5.

[169] Carlson, *Theories of the Theatre*, p. 304.

[170] See Brandt, *Modern Theories*, p. 136.

[171] Pitches, *Vsevolod Meyerhold*, p. 108.

[172] See the section 'Rhythm' in Chapter 1 on Appia on the metaphorical notion of vertical and horizontal, derived from the practice of musical notation in scores.

of music by emphasizing the rhythmic aspects of montage: its swift changes in timbre, mood and genre, all of which music can communicate particularly well as an 'experience of transience'.[173]

His eclectic and often contrast-rich use of music and sound becomes an important technique of the grotesque. Music and musicality play a crucial role in creating the contrasts and distortions that form part of the grotesque aesthetic. By consciously thinking of theatre as a contrapuntal composition, as we have seen earlier, Meyerhold creates a kind of musical montage full of sharp contrasts and contradictions. Montage, as becomes evident, is not merely or predominantly a *semantic* technique for Meyerhold, by which meaning-making becomes a more complex process and activates the audience who create a third semantic element from the juxtaposition of two previous elements. Meyerhold explicitly talks about it as a *musical* technique:

> When we come to examine Eisenstein's pronouncements we shall see how he divides up everything into 'attractions' – that is, into episodes […] He constructs these episodes *according to musical principles*, not with the conventional aim of advancing the narrative. This may sound rather abstruse unless we understand the nature of rhythm.[174]

Consequently, Pitches concludes that 'montage is intrinsically *musical*: the arrangement of the overall production can be likened to a composition. […] The collision of ideas generated by montage naturally lead to the mixing of opposites and hence to the *grotesque*'.[175]

It is in connection with this reading of the grotesque, I argue, that Meyerhold embraces the term and the idea of 'counterpoint' referring to its basic underlying principle, which consists in the combination of two or more elements, independent in rhythm, contour and timbre, which foreground melodic interaction and contrast, rather than the creation of harmonies. Meyerhold combines this musical principle with Mikhail Bakhtin's[176] ideas of dialogism and polyphony; the co-presence and interweaving of a variety of voices from different classes and in different idioms in the prose of Rabelais or Dostoyevsky. Thinking of the theatre as a polyphony of voices and directing as an exercise in theatrical counterpoint is certainly one of Meyerhold's striking and innovative contributions to the development of the art form and has proven, as we will see, highly influential. Not only did he, as Robinson says, 'incorporate music into his productions in unusual and aggressive ways, sometimes matching the emotional mood and rhythm of the stage action,

---

[173] Maconie, *The Concept of Music*, p. 66.

[174] Meyerhold in Leach, *Vsevolod Meyerhold*, p. 124, my emphasis.

[175] Pitches, *Vsevolod Meyerhold*, p. 75, original emphasis.

[176] See also Jane Milling/Graham Ley, *Modern Theories of Performance* (Basingstoke, 2001), p. 56 on Bakhtin's influence on Meyerhold.

and sometimes contradicting it, in highly self-conscious counterpoint';[177] he also transferred this as a principle onto the technique of acting, the use of language, lighting and design. Counterpoint, here, is not a mere juxtaposition – point against point[178] – of *meanings*, creating contrasts, contradictions and ironies on stage, but is also a deconstruction of theatre into units that correspond to musical intervals, rhythms and motifs, so that they can be composed *structurally* as counterpoint, too.

What is interesting about all this, and I have already hinted at this earlier, is that Meyerhold uses musicality as a vehicle – in training, directing, structuring, rehearsing for theatrical performance – for the reorientation towards and rediscovery of the *theatrical*. He has that in common with several of his contemporaries, such as Vakhtangov, Fuchs or Tairov (even though their notions of musicality and theatricality may be quite different in detail). 'Theatre is theatre',[179] Tairov states at the end of his *Notes of a Director*, and Brecht uses the same phrase to summarize Vakhtangov's approach:[180] but in both cases the idea of the uniqueness and autonomy of theatre as an artistic medium is inherently combined with the idea that '"theatricality" also meant "musicality"'.[181]

Musicality as a Means of Re-theatricalization

Musicality – alongside a highly developed sense of professionalizing physical and vocal training for the actors – is used by Meyerhold as a guarantor for the artistic difference between theatre and life. When he says that 'the theatre is art and everything in it should be determined by the laws of art. Art and life are governed by different laws',[182] we need to remember that he also often refers specifically to the 'laws of music' as an essential guideline for acting and directing. Or, to put it differently, when Meyerhold quotes Grillparzer in saying that 'art is to reality as wine is to the grapes',[183] one could say that for Meyerhold *musicality* is the process of winemaking: creating a deliberately *crafted*, refined and transformed essence of life, rather than its imitation. Meyerhold underlines this distinction using rhythm – one of the most prominent aspects of his musicality as we have seen – as an example:

---

[177] Robinson, 'Love for Three Operas', p. 287.

[178] 'Punctus contra punctum' is where the term originated from.

[179] Tairov, *Notes of a Director*, p. 143.

[180] In Vera Gottlieb, 'Vakhtangov's Musicality: Reassessing Yevgeny Vakhtangov (1883–1922)', *Contemporary Theatre Review*, 15/2 (2005), pp. 259–68, p. 260.

[181] Gottlieb, 'Vakhtangov's Musicality', p. 268.

[182] Meyerhold, *Meyerhold on Theatre*, p. 147.

[183] Gladkov, *Meyerhold speaks*, p. 168. Original: 'Die *Kunst* verhält sich zur Natur wie der Wein zur Traube' (Franz Grillparzer, *Grillparzers sämtliche Werke in zwanzig Bänden. Volume 15* [Tübingen, 1892], p. 30).

Music, which determines the tempo of every occurrence on the stage, dictates a rhythm which has nothing in common with everyday existence. The life of music is not the life of everyday reality. 'Neither life as it is, nor life as it ought to be, but life as it is seen in our dreams' (Chekhov). The essence of stage rhythm is the antithesis of real, everyday life.[184]

Music, rhythm and musicality are instruments for Meyerhold to create a clear distance between life and theatre, to support his quest for a grotesque and explicitly *theatrical* performance. If we use Helmar Schramm's 'magic triangle' of '*aisthesis, kinesis* and *semiosis*', which mark the 'conceptual cornerstones' of a 'virulent field, on which to elaborate *theatricality* in relation to the disparate whole of culture and scholarship',[185] we can differentiate some of the main connections between musicality and theatricality in Meyerhold's artistic credo. For Schramm, theatricality is characterized in a triangular relationship of powers – a 'style of perception' (aisthesis), a 'movement style' (kinesis) and a 'semiotic style' (semiosis)[186] – whose influence on each other may manifest itself as 'amplification or attenuation of influence, as dissonant friction or harmonic configuration, as mirroring or shadowing'.[187]

Aisthesis

With regard to the 'style of perception', Meyerhold's theatricality aims at creating a continuous awareness in the actor and spectator of the fact that they are performing/witnessing *theatre*. Vakhtangov, one of Meyerhold's students, said: 'Meyerhold calls a performance "good theatre" when the spectator does not forget for a moment that he is in a theatre. Stanislavski on the contrary, wants the spectator to forget that he is in the theatre.'[188] Another director closely associated with Meyerhold, who actually coined the term 'theatricality' (*teatralnost*[189]), Nikolai Evreinov, emphasizes this as the transformational aspect of theatre:

> According to Evreinov, stage-related theatricality rests essentially on the theatricality of an actor who, moved by a theatrical instinct, attempts to transform the reality that surrounds him.[190]

---

[184] Meyerhold, *Meyerhold on Theatre*, p. 85.

[185] Helmar Schramm, *Karneval des Denkens. Theatralität im Spiegel philosophischer Texte des 16. und 17. Jahrhunderts* (Berlin, 1996), p. 251.

[186] Schramm, *Karneval des Denkens*, p. 254.

[187] Schramm, *Karneval des Denkens*, p. 251.

[188] Vakhtangov in Toby Cole/Helen Krich Chinoy (eds.), *Actors on acting* (New York, 1970), pp. 506–7.

[189] See Josette Féral, 'Theatricality: The Specificity of Theatrical Language', *SubStance*, 31/2 and 31/3 (2002), pp. 94–108, p. 95.

[190] Féral, 'Theatricality', p. 99.

In Meyerhold's theatre-making and his 'concept of theatricality'[191] this manifests itself in the 'actor's ostentatious demonstration to the spectator that he is at the theater; his is an act that designates the theater as distinct from reality'.[192] The 'theatrical instinct', which Evereinov describes as similar to sexual desire or other fundamental human needs, however, is a more trained and cultivated affair in Meyerhold's theatre: it is a craft acquired not least through musical training. Re-theatricalization means a return to theatre as a craft, not an illusion, and to a consciously and overtly artistic (as opposed to 'naturalistic') design of its foremost components: movement, space and time. Music provides an artistic language not expected to be a realistic imitation of nature, and musicality thus acts as a filter and transformative power. For Meyerhold the theatrical *aisthesis* not only means shifting the audience's perceptive attention to the *form* of theatre, to its construction and rhythmic shape in time,[193] but also nurtures a different kind of perception and attention in the *actor* in rehearsal and training – guided by musicality, as we have discussed earlier.[194] As Feral reminds us, 'theatricality is a process that is above all linked to the conditions of theatrical production'[195] and for Meyerhold musicality has a decisive impact on shaping these conditions.

It is interesting to see how this idea resonates with other theatre-makers with certain shifts of emphasis. The idea of what theatre is – essentially – and thus what constitutes theatricality is often associated with qualities conventionally associated with music: rhythm, form, harmony, purity. Tairov, for example, would

> recognize music as the most independent and most pure of all the arts. And it of course follows that he should, therefore, seek to make his productions approach music so far as possible. Thus the dialogue of his productions was not so much spoken as intoned, not quite in recitative, but in richly rhythmic and sustained tone, poetic utterance. His movement was not quite dance, but nevertheless choreographed, flowing, sustained, rhythmic, and elevated, artistically designed movement.[196]

Similarly, Jacques Copeau and later Peter Brook also 'stress the differences between theatre and life', as Philip Auslander has demonstrated, but

---

[191]   Féral, 'Theatricality', p. 103.

[192]   Féral, 'Theatricality', p. 103.

[193]   See also Claus Mahnkopf's thoughts on the 'artificial nature of time in music' ('Vermag Musik die Zeit vergessen zu machen? Überlegungen zur Künstlichkeit der Zeit', in Nikolaus Müller-Schöll/Saskia Reither (eds.), *Aisthesis. Zur Erfahrung von Zeit, Raum, Text und Kunst* (Schliengen, 2005), pp. 163–71, p. 163.

[194]   See the section Directing, Actor Training and Rehearsing earlier in this chapter.

[195]   Féral, 'Theatricality', p. 103.

[196]   Kuhlke in Tairov, *Notes of a Director*, pp. 32–3.

like Aristotle, they believe that the spectator leaves the theatre in a condition close to an ideal affective state. The spectacle accomplishes this in much the way music does – through abstract theatrical elements (rhythm, sound, archetypal imagery) rather than through mimesis.[197]

'Re-theatralicalization' was a notion strongly entertained by Copeau in contrast to the naturalistic and illusionist theatre as well as to the commercial theatre with its over-abundance of set, costume and spectacle,[198] and by invoking the *commedia dell'arte* as a model for his theatre, Copeau – like Meyerhold – tapped into a theatre tradition that is both highly physical, but also highly rhythmical. For both, the combination of energetic movement with form and stylization, often prompted by musical structures and rhythms, is characteristic for their 'movement style' and their notion of theatricality, which brings us to the kinetic aspect.

Kinesis

Meyerhold once declared, according to Russian philosopher Vyacheslav Ivanov: 'Drama proceeded from the dynamic to the static pole. Drama was born "of the spirit of music, out of the dynamic energy of the choric dithyramb."'[199] Meyerhold did not feel that the often static declamation, which had become so dominant on the theatrical stage of his time, was doing the medium justice. Musicality (or being 'of the spirit of music', in Nietzsche's sense) not only provides form, structure and defamiliarization through stylization, but also injects it with dynamism.[200] Meyerhold's quest was a theatricality that rediscovered the specific kinetic qualities of actors on a stage, by reorienting their training and staging away from a more psychological and emotional approach to character, towards an extrovert physicality of virtuoso mastery of the body and a heightened expressiveness of movement, the achievement of which was aided by musicality and in particular a keen sense of rhythm.

Equally important are Meyerhold's decisions to replace the realistic set designs and the chronological dramaturgies, which sought to represent time as we experience it in everyday life, with rhythmic spaces and musical time structures,

---

[197] Philip Auslander, *From Acting to Performance: Essays in Modernism and Postmodernism* (London, 1997), p. 19.

[198] See Manfred Brauneck *Theater im 20. Jahrhundert* (Reinbeck bei Hamburg, 1998 [1982]), p. 83.

[199] Ivanov in Meyerhold, *Meyerhold on Theatre*, p. 59.

[200] While Meyerhold's idea of dynamism was predominantly based on movement, Kuhlke describes how Tairov felt that Meyerhold's theatre had form, but that it was empty form (see Kuhlke in Tairov, *Notes of a Director*, p. 28). For Tairov, dynamism arose only from the contact of both, form and emotion, becoming an '"emotionally saturated form" […] which was the secret of theatrical art' (ibid., p. 29).

metres, repetitions and the like.[201] Schramm distinguishes here between the 'kinetic perspective (as the dimension of placement) and kinetic mode (as the dimension of temporality)'.[202] With Andreas Kotte I would argue that theatricality, particularly with respect to kinesis, emerges from the coinciding of modes of emphasis (*Hervorherbung*) and abatement of consequence (*Konsequenzverminderung*).[203] A traffic warden's actions are clearly emphasized from other everyday actions by an elevated position, special clothing and unusually 'big' gestures.[204] We do not, however, think of their actions as 'theatre' because these are immediately consequential for the flow and safety of traffic. A game of chess between two friends,[205] conversely, is characterized by the abatement of consequence like most games (unless they are in a professional, competitive context), but is hardly a particularly emphasized action.

Following this distinction, musicality provides Meyerhold firstly with a way of emphasizing voice, gesture and movement, distinguishing them clearly, both in terms of 'mode' and 'perspective', from everyday life. One need only compare his biomechanical exercise of throwing a stone, and someone *actually* throwing a stone to verify this point. And secondly, by emphasizing theatre as theatre and by insisting on its aesthetics and dramaturgies as not naturalistically but musically formed, he also reinforces a continuous sense of 'abatement of consequences'. Inevitably, this has an impact on the kind of *semiotic* engagement the audience has with his theatre.

Semiosis

Theatre as a (hyper)medium[206] facilitates a different process of meaning-making than a novel or a painting. In their desire to re-theatricalize the theatre, Meyerhold and his contemporaries thus objected to the idea that theatre was somehow a branch of literature and merely a vehicle for the 'dissemination' of dramatic writing. As Tairov puts it, theatre should use literature purely as a *material* and cease to act as its 'servant for better or worse'.[207] This also de-emphasizes the *semiotic* aspect of the dramatic substrate:

---

[201] Similarly, Kuhlke talks about 'Tairov's rhythmic orchestration of the movements of actors about these forms [steps and platforms used to give vertical as well as horizontal dimensions to stage movement]' (in Tairov, *Notes of a Director*, p. 32).

[202] Schramm, *Karneval*, p. 258.

[203] Andreas Kotte, *Theaterwissenschaft* (Köln/Weimar/Berlin, 2005), p. 54.

[204] See Kotte, *Theaterwissenschaft*, p. 30.

[205] See Kotte, *Theaterwissenschaft*, p. 54.

[206] See Chiel Kattenbelt's chapter on multi-, trans- and intermediality of theatre, in which he explains that 'due to its capacity to incorporate all media, theatre can be seen as a "hypermedium", i.e. as a medium that can contain other media' (in Henri Schoenmakers et al. [eds.], *Theater und Medien* [Bielefeld, 2008], pp. 125–32, p. 127).

[207] Tairov in Brauneck, *Theater im 20. Jahrhundert*, p. 358.

It has been a long time overdue, to break with a habit of looking at the textual material on stage as something that has no further meaning than expressing this or that idea, this or that thought. It is high time to approach the textual material like you approach the pantomimic material, namely focusing on its inherent rhythm and its intrinsic harmonic and phonetic possibilities. To feel the rhythmical heartbeat of a play, its sound, its harmony and to orchestrate them so to speak – that is the task of the director.[208]

Meyerhold in particular thus utilized (and sometimes idealized) music as a dramaturgical technique towards a formalization and abstraction, but also in particular an abandonment, of the logocentrism of theatre. Roland Barthes's formula 'theatricality = theatre - text',[209] even though developed much later in the 1970s, is of interest here: although the text was by no means abandoned in the Russian avant-garde, musicality provided a shift in focus away from the 'limits imposed on [the master-actor] by literature'[210] towards a notion of theatre as an autonomous art of artistically crafted movement in an artistically crafted time and space.

The kind of theatrical *semiosis* Meyerhold was after is a self-conscious, distanced one. The meaning-making for the audience incorporates a continuous awareness of the theatre as a semiotic *process*, as Silvija Jestrovich explains:

Theatricality [...] can be present in the context of illusion without a self-referential aspect, but whenever theater's conventions and processes become its own topic, theatricality turns into a conceptual approach, often expressing its potential to make the familiar strange. This was the case with Meyerhold's, Tairov's and Evreinov's concepts of the theatricalization and re-theatricalization of theater in the Russian avant-garde. Moreover, these directors practiced the strategy of distancing the familiar using devices of theatricality in ways much closer to the notion of ostranenie as elaborated by Russian Formalists than to Brecht's Verfremdung. Thus theatricality functions as a distancing device when it foregrounds what is immanent to theater, calling attention to the fictionality and incompleteness of the representation.[211]

One aspect of this *ostranenie* is, as we have seen, the musical stylization of speech and movement; another, the intermedial shift by which this theatre invites the

---

[208] Tairov, *Notes of a Director*, p. 119.

[209] See Tracy C. Davis/Thomas Postlewait (eds.), *Theatricality* (Cambridge, 2003), p. 23.

[210] Tairov, *Notes of a Director*, p. 99.

[211] Silvija Jestrovic, 'Theatricality as Estrangement of Art and Life In the Russian Avant-garde', *Histories and Theories of Intermedia (Blog)* [Online] (2008), Blog entry 28.01.2008, http://umintermediai501.blogspot.co.uk/search?q=Theatricality+as+Estrangement [04.11.2011].

audience to abandon the compulsive search for discursive meaning and watch and listen to the theatre 'as music': 'It would seem that the naturalistic theatre denies the spectator's capacity to fill in the details with his imagination in the way one does when listening to music. But nevertheless, the capacity is there.'[212] In a metaphor that strikes a similar chord, Tairov describes the stage as a 'keyboard for the actor's playing';[213] a 'complex and difficult keyboard, which only the master actor can command',[214] which would also paradoxically suggest that employing a *musical* mode of perception, and thus a semiotic style that is quite different from our habitual way of de-coding signs for their *discursive* meaning, affords the spectator a more genuinely *theatrical* experience.[215]

In summary, it has become clear that despite Appia's demonstrable influence on Meyerhold and his contemporaries, there are some significant differences between them, marking an interesting development in how they each use a sense of musicality for quite different theatrical aims.

We should now investigate a parallel and quite distinct development, spear-headed by the Italian Futurists and the French theatre-maker Antonin Artaud, whose writings and practices explore a notably different aspect of the musicality *dispositif*. They draw our attention in particular to the theatricality of sound and the sonic sphere of theatrical performance. Whereas musicality for Appia and Meyerhold had been about form, rhythm, harmony, polyphony, discipline – always inspired by musical and compositional models – Artaud, who will be the focus of the next chapter, was about the raw energy of sound, the cacophony, the deconstructing and destabilizing effects of sound as friction and interference.

---

[212] Meyerhold, *Meyerhold on Theatre*, p. 26.

[213] Tairov, *Notes of a Director*, p. 33.

[214] Tairov, *Notes of a Director*, p. 142.

[215] I have described this elsewhere – and actually with a view to more contemporary theatre forms – as the potential of musicality in theatre to liberate audiences from their reflexive quest for meaning and opens eyes and ears for theatre as a multi-medial audiovisual event: 'Musicality [...] facilitates a communicative process, which affords the spectator [...] the opportunity [...] to switch between "theatrical" and "musical" modes and habits of perception. The spectator *can* go hunting for meaning and try to semantically decipher but may also let his or her attention wander and idle, and in doing that detect structural connections and explore the sonic and rhythmic qualities of the performance' (David Roesner, 'Musicality as a paradigm for the theatre – a kind of manifesto', *Studies in Musical Theatre*, 4/3 [2010], pp. 293–306, p. 296).

Chapter 3
Artaud – The Musicality of Sound, Voice and Noise

In this chapter I will look at the 'phenomenon'[1] that is Antonin Artaud (1896–1948). Artaud has been written about extensively,[2] which allows me to maintain a narrow focus on a few selected aspects for the purpose of this book's central argument. My contention is that Artaud's observations and assertions add a significant aspect to the question of musicality in the theatre by (re-)inventing and 'excavating' the sonic sphere of theatre. Artaud's writings shed light on a particular set of vectors of the musicality *dispositif*, by advocating the performative powers of music and sound as pre-referential, non-narrative, visceral objects.

The relationship of sound and music in this particular argument needs some explanation. How is sound connected with the notion of musicality? If we accept that musicality – at least on a basic level – is about the conscious and intentional organization or disorganization of sounds, and if we further accept that an interest in and attention to sound as a theatrical entity entails considering it as more than a mere semiotic qualifier or accidental by-product in an arena purposefully designed to *exclude* sound (with the exception of the spoken word as producer of meaning), then I would argue that making a case for the autonomy and performativity of sound is to promote theatre's musicality. Artaud himself certainly makes this connection when saying that 'there is a tangible idea of music where sound enters

---

[1]   Jane Milling/Graham Ley, *Modern Theories of Performance* (Basingstoke, 2001), p. 87.

[2]   See for example: George W. Brandt (ed.), *Modern Theories of Drama: A Selection of Writings on Drama and Theatre 1850–1990* (Oxford, 1998); Manfred Brauneck, *Theater im 20. Jahrhundert. Programmschriften, Stilperioden, Reformmodelle* (Reinbeck bei Hamburg, 1998 [1982]); Adrian Curtin, 'Cruel Vibrations: Sounding Out Antonin Artaud's Production of *Les Cenci*', *Theatre Research International*, 35/3 (2010), pp. 250–62; Jacques Derrida/Paule Thévenin, *The Secret Art of Antonin Artaud* (Cambridge, MA/London, 1998), online: http://www.ciasonhar.org.br/PDFS/the_secret_art_of_Artaud. pdf [05.01.2012]; Martin Esslin, *Antonin Artaud. The Man and His Work* (London, 1976); Helga Finter, *Der subjektive Raum. Band 2: Antonin Artaud und die Utopie des Theaters* (Tübingen, 1990); Helga Finter, 'Antonin Artaud and the Impossible Theatre: The Legacy of the Theatre of Cruelty', *TDR*, 41/4 (Winter 1997), pp. 15–40; Christopher Innes, *Avant Garde Theatre. 1892–1992* (London, 1993). Milling/Ley, *Modern Theories*; Edward Scheer (ed.), *Antonin Artaud. A Critical Reader* (London, 2004).

like a character'.[3] It leads him to call for a 'musical condition' at the basis of the kind of theatre he strives for:

> To sum it up more distinctly, something like a musical condition must have existed to produce this staging, everything that is imagined by the mind is only an excuse, a virtuality whose double produced this intense scenic poetry, this many-hued spatial language.[4]

A vital part of this understanding of theatre as the imagination's double is sound. It is commonly known that Artaud's visit to the International Colonial Exposition in Paris in 1931 and his encounter of Balinese Theatre there[5] – John Levack Drever describes the experience as a 'sonic epiphany'[6] – had a pivotal influence on Artaud's vision of theatre.[7] In order to ascertain how, in particular, the sonic qualities of the Balinese theatre impacted his theatrical credo, we need to address a simple but important question: what did Artaud actually hear in Paris in 1931? Following on from that I will extrapolate how Artaud's encounter with the specific Balinese theatrical language and soundscape left its mark on his theatrical vision, which over time has had such an influence on the musical and theatrical experiments of the 1960s and 1970s and beyond.

What Did Artaud Actually Hear?

When concentrating on music and sound amongst the various stimuli in Balinese theatre triggering Artaud's most influential writings, three aspects in particular deserve our attention: what was the soundscape of this theatre like to provoke Artaud's fervent reactions, what were the particular vocal qualities, and how did they interrelate with the performance as a whole?[8]

---

    3   Antonin Artaud, *The Theatre and its Double* (London, 1970), p. 73.

    4   Artaud, *The Theatre and its Double*, pp. 44–5.

    5   See also Laura Noszlopy/Matthew Isaac Cohen (eds.), *Contemporary Southeast Asian Performance: Transnational Perspectives* (Newcastle upon Tyne, 2010).

    6   John Levack Drever, 'Sound effect – object – event. Endemic and exogenous electro-acoustic sound practices in theatre', in Ross Brown (ed.), *Sound: A Reader in Theatre Practice* (Houndmills, 2010), pp. 188–205, p. 189.

    7   See for example: Denis Hollier, 'The death of paper, part two: Artaud's sound system', in Scheer, *Antonin Artaud*, pp. 159–68; Nicola Savarese, '1931 Antonin Artaud Sees Balinese Theatre at the Paris Colonial Exposition', *TDR: The Drama Review*, 45/3 (Fall 2001), pp. 51–77.

    8   Adrian Curtin has explored this question, particularly with respect to Artaud's actual theatrical practice in the production of *Les Cenci*, and demonstrates the immediate influence of Balinese music and theatre on Artaud's sonic design and theatrical aesthetics, 'in which sound attained foreground status, and functioned as a dynamic, destabilizing agent' (Curtin, 'Cruel Vibrations', p. 257).

The Balinese theatre, then and now, is characterized by the visible presence of a small to medium ensemble of musicians, a gamelan, consisting mainly of pitched percussive instruments, such as gongs, metallophones, xylophones and plucked string instruments as well as double-headed drums in various sizes. This orchestra accompanies the theatrical action throughout. While generalizations about the multi-faceted music of Indonesia are, of course, problematic, there are a few musical characteristics which apply quite widely and can be considered 'typical'. I will describe them, intentionally, particularly with respect to how they differ from Western music, classical and popular, not in order to label Indonesian music as 'other', but in an attempt to imagine the level of difference Artaud must have experienced.

Given the range of instruments in a gamelan, the music is ostensibly percussive and very rich in overtones: most of the instruments are made from metal and, given their material and shape, produce a wide range of frequencies and often (to a Western ear) conflicting overtones, in contrast to Western instruments, which are often built to produce a 'purer' tone with a more clearly determined pitch. The impression (again for a Western ear) of unstable tonalities is further enhanced by the different tuning conventions: not all instruments in an ensemble are necessarily tuned to a common point of reference (such as the chamber tone A at 440Hz). In addition, they are also individually tuned within themselves to produce varying intervals and scales, which tend not to be in accordance with the well-tempered tuning conventions established in Western classical and popular music since Bach. This also means that one of the most defining features of Western music, the major/minor dichotomy, does not apply to this music, which makes it emotionally more ambivalent to the Western listener.

Next, the sheer density of the music is noteworthy: R. Anderson Sutton records that scholars speak of 'stratified polyphony'[9] with respect to Southeast Asian music; others prefer to characterize it as heterophonic since 'the pitched parts heard simultaneously are constructed as variations of the single melodic entity either sounded explicitly in one or more voices or held in the performers' minds as a basis for their varied realizations'.[10] Either way, the overlapping of complex musical elements and the 'layering of musical activity in distinct strata'[11] is clearly notable for the listener. As Western ears will struggle to subsume elements due to a particular harmonic or rhythmic function in the music, or in other words to establish hierarchies and economize their attention, the experience – particularly over time – is bound to be overwhelming.

---

[9]   R. Anderson Sutton, 'South-east Asia', in Stanley Sadie (ed.), *New Grove Dictionary of Music and Musicians, 2nd edition*, Vol. 24 (London, 2001), pp. 94–107, p. 94.

[10]   Sutton, 'South-east Asia', pp. 94–5.

[11]   Sutton, 'South-east Asia', p. 98.

The element that is perhaps most accessible at first, is the rhythm: 'Most music of the region is pulsed and organized into cyclical binary groupings with further binary subdivisions.'[12] This is something Western listeners are very familiar with: music of the classical period was largely organized in groupings or 'periods' of eight bars, which again could be subdivided into groups of four or two, and a vast majority of pop music today is also still based on 2-, 4-, and 8-bar units and 4/4 time. However, even this is not a straightforward musical experience due to the unusual variability of tempo on the one hand and the amount of repetition, or the 'prevalence of cyclical musical form'[13] as Sutton calls it, on the other. The teleological nature of much of Western music (working towards a musical climax, exhausting a number of motivic permutative possibilities or presenting a finite number of variations) is – for the Western listener – largely suspended in Indonesian music.

What Artaud heard was a soundscape dominated by comparatively sharp sounds (and his mental illness will have added to the effect[14]), overwhelmingly layered and repeated, and thus in all likeliness a much more *physical* experience than most music available to him at the time.[15] This means that the gamelan pieces not only, like most music, defy discursive meaning, but also resist a *musical* coherence in the sense of the harmonic or rhythmic functionality we have been accustomed to. The music sounds decidedly purposeful, but its rules are not easily understood without training. In other words: the functionality of Western harmonics is displaced by a functionality a Western audience (and Artaud) does not understand.

Before turning our attention to aspects of voice in Artaud's experience of Balinese theatre I will explore in more detail what significance sound (and music experienced *as* sound) has in Artaud's manifestos.

---

[12]   Sutton, 'South-east Asia', p. 95.

[13]   Sutton, 'South-east Asia', p. 99.

[14]   Artaud suffered from lifelong mental illnesses, hallucinations, neuralgia, clinical depression, addiction to opiates and severe headaches following childhood meningitis, all of which are very likely to have resulted in a heightened sensitivity to sound.

[15]   I would argue that the advent of techno in the 1990s, given its volume, repetitiveness, and range of excessive synthetic sounds, can perhaps be compared *in how it affected* listeners to the Balinese music heard by Artaud. As Gina Andrea Fatone reports, there have even been experiments to fuse the two ('*Gamelan*, techno-primitivism and the San Francisco rave scene', in Graham St John [ed.], *Rave Culture and Religion* [London, 2004], pp. 196–208). And interestingly, techno has also had an effect on (some) theatre-makers and dramatic writers at the time, such as Rainald Goetz, which even led to the coinage *TechnoTheater* (Friedrich J. Windrich, *TechnoTheater: Dramaturgie und Philosophie bei Rainald Goetz und Thomas Bernhard* [München, 2007]).

Sound as a Theatrical Element in Its Own Right

Sound as Object

Artaud plays an important role in the advent of sound and also its 'poor cousin' noise[16] as theatrical elements in their own right.[17] Interestingly, despite Artaud's huge influence on sound art, experimental theatre, and sound effects and electronics, his inspiration – the Balinese theatre – was devoid of any 'modern' technologies, sound effects or acousmatic sound; even by the standards of its time (and theatre resisted sound technologies much longer than, for example, film[18]) it was quite 'retro' in terms of the *technical* aspects of its sonic sphere.

What Artaud promoted, ahead of his time, was sound on stage as an autonomous part of performance, which was not – and this was certainly new – a mere extension or illustration of a fictional place, time or character. For analytical purposes I find it useful to refer to the three 'related approaches to the practice of listening and sound making'.[19] that Drever distinguishes in his chapter in Ross Brown's *Sound: A Reader in Theatre Practice* (2010). These are: sound effect, sound object, and sound event. What I am suggesting is that Artaud was essentially promoting the abandonment of sound effects and instead embracing sound objects.

According to Drever, 'sound effect' relates to a predominantly *semiotic* practice of listening to and producing sound in theatre 'confined to the strictures of a standardized convention based on supposed (albeit illusionary) cause related to a rigid system of signification'[20] The aptly named 'thunder sheet', for example, a thin sheet of metal which produces a sound that resembles thunder and has been

---

[16] See Lynne Kendrick/David Roesner (eds.), *Theatre Noise. The Sound of Performance* (Newcastle upon Tyne, 2011).

[17] The other crucial influence is, of course, the Futurists, although their impact was probably more pronounced in music, art and performance rather than in dramatic theatre, which remains the focus of this book. Their treatment of sound and noise is also ideologically different from Artaud's: for Marinetti, Russolo, Kruchenykh and others, exhibiting and celebrating (excessive) sound and noise was a way of glorifying their usual suspects in terms of desirable qualities: being fast, man-made, machine-like, powerful, destructive, etc. Transgression of sound was *the* mode of emphasis (see the discussion of 're-theatricalization' in the final part of chapter 2) towards the very theatricality of their artistic projects, whether these were readings, exhibitions, multi-medial events or concerts. For a detailed discussion on sound dramaturgies of Futurism see Mladen Ovadija, *Dramaturgy of Sound in the Avant-Garde and Postdramatic Theatre* (Montreal, 2013).

[18] The advent of film sound was only a few years before the 1931 Paris Colonial Exhibition. Al Jolson's *The Jazz Singer* (dir. Alan Crosland) from 1927 is widely regarded as the first sound film.

[19] Drever, 'Sound Effect', p. 189.

[20] Drever, 'Sound Effect', p. 197.

a stock item in theatres' sound departments for centuries,[21] is a good example here. Even though the cause of the sound is an illusion, its signification ('there is a thunderstorm') is unequivocal.

Sound objects, in contrast, isolate 'a sound from its context, manipulating it, and thus creating a new sound phenomenon which could no longer be traced directly to its source'.[22] Philosopher Jean-François Augoyard and sociologist Henry Torgue differentiate this concept further:

> The concept of the sound object can be used in three different ways. From a practical and empirical point of view, it describes the interaction of the physical signal and the perceptive intentionality, without which there would be no perception. From the theoretical point of view, it is a phenomenological quest for the essence of sound. Finally, from the point of view of instrumentation, the sound object is intended to be the elementary unit of the general and multidisciplinary solfège of sounds.[23]

The aim of this defamiliarization – described and tested by pioneer sound researcher Pierre Schaeffer – which is often achieved by technical means including the looping of sounds or cutting into its Bell curve (thus erasing its attack, for example), was to help reestablish an 'innocent ear'[24] and a 'new mode of listening […]: *reduced listening*'.[25] Drever elaborates: 'Unlike *casual listening* and *semantic listening*, it requires an unlearning of listening habits. It is only concerned with the relation of listening to the intrinsic qualities of sound.'[26] Artaud, I would argue, paved the way – philosophically, not technologically – for this kind of listening. He already sought after the unheard sound, the sound without context, after estranged and unfamiliar sounds, which would allow and/or force the audience to engage with sound as a physical (or, in Artaud's case also meta-physical) experience rather than a process of signification.[27] The following quotation by Artaud is an indication of this shift:

---

[21]   One of the oldest still functioning theatres from the mid-seventeenth century, the Drottningholm Palace Theatre near Stockholm, for example, lets visitors test and experience this effect to this day.

[22]   Schaeffer in Drever, 'Sound Effect', p. 199.

[23]   Jean-François Augoyard/Henry Torgue, *Sonic Experience: A Guide to Everyday Sounds* (Montreal, 2005), p. 6.

[24]   Gombrich in Drever, 'Sound Effect', p. 199.

[25]   Drever, 'Sound Effect', p. 199, original emphasis.

[26]   Drever, 'Sound Effect', p. 199, original emphases.

[27]   John Collins, sound designer with The Wooster Group and director of Elevator Repair Service, speaks of sound as a 'highly effective creator of a sensation of physical (as opposed to psychological) truth in theatre' (John Collins, 'Performing Sound / Sounding Space', in Kendrick/Roesner, *Theatre Noise*, pp. 23–32, p. 28).

> The noise background is what theater lacks the most, and this is why noises and screams that come from backstage are so ridiculously mangy and grotesque … One should never try to have ten extras sound like a ten-thousand-men crowd. To produce such an effect, one must use recordings of real noises whose intensity could be regulated at will by means of amplifiers and loudspeakers disseminated all across the stage and the theatre.[28]

In order to *signify* a large crowd, the backstage 'proxy' sounds would probably suffice, but for the actual *experience* of a sound of this kind, a different approach is required that uses the *materiality* of sounds, their vibratory qualities and their visceral impact (to which we will return).[29]

In his insistence that theatre should facilitate an experience of sound *as such*, then, Artaud promotes what has later been called 'sound objects', but not what Drever describes as *sound event*. This notion not only attributes a more active, constitutive role to the recipient in the creation of soundscapes, but also emphasizes the *context* of sounds:

> Unlike the self-referential perceptual unit of the *sound object*, the *sound event* however encompasses and extends beyond the intrinsic to include all 'social and environmental' (Truax, 1999) aspects of its original 'spatial and temporal' (ibid.) context: 'a nonabstractable point of reference, related to a whole of greater magnitude than itself'.[30]

The sound sphere of the Balinese theatre, which so impressed Artaud, registered with him neither as a series of sound effects nor sound events, but as sound objects. I am aware of the difference between sound effects and incidental music (which, after all, dominated the Balinese theatre in question), but one can easily draw a parallel between Drever's categories and different functions of stage music: music as effect – as it is very often used in theatre – would describe a music that has a semiotic function, indicating a character's mood or particular place or time. Music as event would carry the 'social and environmental' contexts (Brecht's essay on 'gestic music' from 1938, the same year in which *The Theatre and its Double* was published, comes to mind). But music as object would again describe an attempt to let music not exhaust itself in a particular functionality,

---

[28]   In Drever, 'Sound Effect', p. 191. Adrian Curtin ('Cruel Vibrations') describes and analyzes this envisioned use of sonic technologies in Artaud's production of *Les Cenci* in great detail.

[29]   In contrast, there is also what Martin Welton calls the 'sensuousness of silence' (*Feeling Theatre* [Basingstoke, 2011], p. 83), which transcends the mere physical sense of vibration and 'acoustic resonance' (ibid.).

[30]   Drever, 'Sound Effect', p. 202, original emphases. Quotations are taken from Barry Truax, *Handbook for Acoustic Ecology* (Vancouver, 1999) and R. Murray Schafer, *The Soundscape: Our Sonic Environment and the Tuning of the World* (Rochester, VT, 1994).

but be present as an artistic entity and stage material in and of itself. One could say that Artaud could not help but hear Balinese theatre in this way – due to the lack of prior knowledge or available reference points, in this sense, a pair of 'innocent ears' was forced upon him. His achievement was that he tried to find ways in which to transfer the quality of that experience to the European stage. One aspect of this transfer was the attempt to de-semantize music and sound (and also speech, which we will come to); another aspect, to reclaim the sheer physicality of sound, its visceral qualities.

Visceral Qualities of Sound

Denis Hollier starts his observations on 'Artaud's sound system'[31] with the following quotation by Artaud, which elegantly sums up a programmatic principle of Artaud's thinking with respect to sound:

> Music has an effect on snakes, not by means of the mental ideas it induces in them, but because the snakes are elongated, coil up languorously on the ground, and touch the earth along almost the entire length of their bodies; thus the musical vibrations transmitted to earth affect these bodies as a very subtle and very long massage; well, I propose to treat the public like snakes.[32]

Music and sound, and by proxy also theatre, are not cerebral, lofty, 'airy' phenomena for Artaud; they are physical, 'meaty',[33] primal and chthonic. The stimulus they give – and for Artaud this is a compliment – is skin-deep; to be felt rather than decoded. According to Guido Hiß, it was Artaud's aim to 'affect the mind through the senses':[34] 'in our present degenerative stage, metaphysics must be made to enter the mind through the body'[35] – Curtin thus speaks of a 'concept of vibrational affectivity'.[36] As Christopher Innes confirms, this 'linkage of physical and spiritual [...] is typical of Artaud's approach'.[37] So, one of the reasons why Artaud makes the case for the snake as a model of aesthetic experience, is that he believes metaphysics and spirituality, which are central qualities of his idea of a 'pure theatre',[38] are pre-linguistic and sensual phenomena. More than seeing, hearing as the more physical of the two far senses – Helga Finter even speaks of

---

[31]   Hollier, 'Death of Paper', p. 159.
[32]   Artaud in Hollier, 'Death of Paper', p. 159.
[33]   See Douglas Kahn, *Noise Water Meat. A History of Sound in the Arts* (Cambridge, MA, 1999).
[34]   Guido Hiß, *Synthetische Visionen: Theater als Gesamtkunstwerk von 1800 bis 2000* (München, 2005), p. 245.
[35]   Artaud, *The Theatre*, p. 77.
[36]   Curtin, 'Cruel Vibrations', p. 257.
[37]   Innes, *Avant Garde Theatre*, p. 60.
[38]   Artaud, *The Theatre*, p. 39.

the 'the sound-body of music'[39] – lends itself particularly well to facilitate this kind of artistic encounter. Artaud's 'insistence on the specifically physical disposition of theatre'[40] is thus strongly connected to his sense of a musicality or 'musical condition'[41] of theatre, and part of a transcendental vision of theatre's role, not unlike Appia's understanding. Quite in contrast to Appia, however, musicality is not a vehicle for a harmonic form and an enlightened self, but an expression of a profound discomfort of the self in the world, while at the same time celebrating the 'jouissance'[42] of body, exhilaration and excess. Like the scream that Artaud uses as a metonymy of theatre, it can be an expression of 'triumph or pain'.[43] In short, one could perhaps call Appia's approach an Apollonian concept of musicality in theatre, and Artaud's a Dionysian.

This is also manifest in his ideas on voice, which, as Finter has analyzed in detail, celebrate 'the work on the sound, the rustle, and the timbre of the voice' and seek the 'jouissance of a "pure" voice [...] as the transitional object prior to language'.[44]

Voice, Body and Incantation

Artaud's desire for a theatre that 'bewitches our senses by using a truly Oriental concept of expression'[45] is also an indication of his rejection of Western theatre traditions, in particular its relationship with the spoken word on stage. Artaud was frustrated with the logocentric nature of Western theatre, which is 'enslaved to a writing more ancient than itself'[46] and instead sought to explore 'the way text operated as an evocative, pre-literate sound prior to being attached to semantic meanings',[47] liberating the word by turning it into incantations, by extending the voice, by transforming it into bodily expression and a 'new lyricism of gesture'.[48] Artaud insisted that 'we must first break theatre's subjugation to the text and rediscover the idea of a kind of unique language somewhere in between gesture

---

[39]   Finter, 'Antonin Artaud', p. 34.
[40]   Hiß, *Synthetische Visionen*, p. 250.
[41]   Artaud, *The Theatre*, p. 44.
[42]   Finter, 'Antonin Artaud', p. 28.
[43]   Stephen Barber, *The Screaming Body* (London, 1999), p. 107.
[44]   Finter, 'Antonin Artaud', p. 28.
[45]   Artaud, *The Theatre*, p. 69.
[46]   Artaud, cit. in Jacques Derrida, *Writing and Difference* (London/New York, 1978 [1967]), p. 174.
[47]   Zachary Dunbar, 'Melodic Intentions: Speaking Text in Postdramatic Dance Theatre', in Kendrick/Roesner, *Theatre Noise*, pp. 164–73, p. 169.
[48]   Artaud, *The Theatre*, p. 91. Artaud is neither the first nor the only theatre-maker of his time to express this desire; in 1909, for example, Edward Gordon Craig said: 'I wish to remove the word with its dogma but to leave the sound' (cit. in Uta Grund, *Zwischen den Künsten. Edward Gordon Craig und das Bildertheater um 1900* [Berlin, 2002], p. 161).

and thought'[49] – he found this language in a kind of 'primitive' musicality and in a quality of vocal delivery he called 'intonation'.[50] Jacques Derrida cites a lecture at the Sorbonne from 1931, the same year as the Paris Colonial Exhibition, where Artaud emphasized the sonorous and musical qualities of language on the theatre stage:

> Words themselves have their own potential as sound, they have various ways of being projected into space, which are called intonations. And there is a great deal that could be said about the concrete value of intonation in the theater, about this quality that words have – apart from their concrete meaning – of creating their own music according to the way in which they are uttered, which can even go against that meaning – of creating beneath language an undercurrent of impressions, correspondences, analogies ... .[51]

Mihai Lucaciu, who reads Artaud in terms of theories of hysteria and representations of the body, puts it this way:

> The hysterical Artaud moves from a linguistic position to a more blurry one on the borders of language. The performative language of the hysteric uses sounds, noises, words and speech to act, for the sake of their musicality and intonation, to get what is wanted and to throw out only what is strongly felt. The hysterical sounds are not part of a signifying chain; they are reduplicated things beyond representation and full of their materiality.[52]

Artaud attributed these qualities to the Balinese theatre and called the resulting vocal aesthetics he claimed to have found in it 'incantations'. This word, *l'incantation* in the French original, forges an interesting set of connections between two core Artaudian ideas: it combines the idea of a transformative speech-act, an act of magical evocation or conjuring, with a musical quality of speech, given its etymological connection with *cantare* (Latin for 'singing'). Considering the latter, the musical qualities of language, first, here is how Artaud promotes the abandonment of 'our Western ideas of speech':[53]

---

[49]   Artaud, *The Theatre*, p. 68.

[50]   For an in-depth discussion of philosophical connections between voice, gesture and mediality see Petra Maria Meyer's chapter 'Stimme, Geste und audio-visuelle Konzepte' in her book *Acoustic turn* (Tübingen, 2008), pp. 291–351.

[51]   Antonin Artaud, *Selected Writings. Edited by Susan Sontag* (Berkeley/Los Angeles, CA: University of California Press, 1988), p. 232.

[52]   Mihai Lucaciu, '"This scream I've thrown out is a dream": Corporeal Transformation Through Sound, an Artaudian Experiment', *Studies in Musical Theatre*, 4/1 (2010), pp. 67–74, p. 71.

[53]   Artaud, *The Theatre*, p. 70.

It turns words into incantation. It expands the voice. It uses vocal vibrations and qualities, wildly trampling them underfoot. It pile-drives sounds. [...] It liberates a new lyricism of gestures which because it is distilled and spatially amplified, ends by surpassing the lyricism of words.[54]

Again, he emphasizes a kind of musicality that is not airy, lofty or 'lyric' in the sense of romantically beautiful, but earth-bound and gritty.[55] He celebrates vocal qualities that are not ethereal but 'grainy' – to use Roland Barthes's famous coinage – and uniquely marked by the emitting body, like striation on a bullet: 'through its timbre, the voice, as sound, manifests the body as prompted presence'.[56] These qualities are brought to the fore at the expense of semantic meaning, which was decidedly the case in the way in which Artaud encountered the Balinese theatre:

What little dialogue Balinese spectacle contained was in an archaic tongue that apparently neither performers, nor the Balinese audience (let alone the French spectators), nor even priests understood. It thus became an incantation. The only other vocal communication was on the level of pure sound, so that meaning was transmitted on a physical level through attitudes, which, while not directly allegorical, had an intrinsically symbolic effect through their highly formalized codification.[57]

Interpreting Artaud's intentions (and in particular his snake 'allegory'), Paul Arnold claims:

There must be no caesura between this incantatory, vibratory function of the word and the musicality of all other elements in the spectacle: 'sounds, noises, cries are sought first for their vibratory quality, then for what they represent.' For vibration itself has a quality that acts magically upon us.[58]

This notion of the 'magical' and transformative was described by other witnesses of the Balinese theatre as well, even by more sober observers than Artaud.

---

[54]   Artaud, *The Theatre*, p. 70.
[55]   Jennifer Shryane makes an interesting case for the German avant-garde rock band Einstürzende Neubauten with their 'expanded gestural vocalisation and their use of the scream' to be truly Artaudian artists (Jennifer Shryane 'Sprich zu mir in Seuchensprache/ Speak to me in plague language [Vanadium-i-ching, 1983]: An analysis of Einstürzende Neubauten as Artaudian artists', *Studies in Theatre and Performance*, 30/3 [2010], pp. 323–40, p. 323).
[56]   Finter, 'Antonin Artaud', p. 24.
[57]   Innes, *Avant Garde Theatre*, p. 15.
[58]   Paul Arnold, 'The Artaud Experiment', *The Tulane Drama Review*, 8/2 (Winter 1963), pp. 15–29, p. 23.

André Levinson, a famous dance critic and historian, and not prone to poetic license, wrote equally enthusiastically about the Balinese dancers. He studied their performances carefully and, with customary precision, drew attention to the technical aspects of their dancing: 'But it is time for [...] the curtain to rise and for us to enter the magic circle ... We then see the performance being born from the very soul of the music! Even visually, the indigenous gamelan orchestra [...] has a strange and fascinating effect.'[59]

Levinson, like Artaud, connects the impact of the theatrical experience to a notion of musicality – 'being born from the very soul of music' – with a distinct nod to Nietzsche. It is important to note this connection as it sets Artaud clearly apart from some of his contemporaries' attempts, which at first glance seem to operate with quite similar ideas in terms of sound, language and performance: excessive noise, deconstructing, de-semanticizing and thus destabilizing language, layering of unconnected actions, etc., as found in Futurist and Dadaist performances. As we have seen, Artaud instead wanted to transform and 'elevate' language (and theatre) beyond its mundane *functionality* to something magic, metaphysic and transcendent: 'incantation is the magic function of language'.[60] By freeing language from its semiotic duality (signifier-signified), Artaud hoped to also reconcile or transcend the duality he saw between body and soul, 'fact and idea, [...] matter and mind'.[61]

After exploring the transformative strategies of a kind of primitive musicality with which Artaud sought to make the theatrical experience a metaphysical act *through* the visceral impact of music and sounds, there is a second set of vectors in Artaud's musicality *dispositif* worth looking at. His writings draw attention to the complex connections of sound, music and gesture in a way that goes further, I would argue, than Appia's or Meyerhold's attempts to organize movements on stage musically.[62]

Sound and/as Gesture

'Artaud sought to discover new signs and symbols, inspired from hearing, viewing and feeling sound and gesture.'[63] Extending this observation by Hypatia Vourloumis, I would argue that Artaud wants theatre to provide an experience in which sound and music do not merely interact with bodies and spaces on stage, but

[59]   Savarese, 'Antonin Artaud', p. 66.
[60]   Arnold, 'The Artaud Experiment', p. 22.
[61]   Naomi Greene, 'Antonin Artaud: Metaphysical Revolutionary', *Yale French Studies*, 39/Literature and Revolution (1967), pp. 188–97, p. 190.
[62]   See Chapters 1 and 2.
[63]   Hypatia Vourloumis, '"My Dog Girl": Cok Sawitri's Agrammaticality, Affect and Balinese Feminist Performance', in Noszlopy/Cohen, *Contemporary Southeast Asian*, pp. 107–31, pp. 126–7.

become a quasi-extension of the body, as movement and gesture in space. They do not serve as an accompaniment of gesture, but *are* gesture; a gesture that dissolves the ontological differences of sonic and bodily movement. In the following, Artaud still describes gestures and sounds as separate entities, but the image of the 'hollow limbs' already indicates a convergence and suggests a blurring of their distinctness: the limb becomes a drum, the gesture a sound and vice versa:

> Their gestures fall so exactly on that woody, hollow drum rhythm, accenting it, grasping it in flight so assuredly, on such summits it seems this music accents the very void in their hollow limbs.[64]

In an earlier section of *The Theatre and its Double*, the idea of an amalgamation of sound and gesture is even more clearly developed:

> There is no transition from a gesture to a cry or a sound; everything is connected as if through strange channels penetrating right through the mind! There is a horde of ritual gestures in it to which we have no key, seeming to obey a very precise, musical indication, with something added that does not usually belong to music and seems to be aimed at encircling thought, hounding it down, leading it into a sure, labyrinthine system.[65]

Both gesture and music (or sound) lose their ontological status to form a union in the mind, to merge into a new 'labyrinthine' system. In including this kind of gesture, which – like the Balinese theatre's soundscape – defies the audience's compulsion of meaning-making and interpretation, in his musicality *dispositif*, Artaud anticipates a particular discourse on gesture, which accentuates its 'opacity'. Historically, the discourse on gesture seems to veer between a tendency to see this as either an authentic expression of a character's innermost sensations ('the movements of the soul find their natural expression in the movements of the body'[66]), or as an abstracted or allegorical code signifying these emotions, but perhaps more importantly relationships, status, social etiquette, etc.[67]

More recently, authors like Vilém Flusser and Giorgio Agamben have argued that gestures do not 'dissipate' in a simple process of representation. Jens Peters refers to Flusser when saying that 'any gesture has a certain opacity where meaning ceases to be easily readable':[68] for Flusser gestures are 'movements of the body

---

[64]   Artaud, *The Theatre*, p. 48.

[65]   Artaud, *The Theatre*, pp. 39–40.

[66]   Alexander Kuba, 'Geste/Gestus', in Erika Fischer-Lichte/Doris Kolesch/Matthias Warstat (eds.), *Metzler Lexikon Theatertheorie* (Stuttgart, 2005), pp. 129–36, p. 130.

[67]   See Kuba, 'Geste/Gestus', p. 132 and Jens Roselt, *Seelen mit Methode* (Berlin, 2005).

[68]   Jens Peters, *Narration and Dialogue: Representation of Reality in Contemporary English and German-language Drama (Texts – Translation – Mise-en-scène)* (PhD Thesis, University of Exeter, 2013).

or of a tool connected to it for which there is no satisfactory causal explanation'.[69] This point seems to be supported by Agamben, who suggests that gesture is 'that dimension of language that is not exhausted in any communication of meaning and that, in this way, marks the point at which language appears in its mere capacity to communicate'.[70] For Agamben, gesture goes beyond that point and shows 'language as irreducible, absolute potentiality'.[71] As a consequence, gesture undermines the false alternative between aims and means, as Agamben suggests: 'gesture is a display of mediation, the making visible of a means as such'.[72]

Gestures, then, can be characterized as opaque, liminal, suggestive and 'potential' and the way in which Artaud was willing and able to see the gestural code of the Balinese theatre corresponds with this, particularly because his 'innocent gaze' (in correspondence with Schafer's 'innocent ears' I mentioned earlier) could only penetrate the cryptic surface of the movements.

There is a close parallel between the perception of 'sound objects' and the gamelan music described earlier, and the way in which a Western spectator, whether in 1931 or today, would perceive the Balinese *gestural* code of performance. In Christoph Wulf and Erika Fischer-Lichte's terminology, Artaud was confronted with 'metaphoric gestures, which only become legible if one understands their cultural reference points'.[73] Being indecipherable to the uninitiated listener or viewer, they both allow for an 'innocent' experience, if the recipient resists – while perhaps not being entirely unassuming or non-predisposed – certain habits of categorization and interpretation. Without intimate knowledge of the cultural encoding of the sounds and gestures, they remain cryptic with regard to their function or reference. What Artaud adds to this is to interrelate sound, music and gesture inextricably, which further enhances their suggestiveness and 'potentiality'. There is, on one level, what Delalande calls the 'suggested gesture'[74] of musical sound: he asserts that 'the first meaning attached to the sound of an instrument is the gesture that produces it'.[75] As a consequence, we tend to ascribe or fantasize gestures to sounds even when we cannot see them or when they do not exist as such (for example with digital sounds): 'If a sound […] were produced by a synthesizer, it would also suggest a movement, but an imaginary movement that could have produced such a sound.'[76]

---

    [69]   Vilém Flusser, *Gesten* (Bensheim/Düsseldorf, 1991), p. 8.

    [70]   In Eric Manning, *Politics of Touch. Sense, Movement, Sovereignty* (Minneapolis, MN, 2007), pp. 7–8.

    [71]   In Manning, *Politics of Touch*, p. 8.

    [72]   Giorgio Agamben, 'Notes on Gesture (1978)', in Giorgio Agamben (ed.), *Infancy and History: The Destruction of Experience* (London/New York, 2007), pp. 155–67, p. 155.

    [73]   Christoph Wulf/Erika Fischer-Lichte (eds.), *Gesten. Inszenierung, Aufführung, Praxis* (München, 2010), p. 11.

    [74]   Francois Delalande, 'Sense and Intersensoriality', *Leonardo* 36/4, August (2003), pp. 313–16, p. 315.

    [75]   Delalande, 'Sense and Intersensoriality', p. 314.

    [76]   Delalande, 'Sense and Intersensoriality', p. 314.

Linking sounds and gesture is, however, not merely an activity of the mind and not limited to the audience's experience:

> The instrumentalist's experience is of a sensorimotor type. The performer uses body and gestures not only to produce sounds but also to receive them. The performer perceives with the hands, mouth, breath, ribcage and so forth. Between production and reception, a tight imbrication is established, quite comparable to what can be observed during infancy.[77]

This childlike (read also: 'innocent') embodied process of an iteration between sounds, gestures, imagination and the physical experience of resonance is in many ways analogous to the *theatrical* experience Artaud celebrates and hopes to create.

If we consider the detailed discussion of musical gesture and 'gestic' music by Asja Jarzina and her reflections on Theodore W. Adorno's writings on music and gesture, yet another level of this interplay emerges. She cites his assertion that 'music is not about meaning but about gestures':

> Insofar as it is language, it is, similar to notation in its history, a language of sedimented gestures. One cannot ask what music communicates as its meaning, but instead its theme is: how can gestures be immortalised.[78]

This would indicate that music and sound not only 'suggest' the immediate gestures we (as producers or recipients) ascribe to them, but also evoke a *history* of gestures, layers of embodied meanings. This takes us back to aspects that Artaud was keenly interested in: the archaic, ritual, the 'primitive' and 'pre-civilized'[79] that he felt would reinject life into what he considered a stale and outdated model of theatre. While gesture is generally characterized by a tension between its ambition (or even requirement) to communicate something[80] and the fact that there tends to be inexplicable surplus, a certain level of opacity,[81] Artaud seeks to steer it towards the latter. The musicality of gesture – its combination with sound and its transformation into gesture *in* or *through* sound accentuate the pre-discursive: the musical gesture thus becomes a meaningful element that can be embodied rather than articulated with words, which carries layers of historical *practices* rather than theories or concepts.

---

[77]   Delalande, 'Sense and Intersensoriality', p. 314.

[78]   Adorno in Asja Jarzina, *Gestische Musik und musikalische Gesten* (Berlin, 2005), p. 44.

[79]   By putting both terms in inverted commas I want to mark the post-enlightenment, colonial position they have come from, which contains a value judgement I do not share, which Artaud, despite celebrating these characteristics as qualities of his vision of theatre, reiterates quite uncritically.

[80]   See Jarzina, *Gestische Musik*, p. 47.

[81]   I owe thanks to Jens Peters for this notion.

How Did Artaud's Sense of 'Musicality' Influence His Notion of Theatre?

One of the ideas Artaud puts forward by summarizing his experience of the Balinese theatre is that of a 'pure' theatre:

> In fact, the most striking thing about this show – so well-contrived to baffle our Western concept of theatre that many may well deny it any dramatic qualities whereas it is the finest demonstration of pure theatre we have ever been privileged to see here – what is striking and disturbing about it for us as Europeans is the wonderful intelligence seeming to spark through the compact textural gestures, in the infinitely varied voice inflections, in that tempest sound resounding as if from a vast, dripping rainforest, and in the equally sonorous interlacing moves.[82]

This quotation contains a few expressions worth pausing on, before looking at the notion of 'pure theatre' itself.

'Sonorous interlacing moves'

Generally speaking, the emphasis on the *sonic* qualities of theatre is particularly evident here and certainly, looking back at Artaud's contribution to theatre from a 70- to 80-year distance, one of his important legacies. More specifically, though, it is his continuous insistence on metaphorical and literal connections, an 'interlacing', of sound and the body, of visceral vibrations and 'sonorous' movement that characterizes (and distinguishes) his idea of a musicality of theatre: when he speaks of 'the evocative power of rhythm, the musical quality of physical movement'[83] he goes further than Appia or Meyerhold: whereas they are interested in an analogy, which involves a level of abstraction exploring how to apply certain principles of music to certain aspects of physical movement, Artaud aims for a musicality not at the level of abstract concept and forms, but at a physical level of vibration; a marriage of sound and flesh.

With reference to a theatre production[84] that involved the Artaudian avant-garde music collective 'Einstürzende Neubauten', Jennifer Shryane speaks of 'music produced from the physical effects of the theatre itself'.[85] This seems to be a good working definition of one of the poles between which Artaudian theatre aesthetics are 'suspended' – the other, I would argue, could sensibly be described as 'theatre produced from the physical effects of music itself'.

---

[82] Artaud, *The Theatre*, pp. 39–40.
[83] Artaud, *The Theatre*, p. 38.
[84] Werner Schwab's *Faust, mein Brustkorb, mein Helm*, directed by Thomas Thieme (Hans-Otto Theater, Potsdam 1994). See http://www.neubauten.org/faustmusik [15.01.2012].
[85] Shryane, 'Sprich zu mir', p. 332.

'Infinitely varied voice inflections'

The second aspect of Artaud's musicality *dispositif*, which I have already briefly referred to, is his fascination with the materiality of voice, which has since been explored by theatre-makers from Valère Novarina to Einar Schleef, from The Wooster Group to the Societas Raffaele Sanzio.[86] It is a vocality that is neither in the service of language and communication, as it has been reflected, theorized and trained from ancient schools of rhetoric to today's leading voice teachers,[87] nor necessary in pursuit of an anti-language, whether in the form of Dadaist non-sense or Futurist noise. It is what Alice Lagaay in her '(negative) philosophy of voice'[88] describes as an 'increased attentiveness to the embodied and acoustic nature of human utterance and communication'.[89] Artaud wants a voice on stage that, analogous to Agamben's already cited description of gesture, no longer transmits or mediates but is the making audible 'of a means as such'.[90]

'Wonderful intelligence'

Insisting equally on the 'primitive' and pre-discursive nature of the Balinese theatre, and its 'wonderful intelligence', Artaud promotes a 'special *kind* of intelligence'[91] for the theatre. Like the rituals, screams, sounds and gestures he conjures up, he wants theatre to be a form of knowing (rather than a mere representation of it), a translation of the kinds of 'pre-conceptual and pre-linguistic',[92] perceptual and cognitive experiences which music affords, onto the stage. Music is a model for the kind of intelligence hailed by Artaud.

---

[86] See Claudia Castellucci/Romeo Castellucci/Chiara Guidi/Joe Kelleher/Nicholas Ridout, *The Theatre of Societas Raffaello Sanzio* (London, 2007); Doris Kolesch/Jenny Schrödel (eds.), *Kunst-Stimmen* (Berlin, 2004).

[87] See, for example, Cicely Berry's *Voice and the Actor* (New York, 1973), Patsy Rodenburg's *The Actor speaks* (London, 1997), or Kristin Linklater's *Freeing the Natural Voice* (London, 2006) to name but a few.

[88] Alice Lagaay, 'Towards a (Negative) Philosophy of Voice', in Kendrick/Roesner, *Theatre Noise*, pp. 57–69.

[89] Lagaay, 'Towards a (Negative) Philosophy', p. 58.

[90] Agamben, 'Notes on Gesture', p. 155.

[91] I am using Susanne Langer's phrase here (cit. in Wayne D. Bowman, *Philosophical Perspectives on Music* [Oxford, 1998], p. 199, my emphasis) who refers to music in this way. See also the section on cognition in the Introduction.

[92] Ramón Pelinski, 'Embodiment and Musical Experience', *TRANS. Revista Transcultural de Música*, 9 [Online] (2005), http://redalyc.uaemex.mx/pdf/822/82200914.pdf [16.08.2011].

'Pure theatre'

I would argue that Artaud's notion of a 'pure' theatre contains at least two aspects: an interest in a 'purist' aesthetic and a quasi-religious sense of purity. As we have seen, there are a lot of things Artaud wants to strip the theatre of: the constraints of a predominantly semantic language, the clutters of 'décor' and more generally the 'dramatic qualities' as they have conventionally been understood. As Philip Auslander puts it: 'Although Artaud's descriptions would seem to indicate interest in "total theatre," Timothy Wiles has argued that because Artaud is primarily concerned with the essence of the theatrical event, his theory is actually reductive.'[93] His inability to fully 'read' the Balinese performance, to decode the gestures and the music/sounds of Balinese theatre, inspired a notion of a pure, visceral, and shockingly immediate theatre; an essentialist aesthetics. But 'essence' for Artaud is also a transcendental idea: 'Artaud's belief that theatre could express what he calls "la métaphysique" corresponds to Copeau's efforts to reach a level of universal truth.'[94] There is already a distinct messianic note in Appia's writings and his concept of theatre[95] and I would argue that in both his and Artaud's case it is *musicality* that serves as one of the main 'vehicles' for the divine, the transcendent, the metaphysical. The 'God' each of them worships, however, is of course a very different one, as we have seen.

There is a tangible Baroque influence in this connection of music with the religious or spiritual,[96] even (or particularly) for Artaud, who on the surface seems to tap into the altogether different connection of music and religion inspired by Southeast Asian rituals and Balinese Hinduism. Baroque music exalted the Christian God through a highly developed semantic code of forms, intervals and affective motifs.[97] Even if Artaud strove for the expression of a different spirituality and by means of a very different kind of musicality, there seems to be a (perhaps involuntary) concurrence in the conviction that 'access to such spiritual experiences is only available in ways or forms – in this case musical works – that defy linguistic or other forms of rational expression or articulation'.[98]

As Iris M. Yob suggests, also referring to Susanne Langer, 'the various aspects of religion, especially its mythical and ritual elements, shared common roots with

---

[93]   Philip Auslander, *From Acting to Performance: Essays in Modernism and Postmodernism* (London, 1997), p. 20.

[94]   Auslander, *From Acting to Performance*, p. 20.

[95]   See Milling/Ley, *Modern Theories*, p. 87.

[96]   I am not using the two as synonyms, but follow Iris M. Yob, who with reference to Catherine Albanese describes the spiritual as 'the personal, experiential element in religion' (p. 146) whether that religion is collective or individual, or centered on God, or the self, or Nature, or an Ideal worth dying for (Iris M. Yob, 'Why is Music a Language of Spirituality?', *Philosophy of Music Education Review*, 18/2 [Fall 2010], pp. 145–51).

[97]   Appia, for example, certainly still maintained this idea of a connection between a balanced musical form and spiritual 'truth'.

[98]   David Carr in Yob, 'Why is Music a Language of Spirituality?', p. 149.

the arts including music'.[99] For some practitioners, then, music is a vehicle and template for spirituality in the theatre.

There is a further connection, however: as I suggested earlier (see the Introduction), the musical *dispositif* is not an objective 'thing' or tangible process; musicality in theatre is an embodied practice of perception, cognition and creative activity. It is not an intrinsic quality to certain plays, productions or even actors, but a negotiated agreement to search for and instil musical qualities – whatever they are in the individual case – into the theatrical process. With regard to spirituality, Yob asks a question that resonates with my understanding of musicality: 'What would happen to our inquiry if we began with the premise that spirituality does not reside in the music but in the music maker and the music listener?'[100] Adapted to the research questions of this book, this could be rephrased as: 'What would happen to our inquiry if we began with the premise that musicality does not reside in the theatre but in the theatre-maker and the theatre audience?' Each chapter seeks to give answers to this question, and in the case of Artaud one of the answers I offer is that, for him, musicality manifests itself as an attention to sound and voice as raw and sometimes primitive materials in order to give access to an immediately physical and thus spiritual experience of theatre. By contrast, we will encounter an altogether more 'profane' musicality in the following chapters.

A final aspect that is worth remarking on is a reflection on where the idea of musicality is located in Artaud's theoretical edifice. In comparison to most practitioners we have encountered, be it Appia, Meyerhold, Copeau or others, Artaud's musicality *dispositif* is a more abstract one and mainly concerned with a hypothetical audience. Whereas before we have seen a strong emphasis on the actor and director and a series of often very practical and concrete considerations about their training, practices and processes, Artaud's manifestos are much more speculative, and his own, sparse practice altogether more divorced from his claims and visions on paper.[101] It remains a curiosity of theatre history then, perhaps, that Artaud's legacy has been so remarkably strong, as Finter attests:

> Could such an analysis of theatre be said to have its successors or imitators? Apparently yes, since several decades of theatre experimentation have been associated with Artaud's name (see Virmaux 1979, 1980).[102] Yet, as the diversity of these examples would seem to indicate, it has been the questions Artaud posed rather than the individual answers he offered that have contributed to the development of a tradition around his ideas on the theatre.[103]

---

[99] Yob, 'Why is Music a Language of Spirituality?', p. 148.

[100] Yob, 'Why is Music a Language of Spirituality?', pp. 148–9.

[101] This has been documented extensively, for example in Innes, *Avant Garde Theatre*.

[102] Finter refers to Alain and Odette Virmaux's books *Artaud: un bilan* (Paris, 1979) and *Artaud vivant* (Paris, 1980) here.

[103] Finter, 'Antonin Artaud', p. 18.

The resonances with Artaud are varied and too many to list here, but besides a considerable body of physical theatre that shows Artaudian 'pedigree', it is particularly the numerous experiments with sound and/or vocality in performance which from the 1960s onwards have continued to grate against the mainstream sonic and vocal landscapes on European theatre stages that Artaud can still take some credit for.[104] Artaud is a rare (and by the laws of physics impossible) case where the 'echo' is louder, more varied and more persistent than its 'input signal' could have ever been.

---

[104] The deconstruction of language in the early works of Robert Wilson or Richard Foreman, and the vocal theatricality of Meredith Monk, Jaap Blonk, Diamanda Galás or Cathy Berberian are a few examples. See Helga Finter, 'Die Theatralisierung der Stimme im Experimentaltheater', in Klaus Oehler (ed.), *Zeichen und Realität, Bd. 3* (Tübingen, 1984), pp. 1007–21; Theda Weber-Lucks, *Körperstimmen. Vokale Performancekunst als neue musikalische Gattung* (PhD thesis, TU Berlin 2005); Meyer, *Acoustic Turn* (in particular pp. 291–351) for more detail and further examples.

Chapter 4
Writing with Your Ears –
The Musicality of Playwriting

One ought to write like composing.

—Novalis[1]

How could it not be permitted and possible to think in tones and to make music in words and thoughts?

—Ludwig Tieck[2]

I have found [...] a mixture between writing and composing, a way of dealing with language compositionally.

—Elfriede Jelinek[3]

Introduction

Any writer worth their salt will have an awareness of the rhythmic and sonic qualities of language and will consider formal and structural aspects of narrative, dialogue or poetry. What I am looking at in this chapter, then, is not musicality as a *new* quality in dramatic writing, but rather at a different level of its manifestation. I will seek evidence of instances where musicality has been a particularly central consideration and driver in the process of writing a text for theatrical performance rather than a by-product or afterthought. At the risk of stating the obvious, this is not always the case: not all writers foreground musicality quite in the same way as those mentioned in this chapter. Some writers use tactile and visual metaphors to describe 'two fundamental states of consciousness'[4] they require when writing plays: 'an awareness of evanescence and of solidity, of emptiness and of too

---

[1]   Novalis in Christian Klug, *Thomas Bernhards Theaterstücke* (Stuttgart, 1991), p. 203.

[2]   Tieck in Monika Schwarz, *Musikanaloge Ideen und Struktur im französischen Theater* (München, 1981), p. 9.

[3]   Jelinek in Barbara Basting, 'Drastische Töne. Die Komponistin Olga Neuwirth und ihre Zusammenarbeit mit Elfriede Jelinek: unerhörte musikalische Sprachen', *du*, 700/10 *Elfriede Jelinek. Schreiben. Fremd bleiben* (1999), pp. 22–5, p. 22.

[4]   Ionesco in Toby Cole (ed.), *Playwrights on Playwriting. From Ibsen to Ionesco* (New York, 2001 [1960]), p. 145. I am merely commenting on a particular statement by Ionesco here, but as Monika Schwarz has argued convincingly elsewhere (*Musikanaloge Ideen*), Ionesco's writing *does* actually also invite being looked at under the musicality heading as well.

much presence, of the unreal transparency of the world and its opacity, of light and of thick darkness'.[5] Others refer to smell and taste: 'Flavour! An impalpable quality, less easily captured than the scent of a flower, the peculiar and most essential attribute of any work of art!'[6] Most commonly, however, playwrights put characters, narrative and genre at the centre of their concerns.[7]

Breaking with the relatively chronological approach of this book so far, I will now look at a range of playwrights across a period of approximately 100 years,[8] comparing them thematically rather than suggesting lineages. While there are of course historical lineages and evidence of influences, it is my impression that the field is hardly cohesive and that it might be more productive to highlight similarities and differences right across the chronological and geographical spectrum. The writers covered in this chapter have occasionally been looked at in terms of their 'musicality', but rarely compared and contrasted – something I will undertake in this chapter.

This chapter also differs methodologically from the previous ones in that not all the writers in question have described or documented their process or left statements of intention or manifestos as we have seen with Appia, Meyerhold, Tairov or Artaud. None of the writers I mention is, for example, represented in Dukore's 1,000-page selection of *Dramatic Theory and Criticism* (1974). So my intention of focusing on process and discourse is more difficult to carry out. Moreover, musicality becomes a potentially more metaphorical (and for the purposes of this book, slippery) ground, since looking at dramatic writing rather than acting, training and directing means that we are no longer confronted with an activity that shapes time with the same level of determinacy as music does. A spoken monologue creates a definite musical shape: a melody, timbre, rhythm, duration, etc. – a *written* monologue bears the *potential* of this musical shape, and

---

5   Ionesco in Cole, *Playwrights on Playwriting*, p. 145.

6   John Galsworthy in Cole, *Playwrights on Playwriting*, p. 49.

7   See Bernard F. Dukore (ed.), *Dramatic Theory and Criticism: Greeks to Grotowski* (Boston, 1974); Manfred Pfister, *The Theory and Analysis of Drama* (Cambridge, 1991); Cole, *Playwrights on Playwriting*.

8   In terms of determining the historical period to focus on, Monika Schwarz, who has discussed music-analogue concept(ion)s in Ionesco's and Tardieu's writing for the theatre, reminds us that the musicality *dispositif* became productive relatively late in drama, having already enjoyed currency in literature and poetry since early Romanticism, particularly in Germany through writers such as Wilhelm Heinrich Wackenroder (1773–1798), Johann Ludwig Tieck (1773–1853), and Georg Philipp Friedrich Freiherr von Hardenberg (1772–1801) (better known as Novalis), two of which I have quoted at the beginning of this chapter. For further research into the role of music for these writers see Jürg Kielholz, *Wilhelm Heinrich Wackenroder. Schriften über die Musik. Musik- und literaturgeschichtlicher Ursprung und Bedeutung in der romantischen Literatur* (Frankfurt am Main, 1972); Christine Lubkoll, *Mythos Musik. Poetische Entwürfe des Musikalischen in der Literatur um 1800* (Freiburg, 1995); and Barbara Naumann (ed.), *Die Sehnsucht der Sprache nach der Musik. Texte zur musikalischen Poetik um 1800* (Stuttgart/Weimar, 1994).

its musicality can still be articulated in a variety of ways. The dramatist makes what could be called a strong 'offer' towards a musical realization,[9] demanding the consideration of rhythm, timing, vocality, pauses, etc. in the production process and the acting style, but cannot fully determine its musical shape in production: 'the dramatic text is not autonomous and complete since it possesses a scenic virtuality awaiting its realization'.[10]

Two Leading Musical Models: Score and Instrument

Unsurprisingly, then, two metaphors crop up frequently wherever musicality becomes an aspiration and working principle for playwrights – both designed to increase the level of control and determinacy of the musicality of the performed text: the notion of the play as a score[11] and the actor as a (musical) instrument. Beckett is a case in point: 'whether read aloud or silently, Beckett's careful words resemble elements of a musical score, coordinated by and for the ear, to sound and resound'.[12] Theatre-maker George Devine echoes this closely:

> One has to think of the text as something like a musical score wherein the 'notes', the sights and sounds, the pauses, have their own interrelated rhythms, and out of their composition comes the dramatic impact.[13]

Ackerly and Gontarski give an example of this practice of 'scoring': 'In *Play*, everyday banality is orchestrated like a musical score: characters respond to the light as to a conductor; stage directions about tempo, volume, and tone; and instructions for a repeat, da capo.'[14]

The notion as such is not new, of course. Already in 1950, Clifford J. Turner in his standard work on *Voice & Speech in the Theatre* – which in itself does not promote a particularly experimental approach – writes:

---

[9]   This includes the possibility for a composer to actually put it to music, which we find frequently with Beckett's texts, for example. See Klaus Kanzog/Hans Joachim Kreutzer (eds.), *Werke Kleists auf dem modernen Musiktheater* (Berlin, 1977) and Chris J. Ackerley/Stanley E. Gontarksi, *The Grove Companion to Samuel Beckett* (New York, 2004), pp. 389–96.

[10]   Sophia Totzeva, *Das theatrale Potential des dramatischen Textes: ein Beitrag zur Theorie von Drama und Dramenübersetzung* (Tübingen, 1995), p. 65.

[11]   See also Totzeva's chapter 'Der dramatische Text als Partitur' ['The dramatic text as score'] in Totzeva, *Das theatrale Potential*, pp. 64–7.

[12]   Mary Bryden (ed.), *Samuel Beckett and Music* (Oxford, 1998), p. 2.

[13]   Devine in Catherine Laws, 'The Music of Beckett's Theatre', in Danièle De Ruyter-Tognotti et al. (eds.), *Three Dialogues Revisited (Samuel Beckett Today)* (Amsterdam, 2008), pp. 121–33, p. 121.

[14]   Ackerley/Gontarski, *The Grove Companion to Samuel Beckett*, p. 393.

The text of a play has often most aptly been compared with a musical score. The actor is the link between the dramatist and the audience. His voice is the means by which the dramatist's work is bodied forth, and it is the main channel along which thought and feeling are to flow. His voice, in fact, is an instrument, a highly specialized instrument, which is activated and played upon by the actor's intelligence and feeling, both of which have been stimulated by the imaginative power he is able to bring to bear upon the dramatist's creation.[15]

Turner, however, uses 'score' and 'instrument' clearly as metaphors, whereas Beckett – to stay with this prominent example – seeks to genuinely exploit the analogy much more literally in order to arrive at a different kind of theatrical aesthetic: 'It may indeed be that music, heard or unheard, is in some sense intrinsic to Beckett's sense of the possibilities of theatre.'[16]

A number of reports and anecdotes further illustrate this musical approach of Beckett. Danijela Kulezic-Wilson writes about his use of a metronome to control the tempo of his actors' speech, but also mentions the use of a piano to fix their pitch.[17] In addition there is Beckett's 'tendency to use musical terminology (especially Italian terms) in rehearsal',[18] and, as actor Billie Whitelaw describes, 'Beckett's preference for directing her by "conducting" the lines'.[19] Kevin Branigan tells us that consequently 'on numerous occasions, Whitelaw compares the effect of performing as a Beckett character to a musical instrument'. His interpretation of this marks the difference to Turner again: 'The purpose of such an instrumental character was to act as a resonating channel for the music *without seeking to comment upon or interpret the text*.'[20] The instrument metaphor, which as we have seen in Chapters 1 and 2 is often accompanied by the notion

---

[15]   J. Clifford Turner, *Voice & Speech in the Theatre* (London, 1993 [1950]), p. 2.

[16]   Nicholas Till, 'Stefano Gervasoni's "Pas Si": Staging a Music Theatre Work Based On a Text by Samuel Beckett', *Contemporary Theatre Review*, 23/2 (2013), pp. 220–32, pp. 221–2.

[17]   Danijela Kulezic-Wilson, 'From Musicalisation of Theatre to Musicality of Film: Beckett's *Play* on Stage and on Screen', in Lynne Kendrick/David Roesner (eds.), *Theatre Noise. The Sound of Performance* (Newcastle upon Tyne, 2011), pp. 33–43, p. 37.

[18]   Ruby Cohn in Laws, 'The Music of Beckett's Theatre', p. 121.

[19]   Whitelaw in Laws, 'The Music of Beckett's Theatre', p. 121. See also W.D. Asmus, 'Practical aspects of theatre, radio and television. Rehearsal notes for the German premiere of Beckett's *That Time* and *Footfalls* at the Schiller-Theater Werkstatt, Berlin (1.9.76)', *Journal of Beckett Studies*, 2 [Online] (1977), http://www.english.fsu.edu/jobs/num02/Num2WalterAsmus.htm [28.02.2012] for a detailed account of Beckett's rehearsal process for the German production of *Footfalls* (1977).

[20]   Kevin Branigan, *Radio Beckett. Musicality in the Radio Plays of Samuel Beckett* (Oxford, 2008), p. 217, my emphasis.

that the actor is also the instrumentalist,[21] changes in relation to Beckett's work, where actors were, as Bryden puts it, actually 'being played or sung by Beckett'.[22]

To use a more contemporary example, playwright Martin Crimp problematizes the notion of the score and the instructions an actor needs in contrast to a musician in an interview with Aleks Sierz:

> MC: So when I started at the Orange Tree,[23] I saw text as a musical score. And I expected people just to get on with it – and do the music.
> AS: It's a good analogy.
> MC: It's *quite* a good analogy. *(Pause.)* Because obviously actors are more complex than that, they need more than musicians do. With a musical score, if it says *forte* and someone is playing *piano*, it's easy to correct, but acting is more complicated, and the more experienced you get, the more you realise that perhaps *piano* might be a better choice than *forte*.[24]

Notwithstanding this difference, there have been recurring attempts by playwrights to incorporate aspects of notation in their playtexts, which are not stage directions in a conventional sense, but musical performance instructions and provide an indication towards a more literal sense of the drama as score. Examples of these are Beckett's frequent use of '[Pause.]'[25] to indicate where a beat should be placed, or the ways in which Caryl Churchill precisely organizes overlaps of different characters' speeches. She takes this to a level which is no longer just a representation of a character's impatience or rudeness but facilitates a more polyphonic layering of utterances, a heteroglossia of social, political and historical voices, for example, in the opening scene from *Top Girls* (1982), which Elaine Aston calls an 'aural choreography of the lines, rhythms and silences'.[26] Similarly (and with influence from Churchill and Beckett), Crimp provides a number of notational devices to determine the musicality of his play *The Treatment* (1993):

> An oblique stroke / indicates the point of interruption in overlapping dialogue.
> Brackets () indicate momentary changes of tone (usually a drop in projection).
> A comma like this on a separate line
>
> ,
>
> means a pause.[27]

---

[21] See Bella Merlin, *Acting – The Basics* (London/New York, 2010), p. 27.

[22] Bryden, *Samuel Beckett*, p. 44.

[23] The Orange Tree Theatre in Richmond produced the first six plays of Martin Crimp.

[24] In Aleks Sierz, *The Theatre of Martin Crimp* (London, 2006), p. 87, original emphasis.

[25] For example in *Happy Days* (1961).

[26] Elaine Aston/Elin Diamond (eds.), *The Cambridge Companion to Caryl Churchill* (Cambridge, 2009), p. 150.

[27] Martin Crimp, *The Treatment* (London, 1993).

Crimp thus introduces instructions that suggest certain *tempi* (quick succession to the point of overlaps versus deliberate pauses) but also changes in timbre and dynamics of speech, which playwrights rarely define except implicitly by stating a change of emotion, intention or atmosphere in the *didascalia* or through the dialogue.

Despite any notational attempts, however, plays will struggle to get anywhere close to the level of precision in terms of musical instructions that practices of musical notation and interpretation have reached in the last centuries of Western classical music. Still, the change in perception and textual practice that is triggered by these written gestures towards musical notation and the metaphor of the 'drama as score' are not to be underestimated. With this in mind I will take into account what Andreas Höfele calls 'implicit stagings'[28] when analyzing the musicality of plays. These 'implicit stagings' are more or less firmly established in the text itself (or a certain tradition of staging, conducted or authorized by the playwright, as we find it with Beckett, Bernhard or Churchill) and allow us to ascertain how a dramatic text may convey a musicality which impacts on the processes of directing and acting.

So who are these playwrights? The following list is not meant to be comprehensive, but provides a first orientation and an idea of the scope and variety: George Bernard Shaw (1856–1950), Alfred Jarry (1873–1907), Gertrude Stein (1874–1946), Antonin Artaud (1896–1948), Jean Tardieu (1903–1995), Samuel Beckett (1906–1989), Heiner Müller (1929–1995), Brian Friel (1929–), Thomas Bernhard (1931–1989), Edward Bond (1934–), Caryl Churchill (1938–), Sam Shepard (1943–), Elfriede Jelinek (1946–), Howard Barker (1946–), Valère Novarina (1947–), Martin Crimp (1956–), David Ian Rabey (1958–), Werner Schwab (1958–1994), Enda Walsh (1967–), and Sarah Kane (1971–1999) have all been associated with 'musicality' or have claimed it for themselves. Variably, this manifests itself as an influence of actual music (e.g. Shaw, Friel, Bernhard), an affinity to musical principles, ideas or modes of perception (Tardieu, Novarina, Shepard) a particular concern with rhythmical, sonic and paralinguistic qualities of speech (Artaud, Stein, Shepard, Walsh) and/or a sceptical view on the established communicative strategies of dramatic dialogue (Bernhard, Barker, Jelinek).

At first sight, there is plenty of evidence for musicality in/of playwriting, but this *dispositif* needs further unpacking and differentiation since 'the term musical is simply too vague a description'[29] as Branigan already admonishes in relation to Beckett. I will thus attempt to tease out different aspects of this association between writing and music, this 'musical attunement'[30] of playwrights, and

---

[28] Höfele in Gerda Poschmann, *Der nicht mehr dramatische Theatertext. Aktuelle Bühnenstücke und ihre dramatische Analyse* (Tübingen, 1997), p. 290, transl. by Jens Peters. See also Totzeva's chapter 'Die implizite Inszenierung' ['The implicit staging'] in *Das theatrale Potential*, pp. 59–62.

[29] Branigan, *Radio Beckett*, p. 218.

[30] Branigan, *Radio Beckett*, p. 218.

interrogate some of the consequences this has for the theatre. The following aspects in particular seem to warrant a closer look: music as a condition for dramatic writing, the relationship of dramatic and musical form(s), the impact of musicality on language and utterance, followed by a discussion of the core implications of the above.

Music as a Condition for Dramatic Writing

A Ground to Walk On

For some playwrights, musicality is not only a quality (however defined) to aim for in the writing process, but even more profoundly a *conditio sine qua non*, a condition *a priori* of any actual dramatic writing. For Thomas Bernhard, for example, whose childhood was overshadowed by recurrent life-threatening illnesses, music played an important psychophysical role in his healing process.[31] After his musical training and the realization that due to his conditions he would never be able to be a professional singer, he channelled his musicality into the development of a unique writing style. Combined with his notorious tirades against Austria, his home country, this made him one of the most successful, controversial and critically acclaimed playwrights in German-speaking theatre until today.[32] For Bernhard, music played an existential role as a writer: Bürgers speaks of the 'self-invention [die Selbst-Erschaffung] of the writer Bernhard from the spirit of music'.[33] Bernhard himself describes this primacy of a musical concept for his writing as follows:

> I would say it is a question of rhythm and has a lot to do with music. Yes, you can only understand what I write when you realize that it is first and foremost the musical component that counts, and that what is being told is secondary. Once the first thing is there, I can begin to describe things and events. The problem is in the 'How?'.[34]

---

[31] Manfred Mittermayer, *Thomas Bernhard* (Stuttgart/Weimar, 1995), p. 184.

[32] While several of his 18 plays have been translated into English – for example: *The Force of Habit* (original production 1974/translation 1974), *The President* (1975/1982), *Eve of Retirement* (1979/1982), *A Party for Boris* (1970/1968), *Ritter, Dene, Voss* (1984/1984), *Histrionics* (1984/1984), *Heldenplatz* (1988/1988), *Over All the Mountain Tops* (1981/2004), and *The World-fixer* (1979/2005) – they have rarely been put on stage in the UK, arguably due to their topicality and their strong web of references to German-Austrian culture and philosophy.

[33] Irmelin Bürgers, '"Es ist immer die Musik, die mich rettet ...".Thomas Bernhards Sprachpartituren', in Hans Werner Henze (ed.), *Musik und Sprache. Neue Aspekte der musikalischen Ästhetik IV* (Frankfurt am Main, 1990), pp. 173–91, p. 179.

[34] Bernhard in Mittermayer, *Thomas Bernhard*, p. 184.

Bernhard's fellow Austrian playwright, Elfriede Jelinek, won the Nobel Prize for Literature in 2004 'for her musical flow of voices and counter-voices in novels and plays that with extraordinary linguistic zeal reveal the absurdity of society's clichés and their subjugating power'.[35] She uses the metaphor of music as being the ground on which she moves as a writer, but also expresses a complex and ambivalent relationship to this. Music is both foundational and defamiliarizing, unachievable and always already present:

> As if music (and later, for me, as so to speak the last stop, language) were the earth on which one walks, but one always wants to run away from this ground one moves on, which naturally is not possible, because one would fall into the abyss. One walks therefore on something, on a ground one would like to flee, which is precisely impossible. But what one does while one is going toward that one place one so much seeks for and never finds (one stands on top of it!): one remains strange. Doesn't know why, though. For that there under the feet, one can't see it. It is hidden by oneself. Music makes one strange ... when one produces it, music, one becomes oneself, even for oneself, at the same time something strange, not as strange as the composers were, and yet, since one is following their calls, and where they call one to, one should know, if one has properly practiced (Oh dear!), but when we get there, then this ground underneath us breaks away, we ourselves are completely gone away, and we know we are not cozily amongst ourselves, but that that which is beneath us, moves like time. No salvation.[36]

Jelinek, who trained as a pianist and organist (the above quotation is from an homage to her organ teacher), seems to liken the quest for music and the quest for language, which in her case acts almost as sublimation for music: the *dispositif* for both is the impossibly to grasp and make familiar these ephemeral, time-based forms of expression. One indication of this musical relationship to language in Jelinek's work is the increasing tendency to write plays which lack the most traditional hallmarks of the dramatic genre: actions, characters, dialogue. They consist of blocks of texts or 'language planes' (*Sprachflächen*[37]), which require orchestration and editing. She sometimes even continues to write and amend the texts during the run of the original production, as in the case of *Die Kontrakte des Kaufmanns* [*The Merchant's Contracts*] (directed by Nicolas Stemann, Cologne 2009, see Figure 4.1).[38]

---

[35]   The Nobel Prize Committee, http://www.nobelprize.org/nobel_prizes/literature/laureates/2004/ [17.02.2012].

[36]   Jelinek in Larson Powell/Brenda Bethman, '"One must have tradition in oneself, to hate it properly": Elfriede Jelinek's Musicality', *Journal of Modern Literature*, 32/1 (2008), pp. 163–83, p. 170, translation by Larson Powell.

[37]   See Karen Jurs-Munby, 'The Resistant Text in Postdramatic Theatre: Performing Elfriede Jelinek's Sprachflächen', *Performance Research*, 14/1 (2009), pp. 46–56.

[38]   For reviews and a short video example see http://www.nachtkritik.de/index.php?option=com_content &task-view&id=2688 [17.02.2012].

Figure 4.1   Nicolas Stemann's production of Jelinek's *Die Kontrakte des Kaufmanns* (Schauspiel Köln 2009) with the director on guitar

An Attunement of the Senses

Musicality as a condition for dramatic writing is more than a philosophical question, though. It also manifests itself in the descriptions of a heightened sensitivity towards sound and silence that authors put forward and reflect on.[39] Staying with Bernhard and Jelinek for the moment, we can see that they highlight different aspects of this sensitivity.

For Bernhard, who has incidentally been called the 'Beckett of the Alps',[40] the compositional aspects of assembling and constructing language as sounds is a fundamental approach to his writing: 'like a composer', he is quoted as saying, 'he collects tones, by the box-load, which are then put in order and succession'.[41] Bürgers calls this the 'alchemistic-structuralist' recipe of deconstruction and reassembly, destruction and recreation [...]',[42] which characterizes Bernhard's

---

[39]   Another indicator, as we will see in more detail later, is a particularly strong sense of rhythm and form, both on a micro- and a macro-structural level.

[40]   Fritz Rumler dubbed him 'Alpen-Beckett' (cit. in Friedrich J. Windrich, *TechnoTheater: Dramaturgie und Philosophie bei Rainald Goetz und Thomas Bernhard* [München, 2007], p. 19).

[41]   Bürgers, 'Es ist immer die Musik', p. 187.

[42]   Bürgers, 'Es ist immer die Musik', pp. 187–8.

writing process. She even refers to it as 'linguistic serialism' ('sprachliche Reihentechnik'[43]) in analogy to serialism in music, which was concerned with an objectified, algorithmic approach to musical tones aiming to escape the long-established hierarchies of intervals and harmonies. Bürgers (and others) attest to a fraught relationship between Bernhard and the world in general – and Austria in particular – similar to Jelinek's withdrawn but poignantly critical stance. Bürgers thus claims musicality to be a coping mechanism of the author:

> In a chaotic world full of discordant harmonies Thomas Bernhard at least in his books created a new musical order. [...] he has got the ability, to capture the musicality in language and thus to come to terms with being horrified by the world, by distancing himself from it through the act of writing.[44]

Musicality certainly enabled Bernhard to write in the first place and is also employed as a particular way of capturing and bringing into expressive form Bernhard's ardent rage at some of his fellow human beings. I am, however, less sure that this had (or was meant to have) the consoling effect Bürgers describes. Musicality provided a channel and perhaps a valve for Bernhard, not a cure.

While Bernhard's musical attunement shows strong influences from Bach, Mozart and the New Vienna School,[45] Jelinek's work is deeply rooted in the music and philosophy of German romanticism and plays with multiple syntactic and semantic connections and combinations, or 'metonymic constructive techniques'[46] as Powell and Bethman call them. She has a strong sense of the 'musicality or sonority' of her writing and the rhythmicity of her style; both phenomenologically and semantically her writing creates many resonances due to the array of references, quotations, puns and neologisms,[47] all of which are based on an approach to language as a sonic event rather than just a carrier of meaning.

Jean Tardieu's work presents an interesting contrast here: while 'the acoustic realization is a vital aspect of his notion of analogy [between plays and music, DR], a condition for the aesthetic validity of the intention of [the music] analogy in his plays',[48] his language is not – like Jelinek's – tending to a glut of references, but exposes the blandness and the non-sense of everyday-life communication. This approach to dramatic writing though hearing and a musical exploration of the futility (and at times comedy) of everyday speech is shared by Beckett – albeit in a different context and with different results. Where Jelinek's musicality

---

[43]   Bürgers, 'Es ist immer die Musik', p. 188.
[44]   Bürgers, 'Es ist immer die Musik', pp. 188–9.
[45]   See Bürgers, 'Es ist immer die Musik', p. 180.
[46]   Powell/Bethman, 'One must have tradition', p. 167.
[47]   All of this makes her work almost 'untranslatable as only Mallarmé or Joyce, two writers centrally concerned with music' are (Powell/Bethman, 'One must have tradition', p. 167).
[48]   Schwarz, *Musikanaloge Ideen*, p. 31.

tends to an aesthetics of plethora, of overabundance, and where Tardieu explores repetition and rigorous musical 'architecture', Beckett's 'writing-by-ear' seeks out reduction, pauses and silences. Bryden makes a convincing and nuanced case for Beckett's musicality based on Berio's statement that 'music is everything that one listens to with the intention of listening to music'.[49] She rightly claims, however, that 'one still needs an explanation of what predisposes to that intention in specific contexts'.[50] Bryden suggests that there are two main reasons: 'The first is that Beckett's texts exhibit an extraordinarily acute attunement to sound: not just noise, but intimate ambience sound. The second is that there is a peculiarly rich role allocated to silence in Beckett's writing.'[51] Again, a highly developed acoustic sensitivity is the condition from which this kind of writing thrives:

> All of Beckett's texts, whether they be prose, poetry, or drama, are the product of one who, by his own account, *heard* them in advance of writing them. They abound with evocations of oral memories, sounds and their withdrawal, acoustic qualities, rhythms and melodies. If Beckett heard them in advance, however, he was not merely a passive receptor or conduit for them. On the contrary, the achievement of a satisfactory auditory balance was a matter – as his many draft manuscripts demonstrate – of multiple refinements, cancellations, retunings.[52]

In Beckett's writing there is not only evidence for this careful crafting of language from a perspective of sound and rhythm, but also an awareness of the important function of silence, not so much as a mere absence of sound,[53] but as its essential breeding ground and 'endpoint', as Branigan calls it (in relation to Beckett's radio plays):

> Beckett's aesthetic [...] involves a gravitation of all voices, sounds, and music towards this gaping hole in the sonic texture of the broadcasts. This requires painstaking attention by actors, producers and composers to a musicality which makes silence the unattainable endpoint.[54]

---

[49] Berio in Bryden, *Samuel Beckett*, p. 24.

[50] Bryden, *Samuel Beckett*, p. 24.

[51] Bryden, *Samuel Beckett*, p. 24.

[52] Bryden, *Samuel Beckett*, pp. 1–2, original emphasis.

[53] After Cage's much discussed experience of the impossibility of total silence in the anechoic chamber at Harvard University in 1951, it is probably obvious that I don't mean 'silence' in an essentialist, absolute or physical-acoustic way, but as a cultural construct; an agreement that we call moments of a *relative* absence of *some* sounds 'silence'. We enjoy, for example, the 'silence' of a walk in the woods despite rustling branches, birdsong and the sound of our feet, due to the absence of traffic noises. We appreciate a break in dialogue on stage as a moment of silence, despite the hum of the light and sound systems, ventilation and the ambient sounds of the audience.

[54] Branigan, *Radio Beckett*, p. 249.

Two aspects of silence – being both a *musical* entity and a *theatrical* device creating presence, anticipation, as well as atmospheric and narrative meaning – are brought to converge congenially by Beckett.[55] Bryden uses a poetic quotation from the philosopher and musicologist Vladimir Jankélévitch to characterize this quality of Beckett's writing: 'music can only breathe in the oxygen of silence.'[56] Bertha, when talking about Beckett's compatriot Friel, however, uses another very succinct characterization when musing about Friel's work's purpose: is it about 'the ultimate refinement of the arts through music into silence'?[57] I think refinement, sublimation, transcendence are certainly part of the array of strategies writers employ when contextualizing their practice in the musicality *dispositif*, but there are others, as we will see. One particularly frequent trope is, again, the idea that music provides strong formal models and templates and can lend structural coherence to a kind of dramatic writing that may have abandoned or weakened other structural devices.

Musicality and Form(s)

Forms

From Strindberg's *Ghost Sonata* (1907) to Caryl Churchill's *Fugue* (1988) dramatic writing has often explicitly referred to musical forms. We need to distinguish between playwrights explicitly using particular forms as templates or models and scholars resorting to labelling dramatic form as symphony, fugue, theme with variations, etc. in an attempt to provide analytical insight. In the first case I would argue that trying to verify or falsify the author's poetological intention, i.e. trying to prove whether they succeeded in transferring the formal qualities of a fugue into language, misses the point. It is more productive to try to uncover what theatrical strategies lie behind the musical claim and what consequences the analogy has for the process and the aesthetics of the writing. The second case has understandably been met with scepticism since a lot of analytical rigour will inevitably be lost when one ignores the material differences of music and language and their respective rules of organization. Calvin Brown warns, in Steven Paul Scher's seminal collection on literature and music, against an unreflected metaphorical transfer of terms.[58] Schwarz echoes this mistrust when

---

[55]   See also Kulezic-Wilson, 'From Musicalisation'.
[56]   Jankélévitch in Bryden, *Samuel Beckett*, p. 27.
[57]   Csilla Bertha, 'Music and Words in Brian Friel's *Performances*', in Donald E. Morse/Csilla Bertha/Mària Kurdi (eds.), *Brian Friel's Dramatic Artistry: The Work Has Value* (Dublin, 2006): p. 71.
[58]   Calvin S. Brown, 'Theoretische Grundlagen zum Studium der Wechselverhältnisse zwischen Literatur und Musik (translated into German by Margaret Robinson)', in Steven Paul Scher (ed.), *Literatur und Musik* (Berlin, 1984), pp. 28–39.

'the "reciprocal enlightenment of the arts" exhausts itself in an indiscriminate use of metaphorical language, when theoretical terms are being transferred from one art to the next [...] without consideration'.[59] Nonetheless Brown, Schwarz and others see the wealth of possible interart interplays and seek ways to describe and analyze them.

Brown lists four ways in which literature and music may relate: a) combination, b) replacement, c) influence, and d) analogy or parallel.[60] These four ways often overlap, he says, but usually one of them dominates. Vocal music, for example, is a case of combination; replacement is sought in programme music or, vice versa, musical analysis or verbal music – 'the attempt to reproduce the immediate effect of a piece of music with words'.[61] Influence manifests itself for example in carrying over particular techniques (e.g. the leitmotif in music or the stream of consciousness in literature) or structures (e.g. the sonata or rondo form) into the neighbouring art.[62] Analogy or parallel cover similar phenomena as those covered by 'influence' according to Brown, but here the parallels are distinct from each other: 'the similarities between musical and literary metric are an example of independent phenomena'.[63]

In Thomas Bernhard's work we can find both replacement and influence quite explicitly: there is more than 'just' a general sense of musicality in the sense of a heightened awareness of sonic and rhythmic qualities of speech and musically informed structures. As Gudrun Kuhn (1996) and Liesbeth Bloemsaat-Voerknecht (2006) in particular have documented and analyzed in great detail,[64] Bernhard refers to existing musical pieces, such as Mozart's *Magic Flute* or Schumann's *Fantasie op. 17* and seeks to imitate structural and rhetorical characteristics of these compositions with words or find equivalences. 'Bernhard does not just copy. He uses material, which he encounters in music and makes use of its inherent musical aspects in order to create his own artwork.'[65] What Bernhard achieves, then, is more an imitation of the 'gestus' of a particular musical form and its semantics than a one-to-one equivalency.[66] In his play *Die Berühmten* (1976) Bloemsaat-Voerknecht identifies a series of discursive themes that Bernhard introduces and works through, closely influenced by how Schumann treats the

---

59   Schwarz, *Musikanaloge Ideen*, p. 7.
60   Brown, 'Theoretische Grundlagen', p. 33.
61   Brown, 'Theoretische Grundlagen', p. 35.
62   Brown, 'Theoretische Grundlagen', p. 37.
63   Brown, 'Theoretische Grundlagen', p. 38.
64   In addition see Manfred Jurgensen (ed.), *Bernhard. Annäherungen* (Bern/München, 1981); Bürgers, 'Es ist immer die Musik'; Mittermayer, *Thomas Bernhard*; Gitta Honegger, 'Fools on the Hill: Thomas Bernhard's Mise-en-Scène', *Performing Arts Journal*, 19/3 (1997), pp. 34–48; and Otto Kolleritsch, *Die Musik, das Leben und der Irrtum: Thomas Bernhard und die Musik* (Wien, 2000).
65   Lisbeth Bloemsaat-Voerknecht, *Thomas Bernhard und die Musik* (Würzburg, 2006), p. 229.
66   See Bloemsaat-Voerknecht, *Thomas Bernhard*, p. 176.

musical themes in his *Fantasie, op. 17* – she detects comparable ways in which
motifs return and vary, or in which certain rhetorical figures are repeated with the
effect of a conclusion.[67]

In the UK, Caryl Churchill played consciously with the form of the fugue in her
collaboration with choreographer Ian Spink for the television piece *Fugue* (1988),
inspired in particular by Bach's *The Art of the Fugue*. According to Sarah Rubidge,
Spink 'asked Churchill to structure her script using the musical principles which
underpin Fugue No 10'.[68] Libby Worth describes the result:

> *Fugue* opens with a series of repetitions with slight variation on the news of the
> father's death being relayed to each of the adult sons and daughters. The short
> sentences such as: 'he'd just got out of the bath', and 'he was already falling
> down the stairs – when I heard him' are reiterated with shifts in emphasis, rhythm
> and order. [...] Flurries of Churchill's half sentences create a specific rhythmic
> pattern that can, like Bach's music that plays through the piece, become material
> to be manipulated, deconstructed and re-built.[69]

Again, I doubt that despite the explicit and very specific relationship of this piece
of writing to a musical compositional technique, the similarity would hold up to
a strict comparative analysis, as the compositional rules of the fugue are based on
uniquely musical characteristics to do with defined pitch and tonality. But it is a
good example of how an author makes certain compositional principles productive
for her writing – here in order to facilitate an experimental fusion of words, dance
and the medium of television.

Another striking example of a very tangible influence of specific musical forms
on dramatic writing can be found in Jean Tardieu's work, as Monika Schwarz has
examined (1981). In plays like *Conversation-sinfonietta* (1951) or *La Sonate et les
trois Messieurs ou comment parler musique* (1952), Tardieu consciously employs
historical musical forms, using them both as schemes and formal outlines 'to be
filled with linguistic material',[70] but also as 'forms of thinking, which express a
dialectic between form and material'.[71]

Schwarz describes how in contrast to Mallarmé, who was under the
influence of Wagner's total work of art, Tardieu oriented himself more to 'the
music of the Vienna classic and the forms it produced, Sonata and Symphony'.[72]

---

[67] See Bloemsaat-Voerknecht, *Thomas Bernhard*, pp. 175–6.
[68] Spink in Libby Worth, 'On Text and Dance: New Questions and New Forms',
in Elaine Aston/Elin Diamond (eds.), *The Cambridge Companion to Caryl Churchill*
(Cambridge, 2009), pp. 71–87, p. 77. She means the *Contrapunctus 10 a 4 alla Decima,* a
Double fugue from J.S. Bach's *Die Kunst der Fuge*, BWV 1080.
[69] Worth, 'On Text and Dance', p. 77.
[70] Schwarz, *Musikanaloge Ideen*, p. 32.
[71] Schwarz, *Musikanaloge Ideen*, p. 32.
[72] Schwarz, *Musikanaloge Ideen*, p. 27.

Consequently, *Conversation-sinfonietta* – his first attempt to use musical form as an immediate point of departure – is not divided into scenes or acts, but into three musical movements,[73] which are identified as Allegro ma non troppo, Andante sostenuto, and Scherzo vivace. As Schwarz notes, this already marks a departure from the musical model: Tardieu's 'Sinfonietta' lacks the customary fourth movement, its finale. Schwarz's analysis as a whole suggests that as much as Tardieu 'flirts' with sonata and symphony as forms, his play is not an attempt to theatrically adapt these forms in a literal sense.[74]

Tardieu takes a particular musical form of sequences and their constituting principles as a model for the design of the dramatic progression since they appear suitable for him to provide the integration of the text, which aims to avoid a causal-determinist setup and the principle of mimesis.[75]

Theatrically, the play's suggested stage set-up is much like a concert situation: 'onstage there are six chairs in a semicircle, a conductor's podium, music-stands as well as two microphones'.[76] The typical *performative* elements of a concert – entrances, bows, an introduction to the piece, etc. – are also all present, but part of the precisely choreographed parody which marks the beginning of the piece.[77] Schwarz notes that the appropriation of musical models into the dramatic writing of Tardieu creates something in between: no longer drama, not yet music. The 'exposition' of the play, for example, is 'neither the exposition of the Sonata adapted for language, the functional system of which is likely to be impossible to translate onto language anyway, nor does it have anything to do with the common notion of exposition in the theory of drama'.[78] Tardieu creates implicit stagings that occupy a liminal space between art forms; a kind of para-concert and para-theatre (the latter being a term he actually used in reference to his theatre: 'para-théâtre'[79]). The influence of musical form, here, not only shapes the structure of the play and its dialogue (Schwarz analyzes this in detail) but also includes analogies to the performative and discursive rituals of (classical) music. These are – more than we find with other playwrights – actually at the heart of this play's *content* as well as its formal layout. And in contrast to the frequently world-weary plays of Bernhard and Beckett and their musicality of futile repetition or ebbing-away dialogue, Tardieu's work betrays playfulness, parody and irony, for which musicality can equally be an excellent vehicle.[80]

---

[73] See Schwarz, *Musikanaloge Ideen*, p. 33.

[74] See Schwarz, *Musikanaloge Ideen*, p. 47.

[75] Schwarz, *Musikanaloge Ideen*, p. 30.

[76] Schwarz, *Musikanaloge Ideen*, p. 34.

[77] This kind of compositional staging of para-musical aspects of concert rituals has since been exploited by composers such as John Cage, Mauricio Kagel, György Ligeti, Dieter Schnebel, or Manos Tsangaris and others (see Schwarz, *Musikanaloge Ideen*, p. 34).

[78] Schwarz, *Musikanaloge Ideen*, p. 40.

[79] See Schwarz, *Musikanaloge Ideen*, p. 33.

[80] See also my analysis of Filter's work in Chapter 6.

Form

Beyond the more explicit references to and influence from established musical forms, we find a rich variety of formal strategies derived from music that constitute or contribute to the musicality of dramatic writing. The authors in question use musical principles such as repetition, variation, permutation or motivic composition in order to explore alternative structures to those provided by narrative, situation and character. Individually, however, this can range from largely replacing traditional constituents of drama to merely extending and enriching the existing structural models. On one end of this spectrum, we might find Beckett's *Breath* (1969) – a radically short play lasting about 25 seconds in performance – consisting of the sound of an in- and out-breath, a littered stage and a single light sequence. On the other end, we could locate plays from Strindberg to Crimp, from Shaw to Friel, which still follow many established 'rules' of playwriting (narrative, dialogue, character, etc.) but use musicality of language and/or structure to accentuate their theatricality, heighten the poetic qualities of speech, avoid too literal a sense of realism or create friction and defamiliarization.

Repetition and Variation
A particularly prominent feature is the interplay between repetition and variation, both on macro- and microstructural levels of dramatic text. See for example this passage in Tardieu's *La Sonate* from its 'First movement: Largo':

>   A: Did it rise fast?
>   C: It rose very fast.
>   A: This fast?
>   B: Faster.
>   C: Even faster.
>   B: Faster.
>   C: Faster.
>   A: Fast, fast, fast, fast?
>   C: Very fast.
>   B: Very fast.
>   C: Very fast.
>   B: Very, very fast.
>   C: Very, very, very fast.
>   *Pause.*[81]

---

[81]   Jean Tardieu, *Théâtre de chambre* (Paris, 1966), pp. 117–18. In the French original this passage reads: 'A: Er ça montait vite? C: Ça montait très vite. A: Si vite ce ça? B: Plus vite que ça. C: Plus vite encore. B: Plus vite. C: Plus vite. A: Vite, vite, vite, vite? C: Très vite. B: Très vite. C: Très vite. B: Très, très vite. C: Très, très, très vite. *Un silence.*'

In this short sequence, Tardieu explores repetition but includes a range of subtle musical differences: he uses what can be described as a question-answer scheme for the first two lines (they are question and answer both musically and grammatically); he then repeats that scheme, but accelerates by diminution (going from 4 words to 2 to 1) and provides a variation in timbre as B responds the second time instead of C. We have identical repetitions between two voices (lines 6–7 and 9–11), and by one voice (line 8), a small variation in line 5 and a climax or augmentation from line 11–13. The more Tardieu explores 'how to speak music' (*comment parler musique*), I would argue, the more the words become sonic material. This word-music plays with the fading referential *meaning* of the words 'fast' or 'very' and facilitates the transformation of the words into an acoustic passage that will, in all likeliness, feature the very musical qualities (rising, fast) which it describes. The banality and redundancy of dialogue are exposed and parodied, but at the same time translated into a kind of word-music in its own right.

Gertrude Stein is also known for an often humorous and sometimes childlike cyclical approach to language, where certain turns of phrases and sounds are repeated with minor variations creating an undulating rhythm and a shimmering of sense and non-sense. As Sarah Balkin writes:

> Repetition with variation is foundational to musical composition, and the text of Stein's play does the work of the absent score. Marc Robinson discusses Stein's notorious use of sound repetition, stating, 'Stein prefers to call it "insistence": A repetition changes nothing, she notes, but insistence keeps pushing at different parts of obdurate surfaces, each push having a changed emphasis and speed and direction'.[82]

Stein's interest in repetition is not aiming at a suspension of time, or the experience of the stagnation and futility of our existence, which we can find in Beckett's works, but a sense of 'being totally absorbed in the present moment as a thing felt'.[83] When she dropped out of medical school in 1901 she 'had nothing to do but talk and look and listen' and 'did this tremendously'.[84] She describes the consequences:

> I began to get enormously interested in hearing how everybody said the same thing over and over again with infinite variations but over and over again until finally if you listened with great intensity you could hear it rise and fall and tell all that there was inside them, not so much by the actual words they said or

82   Sarah Balkin, 'Regenerating Drama in Stein's *Doctor Faustus Lights the Lights* and Woolf's *Between the Acts*', *Modern Drama*, 51/4 (2008), pp. 433–57, pp. 440–41.
83   Johanna Frank, 'Resonating Bodies and the Poetics of Aurality; Or, Gertrude Stein's Theatre', *Modern Drama*, 51/4 (2008), pp. 501–27, p. 519.
84   Gertrude Stein, *Lectures in America* (Boston, 1935), p. 138.

the thoughts they had but the movement of their thoughts and words endlessly the same and endlessly different.[85]

Here are two examples of how this translates onto the page,[86] taken from *Doctor Faustus Lights the Lights* (1938):

Scene II
I am I and my name is Marguerite Ida and Helena Annabel, and then oh then I could yes I could I could begin to cry but why why could I begin to cry.
    And I am I and I am here and how do I know how wild the world is how wild the wild woods are the wood they call the woods the poor man's overcoat but do they cover me and if they do how wild are they are wild and wild and wild they are, how do I know how wild the woods are when I have never ever seen a wood before. [...]

Scene III
[...] The boy has said will you
The woman has said
Can you
And you, you have said you are you
Enough said.
You are not dead.
Enough said.
Enough said.
You are not dead.
No you are not dead
Enough said.
Enough said.
You are not dead.
    All join in enough said you are not dead you are not dead enough said yes enough said you are not dead yes enough said, thank you yes enough said you are not dead.
And at the last
In a low whisper
She says
I am Marguerite Ida and Helena Annabel and enough said I am not dead.[87]

---

[85]   Stein, *Lectures in America*, p. 138.
[86]   It is vital, however, to also experience Stein's writing in performance. Hear, for example, her reading of her poem 'If I Had Told Him a Completed Portrait of Picasso' (1923) at http://writing.upenn.edu/library/Stein-Gertrude_If-I-Told-Him_1923.html [27.02.2012].
[87]   Gertrude Stein, *Last Operas and Plays* (Baltimore/London, 1995), pp. 95, 103.

Stein's repetitive prose, with its nuanced variations and reoccurrences of phonemes, grammatical constructions, expressions, 'word-play and homonym'[88] are all an attempt to both capture and render an experience of the 'here and now' (or: 'hear and now'?[89]) thus bridging the temporal disparity between depiction on stage and emotion of the audience: her 'fundamental discovery' about plays is that 'the scene as depicted on the stage is more often than not one might say it is almost always in syncopated time in relation to the emotion of anybody in the audience'.[90] Where other authors may use repetition in order to destabilize 'natural' time or the accepted patterns of chronological causality and sequence and gesture towards futility, fatality, or loss of communication in a kind of transcendent pessimism, Stein aims, one could argue, to actually stabilize the relationship between performance and experience. It 'makes anybody nervous',[91] she claims, 'that the thing seen and the thing felt about the thing seen [are] not going at the same tempo'.[92] She tries, as Johanna Frank puts it, to 'capture the "melody" of her subject as she feels it in the moment of the portrait's composition'.[93]

Beckett uses repetition quite differently: the dialogue of his characters does not 'descend' into nonsensical sound patterns as it frequently does in Tardieu's and Stein's work. As Mark and Juliette Taylor-Batty write on *Waiting for Godot* (1949):

> The structure of the play is founded on repetition – of words, events, motifs, sequences of movement – and it operates like a musical score in that respect, stating and restating its themes in a series of ever so slightly varied verbal and gestural leitmotifs.[94]

In Beckett's work, repetition is still reflective of the characters and their situation but also provides a sense of purpose and formal structure in an otherwise existentialist avoidance (by and large) of plot and direction. Bernhard shares this use of a more 'architectural' use of repetition against the more playfully sonic style of Stein or Tardieu. Christian Klug observes:

---

[88] Frank, 'Resonating Bodies', p. 508.

[89] With apologies to Eric Vautrin for borrowing this word play from his chapter of the same name in Kendrick/Roesner, *Theatre Noise*, wherein he discusses 'how technologies have changed sound practices' in the theatre (pp. 139–48).

[90] Stein, *Lectures in America*, p. 93.

[91] Stein, *Lectures in America*, p. 95.

[92] Stein, *Lectures in America*, p. 94.

[93] Frank, 'Resonating Bodies', p. 508.

[94] Mark Taylor-Batty/Juliette Taylor-Batty, *Samuel Beckett's Waiting for Godot* (London/New York, 2008), p. 29.

On a *macrostructural level* the function of these stylistic devices [repetition and variation] changes as follows: they not only provide the coherence of larger units through formal recurrence, but also constitute a significant part of the actual dramatic events of the plays such as changes in intensity, accelerations, deceleration or mood swings.[95]

Bloemsaat-Voerknecht demonstrates how Bernhard finds equivalences to music-rhetorical models of repetition such as 'polyptoton (repetition of the words of others)' or 'palillogia (repetition of one's own words)'[96] based on his reverence for Mozart and using actual compositions as structural models. Sometimes, this merely reflects on the characters' (lack of) intelligence, stubbornness or obsessiveness. Minetti, for example, the ageing actor and eponymous hero of Bernhard's play from 1976 (named after the actual actor Bernhard Minetti, who also starred in the original production), expresses his unique relationship to the role of Prospero in this way; a role that he dreamed of playing for 30 years:

Have I told you that Ensor
promised me the mask
for Prospero
When I play Prospero
I said to him
Prospero I should have played
Prospero
he points into the lobby
A storm draws in
There in the corner
Ensor promised me the mask for Prospero
I said
I had time
in twenty years perhaps
said I
Lear now
Prospero in twenty years
Twenty years after Lear Prospero
But Ensor is dead
I never played Prospero
only dreamed of it
playing him
in Dinkelsbühl I always dreamed
of playing Prospero
in Dinkelsbühl

---

[95]   Klug, *Thomas Bernhards Theaterstücke*, pp. 189–90.
[96]   Bloemsaat-Voerknecht, *Thomas Bernhard*, pp. 106, 108.

in the attic
my dear
Thirty years of
getting up
stepping in front of the mirror
and playing Lear
People said
I was crazy.[97]

Here, the musical structures – the obsessive repetition, the slow spiralling forwards of the account by gradually adding new details to the story, the sudden shift when the outside world is acknowledged ('People said I was crazy') – can still be read at the level of characterization, the redundant ramblings of an ageing and bitterly disappointed actor.

At other times, however, the structural affinities to music go far beyond supporting the portrayal of the play's personnel. They become manifestations of Bernhard's continuous scepticism towards language and meaning. Wieland Elfferding puts this beautifully:

> Language spirals out of the horizontal of the continuous narrative meaning into the vertical and becomes its own topic. This is the use of musicality in Thomas Bernhard's work. [...] The signifiers begin to play amongst themselves and thumb their noses at those signifiers which are still indebted to the old metaphysical world of hero and anti-hero. Music [and Bernhard's theatre, DR] do not, as one might think, inevitably result in a *l'art pour l'art* but its relationship to reality just takes a deviation via a demonstrative breaking free of its language from a world, which always presumed to know its meaning.[98]

Bernhard is by no means the only author for whom musicalization of speech is a response to a profound crisis of language and the unchallenged habits of meaning-making – we have certainly seen Artaud express this topos a generation earlier and could trace it further back, for example to Hugo von Hofmannsthal, whose famous

---

[97] Habe ich dir gesagt daß mir Ensor / für den Prospero / die Maske versprochen hat / Wenn ich Prospero spiele / habe ich zu ihm gesagt / Prospero hätte ich spielen sollen / Prospero / *zeigt in die Halle hinaus* / *Ein Sturm kommt auf* / Dort in der Ecke / hat mir Ensor die Maske für Prospero versprochen / ich sagte / ich hätte Zeit / In zwanzig Jahren vielleicht / sagte ich / Den Lear jetzt / den Prospero in zwanzig Jahren / Zwanzig Jahre nach dem Lear Prospero / Aber Ensor ist tot / Ich habe Prospero nie gespielt / immer nur davon geträumt / ihn zu spielen / in Dinkelsbühl habe ich immer davon geträumt / den Prospero zu spielen / in Dinkelsbühl / in der Dachkammer geträumt / mein Kind / Dreißig Jahre lang / aufgestanden / und vor den Spiegel getreten / und den Lear gespielt / Die Leute sagten / ich sei verrückt. Thomas Bernhard, 'Minetti', in Thomas Bernhard, *Stücke 2. Der Präsident, Die Berühmten, Minetti, Immanuel Kant* (Frankfurt am Main, 1988), pp. 245–6.

[98] Wieland Elfferding, 'Thomas Bernhards Musik', *Der Freitag*, 09.02.2001.

Lord Chandos Letter from 1902 expresses the sensation that 'the abstract words which the tongue must enlist as a matter of course in order to bring out an opinion disintegrated in my mouth like rotten mushrooms'.[99]

Where Artaud aimed to steer language towards the condition of the scream, however, Bernhard's musical strategy is quite different: he pulls every stop of musical rhetoric to enmesh language in a web of musical relationships and references. Instead of reducing language to primitive sound, he artfully escalates it in endless motivic permutations. Klug thus summarizes Bernhard's musicality as follows:

> The term covers on a *microstructural level* [...] rhetorical figures such as wordplay and repetition, which are associated with musical termini such as variation, retrograde as well as modulation, 'dissident' semantic relations such as wry pleonasms and paradoxes, generally the emphasis of combination, relation and the breaking free of formal relational patterns. Less often than these horizontal compositional principles terms are being referred to, like contrapuntal, 'symphonic' or fugue, which comprise vertical relationships.[100]

In addition to this motivic work, Bernhard also uses language in a way that strongly suggests formal developments and contrasts, both in rhythm and timbre, to the actor speaking his lines. Bürgers attests:

> The spiralling sentence constructions contract more and more with their recurring motifs and set phrases, appear as a theme with infinite variations and yet structure and define the narrative melody decidedly in timbre and tempo, accelerate and retard, form crescendi and accentuate.[101]

This sense of linguistic and musical accumulation on the one hand – which we also find in Jelinek's writing – and Beckett's ebbing prose, which has been called a 'diminuendo of nothingness'[102] on the other, are testament to the non-normative nature of musicality in playwriting. As we have also seen in relation to acting, training and directing, musicality can be (and has been) utilized in pursuit of quite diverse aesthetics. It is not automatically a vehicle towards balance and grace, for example, but can equally form a kind of perceptive or productive shift of emphasis even to the point of excess:

---

[99] Hugo von Hofmannsthal, *The Lord Chandos Letter and Other Writings* (New York, 2005), p. 121.
[100] Klug, *Thomas Bernhards Theaterstücke*, p. 189, original emphasis.
[101] Bürgers, 'Es ist immer die Musik', p. 187.
[102] Whitelaw in Bryden, *Samuel Beckett*, p. 2.

A unique stylistic feature of Bernhard's prose is a technique of escalation, of exaggeration, of getting caught up in or making presumptions about fixed ideas. This is artfully orchestrated in a technique of repetition, which at once repeats (but also always slightly varies) certain themes, phrases and derogative remarks at a high rate while also stepping them up again – especially when the reader may think this no longer possible. This technique of Bernhard reminds us of compositional methods of Baroque music and Serialism. These passages are often pinnacles of comedy in post-war literature in the German language.[103]

Besides Bernhard's obsessive but intricately composed tirades there are other examples in which the musical *dispositif* seems to encourage writers to break widely accepted rules of dramaturgical balance, unity, equilibrium, entertaining pacing, timing and variation – both in a theatrical and a musical sense.

Gertrude Stein uses musicality as a 'potentially threatening force'[104] and suspends narrative chronology and causality in favour of what she calls plays that are 'exactly like a landscape',[105] which caused Leonard Bernstein to claim: 'Stein has come closer than any other writer except Joyce to the medium of music.'[106] Likening her theatre to experiencing and observing a landscape, Stein explains that she tends to 'constantly think about the theatre from the standpoint of sight and sound and its relation to emotion and time, rather than in relation to story and action'.[107] Considerations of how to avoid potential redundancy or lack of narrative economy thus do not dominate her dramaturgical choices as they would in any well-made play. For Jelinek and Barker[108] this has led to consciously abandoning fixed ideas of 'measure' and instead embracing rather rhizomatic[109] 'plethora'[110] –

---

[103] http://de.wikipedia.org/wiki/Thomas_Bernhard [28.02.2012]). For those sceptical of Wikipedia as a source of scholarship it is worth noting that independent tests in the renowned journal *Nature* have proven that its accuracy and reliability is equal to that of the *Encyclopaedia Britannica* while being inevitably more up-to-date (see http://www.nature.com/nature/journal/v438/n7070/full/438900a.html [28.02.2012]).

[104] Balkin, 'Regenerating Drama', p. 448.

[105] Stein, *Lectures in America*, p. 122. See also Daniel Albright's chapter 'Heaven' in his book *Untwisting the Serpent: Modernism in Music, Literature, and Other Arts* (Chicago, IL/London, 2000), pp. 311–64, in which he discusses Stein and the landscape plays in some depth.

[106] Bernstein in Frank, 'Resonating Bodies', p. 519.

[107] Stein, *Lectures in America*, p. 104.

[108] See Jens Peters, 'Crowd or chorus? Howard Barker mise-en-scène and the tradition of the chorus in the European theatre of the 20th Century', *Studies in Theatre and Performance*, 32/3 (2012), pp. 305–16 for a comparison of their work particularly in relation to the use of chorus.

[109] See the introduction of Deleuze and Guattari's *A Thousand Plateaus* (Minneapolis, 1987) for a full exploration of the rhizome metaphor.

[110] Howard Barker's AHRC-funded creative fellowship at the University of Exeter Drama Department was entitled 'Plethora and Bare Sufficiency'. See the special issue of *Studies in Theatre and Performance* (32/3, 2012) for more details.

creating an overabundance of material using the multiple possibilities of musical (and semantic) combinations, associations and *Fortspinnungen* (ways of spinning-forth). Powell and Bethman thus speak of music as a key to a poetics 'of perverse validation of sound and material or medium against meaning'[111] in Jelinek's theatre. Similarly, Adrian Curtin describes Howard Barker's language as highly musical, finding expression in his 'preoccupation with the importance of actors getting the rhythm of a speech "right"'. Curtin calls this 'an indicator of the power and pervasiveness of his [Barker's] "audial consciousness", which is directed toward the compound exploration of verbo-vocalic-sonic (and visual) scenes'.[112] Barker's interest in an aesthetics of 'plethora' comes with a matching fascination for what he calls 'bare sufficiency' and his attempts in this direction have precedents particularly in Beckett's plays. Both are musically inspired formal extremes that challenge conventional strategies of 'making sense' structurally.

Musicality and Coherence

Despite the often-quoted influences of Mozart, Beethoven and Schubert for a number of playwrights, their musicality also reflects the changes in aesthetics that the *twentieth* century brought in Western classical music. During that century composers have, as we know, often abandoned entertainment and beauty as the profane purposes of music, or celebration and exaltation as its religious aims and have embraced compositional methods and musical aesthetics to reflect the frequently problematic experiences of their time and the lack of unifying points of reference.[113]

Heiner Müller's plays are another striking example of this shift: they not only reflect on the abysses of men and society; his writing methods and dramatic composition also reflect a sense of fragmentation, disintegration and iteration. Barbara Kordes, reflecting explicitly on 'musical readings'[114] of Müller's work, attests that 'the writing- and composition-methods described as montage techniques such as intertextuality, fragmentation, quotation, collage and sampling'[115] are characteristic of Müller's prose.

These techniques deliberately promote separation of elements over unity and amalgamation and clearly turn their back on the looming presence of Wagner's

---

[111] Powell/Bethman, 'One must have tradition', p. 164.

[112] Adrian Curtin, 'The Art *Music* of Theatre: Howard Barker as Sound Designer', *Studies in Theatre and Performance*, 32/3 (2012), pp. 269–84, p. 271, quotations are by Barker.

[113] Freud's psychoanalytic theory, Einstein's theory of relativity, the experience of two wars and the decline of religion may be seen as major cornerstones here.

[114] The German title of her book from 2009 on Heiner Müller and Heiner Goebbels (who collaborated frequently in the 1980s and 1990s), *Musikalische Lesarten*, translates as 'musical readings'.

[115] Barbara Kordes, *Musikalische Lesarten: Heiner Goebbels und Heiner Müller* (Göttingen, 2009), p. 129.

Gesamtkunstwerk in the musicality *dispositif.*[116] They also question grand narratives and the authoritative position of the author, as Barthes and others have famously diagnosed elsewhere.[117] We know all this, so my aim in this context is just to point out that musicality has played a part (and continues to play it) in this post-modern/postdramatic transition.[118] The emergence of sampling, or recording and editing techniques and the possibility of working on and freely combining tracks, as well as the wealth of new playback technologies have clearly left a significant mark for dramatic writing and dramaturgy. Playwrights like Müller or Rainald Goetz are influenced by these advances and think of text as 'samples' that can be freely modified and combined as in the sampler machines that were developed in the 1980s and are now readily available as software on any personal computer.[119] In contrast to Müller, Goetz not only utilized aesthetic techniques, but intensively embraced the rave culture of the 1990s and incorporated its themes and *zeitgeist* into what has since been called 'techno-theatre'.[120]

Whether it is a canon of forms derived from classical musical models, or the appeal of a new technology, or an aesthetic that rejects an affirmative sense of form, then, there is still an argument to be made that in all these instances, the notion of musicality is often employed to provide what Klug calls an 'alternative Stimmigkeit zur diskursiven Kohärenz' [an alternative coherence to discursive coherence].[121] Accordingly, Schwarz has suggested that the 'abandonment of dramatic causality or finality, which holds together language in traditional drama, is compensated by structural principles borrowed from music'.[122] This line of argument which plays 'sense' against (musical) 'sensuality' and linguistic versus

---

[116] Heiner Müller and Heiner Goebbels, whose musicality is analyzed in Kordes's book, are both clearly influenced by Brecht and his rejection of the *Gesamtkunstwerk*. He said: 'As long as the term "total art work" [*Gesamtkunstwerk*] implies that the totality is a smear [*Aufwaschen*], as long as the arts are to be "fused" together, the separate elements will all be degraded in equal measure, and each can be for the others only a supplier of cues. ... Such magic is naturally to be fought against. Everything that attempts to hypnotize will produce unworthy intoxications, will make fog, and must be given up' (cit. in Albright, *Untwisting the Serpent*, p. 119; the bracketed emphases are by Albright).

[117] See his essay 'The Death of the Author', for example (http://www.deathoftheauthor. com/ [20.03.2012]).

[118] It is worth stating, I would argue, since musicality has not been given enough coverage in this context. Hans Thies Lehmann's influential book *Postdramatic Theatre* (1999, translated in 2006), for example, only touches on musicality very briefly in a chapter of two pages.

[119] See Chapter 6, which explores the sampler's influence on theatre-making in more detail.

[120] See Windrich, *TechnoTheater*. I am less convinced by Windrich's arguments for listing Bernhard under the same label.

[121] Klug, *Thomas Bernhards Theaterstücke*, pp. 191–2. *Stimmigkeit* in German means 'coherence', or 'fit', and includes *Stimme/Stimmen*, meaning 'voice' and 'tuning'.

[122] See Schwarz, *Musikanaloge Ideen*, pp. 17–18.

contrapuntal regularity is problematic, though, I would argue, as it does not match the experiences of theatre-makers and audiences, who happily 'oscillate' between these proclaimed opposite ends of a spectrum. I do not think there is a mutual exclusivity, an 'either-or', of semantic and musical coherences. They can coexist in quite a dynamic interplay, which can also be individually redefined by each author and theatre-maker. Klug supports this point in relation to Thomas Bernhard:

> Bernhard's musicality does not threaten the 'significance' or 'meaning' of the linguistic material [...]. The reference of the linguistic material is being obscured already by the choice of words, before musical structuring processes come into play. The range of possible meanings of individual words is not eradicated by the interplay of indeterminate referentiality and musical combination, but set free. Musicality and linguistic meaning do not preclude each other, then.[123]

We are thus not dealing with an automatic replacement of sense or sense-making, but rather a 'critique of sense-making by means of our senses' as Ulrike Haß puts it.[124] Here, my focus is on those sensual perceptions that are attuned to 'musicality' across most of our physical senses. Instead of constructing a rigid dichotomy, then, I suggest to use the evidence of musicality in dramatic writing in particular (and theatre in general) to analyze in detail what are rather dynamic and flexible balancing acts between meaning and its denial, between writing, directing, acting and musicking,[125] between reference and self-reference and to make the difficulties of drawing clear lines and boundaries between them the very subject of the investigation.

Before I turn to the question of how the musicality *dispositif* impacts on voice and speech in dramatic writing I should at least mention an early example of music being seen as an 'alternative coherence': Heinrich von Kleist's famous letter to his confidante Marie von Kleist.[126] If we choose to describe one of the dualisms in the discourse examined so far in this book as the polarity between the 'algebraic' or 'architectural' aspects of musicality on the one hand and the idea that music disrupts

---

[123] Klug, *Thomas Bernhards Theaterstücke*, pp. 191–2.

[124] Haß in Christiane Steiner, *Text und Theatralität in Frank Castorfs König-Lear-Inszenierung* (MA Thesis, FU Berlin, 1996), p. 23.

[125] Musicking, as Christopher Small defines his neologism, emphasizes that music is not a thing, but an activity: 'To music is to take part, in any capacity, in a musical performance, whether by performing, by listening, by rehearsing or practicing, by providing material for performance (what is called composing), or by dancing' (Christopher Small, *Musicking: The Meanings of Performing and Listening* [Hanover, 1998], p. 9).

[126] It is not pertinent to the argument of this book to explore the complex relationship of Kleist to music as a whole – I refer to other scholars who have addressed this question, for example: Detlef Müller-Henning, 'Vom Musikalischen in Kleists Prosa', in Klaus Kanzog/Hans Joachim Kreutzer (eds.), *Werke Kleists auf dem modernen Musiktheater* (Berlin, 1977). See also: Lubkoll, *Mythos Musik*; Kielholz, *Wilhelm Heinrich Wackenroder*; or Naumann, *Die Sehnsucht der Sprache*.

discursive logic and is instead 'the language of feeling itself'[127] on the other, then the former aspect has already been expressed succinctly by Kleist in 1811. He writes:

> I think of [music] as the root, or, rather, to express it more precisely, the algebraic formula of all the others; [...] I for my own part, from earliest youth, have related all my general speculations about literature to tones. I believe that from the principle of the figured bass [Generalbass] there are inferences to be drawn that are of the first importance for literature.[128]

Sigismund Rahmer interprets the letter in a way that echoes the observations at the beginning of this chapter on music as a condition *for* and *of* writing:

> The significance of Kleist's statements on music arises from what we know about his and other excellent dramatists' productive methods. The dramatic imagination, the concept of the playwright, emerges from a musical disposition [Stimmung]. It is music which sparks off the poetic fantasy, one might say. The musical mood inseminates the poetic imagination. This is why Kleist has to see this art as the root of all other arts. Music represents, according to Kleist, the algebraic formula for the other arts. We are reminded of Pythagoras's effort to explain harmony from numerical proportions and of Leibniz's definition of music as als exercitium arithmeticae occultum nescientis se numerare animi [Music is a hidden arithmetic exercise of the soul, which does not know that it is counting].[129]

The notion of the mathematical nature of music, as well as – and as a consequence – its perceived precision and the coherence of its numerical proportion have remained in currency. One of Bernhard's protagonists in his novel *Korrektur* (1975), for example, is quoted saying that 'music was the art closest to the sciences and to the nature of man, and that music was basically mathematics rendered audible'[130] – an idea that refers directly to Schopenhauer and Novalis's notion of an *harmonia mundi*.[131] Unsurprisingly, Bernhard's musical preferences are, as we have already seen, 'Mozart, Bach and the New Vienna School', as it was these composers who 'have most successfully attempted to overcome chintzy emotional indulgence and render music a spiritual and intellectual art, a kind of philosophical mathematics,

---

[127] Leoš Janáček cit. in Bertha, 'Music and Words', p. 61.

[128] Heinrich von Kleist, 'Brief an Marie von Kleist', in Heinrich von Kleist, *Werke und Briefe in vier Bänden, Bd. 4 Briefe* (Berlin, 1995 [1811]), p. 481. My translation is based in part on Powell and Bethman's translation ('One must have tradition', p. 179).

[129] Sigismund Rahmer, *Heinrich von Kleist als Mensch und Dichter* (Berlin, 1909), p. 230. See also Carl Dahlhaus, 'Kleists Wort über den Generalbass', in Joachim Kreutzer (ed.), *Kleist-Jahrbuch* (Berlin, 1984), pp. 13–24 for a detailed analysis from the point of view of musicology.

[130] In Mittermayer, *Thomas Bernhard*, p. 185.

[131] See Klug, *Thomas Bernhards Theaterstücke*, p. 195.

emphasizing its rational ideal and setting free its educational potential'.[132] Bernhard's musical strategy certainly does contain an element of educational insistence in his obsessive lamentations about the chaos of the world, the inevitable physical decay of the body and the perceived ignorance of people, but also a liberating sublimation by turning it into intricate form and fine, bitter humour.

Having looked at the implications of the musicality *dispositif* on form and forms in playwriting, I will now focus on a different aspect by addressing a range of strategies that *in the process of writing* render the (imagined) speaking voice problematic – as a means of communication, natural expression of the self and as a theatrical entity.

Musicality and the Problematization of Voice

The use of musical principles of construction and permutation as well as the various other ways in which playwrights increase our awareness of the musicality of the drama all contribute, as we have seen, to changes in the status of language. Given that dramatic speech is meant to be spoken, realized vocally in front of an audience, musicalization can also become an interrogation, celebration and/or problematization of voice and its relationship to language.

The 'Genosong' of Dramatic Dialogue and the Futility of Language

When looking at Artaud and his influence on subsequent generations of theatre-makers, we have already encountered an increasing interest in the paralinguistic aspects of speech, or what Roland Barthes calls the 'grain' of the voice or the 'genosong' of voice (based on Julia Kristeva's concept of genotext and phenotext).[133] Dominic Symonds has pointed out the difficulties and imprecisions of the terms phenosong and genosong elsewhere[134] and I will not attempt another re-reading of Barthes and Kristeva here, but instead use some of the keywords of this debate as prompts for my investigation. What Barthes's neologism gestures towards is aspects of spoken language that fall at least partly outside of its *communicative* function[135] (in the sense of Roman Jakobson's list[136]), such as spoken language's

---

[132] Bürgers, 'Es ist immer die Musik', p. 180.

[133] Roland Barthes, 'The Grain of the Voice', in Roland Barthes, *Image-Music-Text* (New York, 1977), pp. 179–89.

[134] Dominic Symonds, 'The corporeality of musical expression: "the grain of the voice" and the actor-musician', *Studies in Musical Theatre*, 1/2 (2007), pp. 167–82.

[135] In summary, these are: the referential, aesthetic, emotive, conative, phatic and metalingual functions, which address six aspects of the communicative act: the context, the message, the sender, the receiver, the channel and the code.

[136] See Roman Jakobson, 'Closing Statements: Linguistics and Poetics', in Thomas A. Sebeok (ed.), *Style in Language* (Cambridge, MA, 1960), pp. 350–77.

'very materiality', 'the voluptuous pleasure of its signifier-sounds',[137] its physical, vibratory appeal, the eroticism or repulsion of its texture and timbre.

I would argue that these notions are also prevalent amongst a number of the playwrights in this chapter despite the fact that they are dealing with *potential* and *imagined* voices, unless their writing process is already entwined with the actual actors and directors through work-in-progress arrangements or specific commissions. The effects and strategies of these interrogations of voice naturally vary between authors, as a quick survey will show.

Questioning the Status of Language

Starting with Gertrude Stein, we find that there is an anecdotal 'genesis' account for the origins of her theatre, not dissimilar to Artaud's foundational experience of the Balinese theatre at the International Colonial Exposition in Paris in 1931.[138] This is how Frank relates Stein's story:

> As a young child, she attended a musical production starring the French actress Sarah Bernhardt, who performed and sang entirely in French. As she details in her lectures, Stein, a young English-only speaker, found herself attracted to how the foreignness of the characters and their actions kept them at a distance, so that '[she] did not have to know them' but could experience them [1935, 116]. [...] The sense of distance, however, is what compensated for her other childhood encounter with the theatre: her frustration with the notion of syncopated time. Because, at the Bernhardt production, the young Stein did not understand the words spoken, she could focus her thoughts and energies on the sounds of the words rather than on their meaning as signifiers in a sign-system. Story time on the stage did not conflict with the emotional time of the spectator because, as an English speaker at a French production, Stein could not follow the story of the action on the stage. Instead, meaning was located in the timbre, inflection, gesture, tone, rhythm, sonority, and resonance of the words spoken or sung.[139]

Like Artaud, Stein 'foregrounds voice as sound rather than allowing it to disappear into the signification of words'.[140] The aesthetic consequences, however, are quite different. While Artaud pursues a purity and metaphysical appeal of the spoken word through a particularly *physical* experience of theatre for the audience, Stein provides for a much more contemplative and playful engagement. In both cases, musicality 'contributes to defining the relationship between a text and an audience',[141] but in contrast to Artaud, Stein's 'emphasis on art's materiality serves

---

137   Barthes in Symonds, 'The corporeality', p. 170.
138   See Chapter 3.
139   Frank, 'Resonating Bodies', p. 515.
140   Frank, 'Resonating Bodies', p. 505.
141   Frank, 'Resonating Bodies', p. 523.

to focus attention on the immediacy of the composition as a potential interface with the world, upon the stature of its ordinariness, and also upon its capacity to compose the world in its very immediacy'.[142] She thus embraces the mundane that Artaud seeks to transcend.

In Beckett's work we find a different emphasis yet again: his musicalization of dialogue is a manifestation of 'the tension between the desire for meaningful expression and the sense of its impossibility'.[143] Musicality becomes the vehicle for interrogating and undermining language, but also for creating an emotional response to it. Talking about a passage in *Waiting for Godot* that is particularly evocative sonically Mark and Juliette Taylor-Batty find that

> additional effects are created through manipulation of the phonic qualities of words, many of which are also onomatopoeic, such as 'whisper', 'rustle', 'murmur', 'feathers', 'ashes', 'leaves'. The actress Billie Whitelaw once commented on the 'dramatic rhythms of Beckett's word music' [...], and indeed, Beckett's language here begins to work on us in different ways: like music, such language affects us emotionally rather than signifying anything very clearly, thus leading us towards an experience of language rather than a rational 'understanding' of it.[144]

As we have already seen, Beckett uses a range of musical approaches not just in writing but also in rehearsal, working towards an 'experience of language' and maintaining the 'tension between his repeatedly expressed dissatisfaction with a language system [...] and the impossibility of abandoning our primary mode of expression'.[145] He would, for example, use extreme tempi to get to the 'grain of the voice' qualities, as Branigan attests: 'In his role as a director, this belief in the primacy of sound over intelligibility often resulted in pushing actors to delivering dialogue at breakneck tempo.'[146] Tardieu shares Beckett's scepticism towards language – Schwarz elucidates the connection of Tardieu's 'Sprachkrise' [crisis of language][147] and the critique of language's seemingly unproblematic

---

[142] Brad Bucknell in Frank, 'Resonating Bodies', p. 523.

[143] Laws, 'The Music of Beckett's Theatre', p. 126. Adrian Curtin observes similar aspects in Howard Barker's plays: 'Barker frequently isolates, fragments, and/or repeats single words in his texts, abstracting them from the flow of speech in order to work them over, so to speak, almost obsessively, magnifying their phonic properties and defamiliarising their meaning' ('The Art *Music* of Theatre', p. 274).

[144] Taylor-Batty/Taylor-Batty, *Samuel Beckett's Waiting for Godot*, pp. 49–50.

[145] Laws, 'The Music of Beckett's Theatre', p. 126.

[146] Branigan, *Radio Beckett*, p. 216. Beckett's *Play* from 1962–1963 is a case in point. See excerpts of Anthony Minghella's film version from 2000 at https://www.youtube.com/watch?v=NiEtsVPpjyM [05.03.2012]. Also see Kulezic-Wilson, 'From Musicalisation', and http://www.beckettonfilm.com/plays/play/synopsis.html [05.03.2012].

[147] Schwarz, *Musikanaloge Ideen*, p. 20.

representation of world and thought with his turning to alternative (i.e. musical) principles of construction and coherence:

> The idea of absolute music and the linguistic conception of nonsense converge in shedding their relationship to reality, an ideal which according to Tardieu the absolute total art achieves, but which poetry can only ever strive for as an unachievable aim.[148]

For the actors this has implications for any rehearsal process of Tardieu's plays: the idea and function of dialogue itself is profoundly questioned, so that sometimes, for example, it is no longer the 'sense or meaning of what's being said that is important, but solely its gestus'.[149] Similarly, punctuation becomes an important indicator for the *musical* interpretation, since the actors cannot necessarily use content or context of the utterances as guidelines for their delivery any more.[150] Like Beckett or later Sarah Kane, Tardieu also makes explicit use of timbre in his plays, specifically in *Conversation-sinfonietta*, dividing the actors into groups of lower and higher vocal pitch and timbre and using these contrasts consciously and musically. Where Tardieu's problematization of voice turns out as an often humorous and satirical take on the 'jingle' of mundane conversations, Valère Novarina promotes a more extreme and physical take on the idea of a materiality of language. He demands a 'pneumatic actor',[151] whom he describes as an organ to *excrete* language, a resonant body of meat, fluids and bones: 'You must not be clever, but rather put your abdomen, teeth and jaws to work.'[152] He considers any cerebral approach to text as a sign of repression:

> The actor is not an interpreter because the body is not an instrument. Because it is not the instrument of the head. Because it is not its support. Those who tell the actor to interpret with the instrument of his body, those who treat him as an obedient brain, clever at translating others' thoughts into corporeal signals, those who think that something can be completed from one body to another and that a head could command a body, are guilty of misunderstanding the body, of repressing the body, quite simply guilty of repression.[153]

Instead, his metaphors emphasize a materiality of the speech-act that – unlike the writing of other authors – does not foreground its *sonic* qualities, but the *physical* aspects of their production. One cluster of metaphors circles around acts of ingestion and excretion (and their audibility): 'Chew and eat the text.

---

[148] Schwarz, *Musikanaloge Ideen*, p. 27.
[149] Schwarz, *Musikanaloge Ideen*, p. 43.
[150] See Schwarz, *Musikanaloge Ideen*, p. 44.
[151] Novarina, 'Letter to the Actors', p. 95.
[152] Novarina, 'Letter to the Actors', p. 95.
[153] Novarina, 'Letter to the Actors', p. 102.

A blind spectator should be able to hear it crunched and swallowed [...]. Mastication, sucking, swallowing.'[154] Another cluster is more 'hydraulic' and sees the actor as

> a rhythm machine, where the liquids (chyme, lymph, urine, tears, air, blood) all circulate in torrents, where everything that rushes down the inclines, through the canals, the tubes, the sphinctered passages, to quickly ascend again, overflow, force open the mouth [and] ends up becoming rhythmic, rhythming itself, multiplying its force through rhythm – this rhythm comes from pressure, from repression – and exits, ends up exiting, ex-created, ejected, jaculated, material.[155]

The musicality in Novarina's vision is that of living, breathing actors onstage with all their bodily functions and the rhythms and sounds that this visceral approach to language brings about.

> In different ways, then, we can see authors use notions of musicality to not only problematize language, but also the ontology of the subject onstage whether as performer or character – which is not to say that that distinction can always be upheld in the first place.[156]

Musicality as Characterization

Where Stein, Artaud, Beckett or Tardieu use musicality to shift language's function, foreground its materiality and often create quite opaque characters,[157] other authors have used the 'genosong' of speech to *add* rather than detract from the characterization of their dramatic personnel.

Thomas Bernhard's characters are somewhat in between things in this respect: their musical repetitiveness of speech and their defamiliarizing gestus of the classical singer,[158] despite being in a play rather than an opera, still bear witness to a 'mistrust towards language' which 'finds its expression in the abysmal scepticism

---

[154] Novarina, 'Letter to the Actors', p. 95.

[155] Novarina, 'Letter to the Actors', p. 103.

[156] I will look at this aspect in more detail in the final part of this chapter.

[157] In Beckett's *Play*, the two female and one male speakers are only called M, W1 and W2 and in Tardieu's *Le Sonate* the characters are Monsieur A, Monsieur B and Monsieur C. We find this lack of characterization again in Sarah Kane's *Crave* (1998), whose four protagonists are called A, B, C and M and have been compared to a string-quartet rather than an ensemble of dramatic characters (see for example http://www.iainfisher.com/kane/eng/sarah-kane-link-crave.html [05.03.2012] or http://www.spiegel.de/kultur/gesellschaft/0,1518,70459,00.html [05.03.2012]).

[158] Kuhn and Bloemsaat-Voerknecht speak of 'sängerischer Gestus' (Bloemsaat-Voerknecht, *Thomas Bernhard*, p. 99).

with regard to the possibility of seeing language as an instrument of insight'[159] – which is not unlike the descriptions of Beckett's language we have seen. At the same time, Bernhard's musicality helps to create rich and rewarding characters and food for character actors. Musicality is not seen as incompatible with realistic acting, as one of Bernhard's foremost actors, Minetti, explains:

> When Gorvin[160] recently saw me as a character in a play by Bernhard, which was performed quite realistically, she said: 'you actually make music'. [...] I find Bernhard eminently musical. What you say about rhythm, I feel very strongly. [...] For me, the sentences, when I learn them at home before a performance and confront myself with them, are very rhythmical. Funnily, through rhythm I learn a lot about the characters.[161]

More recently, a number of playwrights have rediscovered musicality not so much as an abstraction, but as a kind of *Kunstsprache*, a heightened, rhythmically and sonically pinpointed vernacular that provides rich layers of association and resonances with respect to class, jargon, idiolect, and regionality while remaining tentative, indeterminate and shimmering with these references.

Caryl Chruchill's *The Skriker* (1994), for example, features an eponymous character described as 'a shapeshifter and death portent, ancient and damaged'.[162] The character's language plays with the musical qualities of language insofar as it uses alliteration and assonances excessively ('so I spin the sheaves shoves shivers into golden guild and geld and if she can't guessing game and safety match my name then I will take her no mistake know mister no missed her no mist no miss no me no'[163]), borders on the nonsensical from time to time ('Is it William Gwylliam Guillaume? Is it John Jack the ladder in your stocking is it a Joke? Is it Alexander Sandro Andrew Drewsteignton? Mephistopheles Toffeenose Tiffany's Timpany Timothy Mossycoat?'[164]) and foregrounds the rhythmicality of language by the use of short and sharp words in quick succession ('Shriek! shrink! shuck off to a shack, sick, soak, seek a sleep slope slap of the dark to shelter skelter away, a wail a whirl a world away. Slit slap slut. That bitch a botch an itch in my shoulder blood. Bitch botch itch. Slat itch slit botch. Itch slut bitch slit'[165]). Ralf Erik Remshardt describes the result as follows:

---

[159] Elisabetta Niccolini, *Der Spaziergang des Schriftstellers: 'Lenz' von Georg Büchner, 'Der Spaziergang' von Robert Walser, 'Gehen' von Thomas Bernhard* (Stuttgart, 2000), p. 207.

[160] Joana Maria Gorvin (1922–1993) was a famous German actor and part of the ensemble of Gustaf Gründgens in the 1940s. Since 1995 the Academy of the Arts in Berlin has awarded an exceptional female performer every year the Joana-Maria-Gorvin Prize.

[161] Minetti in Bloemsaat-Voerknecht, *Thomas Bernhard*, p. 99.

[162] Caryl Churchill, *The Skriker* (London, 1994), p. 1.

[163] Churchill, *The Skriker*, p. 1.

[164] Churchill, *The Skriker*, p. 1.

[165] Churchill, *The Skriker*, pp. 1–2.

Churchill invents a Joycean language which pushes, as she says, 'the verbalness of the text to an extreme': a hodge-podge of resonances, references, and puns; a word-salad and cascade of constantly self-subverting, slippery sentences, as if all human parlance had penetrated the earth's crust in shards and were being manically regurgitated by the Skriker. The phenomenal Kathryn Hunter, a tiny woman with an exceptionally expressive face and body, delivers these tatters and torrents of text as a mixture of incantation and subconscious jazz riff, half possessed by the language and half possessing it. It is a tour de force for both author and actress, with some of Churchill's most powerful and poetic writing in evidence.[166]

Paraphrasing Remshardt, one could say that the Skriker half generates the kind of language that reflects the character's traits (as an untrustworthy, 'mysterious female punk rock earth spirit'[167]) and *is* half generated by the language itself: self-subverting, slippery, regurgitated, incantatious.

Enda Walsh's idiom of two teenage outsiders in *Disco Pigs* (1996) is another kind of *Kunstsprache*, indebted to youth culture, the clubbing scene and Irish provinciality. His language looks at times like a phonetic transcription and ties in with the characters' tendency to vocally create the sound-track and 'Foley effects' to the film inside their heads that is their life. See for example the beginning of the play:

> Lights flick on. PIG (male) and RUNT (female). They mimic the sound of an ambulance like a child would, 'bee baa bee baa bee baa!!'. They also mimic the sound a pregnant woman in labour makes. They say things like 'is all righ miss', 'ya doin fine, luv', 'dis da furs is it?', 'is a very fast bee baa, all righ. Have a class a water!' Sound of door slamming. Sound of heartbeats throughout.
> RUNT. Out of the way!! Jesus out of the way!
> PIG. Scream da fat nurse wid da gloopy face!
> RUNT. Da two mams squalin on da trollies dat do speeding down da ward. Oud da fookin way!
> PIG. My mam she own a liddle ting, look, an dis da furs liddle baba! She heave a rip all inside!! Hol on mam!![168]

This vocal duo not only characterizes itself by means of its rhythm and sound of its speech,[169] but also invokes the entire soundscape through imitating noises, quoting

---

[166] Ralf Erik Remshardt, 'The Skriker by Caryl Churchill', *Theatre Journal*, 47/1 (1995), pp. 121–3, p. 121.

[167] See http://www.youtube.com/watch?v=Dn5RkFywtrs [05.03.2012].

[168] Enda Walsh, *Disco pigs. Sucking Dublin. Two plays* (London, 1997), p. 3.

[169] Another example of the particular rhythmicality of Walsh's text is the frequent use of 'fuck' in *Bedbound* (2001), which becomes more of an energetic, explosive beat than an expletive, rhythmically structuring and driving forward he dialogue. The character DAD's

other speakers, expressions, pop cultural references, the local (Cork) accent, and by creating acoustic spaces through onomatopoeia.

It is noteworthy that similar to Ireland with its relationship to the UK, Austria as another, small(er) country sharing its language with a bigger country (Germany), has also produced playwriting which mixes local dialect, a relatively high proportion of expletives and a heighted sense of rhythm and sound into a *Kunstsprache*. In these invented idioms it seems to be easier, somehow, to take on some of the absurdities of the societal contexts and to playfully use and abuse the prevailing theatricality of Catholicism. Werner Schwab (1958–1994) is the prime example here, but others before (Peter Turrini, 1944–) and after him (Ewald Palmetshofer,[170] 1978–) confirm the trend, as do authors such as Franz Xaver Kroetz (1946–) who, while being German, probably considers himself Bavarian in the first place and thus shares the notion of a strong influence of local and vernacular linguistic soundscapes with his Austrian colleagues.

These dramatic texts thus remind us of what Mikhail Bakhtin identified as 'heteroglossia' and 'polyphony' in Dostoevsky and Rabelais. We have seen this coexistence and simultaneity of autonomous voices of varied character and provenance already in Meyerhold's theatre works – here, however, the polyphony is already premeditated at the stage of writing. What Bakhtin describes, with regard to the novel, as the 'artistically organized system for bringing different languages in contact with one another'[171] can be readily applied to a range of writing practices which provide 'a multiplicity of social voices and a wide variety of their links and interrelationships'.[172] Sticking with the musical metaphor, Bakhtin speaks of the 'movement of the theme through different languages and speech types' and then, using a different image, about 'its dispersion into the rivulets and droplets of social heteroglossia, its dialogization'.[173] As Schwarz points out, this idea of a musical polyphony in writing has had its forerunners in other genres of literature, in particular in romantic and symbolist poetry:

---

first words are: 'FUCK FUCK FUCK FUCK FUCK FUCK fucking hell fucking hell fuck fuck fuck Jesus fuck!! Fucking hell!!' (Enda Walsh, *bedbound & misterman. Two Plays by Enda Walsh* [London, 2001], p. 9).

[170] In his portrait of Palmetshofer for nachtkritik.de, Andreas Klaeui writes: 'The artificial language [Kunstsprache] coloured by marked dialect, which is characteristic of his writing, is part of a problematization of language. Trying to describe it, musical terms impose themselves: fugue, false entries, canon, retrograde … – not to mention the enormously musical speech-rhythm. All this, says Ewald Palmetshofer, is very consciously worked out: "The music inherent in language is meant to continue to narrate subliminally, what can't be said"' (http://nachtkritik-stuecke08.de/index.php/stueckdossier3/portraet-ewald-palmetshofer [05.03.2012]).

[171] Mikhail Bakhtin, *The Dialogic Imagination* (Austin, 1981), p. 361.

[172] Bakhtin, *The Dialogic Imagination*, p. 263.

[173] Bakhtin, *The Dialogic Imagination*, p. 263.

Mallarmé, for example, is fascinated in particular by the ability of music to express different things simultaneously, and is impressed by its purely combinatorial constructions; characteristics, then, which make him look for words which oscillate most polysemantically within the poetic edifice due to their complex richness of references.[174]

More recently, Martin Crimp (in *Attempts on her Life*, 1997) and Caryl Churchill (in *Top Girls*, 1982), for example, have taken on this idea of polyphony of voices and have organized these voices by indicating precise overlaps and accumulations of text for the actors. Where Churchill conjures up a multi-voiced resonance of women's struggles through the ages, Crimp's poly-perspective writing dissects the fragmenting and assembling of personality and subject in a multi-medial world. These kinds of techniques can also be found in Heiner Müller's plays, as Barbara Kordes explains:

> The impression of multiple voices is reinforced on the level of textual editing as a score of regularly surfacing lines printed in majuscules, which break, also purely visually, into the text like another voice. The same is true for the capitalization within verses and the lack of punctuation.[175]

This kind of musicality not only gives voice on a formal level to Müller's profound distrust of authoritative 'grand' narratives, but also creates 'stumbling blocks' on the productive and receptive paths of actors, directors and audiences. This avoids or impedes too smooth a transition from page to stage, and from stage to auditorium. Musicality, here, does not expedite our understanding, but makes it deliberately unwieldy. It rather prevents the actor from illustrating the text too much and anticipating an interpretation and demands quite an active role of the audience in forming *semantic* connections from deliberately separate voices, whose connection is a more compositional than narrative one.

Implications

Having explored and compared a range of 'symptoms', forms and strategies of musicality in playwriting, I will now tease out some further implications these may have. These are: a) the shifts towards non-realistic time and meaning that may come with its musicalization, b) a different sense of autonomy of the play as an art form, c) the 'politics' of a musical approach to form, and d) the impact musicality has on the construction or deconstruction of character and subject in playwriting.

---

[174] Schwarz, *Musikanaloge Ideen*, p. 31.
[175] Kordes, *Musikalische Lesarten*, p. 120.

A Different Sense of Time, a Different Kind of Meaning

Music creates a different time, which is neither real time, nor fictitious time.[176] It also creates a different kind of meaning or meaning-making. This allows authors with a deep-seated suspicion of established meaning-making processes in drama to write this suspicion into the play itself.

An early example of this was Gertrude Stein's impression of 'syncopated time', which I have mentioned before in this chapter. She criticizes the gap between depicted emotion on stage and felt emotion in the auditorium. She explains that 'your emotion as a member of the audience is never going on at the same time as the action of the play'.[177] Her solution for this problem was to 'bring both the time of the play and the time of the spectator into the complete, absolute present'[178] and one of the ways of doing that was to de-emphasize language's communicative functions and highlight its musicality. Frank speaks of 'a similarity between the experience of hearing the sounds of Stein's words and that of hearing the sounds of musical notes, articulations that come to life in performance'.[179] By creating a playful language full of assonances and the rhythms of nursery rhymes, she aimed to facilitate the audience being 'totally absorbed in the present moment as a thing felt',[180] believing that that was how the production of knowledge worked. This is not to suggest that Stein promoted an idea of art as a harmless and naïve pastime, but instead challenged hegemonies of linear causality and what she considered the often 'male' logic and form of arguments or narrative. With her musicality she promoted an experiential form of knowing; something that Ian Sutherland and Sophie Krzys Acord have characterized in a different context as 'an embodied, tacit and contextualized phenomenon, varied and subjective: a verb rather than a noun'.[181]

Beckett's musicality also plays with notions of the tacit and embodied, as Branigan explains: 'The plays are musical in the broadest definition of the word as they invite the listener to react in an intuitive rather than intellectual manner.'[182]

---

[176] See for example – from a range of disciplines, such as neuropsychology, musicology, theatre studies and sociology – Jonathan Kramer, *The Time of Music* (London, 1988); David Epstein, *Shaping Time. Music, the Brain, and Performance* (New York, 1995); Ana Agud, 'Musikalische und sprachliche Zeit', in Albrecht Riethmüller (ed.), *Sprache und Musik. Perspektiven einer Beziehung* (Laaber, 1999); Tia DeNora, *Music in Everyday Life* (Cambridge, 2000); Christa Brüstle et al. (eds.), *Aus dem Takt. Rhythmus in Kunst, Kultur und Natur* (Bielefeld, 2005); and Daniel Levitin, *This Is Your Brain On Music* (London, 2008) for a fuller discussion of this assertion.

[177] Stein, *Lectures in America*, p. 93.

[178] Frank, 'Resonating Bodies', p. 518.

[179] Frank, 'Resonating Bodies', p. 519.

[180] Frank, 'Resonating Bodies', p. 519.

[181] Ian Sutherland/Sophie Krzys Acord, 'Thinking with Art: From Situated Knowledge to Experiential Knowing ', *Journal of Visual Art Practice*, 6/2 (2007), pp. 125–40, p. 126.

[182] Branigan, *Radio Beckett*, p. 248.

The musical *dispositif* allows them to enter what Bryden calls a different 'world' with respect to experience of time and processes of meaning making:

> Beckett concurs with Pater[183] in regarding the art of music as being 'unique' in inhabiting a zone of abstraction and materiality. Thus, in *Proust,* he presents music in Schopenhauerian terms as 'the Idea itself, unaware of the world phenomena, existing ideally outside the universe' [...]. The composer of music, like the composer of mathematics, can work in a self-referential world, a world of virtuality and abstraction.[184]

By emphasizing the here-and-now of the shared theatrical experience and the very materiality of that encounter, musicality thus actually reorients the theatre back from a mere platform of ideas to its material ontology, its theatricality – a thought we have encountered frequently in the writings of Tairov, Fuchs or Meyerhold. But while theatre can aspire to the often abstract and self-referential nature of music, it cannot be as relatively immaterial or 'virtual', as Bryden calls it. If we are in a park, for example, and sounds from a nearby open-air concert drift past, we still experience music. This common experience, which we could call 'acousmatic',[185] is much less likely with regard to theatre. Two rare examples we have of an 'acousmatic' theatre are the 'théâtrophone'[186] and the audio recordings of famous theatre productions in the 1940s–1960s – but both practices only made sense precisely at a point in time when there was a kind of theatre that had largely abandoned its theatricality and had become literature to be read out aloud.

The embodied and not always discursive experience of theatre, analogous to what we have seen described as the 'pre-conceptual and pre-linguistic'[187] cognition of music, changes the role of the audience, as Laws explains:

> Wherein the relative absence of semantics leads the listener into a more active role in the perception of patterns of similarity and difference, and the meaning of the piece develops out of that web of associations. [...] the musical effect

---

[183] This is Walter Pater, whom I have referred to frequently already.

[184] Bryden, *Samuel Beckett*, p. 42.

[185] See Michel Chion, *Audio-Vision. Sounds on Screen* (New York, 1994).

[186] Invented in 1881 by Clement Ader, the 'théâtrophone' 'involved telephonic transmission of live performances of theatres and music halls into domestic households and amplification of the sound through phonograph speakers' (Tim Crook, *Radio Drama: Theory and Practice* [London, 1999], p. 15). Also see Jean-Marc Larrue, 'Sound Reproduction Techniques in Theatre: A Case of Mediatic Resistance', in Kendrick/Roesner, *Theatre Noise*, pp. 14–22, and Adrian Curtin, *Avant-Gard Theatre Sound: Staging Sonic Modernity* [New York, 2014].

[187] Ramón Pelinski, 'Embodiment and Musical Experience', *TRANS. Revista Transcultural de Música*, 9 (2005) [Online], http://redalyc.uaemex.mx/pdf/822/82200914.pdf [16.08.2011], p. 32.

is intimately bound up with the problematics of communication, subjectivity and representation (i.e. with Beckett's 'aesthetics of failure') [...]. For Beckett, unlike Joyce, the aim is not to extend the implicative potential of words, but rather to pare it down, so as to explore the relationship between referential and non-referential meaning.[188]

This model of musical cognition for meaning-making in theatre also impacts on the process of writing, acting and directing. Laws attests that 'much of Beckett's drama involves a sophisticated understanding of the relationship between music, subjectivity and the production of meaning'[189] and Bryden explains what this relationship is for him: Beckett, she says, considers music to be

> 'the highest art form', since 'it's never condemned to explicitness'. By refusing to anatomise or domesticate it, Beckett allows music to retain for the listener its full force of ambiguity.[190]

The music of his language, then, reflecting ambiguities and semantic opacity, requires voices which are 'often frail but tenacious, threatened with extinction and yet committed to utterance'.[191]

Musicality as a way of exploring the 'problematics of communication' and involving the audience at different cognitive levels resonates also with Bernhard, who – with reference to Schopenhauer, whom he read extensively – shared the conviction that 'specifically musical insight, if it exists, cannot be discursive [begrifflich]'.[192] Using a coinage by Novalis, Klug describes Bernhard's 'linguistic musicality' as consisting in the 'indeterminate significance [unbestimmte Bedeutsamkeit] of associative and formulaic speech'.[193] Novalis fittingly describes this as 'alluding, not-affirmative speech, which does not promote particular points of view, but plays on ideas, words and poetic props like on the keys of a musical instrument'.[194] One of the consequences of this approach is that Bernhard encourages an allegorical reception:

> The singular and individual, which appears on stage, is meant to be regarded in mediation in order to capture allegorically the musical-general [...]. The musical-general does not consist in expressing 'this or that singular and specific' existential orientation, but '*the* joy, *the* sadness, *the* pain, *the* shock,

---

[188] Laws, 'The Music of Beckett's Theatre', p. 127.
[189] Laws, 'The Music of Beckett's Theatre', p. 130.
[190] Bryden, *Samuel Beckett*, p. 31. The quotations are from Lawrence Shainberg.
[191] Bryden, *Samuel Beckett*, p. 28.
[192] Klug, *Thomas Bernhards Theaterstücke*, pp. 206–7.
[193] Klug, *Thomas Bernhards Theaterstücke*, p. 205.
[194] Novalis in Klug, *Thomas Bernhards Theaterstücke*, p. 205.

the jubilation, *the* amusement, *the* contemplation *itself,* quasi in abstracto, the essence of it without any frills'.[195]

The ideas of abstraction, the allegorical and the self-referential, which pervade the musicality *dispositif,* are closely connected to another trope that I found particularly pronounced with regard to playwriting in comparison to the discussions and manifestos on acting, directing or designing theatre. It is the claim and the aim for autonomy of dramatic writing as an art form.

Musicality and the Autonomy of Dramatic Writing

Over time, there have been various 'rankings' of the arts in ever-changing hierarchies based on the ascription of purity, complexity, closeness to nature, required craftsmanship, or – autonomy. The ascent of instrumental music and its reception by the literary greats of German romanticism, such as Tieck, Wackenroder and later E.T.A. Hoffmann, triggered a paradigmatic change in how music was seen in the hierarchy of the arts. Having long been considered a servant to the master of literature, it was now hailed as the highest and most autonomous of the arts; the 'queen of the arts',[196] as Walter Pater put it. Dahlhaus summarizes this significant change in music aesthetics: 'If instrumental music was seen by the common sense aestheticians in the 18th century as a pleasant noise below language, it was declared in the romantic metaphysics of the arts to be a language beyond language.'[197] This idea found expression in the term 'absolute music', which has been influential – despite its many flaws[198] – until today. What it also started was a reevaluation of what literature and poetry should be like. Powell and Bethman explain this when discussing Jelinek's literary influences:

> In the German Romantic tradition to which Jelinek's work is so self-consciously indebted, literary music may be described as an aesthetic program […] and was inseparable from a poetics of autonomy. […] As in Romanticism and Modernism, literary musicality is, paradoxically, both a marker of aesthetic autonomy – of resistance to communicative meaning – and also a Utopian revolt against the limits of the medium of literature, of art itself.[199]

---

[195] Klug, *Thomas Bernhards Theaterstücke*, 208, original emphases. Quotations are from Schopenhauer's *The Word as Will and Idea*, 1818.

[196] In Powell/Bethman, 'One must have tradition', p. 164.

[197] Dahlhaus in Schwarz, *Musikanaloge Ideen*, p. 12.

[198] Simply by looking at the production and reception of music from a cultural-materialist point of view renders the idea of a purely 'non-representational' music highly problematic. As Christopher Small, for example, has demonstrated extensively (*Music. Society. Education* [London, 1980]; *Musicking*), the socio-economic conditions are – intentionally or not – always inscribed into the music and its performances.

[199] Powell/Bethman, 'One must have tradition', pp. 164, 178.

In later iterations of 'musical writing' and in particular playwriting, this sense of autonomy did not necessarily mean an attempt to climb up the ladder in the pecking order of the arts, but a vehicle to liberate an art form from its own sets of conventions and restrictions. If we take Tardieu as an example, it is evident that he used a musical-compositional approach in order to 'provide integration to a text, which seeks to avoid a causal-determinist construction and to abstract itself from the principle of mimesis'.[200] Schwarz elaborates on this point:

> For Tardieu music-analogue drama converges with the purity and abstraction of linguistic composition in general, irrespective of whether it is derived from principles which have been developed in the history of musical composition, or by recurring to theatrical techniques such as monologue, dialogue, aside etc., as long as these techniques appeared to be reduced to their pure form as speech, while providing abstraction from any content.[201]

Here, the *idea* of absolute music is transferred onto dramatic literature, but with an eclectic use of writing techniques to achieve a *sense* of non-referentiality, while being fully aware, I would argue, that this is more a gestus than the actual attempt to create a dramatic art that was free from any presuppositions and assumptions and would actually get the audience to abandon any attempt at sense-making. The parodistic streak in Tardieu's plays alone undermines that: parody obviously does not work without bearing references to a world outside the artwork itself, even if that world represents the *dispositif*: the discursive conventions, creative conventions and reception habits of an art form. While pursuing 'purity' in his composed theatre, Tardieu was not a purist about how to achieve that effect.

There is, however, also a utopian undercurrent in Tardieu's plays. While he acknowledges an 'un-translatability in principle'[202] between the arts, he still pursues a common sphere, which they all inhabit,[203] a 'utopian region of the mind, separate from reality'.[204] The advantage that abstract painting and music have over literature, he claims, is that they only meant themselves, i.e. that *signifié* and *signifiant* coincided, whereas the referential quality of verbal language constituted a deviation which made the perception of the spiritual in art more difficult.[205]

Beckett promotes a different kind of purism and autonomy with his theatre, which finds expression in his rejection of the idea of the *Gesamtkunstwerk* that so often makes its appearance in the discourse on musicality in theatre. According to Bryden, Beckett did not espouse what he called 'Wagnerism', saying: 'I don't

---

[200] Schwarz, *Musikanaloge Ideen*, p. 30.
[201] Schwarz, *Musikanaloge Ideen*, p. 30.
[202] Schwarz, *Musikanaloge Ideen*, p. 27.
[203] Cf. Schwarz, *Musikanaloge Ideen*, p. 28.
[204] Schwarz, *Musikanaloge Ideen*, p. 28.
[205] Cf. Schwarz, *Musikanaloge Ideen*, p. 28.

believe in art synthesis: I want a theatre thrown back on its own resources.'[206] For someone who has inspired many composers to create music-theatrical works based on his writings, he is also quite outspoken against opera in general, calling it, with regard to music, 'a hideous corruption of this most immaterial of all the arts'.[207] Musicality in theatre, then, for Beckett is not about mixing or synthesizing art forms or media, but is a route towards reorienting theatre to its essential components.[208] It is not about adding a layer, but using a musical disposition to strip away as much as possible. Musicality helps to make the theatre independent of its own cluttered conventions.

In Beckett's case autonomy also means that musicality 'preserves' the author's vision against too liberal a sense of interpretation by others. It is – reminiscent of Appia's arguments – a way of executing control over the transition from page to stage, to retain a more loyal version of the 'implicit staging' by the playwright (however problematic one may find this notion). By contrast, other authors such as Jelinek seek compositional writing strategies (excess, citation, conglomeration, etc.) that specifically *demand* the director or composer's intervention, interpretation and co-authorship. Jelinek has incorporated this idea into the stage directions of her plays (see Figure 4.2)[209] and also describes this kind of dialogue when talking about her collaboration with composer Olga Neuwirth:

> In principle I give Olga textual material and she then takes from this what she needs. I also do this with directors. They make their own play out of my plays and the best that can happen is that you can see your own work with new eyes.[210]

In any case, the notion of an autonomy of dramatic writing – inspired by ideas of absolute music – is not a naïve or emphatic one for any of the three examples I have given here, Jelinek, Tardieu, Beckett, or for any others one might quote. There are no illusions or ambitions to *actually* create a theatre that is purely

---

[206] Beckett in Bryden, *Samuel Beckett*, p. 33.

[207] Beckett in Bryden, *Samuel Beckett*, p. 33.

[208] We have already encountered this idea in the writings of Meyerhold, Tairov and others, who also see musicality as the ideal vehicle to return to an autonomy and essentialism of theatre; a theatricality of the theatre.

[209] At the beginning of *Ein Sportstück* she writes, as a stage direction: 'The author doesn't give many stage directions, she has learned her lesson by now. Do what you like. The only thing that has to be kept are the Greek Choruses […]' (Elfriede Jelinek, *Sports Play. Translated by Penny Black* [London, 2013], p. 39). Vanda Butkovic, director of the UK premiere of *Sports Play* (Cardiff, Exeter, London 2012, see Figure 4.2), says: 'We focused on how it sounds, not what it's saying. For the choric scenes in particular, you can absolutely hear it. When the chorus applies the rules like in a musical composition – dynamics, pauses, tempo, rhythm, sound of the words, repetitions – then everything is explored against the meaning of the text' (at http://exeuntmagazine.com/features/sports-play-vanda-butkovic/ [25.07.2012]).

[210] Jelinek in Basting, 'Drastische Töne', p. 25.

Figure 4.2   Just a Must's UK premiere of Jelinek's *Sports Play*

self-referential. But there is a clear sense that this gestus of an 'absolute theatre' is a means to interrogate theatre's social, economic or philosophical significance as a sense-making device after all, while questioning its mechanisms. For Jelinek, for example, the idea of autonomy

> stands in some tension with the political engagement often suggested by her work, especially for the theater. [...] Self-reference and autonomy do not simply mean a postmodern 'anything goes,' at least not in Jelinek's case. Autonomy is a cage of meaning, a 'prison house of musicality' against which Jelinek's language frantically batters as a bird against a windowpane.[211]

This tension of a potentially purist, escapist, self-referential musicality for its own sake and a musicality that highlights the problematics and politics of meaning-making is articulated in different ways and intensities for each author. I would like to pause on the idea of what I would call 'gestic musicality' for a moment.

Gestic Musicality

By suggesting a 'gestic musicality in theatre' in relation to Brecht it is worth reminding ourselves of the complex, and at times contradictory, definitions of

---

[211]   Powell/Bethman, 'One must have tradition', p. 165.

'gestic music' (*Gestische Musik*) in Brecht's writings. Kenneth Fowler traces the varying statements Brecht makes in relation to gestus. He sees the main conflicts of Brecht's use of the idea in the fact that he defines gestus as 'socially meaningful gesticulation, not illustrative or expressive gesticulation',[212] but does not explain how gesture can 'demonstrate economically determined social relationships'[213] without illustrating these. Secondly, *all* gestures bear traces of the material conditions they arise from and will thus – willingly or not – be socially meaningful. It does become clear, however, from other references to gestus by Brecht, that he not only means gestures with social meaning, but 'a synthesis of body and facial movement and language'[214] and that gestus as an 'expression of an inner condition' is never 'abstracted from its social context'.[215] What this also means, as Brecht explains in the *Kleines Organon* from 1948, is that gestus combines gesture with attitude.

On a pragmatic level, two main aspects of gestic musicality in theatre emerge: 1) *gestus* as a social attitude *in* music and 2) *gestus* as an attitude when *performing* music. Jürgen Engelhardt defines the first when saying that 'gestic composing [...] means to be dealing with the fact that the predetermined in the musical formation and the specific social and musical awareness of the compositional subject constitute themselves in organized sound behaviour [Klangverhaltung]'.[216] The second meaning becomes clear in the following Brechtian advice:

> It is an excellent criterion for a piece of music with text, to demonstrate with what attitude the interpreter must deliver certain passages, polite or angry, humble or abject, affirmative or dismissive, sly or without calculating. In this the most common, most vulgar, and most banal gestures are to be preferred. Thus, the political value of the music piece can be estimated.[217]

Gestus, as a theatrical principle, tries in part 'to break the mimetic "naturalness" of the artistic material and show art as something made'[218] and also to transform a musical gesture into a social gesture. What this also means is that musicality in theatre is not mere self-indulgent formal experimentation nor a relabelling of

---

[212] Brecht in Kenneth Fowler, *Received Truths: Bertolt Brecht and the Problem of Gestus and Musical Meaning* (New York, 1991), p. 29.

[213] Fowler, *Received Truths*, p. 29.

[214] Fowler, *Received Truths*, p. 31.

[215] Fowler, *Received Truths*, p. 29.

[216] Jürgen Engelhardt et al., *Gestus und Verfremdung. Studien zum Musiktheater bei Strawinsky und Brecht/Weill* (München/Salzburg, 1984), p. 57. The word *Verhaltung* is quite uncommon in German – Engelhardt defines it as follows: 'Verhaltung means the entirety of human forms of action and reaction – form the emotion via fantasy to understanding, as it manifests itself in the opinions, convictions, attitudes and gestures, etc.' (p. 49).

[217] Bertolt Brecht, 'Über gestische Musik', in Bertolt Brecht, *Gesammelte Werke, Band 17: Schriften zum Theater 3* (Frankfurt am Main, 1967), pp. 482–5, p. 485.

[218] Engelhardt, *Gestus und Verfremdung*, p. 57.

poetic devices with musical terminology. How to compose for the theatre and/or *with* the theatre, and how to perform these compositions[219] is political insofar as theatre in its process of creation can be seen as a model for social interaction, and in performance creates a space for perception, which can have political impact and significance.

This latter point has been discussed by theatre scholar Nikolaus Müller-Schöll, who distinguishes between 'political theatre and doing theatre in a political way'.[220] While the former would negotiate and discuss political issues within an established representative framework, the latter would interrogate the framework itself, and thus that which we call the theatre. Müller-Schöll then shows (with reference to Walter Benjamin) that the political aspect of 'doing theatre in a political way' is to express 'the relationship between the performed action and the action of performing itself'.[221] While the former, the 'presented action',[222] can be controlled, there remains a certain amount of uncontrollability for the second, 'the very act of (re)presenting'.[223] This remainder, one might conclude, is a subversive element *vis-à-vis* the circulating political as well as artistic ideologies of power and control.

Musicality in theatre is, I would argue, particularly suited to generating this dual consciousness (about the performance as well as the act of performing) in both the performers and the audience. Writing, acting, directing, etc. *musically* always involves an intermedial transfer which Christopher Balme describes as 'the attempt to realize in one medium the aesthetic conventions and habits of seeing and hearing in another medium'.[224] Due to this intermedial transposition, musicalization almost inevitably undermines certain performative conventions, draws attention to the acts of their creation and creates friction with the expectations and conventions of theatrical writing or performance. This often leads to a degree of productive uncertainty for both practitioners and audiences, how to understand, classify or assess what is being performed, and may open up a utopian margin: the possibility, with regard to every new play or production, of asking 'What *is* theatre? What *is* music?' The necessity, each time, of redetermining their interplay, also provides an opportunity to continue discussing the social interaction between practitioners and recipients, or even the collapse of a clear distinction between

---

[219] Brecht remarks on the difference to conventional musicianship in saying: 'If the music is gestic, then those who make music act' (Brecht in Fowler, *Received Truths*, p. 40).

[220] Nikolaus Müller-Schöll, 'Theatre of Potentiality. Communicability and the Political in Contemporary Performance Practice', *Theatre Research International*, 29/1 (2004), pp. 42–56, p. 42.

[221] Benjamin in Müller-Schöll, 'Theatre of Potentiality', p. 44.

[222] Müller-Schöll, 'Theatre of Potentiality', p. 44.

[223] Müller-Schöll, 'Theatre of Potentiality', p. 44.

[224] Christopher Balme, 'Intermediality: Rethinking the Relationship between Theatre and Media' [Online], http://epub.ub.uni-muenchen.de/13098/1/Balme_13098.pdf [11.06.2013], p. 7.

these categories themselves. As we will see in the final part, this may also mean an interrogation of the status of the subject on stage as a side-effect of musicalization.

Musicality and the Constitution and/or Deconstruction of the Subject

Earlier in this chapter, I talked about how musicalization in playwriting often includes a problematization, celebration or interrogation of voice, both for the actors in the rehearsal and performance process and the audience in watching and hearing the result. Looking at the discursive evidence, it becomes clear, however, that this goes further than causing a change in the aesthetic experience. It could be argued (and has been argued) that – amongst other factors – musicality contributes to problematizing the relationship between voice, speech and the subject itself, or that it is an expression of a more complex interplay of these. Traditionally, *dramatis personae* are pre-existent characters: they are listed and sometimes briefly characterized at the outset of the play and usually confirm, modify or expand their character traits, motivations and psychological profile through the things they do and say during the course of the play.

In the case of quite a few of the playwrights we have talked about in this chapter this idea is under review: the relatively stable idea of a character (including developments and turns in their psyche and behaviour) is no longer reliable: characters may be layered to a degree of irresolvable contradictions, their speech may be a collage of quotations and 'prompted speech' ('soufflierte Rede'[225]) or they may seem to exist only *through* the act of speaking; selves that are constituted only through voice and language.[226] One aspect of this change is embedded in the turn towards musicality, which embraces the already mentioned difference of musical signification compared to discursive communication: in music, signifier and signified usually are one and the same thing,[227] or, as Boris de Schloezer put it: 'In music, the message is immanent in the messenger, its content is in its form to such a degree that strictly speaking music *has* no sense, but *is* sense.'[228]

Gertrude Stein's characters, for example, are not, as Frank puts it, 'described' but 'rendered' through their speech-acts.[229] Her plays are hardly driven by character or plot, but become an 'exploration [...] of the sensory experience of word-sounds

---

[225] Helga Finter, 'Antonin Artaud and the Impossible Theatre: The Legacy of the Theatre of Cruelty', *TDR*, 41/4 (1997), pp. 15–40, p. 26.

[226] Jelinek has made this thought quite explicit: 'I have written plays in which the characters are constituted by their speech, and as long as they are speaking, they exist, but whenever they cease to speak, they also cease to exist' (in Brenda L. Bethman, '"My Characters only live insofar as they speak": Interview with Elfriede Jelinek', *Women in Germany Yearbook*, 16 [2000], pp. 61–72, p. 66). (Thanks to Jens Peters for pointing me to this quotation.)

[227] Cf. Schwarz, *Musikanaloge Ideen*, p. 28.

[228] De Schloezer in Müller-Henning, 'Vom Musikalischen', p. 48, original emphasis.

[229] See Frank, 'Resonating Bodies', p. 508.

and of her attempt to create an immediate, ephemeral, unmediated presentation'.[230] Looking at her play *A List* (1922), for example, Daniel Albright finds that 'the fact that all the names begin with the letter *M* and the fact that the characters say approximately the same thing tend to defeat any sense of individuation'.[231]

In a different corner of the field, which I am seeking to map here, we find some of Sam Shepard's plays.[232] In Elizabeth Hardwick's introduction to his *Four Two-act Plays*, she describes the relationship of language and subject as follows:

> Perhaps the characters are not profitably thought of as characters at all. They are actors, parodists. They slip from style to style; they carry a few props around with them as they change their roles; they 'freeze' when they want to withdraw from the action on the stage. The essence of their being is energy, verbal energy. In the restless inventiveness of their parodies and tirades, a storm of feeling and experience blows across the stage.[233]

Some of this description actually also fits the 'characters' of some of Jelinek's and Kane's theatre texts quite well even though the system of references, the pool of citations, the overall 'sound' of the different playtexts is quite unique in each case, given the different personal and cultural contexts from which they emerge. Jelinek's musicality, for example, 'is a form within this medium, a specific aesthetic practice deeply indebted to the historical inheritance of Romanticism and High Modernism'.[234] But like Shepard, Jelinek uses music as a 'key to a poetics of non-identity',[235] a tool to create and organize a web of references, rhythms and resonances. Her characters have been described as 'Sprachmaschinen' [speech machines], 'which only exist while they speak and otherwise vanish completely'.[236]

In her famous essay-manifesto from 1983 'Ich möchte seicht sein' ('I Want to Be Shallow'),[237] Jelinek proposes a model for a theatre where her texts could be plainly spoken by mannequins on a catwalk:[238]

---

[230] Frank, 'Resonating Bodies', p. 510.

[231] Albright, *Untwisting the Serpent*, p. 326. See my earlier footnote on Beckett's *Play* and Kane's *Crave* in this respect as well.

[232] The next chapter will look into Shepard's musicality in more detail.

[233] Hardwick in Sam Shepard, *Hawk Moon: A Book of Short Stories, Poems, and Monologues* (New York, 1981), pp. 11–12.

[234] Powell/Bethman, 'One must have tradition', p. 178.

[235] Powell/Bethman, 'One must have tradition', p. 164.

[236] Henriette Kunz, *'Ich komme von der Sprache her' – Das Neue Theater der Elfriede Jelinek und seine Konfrontation mit dem herrschenden Code* (München/Ravensburg, 2005), p. 6.

[237] Elfriede Jelinek, 'Ich möchte seicht sein', in Christa Gürtler (ed.), *Gegen den schönen Schein. Texte zu Elfriede Jelinek* (Frankfurt am Main, 1990 [1983]), pp. 157–61; Elfriede Jelinek, 'I Want to Be Shallow. Translated by Jorn Bramann' (1997 [1983]), http://www.elfriedejelinek.com [Follow link 'Zum Theater'] [09.03.2012].

[238] See Jelinek, 'Ich möchte seicht sein'; Jelinek, 'I Want to Be Shallow'.

People shouldn't say things, and pretend they are living. [...] I don't want to bring to life strange people in front of an audience. [...] Actors tend to be false, while their audiences are genuine. For we, the audiences, are necessary, while actors are not. For this reason the people on stage can be vague, with blurred outlines.[239]

As a result, we encounter personnel on Jelinek's stages who give sometimes passionate, sometimes quite distanced accounts of the state of things in a compulsive, prompted way. The impression they make 'oscillates between irony, aggression and desire for a release not only from the real existing unfreedom of society, but also from sexuation as such'.[240] These are themes and aesthetic means we also find in Sarah Kane's work, most clearly in her later plays *4.48 Psychosis* (2001 [OP: 2000]) or *Crave* (2001 [OP: 1998]):

Crave is divided into four voices, identified only by the letters A, B, M and C. The voices speak without concrete context and there is only the most fragmentary hint of a narrative. [...] The effect of the piece when staged is surprisingly musical. The text demands attendance to its rhythms in performance, revealing its meanings not line by line, but, rather like a string quartet, in the hypnotic play of different voices and themes.[241]

Kane employs a music-aesthetic model (the string quartet), the effect of which Goethe (in relation to Beethoven) famously claimed to be 'as if four sensible people are having a conversation with each other',[242] except that the conversation in Kane's play is rather composed as a continuous tightrope walk between making sense and forming connections while disrupting and veiling them just as quickly.

Bernhard's musicality constructs a flipside to the opaque characters of Kane or Jelinek. His protagonists are over-characterized through constant (self-)reflection, expressed in the spiralling repetitions of their speech. Bernhard's musicality is in 'a particular relationship to interiority' in that it constitutes 'a mimesis of the speech act' and of 'psychological thought processes'.[243] In music, he finds a form to represent how his characters think and this portrays their 'penetratingly destructive reflection on their existence'.[244] Where Bernhard blurs his characters by a compulsive self-rendition in speech, Beckett leaves them characteristically under-developed:

---

[239] See Jelinek, 'I Want to Be Shallow'.

[240] Powell/Bethman, 'One must have tradition', p. 178.

[241] David Greig in Sarah Kane, *Complete Plays* (London, 2001), pp. xiii–xvi.

[242] Goethe in Christian Kaden/Volker Kalisch, 'Musik', in Karl-Heinz Brack (ed.), *Ästhetische Grundbegriffe* (Stuttgart/Weimar, 2005), pp. 256–308, p. 283.

[243] Klug, *Thomas Bernhards Theaterstücke*, p. 193.

[244] Herzog in Mittermayer, *Thomas Bernhard*, p. 187.

Many practitioners, for example, clearly relate the musical effect to Beckett's determination that his characters and their words or actions cannot be explained and that actors should avoid imposing an interpretation upon the words. [...] The use of musical terminology provides a directorial method which treats the characters, words, and stage directions as given, the only remaining question being the effective portrayal of their structural relationships.[245]

Musicality, rather than character portrayal and development, is the actor's task in Beckett's theatre.[246] Again, the subject on stage is not a pre-existing condition of the dramatic dialogue and plot, but a by-product of speech-acts held together by musical construction, repetition and contrast.

The critique of the modern or post-modern subject is particularly evident again in Heiner Müller's writing: Hans-Thies Lehmann speaks of 'polyphonic discourse' and 'a new model of epic theatre'[247] (a coinage by Andrzej Wirth) in relation to Müller's plays, making the theatre a '"speaking space" (Sprechraum)'[248] or a resonance chamber for 'sounding out' thoughts in addresses to an audience. Lehmann thus defines Müller's figures as 'speakers [...], who in the absence of an autonomous characterization have to be understood as "vehicles of a discourse"'.[249] As Kordes observes, Müller (and later also Heiner Goebbels) promotes an aesthetic of acting closer to what Michael Kirby calls 'not-acting':[250] 'the text is rather recited, exhibited as a foreign and alien material, than as part of the character'.[251] This also changes the actor's task, Kordes finds: 'Provided there are clearly outlined characters at all, the actors do not get to *be* their "roles"; a one-dimensional empathy with a "character" is also not made possible.'[252]

What I have tried to map in this chapter, then, is a range of different relationships and encounters between playwrights and musicality: as a poetic and philosophical notion, concrete condition and guidance for writing, metaphor for different dramaturgical approaches, and blueprint for new micro- and macrostructures of dramatic composition. Despite all the historical differences, varying national and linguistic characteristics and individual distinctions, there seem to be the common themes of a renunciation of the all-too-well-established dramatic models and an – often implicit – call for reform that pervades this musicality *dispositif*.

---

[245] Laws, 'The Music of Beckett's Theatre', pp. 121–2.

[246] Danijela Kulezic-Wilson writes: 'As Beckett's biographer James Knowlson (1996, 448) noted, "for him, pace, tone, and, above all, rhythm were more important than sharpness of character delineation or emotional depth"' ('From Musicalisation', p. 37).

[247] Hans-Thies Lehmann, *Postdramatic Theatre* (London/New York, 2006), p. 31.

[248] Lehmann, *Postdramatic Theatre*, p. 31.

[249] Lehmann, *Postdramatic Theatre*, p. 32.

[250] Michael Kirby, 'On Acting and Not-Acting', *The Drama Review*, 16/1 (1972), pp. 3–15.

[251] Lehmann in Kordes, *Musikalische Lesarten*, p. 130.

[252] Kordes, *Musikalische Lesarten*, p. 129.

While this chapter developed a strong emphasis on writers whose musicality has been influenced largely by Western classical music and *compositional* practices, there are, as I have hinted at with regard to Shepard or Goetz, other influences, particularly from popular genres such as gospel and jazz, rock or rap, which also foreground the importance of *improvisational* practices. In the following chapter I will explore this area further, focusing on the influence of improvisational techniques in theatre which are derived from or are related to music, and how some of these techniques have been incorporated into or adopted for processes of devising, writing or performing theatre.

Chapter 5
Theatre and Jazz

Introduction

There is a strong and vital relationship between theatre-making and popular music, despite the dominance of analogies to Western classical music ('symphony', 'orchestra', 'counterpoint', 'conductor') we have encountered so far. In this chapter I will explore this relationship further, paying particular attention to the role that 'jazz' and related concepts of improvisation have played for the processes and imaginations of theatre-makers. While the previous chapters have dealt with notions of musicality much less specifically attached to a genre or style other than being preoccupied with classical rather than 'popular' music, this chapter focuses on the influence of 'jazz' as a quite distinct *dispositif*. I will therefore develop this chapter from the discussion of jazz as an idiom, ideology and habitus, while analyzing its impact on selected practices in a second step.

Initially, I will tease out a few cornerstones of what might constitute 'jazz musicality'[1] and in particular examine jazz improvisation as a model for creating and/or performing theatre. This is followed by three case studies from different times and cultural contexts to analyze how jazz musicality is employed: first I will investigate the collaboration of playwright Sam Shepard and actor and director Joseph Chaikin in the 1970s, and then two more recent European projects: Thorsten Lensing and Jan Hein's German production *Der Lauf zum Meer* from 2009 and Bred in the Bone's British-Polish production of *Unreal City* (2006).

As Marshall Soules quite rightly attests, 'there are countless examples of theatre practitioners inspired by the organization, expressive goals, and discipline of the jazz ensemble'[2] and I will not attempt to make a comprehensive list.

---

[1]   Catherine Bouko, 'Jazz Musicality in Postdramatic Theatre and the Opacity of Auditory Signs', *Studies in Musical Theatre*, 4/1 (2010), pp. 75–87. While I like Bouko's term 'jazz musicality', her text has a quite different focus from what I am attempting with this chapter. Bouko's exploration is more reception-oriented and asks how meaning making works with regard to the musicality of performance. At the same time her approach seems a bit eclectic in terms of the musicological aspects, mixing models and metaphors from quite diverse musical idioms and backgrounds.

[2]   Marshall Soules, 'Improvising Character: Jazz, the Actor, and Protocols of Improvisation', in Daniel Fischlin/Ajay Heble (eds.), *The Other Side of Nowhere: Jazz, Improvisation, and Communities in Dialogue* (Middletown, CT, 2004), pp. 268–97, p. 284.

David Savran's seminal study *Highbrow/Lowdown: Theater, Jazz, and the Making of the New Middle Class* (2009) already demonstrates the strong mutual influences and sometimes dissolving boundaries between jazz and theatre, and focuses on the earliest forms of this interplay in the 1920s. Given the hybrid nature of popular performance (dance halls, musical comedy, vaudeville, etc.) at the time, as well as the increasingly performative nature of jazz music, Savran summarizes: 'theatre was jazz – and jazz was theatre.'[3] He paints a vivid picture of 'what F. Scott Fitzgerald dubbed the Jazz Age'[4] and gives an extensive account of the pervasive nature of jazz in theatrical performance, seen either as a model to aspire to or a perceived cultural downfall to be avoided at all costs. While a lot of the early examples of jazz musicality in theatre could be described as attempts to *integrate* jazz and theatre in an evening's entertainment[5] and to appeal to a different *zeitgeist* and audience than the 'legitimate' theatre,[6] there are some early but relatively singular examples of *experimental* fusions of theatre and jazz practices. Scott D. Paulin quotes Edmund Wilson's failed attempt in the 1920s to create a ballet called *Cronkhite's Clocks*, for example, which by his own account was 'written for Chaplin, a Negro comedian, and seventeen other characters, full orchestra, movie machine, typewriters, radio, phonograph, riveter, electromagnet, alarm clocks, telephone bells, and jazz band'.[7] Perhaps unsurprisingly, it never came to fruition. In contrast, Savran mentions the much-talked-about play *Processional* (1925) by John Howard Lawson, subtitled *A Jazz Symphony of American Life*, in which Lawson 'explicitly attempted to mimic, that is, find a theatrical analogy for, the form, spontaneity, and unruliness of jazz'.[8]

So, what might such a theatrical analogy look like? What are the characteristics, attitudes, techniques or working models that theatre has tried over time to incorporate from however it understood 'jazz' at the given moment?

Jazz Musicality and the Theatre

Jazz as Habitus

For the purpose of the following discussion, I have decided to focus on aspects of jazz as a musical practice that – despite being multi-faceted and historically

---

[3]   David Savran, *Highbrow/Lowdown: Theater, Jazz, and the Making of the New Middle Class* (Ann Arbor, 2009), p. 4.

[4]   Savran, *Highbrow/Lowdown*, p. 1.

[5]   See Richard Koszarski, *An Evening's Entertainment. The Age of the Silent Feature Picture, 1915–1928* (New York, 1990).

[6]   See Savran, *Highbrow/Lowdown*, p. 10.

[7]   Wilson in Scott D. Paulin, 'Chaplin and the Sandblaster: Edmund Wilson's Avant-Garde Noise Abatement', *American Music* (Fall 2010), pp. 265–96, p. 265.

[8]   Savran, *Highbrow/Lowdown*, p. 16.

and contextually highly contingent – can be associated with a number of key characteristics which have also featured most prominently in the analogies and appropriations proposed within the world of theatre. I am aware, however, that jazz is more than just a *musical* phenomenon. With reference to jazz's first heyday in the 1920s (it arguably never reached such widespread currency again), Savran asserts:

> For the producers and consumers of culture, jazz was a portal to a new world. It described and emblematized the most exhilarating and controversial ways of making music, love, poetry, race, and America.[9]

In a similar vein, jazz has been described as 'a reflection of broader cultural, political, social, and economic factors',[10] 'a form of communal bonding, ritual, and social interaction … a way of living in the world'[11] and a 'particular quality of social experience and relationship'.[12] Savran also emphasizes how pervasive the idea of jazz was across all performative arts:

> Given its many manifestations, guises, contexts, and performance venues, jazz thus represented the most significant form of cross-mediated performance in the 1920s: a form that undermined the autonomy of dance and concert music, cabaret, social dancing, vaudeville, revue, and narrative theatre. It was, in short, less a discrete style than a musical and social energy linking all these performance practices.[13]

This energy could take many forms: feelings of pride and belonging for ethnic minorities, shared political agendas of an anti-establishment America, national identification (jazz has often been referred to as the only true American art form), an artistic manifesto questioning hegemonies of Western art music, and a 'habitus' in Bourdieu's sense.[14]

It is this idea of jazz as a particular mind-set, disposition and 'praxis'[15] that I find particularly potent and widespread in relation to theatre. For some practitioners, this functions more as a metaphor or simile: an attitude to a performance situation or

---

[9]   Savran, *Highbrow/Lowdown*, p. 4.
[10]   Gary Giddins/Scott Deveaux, *Jazz* (New York, 2009), p. xi.
[11]   Savran, *Highbrow/Lowdown*, p. 25.
[12]   Raymond Williams in Savran, *Highbrow/Lowdown*, p. 10.
[13]   Savran, *Highbrow/Lowdown*, p. 16.
[14]   Pierre Bourdieu, *Outline of a Theory of Practice* (Cambridge, 1977).
[15]   Christopher McCullough proposes the term in this spelling in his book *Theatre Praxis* (London, 1998) as a cyclical interplay of theory and practice: 'The precise division between theory as a contemplative activity and practice as all action seems too crude a model. There is surely a form of action in theory in the form of verbal discourse, as there is contemplation and decision-making in practice' (p. 4).

a material they equate with jazz practices. Annemarie Matzke quotes Peter Brook, for example, who asked the actors of his *Midsummer Night's Dream* production to divide up a Shakespeare monologue into three canonical voices, repeating the lines at break-neck speed. He added: 'Take it like a jazz improvisation.'[16] Brook thus uses a range of *musical* instructions to enable and provoke the actors into breaking with certain habits of speaking Shakespeare, in order to arrive at a new tone, a new performative quality. The clue 'like a jazz improvisation' arguably only functions as shorthand here, however; a nudge towards an attitude more than an actual musical technique.

From a training perspective, Clive Barker, who has referred to his workshops as 'Theatre Jazz' also makes the connection at the level of a mind-set, a readiness, an 'access of constantly [being] there in the position of responding to whatever the other person does and not making statements and not blocking off'.[17] Dick McCaw expands on this metaphor in his introduction to the revised edition of Barker's seminal *Theatre Games* (1977/2010):

> The aim is to develop a sense of play within an ensemble, which, as Littlewood pointed out, is less like being an orchestral player under a conductor, and more like playing jazz which 'gives more scope for improvisation but it also requires more sensitivity to the other players. There is much more give and take'.[18]

Interactivity and sensitivity are also at the heart of the exercises which Joseph Chaikin referred to as 'jamming' and which he used in training, rehearsals and sometimes the performances of the Open Theater.[19] Here, I would argue, however, the analogy goes deeper: it is not just about adopting a certain 'habitus' derived from a certain understanding of jazz (which will have differed significantly from 1920 to 1970); rather, jamming seeks to activate jazz musicality as a psychophysical sensitivity and different cognitive practice in opposition to dominant actor training dogmas of the time (in particular: the 'Method') in order to transform the creative process.

Chaikin's practice, as we will see, taps into another aspect of the social energy or 'habitus' of jazz, which arises in the productive tension between the individual and the group. Jazz musicians are very concerned with finding their own voice, their signature, and their individuality as musicians, but almost always develop these qualities in the close interplay with groups of other musicians, who have

---

[16] In Annemarie Matzke, 'Der unmögliche Schauspieler: Theater-Improvisieren', in Hans-Friedrich Bormann, Gabriele Brandstetter/Annemarie Matzke (eds.), *Improvisieren. Paradoxien des Unvorhersehbaren. Kunst – Medien – Praxis* (Bielefeld, 2010), pp. 161–82, p. 177.

[17] Clive Barker, *Theatre Jazz. Workshop held at Warwick University, Spring 2003* (DVD documentation, Exeter Digital Archives, Drama Department, University of Exeter).

[18] McCaw in Barker, *Theatre Jazz*, p. xvii.

[19] See Chaikin 1972, pp. 116–17.

formative influence on the individual. With reference to Victor Turner, Soules speaks of the rise of 'normative communitas' in jazz, which 'seek to strike a balance between the human needs for individual expression and social integration'.[20] While being closely associated, as an artistic practice, with the idea of the ensemble, its discourse is at the same time unashamedly dominated by 'stars', which differ from rock stars or classical music stars. In classical music, it is predominantly the virtuoso *interpreter* who plays someone else's material; in rock, it is not usually the musical abilities that are foregrounded, but the rock star's persona.[21] In jazz, however, it is the combination of the musician as auteur, virtuoso interpreter, improviser and persona that creates the 'buzz'.

Jazz as habitus is riddled with paradoxical tensions (between individual and collective, being cerebral and deeply emotional, requiring preparation and spontaneity, between tradition and innovation, etc.) and can veer between being a vehicle for social acceptance – a sense of belonging to a certain community – and a 'symbol of rebellion',[22] so it is perhaps not surprising that the 'jazz *dispositif*' regains currency in the 1970s. Before analyzing Chaikin's seminal role in this revival and redefinition of the jazz-theatre connection, I will now explore jazz as a musical practice, establishing some fundamental characteristics[23] even though naturally some of them are historically contingent and exceptions can be found to each of them.

Jazz: Some Musical Characteristics

In the concluding chapter of his seminal *Jazzbuch*, Joachim Ernst Behrendt makes an attempt to come to terms with what he calls the 'Qualität Jazz' [the jazz quality]. He describes the main purpose of jazz as the 'production of intentional intensity [gestaltete Intensität]'.[24] If we add to this Paul F. Berliner's notion that jazz is the pursuit of 'expressive freedom in performance',[25] we can already see a shift from some of the ideas of musicality we have encountered in earlier chapters: there, it was often ideas of purity, structure, technical brilliance, sophistication, which theatre-makers aspired to.

---

[20] Soules, 'Improvising Character', p. 276.

[21] See Philip Auslander 'Musical Personae', *TDR: The Drama Review*, 50/1 (2006), pp. 100–119.

[22] Paul F. Berliner, *Thinking in Jazz* (Chicago/London, 1994) [Kindle edition], loc. 992.

[23] Behrendt; Berliner; Gabbard; Savran; Lock/Murray; Hauber, Jost/Wolbert and Giddins/DeVeaux have all provided excellent studies, which form a solid foundation for my inevitably cursory account, in which I consciously do not aim to provide an essentialist view on what jazz *is*, but what jazz stands for in relation to theatre practices that take inspiration from this art form.

[24] Joachim-Ernst Behrendt, *Das Jazzbuch* (Frankfurt am Main, 1989), p. 566.

[25] Berliner, *Thinking in Jazz*, loc. 911.

So, how do the ideas of intensity, expressivity and freedom manifest musically in jazz, and how might these translate onto the theatrical stage? I will look in particular at timbre and phrasing, rhythm, and aspects of training before investigating analogies with regard to improvisation.

Timbre and Phrasing

Giddins and DeVeaux interestingly start their list of characteristics of jazz music not with improvisation or rhythm, but with timbre: 'jazz musicians, much more than their classical counterparts, use timbre to attain stylistic individuality'.[26] Savran calls this 'timbral idiosyncrasies and distortions'.[27] Another element that guarantees individuality and signature style is the use of unique 'licks, motifs and riffs'.[28] In addition to timbre it is the combination of 'tone production and phrasing, in which the individuality of the performing jazz musician is reflected'[29] as well as 'microtonal inflections',[30] like the famous 'blue' notes,[31] which make players unique and recognizable. On the whole, it could be said that jazz pays particular attention to *sound*;[32] *how* to play is often considered more important than *what* to play (I will come back to this when addressing improvisation).

There is thus a clear ideological-aesthetical shift from classical demands of a pure, natural sound as an optimal vehicle for a composer's vision, to the uniqueness and expressiveness in jazz (both for instrumentalists and vocalists), where rough, uneducated, even damaged voices (Billie Holiday), failing intonation and unpolished onset (Miles Davis), jarring, angular phrasings (Dexter Gordon) are celebrated for making a performer stand out.

In theatre, I would argue, we have seen a comparable shift from the ideal of the actor as an extremely versatile instrument with perfect diction and projection in the service of a playwright and director, to a more co-creative 'auteur' of theatrical performances, unafraid to make their idiosyncrasies (even what used to be considered as deficiencies) a defining part of their performances: an unusual physique, for example (Josef Ostendorf, Viviane de Muynck), a unique vocal timbre or even vocal dysfunction (Sophie Rois, Einar Schleef), a detectable dialect or accent (Josef Bierbichler, Graham F. Valentine).[33]

---

[26] Giddins/DeVeaux, *Jazz*, p. 3.

[27] Savran, *Highbrow/Lowdown*, p. 24.

[28] Giddins/DeVeaux, *Jazz*, p. 23.

[29] Behrendt, *Jazzbuch*, p. 564.

[30] Savran, *Highbrow/Lowdown*, p. 24.

[31] These fall somewhere between the minor and major third, around the flatted fifth and the minor seven of a diatonic scale.

[32] I would argue that this is actually true for most popular music genres, which are by and large comparatively simple in terms of rhythm, harmony and melody, but invest a lot of innovative energy and pay great attention to individual and collective sound, whether it is through playing/singing techniques, recording methods and technologies or arrangement.

[33] See also Patrick Primavesi, 'Geräusch, Apparat, Landschaft: Die Stimme auf der Bühne als theatraler Prozeß', *Forum Modernes Theater*, 14/2 (1999), pp. 144–72;

Rhythm[34]
Jazz is further characterized by its rhythmicity; it is 'distinguished from classical music by a particular relationship to time, marked by the word *swing*'.[35] A strong presence of a manifest pulse and equally strong deviations from it are vital elements of jazz, expressed in particular by the layering of rhythms and by syncopation:[36] 'in most classical music, syncopation is an occasional rhythmic disruption, temporary "special effect" injected for variety. In jazz, syncopation is not an effect – it is the very air jazz breathes.'[37]

In theatre this might correspond to a departure from principles of fluency, elegance and measure in speech and movement (as we find them put forward from Greek tragedy to Shakespeare, Goethe or Racine) toward disjointed prose, insistent repetition and syncopated rhythms of sentences or gestures. We have seen examples of this in Gertrude Stein's or Enda Walsh's writing (see Chapter 4) and it is also particularly tangible in Sam Shepard's writing, as we will see below.

Processes of Training and Production
There are a few things that distinguish the creative processes of jazz from other genres of music: first there are, according to Behrendt, the 'spontaneity and vitality of musical production, in which improvisation plays a part'.[38] Also, jazz reminds us, as Derek Bailey puts it, that 'performing music and creating music are not necessarily separate activities'.[39] As a predominantly oral culture, jazz does not separate the 'work' from its performance in written form and for a long time did not tend to entertain a teaching culture based on written course-books, études, or theoretical treatises. It is an art mainly passed on aurally and orally.[40] Until recently there was hardly any formal training available, and young musicians learnt through imitation and through playing with others.[41]

As a consequence, jazz shifts the artistic focus towards the performer and away from the composer or conductor (with exceptions like Duke Ellington or Glenn Miller). In addition, there is clearly an emphasis on the collective in jazz,

Doris Kolesch/Jenny Schrödel (eds.), *Kunst-Stimmen* (Berlin, 2004); Mareike Hölker, *Vom Sinn zur Sinnlichkeit* (Diplomarbeit, University of Hildesheim, 2005).

[34] See also the section on rhythm in Meyerhold's theatre in Chapter 2.

[35] Behrendt, *Jazzbuch*, p. 564.

[36] 'Syncopation is a general term for a disturbance or interruption of the regular flow of rhythm: a placement of rhythmic stresses or accents where they wouldn't normally occur' (http://en.wikipedia.org/wiki/Syncopation [26.04.2012]).

[37] Giddins/DeVeaux, *Jazz*, p. 14.

[38] Behrendt, *Jazzbuch*, p. 564.

[39] Derek Bailey, *Improvisation, Its Nature and Practice in Music* (Ashbourne, Derbyshire, 1980), p. 64.

[40] See Berliner, *Thinking in Jazz*, loc. 873.

[41] Berliner calls this an 'environmental' music education (*Thinking in Jazz*, loc. 746) and also talks about the vital role the local churches played in this, providing continuous opportunity and demand for musicians to accompany the services (see ibid., loc. 873).

a focus on ensemble performance and a range of practices for generating material together as opposed to notions of single authorship or a piece of work that precedes performance and its subsequent interpretation. This implies a different approach to 'material': Shepard, who refers to jazz as a strong influence on his writing, uses the word 'collage' frequently; together with Gershwin's coinage of jazz an 'aural melting pot',[42] this demarcates two ends of a spectrum: jazz is a heteroglossic language in Bakhtin's sense,[43] where different ideas, styles, musical origins and traditions are assembled, at times remaining distinct and recognizable and at other times merging (or 'melting') into something new and unprecedented.

These ideas correspond to certain developments in the theatre: the improv theatre and 'Theatresports' movements of The Second City[44] or Keith Johnstone[45] with their emphasis on the 'spontaneity and vitality' of theatre performance, the interactive role of the audience and the focus on the performer[46] is the most obvious example and R. Keith Sawyer explores this similarity in detail.[47] But also the experimental, environmental and devised theatre of the 1960s–1970s or the postdramatic theatre from the 1980s onwards[48] are – more or less explicitly – influenced by jazz. Like jazz, they often reject the hegemony of the written 'work' and foreground the collaborative and ephemeral aspects of performance, while using the art form as a vehicle for social commentary. The *effect* of jazz – as it enters the musical arena changing modes of training, performing, listening, distribution and criticism – has been transformative in a way not too dissimilar

---

[42]   In Dorothy Chansky, 'Drama', in David J. Nordloh (ed.), *American Literary Scholarship, an Annual, 2006* (Durham and London, 2008), pp. 421–51, p. 450.

[43]   See also Chapter 2.

[44]   See http://www.secondcity.com/ [27.04.2012].

[45]   See http://www.keithjohnstone.com/ [27.04.2012].

[46]   Chaikin's idea of the 'Creative Actor', for example, reemphasizes the generative importance of the actor and performer over the dominance of the writer and/or director. See Dorinda Hulton, 'Joseph Chaikin and Aspects of Actor Training: Possibilities Rendered Present', in Alison Hodge (ed.), *Actor Training. Second Edition* (London, 2010), pp. 164–83, p. 169.

[47]   R. Keith Sawyer, *Group Creativity. Music, Theater, Collaboration* (Mahwah, NJ/ London, 2007 [2003]) [Kindle edition]. The parallel to improv theatre is interesting in that it operates – like jazz – with strong frames, such as rules of the game, defined parameters, suggestions by the audience, etc., all of which limit and focus the improvisational activity to a certain extent, not unlike standards or stock chord changes (Blues, Rhythm Changes, II, V, I, etc.) limit and focus the jazz musician's improvisation.

[48]   I am not suggesting very clear boundaries between these labels; there are certainly significant overlaps in terms of personnel, aesthetics, modes of production, ideologies between all these forms, with 'devising' being the more common term in the Anglo-American discourse, and 'postdramatic' having stronger central European currency. See Heddon/Milling, *Devising Performance. A Critical History* (Basingstoke, 2006) and Hans-Thies Lehmann, *Postdramatic Theatre* (London, 2006).

(if larger in scale and impact) to the advent of improv theatre, devised theatre, performance art, etc., on the theatrical stage.

It is worth noting that all this clearly contrasts with other concepts of musicality we have encountered so far. While all these concepts are connected by a reformatory impulse, a desire to change and overcome conventions of theatre prevalent at their respective times, we have seen that for Appia, for example, musicality meant elevating the director to a central position, preserving the dramatic author's intentions against the caprice of the actor and disciplining the latter, making performances more precise and repeatable. Now the musical practices and the habitus of jazz are invoked to liberate and stimulate the actor and to make performances unpredictable and unique. What theatre-makers have sought to adopt in the course of this development in particular, is an understanding of improvisation as a *musical* practice. And while musical improvisation has existed for centuries and in many different cultures, the praxis developed in jazz proved the most influential in Western theatre.[49] What are the characteristics of jazz improvisation that have left the clearest marks on this particular musicality *dispositif*?

Theatrical Improvisation as a Musical Practice

I should begin with a clarification: if we accept Bailey's distinction of idiomatic and non-idiomatic improvisation,[50] then I am focusing on the much more common form of idiomatic improvisation throughout this chapter:

> Idiomatic improvisation [...] is mainly concerned with the expression of an idiom – such as jazz, flamenco or baroque – and takes its identity and motivation from that idiom. Non-idiomatic improvisation [...] is most usually found in so-called 'free' improvisation.[51]

My main premise for this section is that jazz inspired a *different* or *additional kind* of theatrical improvisation practice than other forms or traditions of improvisation. I describe this as a shift of emphasis from a mainly narrative model of inventing stories, situations, puns and dialogue[52] – or what one could call 'what' improvisation – to 'how' improvisation: playing with form, musical qualities, pure expression.

---

[49]   'While improvisation has deep roots in the dramatic practices of the world, there has been a resurgence of interest in the European and North American contexts in the twentieth century, during which it developed in close juxtaposition to jazz' (Soules, 'Improvising Character', p. 284).

[50]   Bailey, *Improvisation*, p. 4.

[51]   Bailey, *Improvisation*, p. 4.

[52]   This can be found from the commedia dell'arte to improv theatre.

Most models of *musical* improvisation are based on more or less firm premises: a theme, a chord schema, a basic rhythmic pattern or even a complex set of instructions. While there is of course an interest in *what* the performer comes up with, it is usually matched by at least as strong an interest in *how* they are going to treat the material, engage with the premises, the 'protocols'[53] of the improvisation. Soules describes one way in which 'improvised music and improvised acting as performative practices'[54] intersect:

> In a seeming paradox which threatens to erase the traces of identity, improvisation thrives when the performance of character is given latitude of expression within the framework of the ensemble. Michael Chekhov, renowned Russian actor and teacher confirms the legitimacy of this approach for the actor: '... every role offers an actor the opportunity to improvise, to collaborate and truly co-create with the author and director. This suggestion, of course, does not imply improvising new lines or substituting business for that outlined by the director. On the contrary. The given lines and the business are the firm bases upon which the actor must and can develop his improvisations. *How* he speaks the lines and *how* he fulfills the business are the open gates to a vast field of improvisation. The "hows" of his lines and business are the ways in which he can express himself freely.'[55]

Daniel Belgrad's description of jazz improvisation makes the analogy even more apparent:

> Improvising jazz solos does not consist mainly in inventing new links, but in stringing together learned links and references in new and appropriate combinations – just as new usages and phrasings are a greater part of the poet's work than coining neologisms is.[56]

Jazz improvisation, then, provides a model of improvisation that does not foreground 'the spontaneous invention of performance',[57] but that combines aspects of innovation and invention firmly with practices of collage, montage and assemblage. It is, as Wynton Marsalis calls it, 'a very structured thing',[58] which plays with the tension between a strong sense of form, tradition and legacy and the desire and demand for freedom and inspiration. This also means that the

---

[53]   Soules, 'Improvising Character', p. 270.
[54]   Soules, 'Improvising Character', p. 269.
[55]   Soules, 'Improvising Character', p. 269, my emphasis.
[56]   Daniel Belgrad, *The Culture of Spontaneity. Improvisation and the Arts in Postwar America* (Chicago/London, 1998), p. 180.
[57]   Paul Allain/Jen Harvie, *The Routledge Companion to Theatre and Performance* (London, 2006), p. 161.
[58]   In Berliner, *Thinking in Jazz*, loc. 1599.

seeming opposition between composition and improvisation is problematic: the two generative practices are connected and form a continuum of praxis:[59] 'One the one hand: composing is no creatio ex nihilo. On the other: improvising isn't an act of God.'[60]

So what is the most common practice of jazz improvisation, what are its protocols? Usually, it means playing a well-known melody ('standard') over a chord progression and then taking turns to improvise over these so-called 'changes', using the harmonies as both grounding and leaping off points for paraphrasing and ornamenting the melody of the song, melodic and rhythmic inventions, citations and prepared riffs.[61] These are, as Soules remarks, the 'voluntary guidelines used by performers [...] to ground the play of creativity within a matrix of constraints'.[62] He adds: 'Improvisation for performance – both in jazz music and otherwise – is not typified by unrestrained freedom, though it does provide unique expressive opportunities for individual performers within the ensemble.'[63]

There are additional criteria that distinguish jazz improvisation from, say, speaking *ex tempore* in theatre. Jazz improvisation is generally a collective endeavour,[64] even when there is a clear distinction between a soloist and their accompaniment, since even those who accompany improvise. The band usually seeks to strike a balance between fulfilling the harmonic and rhythmic functions that establish and maintain the chorus while also playing inventively

---

[59] See Ronald Kurt, 'Komposition und Improvisation als Grundbegriffe einer allgemeinen Handlungstheorie', in Ronald Kurt/Klaus Näumann (eds.), *Menschliches Handeln als Improvisation* (Bielefeld, 2008), pp. 17–46, p. 25. In this continuum, we also find what Bormann, Brandstetter and Matzke call the 'effect of spontaneity' or the 'perfect simulation of spontaneity, the strategic control of the non-premeditated' (Bormann/Brandstetter/Matzke, *Improvisieren*, p. 7). In the paradox of rehearsing the spontaneous, in preparing for the ad hoc, Matzke describes tendencies to use improvisation as 'an impression of immediacy' (Matzke, 'Der unmögliche Schauspieler', p. 169) or 'a mediated immediacy' (ibid., p. 181).

[60] Kurt, 'Komposition und Improvisation', p. 26. See also David Davies's chapter 'The Nature of Improvisation' in his *Philosophies of the Performing Arts* (Malden, MA/ Oxford, 2011), pp. 150–64.

[61] See Berliner, *Thinking in Jazz*, loc. 1606 and also the relevant section in Chapter 2 on the analogy between improvisation in jazz and commedia dell'arte given the use of prepared routines, 'business' and stock phrases in the latter. It is worth noting that a lot of these so-called 'standards' originally came from the music-theatre repertoire – 'a repertory of popular songs, often from Broadway musicals' (Bruno Nettl et al., 'Improvisation', in Stanley Sadie (ed.), *New Grove Dictionary of Music and Musicians, 2nd edition, Vol. 12* (London, 2001), pp. 96–133, p. 96). As melodies, they were designed not merely for musical but also dramatic effect, to characterize a situation and its protagonist.

[62] Soules, 'Improvising Character', p. 270.

[63] Soules, 'Improvising Character', p. 271.

[64] This also distinguishes it largely from classical improvisation, which is more commonly a solo activity (organ or piano improvisations for example).

and imaginatively within the constraints of the 'changes' and responding to the changing melodic patterns, rhythmic structures, and intensity of the soloist. This aspect of the collective and the interactive has been captured (and sometimes glorified) with one word: jamming:

> The term *jamming* was first used by jazz musicians; a 'jam session' is an impromptu gathering of musicians with the purpose of improvising together. The term has a positive connotation; when a performance goes particularly well, the musicians might say 'we were really jamming tonight'. In the last several decades, the term has been widely used outside of jazz to describe any free-flowing creative group interaction [...].[65]

There are two further aspects of jamming that have formed part of its attraction to theatre practitioners: the fact that it is a mode of both training *and* performance and that its interactive quality includes the audience, who have a stronger impact on a jazz performance and more interactive agency than in, say, a classical concert:

> Like a vaudeville and musical comedy, in which it was regularly featured, jazz is a partly improvisatory practice that happens in the space between performer and spectator. A jazz solo, a song, or a piece of shtick is a virtuoso turn whose effectiveness is dependent upon the skill and inspiration of the performer, who, if the chemistry is right, will be encouraged and egged on by the audience's spontaneous and often raucous participation.[66]

This is also, as Sawyer describes, one of the main aspects to become a hallmark of improv theatre, where audience participation is often quite welcome and direct, setting the scene or defining the protocol for individual games, seeking to challenge the performers.

Challenging actors to abandon creative behaviour that had become routine and seeking to develop as performers and, importantly, as a group, was also at the heart of Chaikin's use of 'jamming' in his Open Theater. He sought to integrate improvisation into training, creation and performance, not just as a technique, but, in Frost and Yarrow's words, as a 'dynamic principle operating in many different spheres; an independent and transformative way of being and doing'.[67] Chaikin's exercises sought to foster the close attunement between improvising actors,[68] to enhance their ability to closely absorb and listen to what others are doing while at the same time responding or proposing creatively towards an overall performance

---

[65]   Sawyer, *Thinking in Jazz*, loc. 122.
[66]   Savran, *Highbrow/Lowdown*, p. 15.
[67]   Anthony Frost/Ralph Yarrow, *Improvisation in Drama* (London, 1990), p. 13.
[68]   See also Sawyer, *Group Creativity*, loc. 938.

which is constantly shifting.[69] Sawyer calls this an 'interactional synchrony'.[70] By using a strong sense of musicality for the exercises and improvisations through working on tempo, excessive repetition, gradual variation, rhythmic and 'melodic' qualities of vocal and physical expression, Chaikin sought to overcome the performers' habits of planning, intention and interpretation, and tap into a more intuitive and immediate physical reaction to stimuli, creating what Belgrad calls a 'poetics of presence'.[71] One of the members of the Open Theatre, Peter Feldman, sums this up as follows: 'to let the body do the thinking rather than to work it with the mind'.[72] This forms an important part in Chaikin's 'fundamental interest […] to heighten the sense that living people are sharing immediate fleeting moments – to emphasize presence'.[73] The musically informed exercises (and performance strategies) are designed to strengthen the sense of the 'here and now' of performance and the agency of the performer.[74] Improvisation requires both a particularly strong 'interactional synchrony' of the performers, and it highlights the ephemeral nature of music and performance: no 'work' precedes or survives the performance itself, or as Bailey puts it:

> Improvisation is completely unconcerned with any preparatory or residual document and is completely at one with the non-documentary nature of musical performance. Their shared ephemerality gives them a unique compatibility. So it might be claimed that improvisation is best pursued through its practice in music. And that the practice of music is best pursued through improvisation.[75]

Musical improvisation also opens up new dramaturgies and aesthetical perspectives for the theatre. Peter Feldman, a core member of the Open Theatre, when asked about the aims and consequences of this approach, highlights its tendency towards the non-naturalistic:

---

[69]   That is a notably different premise and/or aim to what the analogy of the orchestra and the classical concert conjures up, as we have encountered it before: there, we have a predetermined text and an institutionally established main interpreter, the conductor, here a situation in which a group of people follow a continuously changing goal, which they determine together in an emergent process (see also David Roesner, 'Musicking as *Mise en scène*', *Studies in Musical Theatre*, 4/1 [2010], pp. 89–102, on the question of emergence in performance).

[70]   Sawyer, *Group Creativity*, loc. 942.

[71]   Belgrad, *Culture of Spontaneity*, p. 218.

[72]   Peter Feldman, 'The Sound and Movement Exercise as Developed by the Open Theatre. An Interview with Peter Hulton', *Theatre Papers*, 1/1 (1977), pp. 1–14, p. 13.

[73]   Eileen Blumenthal, *Joseph Chaikin: Exploring at the Boundaries of Theater* (Cambridge, 1984), p. 71.

[74]   With respect to improvisation for musicians, Bailey attests: 'It exists because it meets the creative appetite that is a natural part of being a performing musician and because it involves him completely, as nothing else can, in the act of music-making' (*Improvisation*, p. 153).

[75]   Bailey, *Improvisation*, p. 153.

> I think that rhythm is one of the things you have to come to if you want to break
> down naturalism, which tends to be a-rhythmical. It is certainly one of the things
> you have to have if you want a group operating together as a group because
> otherwise you have just got chaos. […] When you begin to work on rhythm, you
> immediately begin to move away from everyday behaviour, because that behaviour
> is not rhythmical, not rhythmical in a directed semi-ritualised sense anyway.[76]

Using musicality as a vehicle towards a non-naturalistic aesthetics does not,
however, mean the abandonment of character, but provides a different approach:

> Both jazz and improv acting are procedural systems which challenge restricting
> constructions of character; both seek to open up character to greater expressive
> potential, wider freedoms and responsibilities. Improvised jazz and acting
> both refashion character to provide alternate models of human aspiration
> and interaction.[77]

Jazz improvisation as a model for drama embraces an understanding of character
as a much more fluid and layered self, contingent on the interaction between the
individual and the group or society. In Chaikin's theatre practice this could mean
that character derives much less from a scripted pre-text than from processes of
jazz-like improvisation, but even when there is a strong presence of a writer, like
Sam Shepard, in the process, the jazz influence leaves its imprint: David DeRose
describes how in the mid-1970s Shepard began 'collaborating with a small group
of local musicians and actors'[78] on 'ways in which "character development" might
evolve directly from music and sound'.[79] This led to his often-cited 'Note to the
Actors' preceding his play *Angel City*, premiered and published in 1976:

> The term 'character' could be thought of in a different way when working on
> this play. Instead of 'whole character' with logical motives behind his behaviour
> which the actor submerges himself into, he should consider instead a fractured
> whole with bits and pieces of character flying off the central theme. In other
> words, more in terms of collage construction or jazz improvisation.[80]

Shepard encourages embracing the fractured, assembled and 'unfinalizable'[81]
nature of 'character' through the notion of jazz improvisation. Character is no
longer an entity, but a range of potentialities. What is remarkable is that the process

---

[76]   Feldman, 'The Sound', p. 10.
[77]   Soules, 'Improvising Character', p. 284.
[78]   David J. DeRose, 'Sam Shepard as musical experimenter', in Matthew Roudané
(ed.), *The Cambridge Companion to Sam Shepard* (Cambridge, 2002), pp. 227–46, p. 234.
[79]   Shepard in DeRose, 'Sam Shepard', p. 234.
[80]   Shepard in DeRose, 'Sam Shepard', p. 239.
[81]   Mikhail Bakhtin, *Problems of Dostoevsky's Poetics* (Minneapolis, MN, 1984), p. 61.

of performing does not mean having to decide on one or the other, to finalize an interpretation, but to keep all options open, to keep presenting different, even contradicting aspects and layers of the dramatic personnel.

From an audience perspective the jazz analogy also stimulates a shift in perception; James Dennen distinguishes between two modes of listening, which improvised music *necessarily* combines (in contrast to other music): there is 'object-centered listening', for which 'the material sound [...] provides the substance from which a listener will derive any affect, will "feel," take an emotional journey, find a "story," etc.'[82] In jazz and other improvised music, however, the listener will also get involved in 'subject-centered listening', in which he/she 'is concerned with John Coltrane the musician, the saxophonist, the virtuoso, the brilliant improviser, the genius, the legend'.[83] In order to appreciate the music as improvised, as an expression of the musician there and then, the listener keeps the performer present. Transferred to the theatre, this stands in clear opposition to those philosophies of performance in music and theatre where the performer is meant to vanish behind the object (of the score, the text, the character, the work).[84]

All this is not merely a different performative paradigm, but what we might call – quoting Adorno's famous reference to music – a 'form of social mediation'.[85] Musicologist Christian Kaden summarizes the aesthetic and ethical position of improvisation as the difference between an attitude of 'so, und nicht anders' [like this, and only like this], which is characteristic of music that is composed and notated in detail, and an attitude of 'so, und auch anders' [like this, and also different to this].[86] It is an ethics that questions individual authorship, that strives for emergence in collective creativity, that undermines categories of highbrow and lowbrow culture and that embraces the unfinished, contradictory, potential and ephemeral. In comparing literature and jazz in the 1950s Belgrad observes: 'beat poetry and bebop jazz shared a common cultural project: to oppose the culture of corporate liberalism with the spontaneous prosody embodying the tenets of intersubjectivity and body mind holism'.[87]

Jazz theatricality as a 'form of social mediation' runs through the three following case studies. Continuing the already started discussion of Chaikin, the Open Theatre and Shepard will act as my first, more extensive case study,

---

[82]   James Dennen, 'On Reception of Improvised Music', *TDR: The Drama Review*, 53/4 (2009), pp. 139–49, p. 139.

[83]   Dennen, 'On Reception of Improvised Music', p. 140.

[84]   See Davies, *Philosophies of the Performing Arts*, pp. 112–20.

[85]   Adorno in Savran, *Highbrow/Lowdown*, p. 7.

[86]   Klaus Näumann, 'Improvisation: Über ihren Gebrauch und ihre Funktion in der Geschichte des Jazz', in Kurt/Näumann, *Menschliches Handeln*, pp. 133–58, p. 134.

[87]   Belgrad, *Culture of Spontaneity*, p. 197. I am fully aware that both beat poetry and the corresponding cultural project of a jazz musicality in theatre are naturally based at least in part on a range of idealizations and glorifications of jazz, improvisation and the idea of collective, holistic, freely expressive art. But it is not my intention to correct the image of jazz that inspired theatre-makers, but to look at some of the fruit this *dispositif* bore.

followed by two more contemporary ensembles and productions, which will form both a contrast and extension of the close relationship of theatre and jazz formed in the 1920s and 1930s and revitalized in the 1970s. They will also take us into the realm of the contemporary, which I will explore in the final chapter.

Case Studies

Joseph Chaikin, Sam Shepard and The Open Theatre[88]

The Open Theater was not only 'the first well-known American group to explore collaborative creation'[89] but arguably also the first experimental theatre company to employ ideas of a jazz musicality so explicitly in their creation and performance processes. Although Chaikin frequently expressed his affinity to music ('the musical dimension is always important to me'[90]) – particularly to improvised music and jazz – it seems to me that in his case the musicality is less manifestly reflected, postulated and theorized in his writings than contained strongly in his practice. In particular, we find musicality at the heart of many of the exercises and training of the Open Theater, their scenic experiments of confronting musical improvisation and improvised acting,[91] as well as in Chaikin's collaborations with Sam Shepard, in which the interplay between music and story is inextricably linked to the process of script development (as we will see in more detail later).

Both for the training and development processes and the culture of performance, musicality became one key 'system of perception';[92] a disposition with particular perceptive, somatic and cognitive potential.[93] Chaikin says: 'Each man-made object which we see carries within it a recommendation to be seen within a given

---

[88]   Thanks to Stephen Bottoms and Jerri Daboo, who pointed me to Shepard and Chaikin in the first place.

[89]   Hulton, 'Joseph Chaikin', p. 167.

[90]   Chaikin cit. in Lois Oppenheim, *Directing Beckett* (Ann Arbor, 1997), p. 126.

[91]   Eileen Blumenthal, in evaluating the Open Theater's and the subsequent Winter Project's work, describes how in their explorations actors and musicians influenced and inspired each other: sometimes the actors used the sounds and rhythms produced by the musicians to 'find an emotional state', sometimes the musicians took their cues from noises, sounds and gestures the actors made incorporating them in their compositions (see Blumenthal, *Joseph Chaikin*, p. 97). And further: 'Chaikin even explored how speech can harness the expanded sound possibilities of various instruments. In one Winter Project session, an actor tried to speak through a French horn, keeping his words comprehensible while taking on the horn's resonance' (ibid.).

[92]   Joseph Chaikin, *The Presence of the Actor* (New York, 1972), p. 128.

[93]   See also my Introduction.

system of perception.'[94] What we find in the context of the musicality *dispositif* is that systems of perception are playfully and productively brought into conflict: a 'man-made object' may say: 'I am a play, but perhaps you should read me like a musical score.' Chaikin talks about this kind of transference of systems of perception, given the following example: 'In the song, "Good Vibrations," sung by the Beach Boys, they move from one to another to another realm and key within the song. Structurally, this is clearer to understand in music, but it is no less present in acting.'[95] I would argue that significant aspects of the Open Theatre's developmental work are based on shifts like these – improvising with theatrical gesture and vocal sound within the system of perception of jazz.

Exercises and Processes: from 'Chord' to 'Jamming'
The Open Theater worked with a range of exercises that sought to liberate the performers from pre-conceived ideas of 'acting', enhance their presence in the here and now, and foster a strong lateral awareness to support collaborative working methods and ensemble performance. Jazz musicality provided the vehicle towards these aims and shaped a range of exercises, such as the 'chord', 'sound-and movement' and 'jamming'.

For the 'chord', for example, the ensemble would get together an create 'drones, hums, vowel sounds, and even movement, all the actors adjusting to the ensemble so that their gestures formed a single, organic shape'.[96] Already, the musicality embedded here is one of complementarity: it was not about synchronizing or imitating sounds, but finding a range of expression to form an 'organic shape'. That in itself may not seem to be a terribly clear aim, but I would argue that part of the exercise was precisely to define, as a group and through practice, what they would agree to be 'organic'. Jazz ensembles have often found their 'sound' – a matrix of timbre, texture, improvisational freedom and restraint, key harmonic and rhythmic decisions – in a very similar way.

The sound-and-movement exercises,[97] which were not merely a means to an end, but also became a performative strategy that made its way into some of the productions of the Open Theater, emphasize another aspect of jazz musicality: an improvisatory practice based on the imitation and instant transformation

---

[94] Chaikin, *The Presence*, p. 128. This also resonates strongly with the kind of intermediality I referred to in Chapter 4 by quoting Christopher Balme's formula 'the attempt to realize in one medium the aesthetic conventions and habits of seeing and hearing in another medium' (Christopher Balme, 'Intermediality: Rethinking the Relationship between Theatre and Media' [Online], http://epub.ub.uni-muenchen.de/13098/1/Balme_13098.pdf [11.06.2013], p. 7).

[95] Chaikin, *The Presence*, p. 128.

[96] Blumenthal, *Joseph Chaikin*, p. 74.

[97] Robert Pasolli describes the sound and movement exercises as formative for the aesthetic of the Open Theatre (*A Book on the Open Theatre* [New York, 1970], p. 5), claiming they became 'the Open Theater's basic unit of expression' (ibid., p. 20).

of themes, rhythms or motifs. In jazz, improvisation did not emerge from free invention, but started from embellishing and ornamenting popular melodies. Repeating, transforming and adding were the main principles. These are also at the heart of the sound-and-movement exercises:

> One actor would begin a simple, repeatable gesture using both body and voice, not selecting in advance what the action should express, but playing with it until it touched on a clear condition; that actor then approached a second, who tried to copy the forms exactly, thereby being led to their emotional content; the second then altered them and transferred a new sound and movement to a third actor, and so forth. Using kinetic impulses to locate inner states, actors were able to discover emotions that have not been in the experience before.[98]

There is also a sense, I would argue, analogous to jazz, of exploring something simple – a note, a sound, a gesture – from a range of angles: investigating it rhythmically, harmonically, with respect to sound and timbre, intensity, etc. Berliner quotes an example in his impressive ethnographic study *Thinking in Jazz* (1994):

> [...] during an interview with a young drummer, a soft background recording featured flugelhornist Wilbur Hardin, who was generating tremendous excitement with a stream of single-pitched rhythmic patterns at his solo's opening. Carrying on the tradition of soloists like Louis Armstrong who could also create great variety in this manner, Hardin manipulated timbre and articulation subtleties to form different rhythmic groupings, in effect superimposing varied metric schemes upon that of the piece. The drummer suddenly burst out laughing and, with an apology for his distraction, added: 'Did you hear that? That's what our music's about. Listen to all that brother can say with one note!'[99]

The drummer's excitement is generated by an inventive and daring exploration of musical form, while playing within chosen limitations – in this case restricting yourself to a single pitch. Playing with *form*, one could say, can thus generate emotion – whereas conventionally the emotion often precedes a musical form yet to be found. With respect to the Open Theater Blumenthal describes this as a reversal of conventional acting techniques:

> In contrast to Method techniques, which rely on actors' emotional engagement with a condition to generate its physical form, sound and movement was an attempt to work from the outside in.[100]

---

[98]   Blumenthal, *Joseph Chaikin*, p. 83.
[99]   Berliner, *Thinking in Jazz*, loc. 3476–94.
[100] Blumenthal, *Joseph Chaikin*, p. 83.

Another important aspect and result of the sound-and-movement exercises is how they de-emphasize discursive meaning or interpretation of dramatic dialogue as main drivers of theatre:

> Chaikin has explored both how music works in the theater and how theater can enter the less literal, less literary realms that music addresses. A part of this study […] has been simply examining nonlinguistic dimensions of sound.[101]

It is a kind of exercise which is aimed at 'tuning in' to someone else's expression and then offering transformations, variations and developments, which works without the need to explain, rationalize or verbally conceptualize this process.[102] It is a kind miniature embodied oral history, a passing on and incorporating not of texts, but of renditions of pre-texts. Jazz, in contrast to other, more notation-based forms of music, is quite similar in this sense: tunes and modes of playing (but also dress-codes, postures, attitudes, habitus, etc.) are passed on in this kind of way. Many jazz musicians learned to play by copying other artists at first, learning their soli note by note, until they were skilled enough to introduce their own take on the material.

More consciously than in jazz, I would argue, the sound-and-movement exercise also explores the relationship of sound and gesture, aural and visual, within the musical parameters of improvising, finding variations and 'riffing' on certain motifs. By continuously putting vocal or percussive sounds and gestures and movements in relation, and exploring unconventional, non-semantic relations between them, Chaikin's exercises transfer principles from jazz onto the expressive codes of the acting body, seeking to reestablish 'two interrelated dialogues', as Dorinda Hulton describes: 'the first between the "inside" and the "outside", and the second between the body and the mind'.[103]

'Jamming', as we have already seen, presents a next stage up from the still relatively regulated process of 'sound-and-movement', taking the same principles into a freer form:

> Using all kind of vocal sounds, including hisses, clicks, huffs, syllables, and words, actors improvised a musical piece; or using various types of movement, they created a group dance. Jamming was then extended to sentences: While one person said a line straight, another took off from it, making echoes and reverberations; an actor could also jam (or scat) alone, either starting with

---

[101] Blumenthal, *Joseph Chaikin*, p. 96.

[102] It is perhaps amusing to note in this context, that while actors resort to non-linguistic explorations of sound and movement inspired by jazz, jazz musicians frequently employ metaphors of language and story-telling in reflecting on their improvisation practice (see the chapter 'Composing in the moment: The inner dialogue and the tale', in Berliner, *Thinking in Jazz*, loc. 4518–5195).

[103] Hulton, 'Joseph Chaikin', p. 173.

sounds and words and building to a comprehensible line, or beginning with the whole phrase and then, as in a musical development, improvising with its elements. [...] Chaikin felt that this exercise should help sensitise actors to the progressive line and texture of any performance piece. He told the Open Theatre before a run-through of *Nightwalk*: 'Rhythms, jamming [are the] most important thing. Each performance should be a jamming.'[104]

It thus makes the transition from a purely musical play to the creation of meaning and narrative and reconnects the improvisatory practice to forms of storytelling, as Chaikin explains:

> Jamming is the study of an emblem. If we have an emblem, 'I see you, I don't see you dying', the jamming becomes a kind of contemplation of that emblem. The term comes from jazz, from the jam session. One actor comes in and moves in contemplation of a theme, traveling within the rhythms, going through and out of the phrasing, sometimes using just the gesture, sometimes reducing the whole thing to pure sound, all of it related to the emblem. Then another comes in and together they give way and open up on the theme. During the jamming, if the performers let it, the theme moves into associations, a combination of free and structured form.[105]

Jamming thus means to collectively find a symbolic language and emotional presence for an aspect of story, a state, or a situation. The 'emblem' as Chaikin calls it – a verbal, visual or aural aggregation of a particular meaning or problem – guides the improvisation like the melody and chords of a standard guide the jazz jam session.

I have gone into some detail in order to characterize the relationship of 'jazz' and 'theatre' in Chaikin's work (and quite a lot of it resonates with other practices), but have not yet addressed what opportunities these exercises and more broadly the use of jazz musicality provide for Chaikin and his ensemble. I will focus on three aspects: agency, collaboration and presence.

Aims and Strategies: Agency, Collaboration and Presence
The musical approach to developing the actor's tools, awareness and connection with a given material and him/herself is a vital part, I would argue, of Chaikin's vision of a 'creative actor',[106] a co-creator of the theatrical event rather than an interpreter of an author's and a director's vision.

Jamming and other rehearsal methods provide a framework, according to Chaikin, to generate performance material by unlocking the 'inner material' of the actor: 'There is a very great amount of inner material and music to draw from

---

[104] Blumenthal, *Joseph Chaikin*, pp. 75–6.
[105] Chaikin, *The Presence*, p. 116.
[106] Hulton, 'Joseph Chaikin', p. 169.

while staying with the same intentions and words.'[107] It is the combination of improvisatory freedom paired with the patient insistence on playing with a very limited amount of material (a single word or sentence, for example) that uncovers emotions and insights in the actor and the material, which would have been lost to the single pair of eyes and ears of one director.

Through a musical process of improvisation, the actors make the material (the words, the story, the gestures, etc.) their own, embodying them and taking agency over their performance. Incorporating a great deal of the improvisatory freedom and unpredictability into the performances themselves, as Chaikin did with *Terminal* (1969–1971) or *Nightwalk* (1972–1973),[108] for example, is a consequent development of this idea (and one that resonates with contemporary theatre-makers such as Leloup or Lensing, as we will see later).

The agency in this case is both a personal one and also strongly related to the collaborative ethics of making work, which are at the heart of the Open Theater. Jamming, as Blumenthal underlines, 'was designed to help performers integrate their work with one another's during the course of a performance'.[109] In talking about ensemble work, Chaikin highlights a musical quality as one of the core connecting factors (aside from promoting empathy over competing for attention): rhythm:

> [It] has to do with rhythm, with dynamics and with a kind of sensitivity which would be rhythmically self-expressed. For example, there is a kind of inner rhythm going on all the time in any single person. If you would let the body go with that rhythm, you would discover that there is a pattern and a dynamic and an intensity that would change as experience changed during the day, a quality which, if you knew somebody else well, you could say is the theme of that person's rhythm. This is the rhythm in a room and it affects the room and it charges the room and it charges the people.[110]

Through an attention to rhythm and through improvisation practices inspired by jazz, Chaikin seeks to create a kind of ensemble play from which a presence emerges that is no longer attributable to any individual or even merely the sum of all the contributing individuals. Jazz musicality, here, fosters a 'collective creativity',[111] an emergent process of creation and performance. Robert Pasolli's description of the 'chord' supports this notion: the 'chord' has the ensemble in a

---

[107] Chaikin, *The Presence*, p. 117.
[108] See Hulton, 'Joseph Chaikin', pp. 176–80.
[109] Blumenthal, *Joseph Chaikin*, p. 75.
[110] Chaikin, *The Presence*, p. 59.
[111] See Sawyer, *Group Creativity*; Stephan Porombka/Wolfgang Schneider/Volker Wortmann (eds.), *Kollektive Kreativität. Jahrbuch für Kulturwissenschaften und ästhetische Praxis* (Tübingen, 2006); Hajo Kurzenberger, *Der kollektive Prozess des Theaters: Chorkörper – Probengemeinschaften – theatrale Kreativität* (Bielefeld, 2009).

circle, arms around each other, eyes closed, breathing, droning, humming. They create a sound-scape that is in some way part of them, but also seems independent of them, removed from the individual's contribution or intention: 'I don't want to alter it, but to let it alter me.'[112] Pasolli concludes: 'The Chord affirms the Open Theater as a collective. In it, the actor perceives the group as an entity of which he is a part. [...] the chord does not submerge his ego but subsumes it.'[113]

A New Notion of Conducting?

In this context it is interesting to reencounter a musical notion that was already central to earlier practitioners, such as Appia and Meyerhold, and to see it transformed: the idea of the 'conductor'. For Appia and Meyerhold, the conductor was a useful analogy to what they saw as the director's job. A single person with a unifying vision, forming an ensemble through their outstanding abilities, but also (in Appia's case) a stern guardian of the playwright's (and/or composer's) work. Yet, as Pasolli claims, 'the single most important *ensemble* device of the Open Theater is the "conductor"'.[114] Blumenthal expands:

> The most subtle, and interesting, of Chaikin's attempts to unite the ensemble in one dynamic were his 'conductor' exercises. Performers were to tune directly into someone else's energy without imitating the form of the other's action. [...] One performer initiated a gesture and/or sound with a distinct rhythm and tone; the others then tried to meet it with *different* gestures and/or sounds of their own that have the same pulse and feeling as the original. Sometimes the conductor worked with sounds alone and the others only with movement, or vice versa.[115]

As we can see, Chaikin uses a quite different notion of 'conducting' to what may commonly be associated with it in the wake of the great autocratic conductors (Toscanini, Furtwängler, Karajan, etc.). Here, the 'conductor' is not described as a directorial device, a metaphor of authority, or a locus of the interpretative power over a dramatic or musical text, but as an 'ensemble device'. The 'conductors' in turn express their ideas not in a *codified* system of instructions through agreed symbols that strive for clarity and unequivocality of meaning, but use their whole body 'to feed rhythmic impulses to the others',[116] who respond with their own creative associations, 'with *different* gestures and/or sounds of their own',[117] merely trying to adopt the 'same pulse and feeling'[118] as the conductor.

---

[112]   Pasolli, *A Book*, p. 33.
[113]   Pasolli, *A Book*, p. 33.
[114]   Pasolli, *A Book*, p. 26, my emphasis.
[115]   Blumenthal, *Joseph Chaikin*, p. 74, original emphasis.
[116]   Pasolli, *A Book*, p. 27.
[117]   Blumenthal, *Joseph Chaikin*, p. 74, original emphasis.
[118]   Blumenthal, *Joseph Chaikin*, p. 74.

Importantly, actors also take turns in being the conductor, and there is even an exercise called 'conductorless conductor',[119] in which no one is specified as the conductor, but instead the group as a whole carefully negotiates impulses and reactions to each other in a continuous flow of offering and receiving musical stimuli.

In contrast to some of the strategies of musical *dispositifs* we have seen earlier – including abstraction, formalization, defamiliarization or emphasizing the visceral aspects of performance – Chaikin's overriding aim and 'fundamental interest has always been to heighten the sense that living people are sharing immediate fleeting moments – to emphasize presence'.[120] Chaikin defines presence as 'a quality that makes you feel as though you're standing right next to the actor, no matter where you're sitting in the theater'.[121] He also talks about an ideological aspect of presence: his ambition to make presence non-teleological, not simply a means to an end, but a virtue in itself:

> The industrial mainstream of society is always a pressure to make us 'achievers', to make of us 'goods'. Many of our appetites are developed by the industrial society, and most of our models are not picked by us. We are trained and conditioned to be 'present' only in relation to the goal.[122]

Jazz musicality, which also foregrounds being in the here and now and embracing the ephemerality of 'kairos', is a model and vehicle for this kind of presence.[123]

'Jazz-sketching with words' – Sam Shepard
Before examining Shepard and Chaikin's collaborative works, *Tongue* (1978) and *Savage/Love* (1981), I will also briefly look at Shepard's dramatic musicality independently. For this playwright, actor and director's work rock and jazz have played a crucial role: as a topic, as incidental music (Shepard often provided lyrics

---

[119] Pasolli, *A Book*, p. 28.

[120] Blumenthal, *Joseph Chaikin*, p. 71. It is interesting to note that presence in Chaikin's case is not, like in the prevalent Method acting at the time, a particularly 'credible' or 'compelling' *representation* of a (fictional) character, but what Blumenthal calls '*presentational* performing' (p. 79, my emphasis): 'Chaikin has experimented with several quasi-theatrical forms that acknowledge the reporter along with the report. Storytelling, singing, and interviews all involve someone addressing others here and now but testifying about something that may be from another time or even another mode' (p. 79). Music, Blumenthal adds, 'has provided Chaikin with a general model and tool for drawing theater into more subtle and abstract types of address' (p. 97).

[121] Chaikin, *The Presence*, p. 20.

[122] Chaikin, *The Presence*, p. 65.

[123] For a wider range of concepts of presence see Gabriella Giannachi/Nick Kaye/ Michael Shanks, *Archaeologies of Presence* (London 2012), in particular the chapters of Rebecca Schneider and Phillip Zarrilli.

and music to songs that were an integral part of the play), but also as a *dispositif*: a container of zeitgeist,[124] a mode of performing, a rhythmical model of writing:

> The rock star as American pop archetype; Shepard as rock-and-roll playwright; jazz improvisation as a model for play-making and for the perception of reality; an equal expression between music and the actor; and, the rhythmic and percussive qualities of Shepard's language: these are the alternate tracks that music has cut through the landscape of dramatist Sam Shepard.[125]

DeRose describes the importance of music for Shepard's work in detail; the use of rock songs as 'emotional comment' or 'emotional amplifier',[126] rock music becoming 'a central element in Shepard's dramaturgy',[127] and the 'keen awareness of the emotional and physical power that music exerts over an audience'.[128]

Shepard's musicality does not stop at an imaginative use of music or the combination of song and dialogue, but seeks to translate jazz and rock musicality into the writing itself:

> Even when there is no band, no musical score, no songs: there is a rhythmic, frequently percussive, quality of the language of Shepard's characters that makes music of his plays. Words as percussion, as vibration and breath which hit and move the air, have been a trademark of Shepard's work since his earliest plays.[129]

In contrast to some of the approaches we have considered in the previous chapter, where musicality was seen to be consciously used to abstract and formalize language, Shepard finds and lays bare the immanent musicality of various American idioms, which have shaped and are shaped by the pulse, the repetitiveness and the insistence of rock, rap and jazz. We can see this in this example from *Operation Sidewinder* (1970):

> *Young Man*: You can't always have everything your own way. You'll be arrested. You'll be arrested, accosted, molested, tested and re-tested. You'll be beaten, you'll be jailed, you'll be thrown out of school. You will be spanked, you will be whipped and chained. But I am whipped. I am chained. I am prisoner to all your oppression. I am depressed, deranged, decapitated, dehumanised, defoliated, demented and dammed! I can't get out. You can get out. You can smile and

---

[124] According to David DeRose, Shepard 'was [...] incorporating a jazz world view and jazz musicians as characters in his plays' (DeRose, 'Sam Shepard', p. 237).

[125] DeRose, 'Sam Shepard', p. 228.

[126] DeRose, 'Sam Shepard', p. 232.

[127] DeRose, 'Sam Shepard', p. 231.

[128] DeRose, 'Sam Shepard', p. 232.

[129] DeRose, 'Sam Shepard', p. 241.

laugh and kiss and cry. I am! I am! I am! I am! I am! I am! I am! I am! I am! I
am! I am! Tonight. In this desert. In this space. I am.[130]

This speech taps into the specific rhetoric of this character, but also carefully plays
with assonances and alliterations and strong motifs ('You'll'; 'I am'), which are
used with a jazzy-musical sense of balance of repetition and variation. They do
not appear carefully composed and developed, however, but impulsive and quasi-
improvised. Shepard's prose also differs from other playwrights' rhythmicality
insofar as it does not

> fall into the more commonly recited standards of poetic language: it is not
> iambic pentameter, nor does it possess the natural poetic rhythms of modern
> spoken English notable in the loquacious urban fast talkers of playwrights like
> David Mamet.[131]

In *The Truth of Crime* (1973), Shepard famously chose to create a central scene
between the characters Crow and Hoss as a kind of musicalized boxing match. His
stage action reads as follows:

> An off-stage bell rings. The band starts slow, low keyed lead guitar and bass
> music, it should be a lurking evil sound like the 'Sister Morphine' cut on 'Sticky
> Fingers'. HOSS and CROW begin to move to the music, not really dancing
> but feeling the power in their movements through the music. They each pick
> up microphones. They begin their assaults just taking the words in rhythmic
> patterns, sometimes going with the music, sometimes counterpointing it. As the
> round progresses the music builds with drums and piano coming in, maybe a
> rhythm guitar too. Their voices build so that sometimes they sing the words or
> shout. The words remain as intelligible as possible like a sort of talking opera.[132]

In this face-off the 'weapon of choice for the ultimate showdown is neither
knives nor guns, but language: that is, chanted, intoned language accompanied by
rock-and-roll music'.[133]

Influenced by jazz musicians, Shepard then became increasingly interested in
the more complex structures of jazz and the ethics and aesthetics of improvisation:

> Jazz could move in surprising territories, without qualifying itself ... You could
> follow a traditional melody and then breakaway, and then come back, or drop
> into polyrhythms ... But, more importantly, it was an emotional thing. You could

---

[130] Sam Shepard, *Four two-act plays* (London, 1981), p. 183.
[131] DeRose, 'Sam Shepard', p. 242.
[132] Shepard, *Four two-act plays*, p. 97.
[133] DeRose, 'Sam Shepard', p. 231.

move in all these *emotional* territories, and you could do it with *passion* ...
There was a form in a formless sense.[134]

Shepard began to invoke jazz musicality in the devising process of his
works: *Inacoma* (1977), for example, was 'composed improvisationally and
collaboratively, in rehearsals, with the contributions of musicians playing
an equal role to the spoken word and dramatic action'.[135] Two plays written
in 1976, *Suicide in B-Flat* and *Angel City* feature improvisation both as a
subversive practice[136] and a path to a 'spontaneity of expression', as Bonnie
Marranca explains:

> Characterisation in the play [*Angel City*] follows the structural make-up of
> improvisation to the point of building into a musical finale in Act I that has
> the actors (or are they performers?) jamming. The appeal of jazz is more than
> structural. As an approach to composition it embodies an attitude that is at the heart
> of Shepard's work: spontaneity of expression. Not chance, but improvisation.[137]

One of the effects, according to Marranca, is the erotic power, the seductiveness
of Shepard's plays: it is 'what makes his writing sexy though there's no actual sex
[...] it's the rhythm of sex not the representation of it'.[138]

For the writer and his actors, embracing jazz musicality has been described in
terms of 'surrender' to an external creative force; a way of giving up learned modes
of planning, meaningful intention and purpose. Shepard does not romanticize this
idea, however, but describes it in quite dark terms:

> From time to time I've practiced Jack Kerouac's discovery of jazz-sketching
> with words. Following the exact same principles as a musician does when he's
> jamming. After periods of this kind of practice, I begin to get the haunting
> sense that something in me writes but not necessarily me. At least it's not the
> 'me' that takes credit for it. This identical experience happened to me once
> when I was playing drums with The Holy Modal Rounders, and it scared the
> shit out of me.[139]

The way in which actor Joyce Aaron talks about performing in Sam Shepard's
plays resonates with the metaphor of being 'haunted':

---

[134]   Shepard in DeRose, 'Sam Shepard', p. 234, original emphasis.
[135]   DeRose, 'Sam Shepard', p. 234.
[136]   See DeRose, 'Sam Shepard', p. 239.
[137]   Bonnie Marranca (ed.), *American Dreams: The Imagination of Sam Shepard* (New
York, 1981), pp. 20–21.
[138]   Marranca, *American Dreams*, p. 21.
[139]   Shepard in Marranca, *American Dreams*, p. 217.

> You can't approach Sam's plays according to the usual acting terms and conditions – there are no rules, because he has broken them. [...] What you have to do is let that rhythm take you instead of you taking it – you have to surrender to the dynamics of that rhythm, let it possess you.[140]

Spalding Gray, who was Hoss in Richard Schechner's production of *The Tooth of Crime* (1973), also highlights the rhythmical impact of Shepard's language on the creation of characters, describing Shepard's writing as a 'terrific language structure that was like living a rock beat, a drum beat, because Sam was a drummer. [...] I didn't have to worry about psychological approaches to character because the language itself and the voice made this kind of music [...]'.[141]

Shepard thus uses musicality as a vehicle towards characters with a strong sense of idiom and being rooted and located, but at the same time as a means of letting those characters fray and fragment. In this the actors no longer hold on to the character's identity or 'core', but to the rhythm of the writing.

Shepard and Chaikin's *Tongues* (1978)

Tongues united Shepard and Chaikin, who had recognized each other as kindred spirits and exchanged ideas for some time,[142] one strong common denominator in their work being a shared sense of musicality. The project was a joint process of writing for a performance explicitly exploring notions of voice and rhythm, and the final script contained detailed instructions for a percussionist, who accompanies the actor's monologue.[143] Chaikin and Shepard themselves performed the original production at the Magic Theatre in San Francisco.

The process already departed from more literary traditions of playwriting, using the rhythm of long walks and oral conversations and musical exchanges at first to generate and shape material (see Figure 5.1). This exploration of what Chaikin came to call 'thought music'[144] left its mark on the dramaturgy of the piece:

> Shaping the dozen-plus sections of *Tongues* into a performance piece, Chaikin and Shepard use principles drawn more of a musical composition than traditional dramaturgy. [...] Chaikin, whose ensemble creations have mostly been constructed this way, says: 'one of the things which we share, Sam and

---

[140] Aaron in Marranca, *American Dreams*, p. 172.

[141] Gray in Marranca, *American Dreams*, p. 176.

[142] See their letters in Barry Daniels (ed.), *Joseph Chaikin & Sam Shepard: Letters and Texts 1972–1984* (New York, 1994).

[143] See Daniels, *Letters and Texts*, pp. 84–93 and Joseph Chaikin, 'Joseph Chaikin: Continuing Work. An Interview with Peter Hulton, Paris 1981', *Theatre Papers: The Fourth Series (1983–84)*, 4/1 (1983), pp. 1–40, for more detail on the creation process.

[144] Blumenthal in Marranca, *American Dreams*, p. 139.

Figure 5.1   Joseph Chaikin and Sam Shepard during a rehearsal of *Tongues* at
                the Eureka Theatre, San Francisco, 1979

me, is our intense involvement with music. We're never looking for the dramatic
structure. We're looking for [a] … shape that's musically tenable'.[145]

DeRose describes the results in quite similar terms when talking about *Tongues*,
Savage/Love (1981) and *Superstitions* (1981):

> None of these three pieces follows the conventional dramatic action. Instead,
> they are, collage-like in structure, incorporating monologues, poems, dialogues,
> even chance in a variety of voices and characterisations. […] Motifs are
> introduced, as in a musical composition, and then repeated and commented upon
> in different voices and variations.[146]

And Bernard Weiner, in writing about *Savage/Love* calls it 'a tantalizing,
beautifully executed piece of musical theatre. […] It is musical theatre in the sense
of verbal and instrumental jazz'.[147] These plays and performances can clearly be
described as 'jazzed theater and theatricalized jazz'.[148] For *Tongues*, the writing of
the Speaker's part works with many musico-poetic techniques such as assonance,
motif repetition and variation, while the instructions for the percussionist include

---

[145]   Marranca, *American Dreams*, p. 139, p. 141.
[146]   DeRose, 'Sam Shepard', p. 236.
[147]   Weiner in Daniels, *Letters and Texts*, p. 177.
[148]   Savran, *Highbrow/Lowdown*, p. 18.

many theatrical aspects, seeking to clearly stage his actions and presence in relation to the actor: 'Chaikin's work with the actor to create emblems and rhythms for character parallels the poetic and musical structures of Shepard's writing.'[149]

Here are two brief examples from *Tongues*: from the opening section onwards the speaker and the percussionist's parts are tightly interwoven, framing the already rhythmically highly suggestive text (there are many repetitions and reoccurrences at different levels, as well as deliberate work with similar and contrasting phonemes) within a 4/4 rhythmic beat, interspersed with accents:

Speaker:
He was born in the middle of a story which he had nothing to with.
In the middle of a people.
In the middle of a people he stays.

All his fights.	(Percussion accent within 4/4.)
All his suffering.	(*Accent.*)
All his hope.	(*Accent.*)
Are with the people.	(No accent, continues 4/4.)
All his joy	(*Accent.*)
All his hate	(*Accent.*)
All his labors	(*Accent.*)
Are with the people.	(No accent, continues 4/4.)
All the air	(*Accent.*)
All the food	(*Accent.*)
All the trees	(*Accent.*)
All colors	(*Accent.*)
All sound	(*Accent.*)
And smell	(Accent, continues 4/4.)
All the dreams	(*Accent.*)
All the demons	(*Accent.*)
All the saints	(*Accent.*)
All taboos	(*Accent.*)
All rewards	(*Accent.*)
Are with the people.	(No accent, continues 4/4.)[150]

In terms of 'theatricalized jazz', there is a clear sense in this play that the theatrical presence of the musician is important. While he is not presented as a fictional character or as part of a narrative, Shepard's instructions are also

---

[149] Daniels, *Letters and Texts*, p. 6.
[150] Shepard in Daniels, *Letters and Texts*, pp. 75–6.

not merely pragmatically musical, but indicate a staging that frames the music-making as *theatrical*:

> (*Gnawing rhythm picks up tempo and volume through next passage. Both hands and arms of percussionist appear on right and left sides of* SPEAKER, *playing wood scraper gourd. This motion is a large, sweeping half circle so that percussionist's arms appear on one side, disappear behind* SPEAKER, *then reappear on the other side continuously. [...] Abrupt stop of voice and sound, pause, sudden movement of percussionist's right arm jabbing out horizontally, holding a string of small brass prayer bells that dangle down, pause. Wrist of percussionist makes a downward spasm, causing bells to jingle [...].*)[151]

Musicality, then, is the central connecting factor in this collaboration, the shared principle on which to develop the writing, directing and performing of a piece, which itself strongly foregrounds its musical conception. Jazz musicality inspires a hybrid working process and performance aesthetics, oscillating between dramatic monologue, storytelling, concert and live improvisation.

Thorsten Lensing/Jan Hein: Der Lauf zum Meer [The Run to the Sea] *(2009)*

Director Thorsten Lensing and co-director and dramaturg Jan Hein, who are at the core of the theatre group 'Theater T1', have worked together since 1994 and gained notoriety for their rare and radical theatrical productions, which started off in the so-called 'Freie Szene'.[152] Since then, they have been recognized by the cultural establishment with invitations to the Berliner Festspiele and many major German theatres, and reviews in all major newspapers, indicating the increasing exposure of their work.

On seeing their production of Jakob Michael Reinhold Lenz's *Catharina of Siena* (2001) at the Sophiensæle Berlin, I was already struck by its formal clarity and decisiveness, and particularly by how the emotionality and mystic visions of the eponymous character were translated into a simple and immediate musicality.[153]

---

[151] Shepard in Daniels, *Letters and Texts*, p. 84.

[152] This is shorthand for the wide range of theatre-makers, venues and productions working outside of the established and often subsidized theatres. Recently, however, much of the personnel and the aesthetics and working methods of the 'Freie Szene' have become incorporated into the municipal theatres.

[153] At the time, I noted: 'In Thorsten Lensing's production [...] the actor playing Catharina (Ursina Lardi) steps in front of the stage, close to the audience, for an inserted monologue. She speaks from texts which nuns have noted down during religious ecstasies of their fellow nuns and does so quite held back and musically formalized. With her hands she seems to suggestively conduct the phrasing of the short, repetitive sentences, which time and again slip into metrically regular passages. The whole scene remains in commanding and captivating abeyance between indication of clear measure in the rhythmicity of the

Der Lauf zum Meer, based on part four of William Carlos Williams's epic poem *Paterson* (1946–1958), premiered in 2009 and was developed and performed by three musicians (guitarist Jean-Paul Bourelly, percussionist and singer Gilbert Diop and drummer Willi Kellers) and three actors (Viviane DeMuynck, Katharina Schüttler und Charly Hübner). Lensing describes the creation process as an entirely integrated play between musicians and actors as 'equal partners'.[154] Music and musicality proved 'a central theme'[155] for the production. Music wasn't merely an ingredient, responsible for the atmosphere, but instead 'everything developed from music and together with music';[156] specifically from a practice of improvisation – a 'culture of spontaneity',[157] which all three musicians brought to the process, drawing on different musical backgrounds ranging from African chant and storytelling to European free jazz.

Lensing did not approach rehearsals with a particular vision, instructions or interpretation of the text – he is fiercely opposed to the idea of theatre as 'Umsetzung'[158] [realization] of his understanding of a text, but seeks to retain a strong element of surprise and friction between the text and the performers, rather than settling for fixed interpretations. He says he rarely actively asks the performers to agree on a particular scenic 'solution', in order to avoid giving them a false sense of security or contentment, which would stop their continued movement of searching and disrupt the presence of chance. This did mean that the performance maintained a high level of risk for quite a long time into the run, as he says. Simone Kaempf echoes this impression in her portrait of Lensing:

> The strong focus on the energy of the actors and on specific details does not only meet with applause. What is more, the quality of the performances differs from one day to the next, even more than is normally the case in the theatre. In weaker moments the actors run the risk of acting at cross purposes, while on strong evenings, as the audience was fortunate enough to experience in 2009 in 'The Run to the Sea', the dynamism of the play is fully unleashed. Katharina

---

ecstatic phrases and the dissolution through changes of rhythms and long pauses' (David Roesner, *Theater als Musik* [Tübingen, 2003], p. 172).

In my interview with Lensing in 2012, however, he clarified that this scene had actually not been the result of a conscious exercise in musicalizing or even composing the monologue, but emerged from the way in which Lardi had helped herself memorize the erratic, syntactically and semantically illogical text. Rhythm and (musical) gestures served primarily as a mnemonic aid, but Lensing decided there and then not to rehearse the monologue any further and preserve the particular theatrical effect Lardi's form of recollection had for the performances.

[154] Thorsten Lensing, 'Director Thorsten Lensing interviewed by David Roesner' (phone conversation, 07.05.2012).

[155] Lensing, 'Director Thorsten Lensing'.

[156] Lensing, 'Director Thorsten Lensing'.

[157] Belgrad, *Culture of Spontaneity*, p. 1.

[158] Lensing, 'Director Thorsten Lensing'.

Schüttler and Viviane de Muynck played the roles of a young woman whose future still lies ahead of her and an older woman who is looking back over her life. Lensing brought them together with three jazz musicians specialized in improvisation. The result was 75 intensive minutes in which the music underlined the highlights and commented on what remained unsaid, while the actors – with the aid of a textual framework – gave concrete form to the moods created by the music.[159]

Lensing describes his rehearsal process as deliberately chaotic and his task as the need to bear with this chaos. At the best of times, though, rehearsals for *Lauf zum Meer* resembled parties, he says. Theatrical form is not composed or premeditated in this process, but slowly emerges out of continued 'doing'[160] as a small set of agreements and arrangements between the performers within which a great deal of freedom (and risk) are maintained. The task, as Lensing describes it, is to arrive at a point where there is a shared understanding in each moment about what 'works', what 'has a life'.[161] This may of course differ from one performance to the next, and there is a constant need to find an equilibrium between each performer's freedom, so that their individual expressions do not obstruct each other or cancel each other out.

Lensing is however not interested in formal experiments *per se* – he does work in great detail on the text with the actors (and here also the musicians, since everybody attended all rehearsals): he strives for a great amount of clarity for the actors about what they are saying, which then gives them the freedom to find the 'right' form each night to give expression to the text. For him 'form is just an extension of content',[162] and in this case this meant that the actors had to learn how to 'make music with the text'.[163] He found this particularly appropriate for Williams since music plays a central role in the text and the cultural context of the writer, but wouldn't have considered a similar premise and process for other plays, such as Chekhov's.

There are clearly some similarities to Chaikin's musicality: while Lensing doesn't use the word 'presence' a lot, he describes the actors he carefully chooses to work with as interesting to look at and listen to: 'when they continue to surprise me, when they are unpredictable'.[164] It is a *quality* of improvisation – not necessarily a practice – that these actors bring with them: a disposition and attitude towards the text and the performance that truly remains in the *spirit* of jazz as a celebration of the here and now.

---

[159] Simone Kaempf, 'Thorsten Lensing, Jan Hein (Theater T1): Portrait' (2012), http://www.goethe.de/kue/the/pur/tuj/enindex.htm [30.05.2012].

[160] Lensing, 'Director Thorsten Lensing'.

[161] Lensing, 'Director Thorsten Lensing'.

[162] Lensing, 'Director Thorsten Lensing'.

[163] Lensing, 'Director Thorsten Lensing'.

[164] Lensing, 'Director Thorsten Lensing'.

There is also an analogy in the emphasis on playfulness and freedom, which Lensing also grants himself (or forces himself to bear with): based on a long and intensive study and interrogation of the chosen text, he then comes to rehearsals fully unprepared, trying to facilitate 'pure play'[165] rather than arming himself with ideas, concepts or strategies. He improvises 'directing' as much as his performers improvise 'acting' or 'playing music'. By coming to rehearsal without a plan or preconceptions, he says, the resulting performance really belongs to those who perform it. Not unlike Chaikin's actors, there is a very different sense of agency here than we find on many other stages with strong authorial director figures.

Lensing – in contrast to Chaikin or others we have encountered – does not however *train* his actors, does not conduct exercises, and does not establish a theatrical or musical meta-discourse with them, but 'simply' talks about the text and initiates an extended period of playing, granting and generating trust and a shared sense of what feels appropriate with respect to the text in question.

The result, to be fair, has had mixed reviews: some critics dismissed it as 'silly water games and secretive laconic poses' (Andreas Schäfer)[166] or as 'irritating and somehow superfluous' (Jürgen Otten);[167] others, however, found a different kind of sense and appeal in this 'anti-theatre':[168]

> The message is: jazz! Yes, this does make sense. Except not the kind of sense that is comfortingly coherent. Everything is in beautiful contradiction here. The lyrical language on the one hand, the jazz-cosmos full of anarchy and dissolute on the other. On the one hand they strive for deliverance with a tendency towards the metaphysical, on the other, everyone on stage behaves as if they were in their private bathroom; relaxed, grounded and vulnerable as they are. The actors don't speak their lines, they crawl around in them, dig themselves into them. They assimilate to the music: letting themselves fall and drift. [...] The more we get into the sound, the rhythm, the closer we are to the soul of this evening. Jazz is the word of redemption. [...] Thorsten Lensing and Jan Hein [...] have created a production of rare beauty – it is the austere, demure beauty of the unfathomable.[169]

---

[165] Lensing, 'Director Thorsten Lensing'.

[166] At http://www.nachtkritik.de/index.php?option=com_content&task=view&id=2331 [30.05.2012].

[167] At http://www.nachtkritik.de/index.php?option=com_content&task=view&id=2331 [30.05.2012].

[168] At http://www.nachtkritik.de/index.php?option=com_content&task=view&id=2331 [30.05.2012].

[169] Dirk Pilz, 'Jazz mich, und ich liebe dich. *Der Lauf zum Meer* – Thorsten Lensing und Jan Hein verwandeln William C. Williams in Jazz' (25.01.2009), http://www.nachtkritik.de/index.php?option=com_content&task=view&id=2331 [06.05.2012].

Jazz musicality in theatre, as this example shows, not only challenges the dominant *dispositifs* of training, creation and dramaturgy, but also needs to be met with a quite different disposition by the audience, inspiring a different kind of sense making and aesthetic appreciation in some, while frustrating others, who hoped for a more focused, more semantically coherent and theatrically purposeful performance.

Bred in the Bone: Unreal City – *A Jazzed Performance (2006)*

In the announcement of a comeback performance of London-based company Bred in the Bone's *Unreal City* in 2012, Paul Fryer wrote (citing the company's PR material):

> Drawing on innovative training of the actor, based on musicality and embodiment of the text, this piece is built on principles of jazz music, where the actors are the embodiment of the music, and the music the characters that we see.[170]

The piece is based on T.S. Eliot's poem *The Waste Land* and was developed by director Matthieu Leloup with actors Krystina Krotoska and Tanya Munday, and musicians Rafał Habel and Jeremy Harrison.[171] I was curious to find out what the explicit claims of musicality and jazz principles ('The notion of jazz, the notion of improvising is still deeply, deeply there.'[172]) at the heart of the production's creation process and the company's training meant and met with Leloup after the performance of the piece at Rose Bruford College on 20 April 2012.

To begin with, Leloup interestingly seems to be guided in his choice of actors and collaborators by qualities that Lensing also emphasized in almost the same words. Leloup: 'They always surprise me and that's what I look for in the actors. So that's why I developed this idea of musicality and I studied it because it seems to be very effective.'[173] There are also some similarities with regard to the process of development of the piece. The text is equally non-dramatic and forms the basis of the whole performance;[174] the two actors are matched by an

---

[170] Paul Fryer, 'Bred In The Bone, "Unreal City", 19th and 20th April' (e-mail to the SCUDD [Standing Conference of University Drama Departments] mailing list) [17.04.2012].

[171] See http://www.bredinthebone.co.uk/productions/46-current-productions/127-unreal-city.html [04.06.2012].

[172] Matthieu Leloup, 'Director Matthieu Leloup interviewed by David Roesner' (Rose Bruford College, London, 20.04.2012).

[173] Leloup, 'Director Matthieu Leloup'.

[174] Big A3 sheets of paper with the text in English and Polish in the centre and instructions for music and movement at the sides became an actual score of the performance, which was visibly present in the performance itself, serving as an *aide memoire* for the performers, but also, I would argue, as an indicator for the audience to expect a performance that was a hybrid of a concert and a theatre performance, and that despite the tangibly improvised nature of the piece there was a clear structure at its base.

equal number of musicians who developed the performance together in a joint organic process. Initially, however, the music was meant to be more of a training device. Leloup wanted the actors to 'work on the text as if they were working with [jazz] standards',[175] raising the question of how to approach something well-known and set in a playful, open and improvised manner.

'Jazz' functions for Leloup's theatre practice on several levels: as an ideal, it serves as an over-arching metaphor for the vitality of a live artform, which continues to reinvigorate itself, remaining playful and unpredictable. Other than for Lensing, the 'jazz approach' for Leloup 'is not strictly linked to the text. It is something we have worked on as a company before'.[176] It is part of the training on musicality in relation to text, which he developed: 'The freedom that musicians have, I also want the actors to have.'[177]

As an actual musical genre, 'jazz' in a traditional sense was not in fact that present in the production (despite the inclusion of the standard 'Summertime') – similarly to Lensing's musicians, the improvisation clearly fed off a variety of sources, including Klezmer, European jazz, sound art, free jazz. Both Lensing and Leloup are more interested, it seems, in the spirit of jazz as improvised music, rather than in the idiom itself in any of its specific historical articulations.

As a particular performance practice, jazz provides a template for how to negotiate structure and 'non-structure' for Leloup. He borrows 'concepts that are used in jazz music', but says: 'I am looking at what the musician actually does and then I extrapolate from that; I don't look at the structure [in an abstract kind of way].'[178] For *Unreal City* this means that there is a clear underlying structure, which organizes the interplay of musicians and actors, of music, text, gesture, movement, pace and lighting, but keeps many of the instructions themselves relatively open. Sometimes all that the musicians have agreed, for example, is whether a section is in minor or major, and the actors haven't trained and memorized specific speaking cadences, movements or gestures, but rather a sense of how to 'follow the text musically',[179] without interpreting or 'intellectualizing' it.[180] The agreed structure is there to organize the *relationship* between all the elements of the performance and also to implement a strong sense of breaks in rhythm and contrapuntal juxtapositions. Within this structure, however, a strong element of freedom remains. Watching the performance, it seemed to me that Leloup had managed thus to integrate two particular qualities of jazz: the potential for surprise and radical changes in direction, tone or rhythm as a key structural characteristic, but also a clear sense of 'flow' of an immersive insistence on a musical idea or 'feel', capturing, savouring and extending a moment in time.

---

175 Leloup, 'Director Matthieu Leloup'.
176 Leloup, 'Director Matthieu Leloup'.
177 Leloup, 'Director Matthieu Leloup'.
178 Leloup, 'Director Matthieu Leloup'.
179 Leloup, 'Director Matthieu Leloup'.
180 Leloup, 'Director Matthieu Leloup'.

Finally, Leloup strongly emphasizes the cognitive aspect of musicality:[181] what he ultimately tries to achieve is that his actors engage their right side of the brain, 'which is connected to music and poetry'[182] in their approach to text in particular and the performance in general. Rather than locating musicality predominantly in the conceptual and dramaturgical process of creation or the receptive disposition of an audience, Leloup's musicality is a *way of thinking* for the actor and an ability of the director to see and hear the difference between what he calls left-brain or right-brain approaches to text, movement or space. This is also why he trusts strongly in the evidence of *listening* in rehearsals and concedes that this approach cannot really be explained or verbally conceptualized[183] – for him, it becomes evident and powerful only in doing it, trying it in training and rehearsal, and experiencing it.

This latter point has, as it turns out, become a recurring theme of this chapter – more classically minded proponents of musicality in the theatre have found it less difficult, it seems to me, to verbalize their approaches and aims for a musicalization of theatre, whereas from Chaikin to Leloup there is a strong element of the pre-linguistic and the pre-conceptual pervading their jazz-influenced theatre practice, to which the well-worn Brechtian dictum that 'the proof of the pudding is in the eating'[184] seems to apply.

For the aesthetics of these performances this has interesting consequences: not unlike Lensing, Leloup also finds that his way of working, the continuous attempt to engage the right brain, means that the *quality* of movement and textual delivery is musical and that performances are kept fresh and alive, even after a long run or long periods of rest (as in the case of *Unreal City*). It requires an openness and courage of the performers: 'Their great craft in this [piece] is that they allow themselves to not know every time what the hell they are going to do.'[185]

---

[181]   See also the Introduction.

[182]   Leloup refers here to the concept of the lateralization of brain function, which means that for certain types of tasks certain dominances can be measured. (See http://en.wikipedia.org/wiki/Lateralization_of_brain_function [30.05.2012] for an overview and problematization of this concept.) Some psychologists even go so far as to call the idea a 'myth' (http://www.psychologytoday.com/blog/brain-myths/201206/why-the-left-brain-right-brain-myth-will-probably-never-die [12.08.12]) – in this context, I am not trying to verify the scientific basis of the concept, but to evaluate what meaning it has as a metaphor for the theatre-maker.

[183]   This is reminiscent of Pelinski's notion cited in my introduction 'that many musical practices have primary significations without any need for the linguistic vehicle of rational thought' ('Embodiment').

[184]   See Peter Thomson/Glendyr Sacks (eds.), *The Cambridge Companion to Brecht. 2nd Edition* (Cambridge, 2006), p. 250.

[185]   Leloup, 'Director Matthieu Leloup'.

Chapter 6
The Eclectic Musicality of Now

Introduction

Starting with the examples analyzed at the end of the last chapter, my focus is now clearly on what we call 'contemporary' practice. In this final chapter I will outline and selectively investigate how the musicality *dispositif* manifests itself in today's theatre, including roughly one generation of theatre-making under this heading.[1] The general context has been well established by a range of publications[2] and many facets have been drawn out already. The purpose of this chapter, then, lies in highlighting how *musicality* drives or connects with some of the central themes, performance aesthetics and productive mechanisms of today's theatre. This interrelation manifests itself in a wide range of ways: from 'an explosive interest in opera and music-theatre', to an 'energetic link to

---

[1]   As with the book throughout, the focus will remain on European theatre. Robert Wilson is an obvious exception, but it could be argued that his work has been produced predominantly in Europe and has had its strongest impact there.

[2]   For example Paul Allain/Jen Harvie, *The Routledge Companion to Theatre and Performance* (London, 2006); Arnold Aronson, *American Avant-garde Theatre: A History* (London/New York, 2000); Philip Auslander, *From Acting to Performance: Essays in Modernism and Postmodernism* (London, 1997); Gabriele Brandstetter et al., *Grenzgänge. Das Theater und die anderen Künste* (Tübingen, 1998); David Davies, *Philosophies of the Performing Arts* (Malden/Oxford, 2011); Maria M. Delgado/Caridad Svich, *Theatre in crisis?: Performance Manifestos for a New Century* (Manchester, 2002); Richard Drain (ed.), *Twentieth Century Theatre: A Sourcebook* (London/New York, 1994); Erika Fischer-Lichte et al., *Ausweitung der Kunstzone* (eds.) (Bielefeld, 2010); Maggie Gale/John F. Deeney (eds.), *Routledge Drama Anthology and Sourcebook: From Modernism to Contemporary Performance* (London/New York, 2010); Emma Govan/Helen Nicholson/Katie Normington, *Making a Performance: Devising Histories and Contemporary Practices* (London/New York, 2007); Deirdre Heddon/Jane Milling, *Devising Performance. A Critical History* (Basingstoke/New York, 2006); Guido Hiß, *Synthetische Visionen* (München, 2005); Hans-Thies Lehmann, *Postdramatic Theatre* (London/New York, 2006); Gerda Poschmann, *Der nicht mehr dramatische Theatertext* (Tübingen, 1997); Frieder Reininghaus/Katja Schneider (eds.), *Experimentelles Musik- und Tanztheater* (Laaber, 2004); Jens Roselt/Christel Weiler (eds.), *Schauspielen heute. Die Bildung des Menschen in den performativen Künsten* (Bielefeld, 2011); Eric Salzman/Thomas Desi, *The New Music Theatre* (Oxford, 2008); Jacqueline Smart/Alex Mermikides (eds.), *Devising in Process* (London, 2009); Stefan Tigges (ed.), *Dramatische Transformationen* (Bielefeld, 2008); Phillip Zarrilli, *Acting (Re)considered* (London/New York, 2002).

club culture' to innumerable 'other experiments in sound and motion [which] have affected the theatre scene'.[3]

Rather than trying to list all the usual suspects that would fit my 'musicality' description, I have thus sought to identify important themes and concerns in my survey of current European theatre practices, which reflect the widened range of aesthetic aims, productive habits and ethics in theatre-making today. It is quite a mosaic picture that presents itself and while this may be partly to do with the relative lack of hindsight, it also reflects, I would argue, the increasingly eclectic nature of music/theatre relationships. There are still gravitational centres for the various discourses and practices, but they have multiplied and become more flexible. The sections of this chapter thus also eclectically focus at times on aesthetic principles in production and reception, at others on changing creative roles and practices, programmatic thrusts or disciplinary contexts. The first part of this chapter explores these gravitational centres, while the second looks at four examples of practice in more detail while covering a cross section from text-based to devised practices.

Gravitational Centres in the Musicality *Dispositif* of Contemporary Theatre

The Scepticism about Representation

As we know from 2,500 years of its history, theatre tends to renew and reinvent itself partly by rejecting a previous generation's premises and practices and partly by remodelling and appropriating these. In this book I have, amongst other things, sought to investigate the role of music in this process. The various streams of contemporary theatre practice – including that which we may call post-modern, postdramatic, *Regietheater*, *théâtre d'auteur*, chorus theatre, devised theatre, etc. – are characterized perhaps most of all by their heterogeneity: previous paradigms (or their clichés), such as mimetic representation or linear narrative have largely been rejected by the pole bearers of contemporary theatre and replaced with an astonishing variety of scenic forms and performative styles, which are often multi-faceted in themselves.

This resonates strongly with previous developments in musical composition and music-theatre as Kaden and Kalisch confirm: 'Despite all the heterogeneity of compositional movements of the Sixties there is a common thrust or rather a common renunciation of the predetermined.'[4] Fundamental, they say, was the

---

[3]   Delgado/Svich, *Theatre in crisis?*, p. 8. While the strong influence of music and musicality on today's theatre is frequently acknowledged and hardly debatable, it still often does not get detailed academic attention; Govan/Nicholson/Normington's *Making a Performance*, for example, does not even have an index entry on 'music'.

[4]   Christian Kaden/Volker Kalisch, 'Musik', in Karl-Heinz Brack (ed.), *Ästhetische Grundbegriffe. Historisches Wörterbuch in sieben Bänden* (Stuttgart/Weimar, 2005), pp. 256–308, p. 307.

'elementary urge to break with the constraints of immanent systems of power'.[5] For the theatre, I would argue, musicality became one of the vehicles in the 'pluralism of compositional [and theatrical, DR] solutions'[6] on this road to rejection of master narratives and their implied hierarchies, as Lyotard described them.[7] Guido Hiß calls this an 'aesthetics of interferences'[6] with respect to two major practitioners of the post-modern: Robert Wilson and Christoph Marthaler.[8] He describes their work as a 'de-composition of correspondences, demanding the momentum of the theatrical expressive dimensions as well as the authorship of the audience [...], modelled formally on musical patterns'.[9] No longer are the arts that constitute a theatre performance together, interrelated with the predominant purpose of telling, modifying and interpreting stories and characters;[10] they are rather used with other rationales of making performance in mind, creating different anchors of coherence for the audience's experience. Musicality is one of these anchors.

New 'Anchors' of Coherence

I will come back to how musicality replaces or enriches the traditional coherence provided by dramatic structure on a macro-structural level, but I want to first look at this development on a smaller scale: language and dialogic communication, as the often dominant carriers of meaning on the theatrical stage, have long been the ground that gives traction and hold for the audience's perceptive 'anchor' when it is 'trailing' for meaning and coherence. As we have seen recurrently from Artaud or Stein to Chaikin or Jelinek, theatre-makers have shown an increasing interest in problematizing linguistic communication, to recapture the materiality of the onstage voice per se and to break with our habit of reducing language to a carrier of (discursive) meaning. Contemporary theatre remains full of examples in which 'priority is given to musicality instead of semantic

---

5   Kaden/Kalisch, 'Musik', p. 307.

6   Kaden/Kalisch, 'Musik', p. 307.

7   See Jean-François Lyotard, *The Post-Modern Condition: A Report on Knowledge* (Manchester, 1984).

8   See also David Roesner, *Theater als Musik. Verfahren der Musikalisierung in chorischen Theaterformen bei Christoph Marthaler, Einar Schleef und Robert Wilson* (Tübingen, 2003).

9   Hiß, *Synthetische Visionen*, p. 10.

10   Wagner's *Gesamtkunstwerk* remains a strong presence in this discourse, not least as something to reject by difference. Marthaler, for example, 'quotes the hopes and utopias associated with the Gesamtkunstwerk without however being completely absorbed by them' (Hiß, *Synthetische Visionen*, p. 10), and Heiner Goebbels explicitly bases his aesthetic and ethic position in opposition to it, as he explains in his chapter 'Gegen das Gesamtkunstwerk: Zur Differenz der Künste' ['Against the Total Work of Art. On the Difference of the Arts'], in Wolfgang Sandner (ed.), *Heiner Goebbels. Komposition als Inszenierung* (Berlin, 2002), pp. 135–41.

content, the text is first considered as *material*, which is above all constructed on musical constraints'.[11]

'Abstraction' and 'de-semantification' are perceived to be the two strategies of this shift and the discipline of musical composition itself has seen a parallel development, partly paving the way for its theatrical counterparts, partly reacting to them and partly independent of them:

> Increasingly the entire sonoric dimension of language is being integrated into music: the phonetic aspect detaches itself from its counterpart that is defined as meaning and transforms into pure sonic material of a composition: the phonetic material aspect of language thus becomes the actual agent of composing.[12]

This description would also fit quite a few recent (and not so recent) attempts of breaking with the hegemony of discursive language on the theatre stage, from Dada to Dario Fo, from Schwitters to Marthaler; Elmar Budde's interpretation of the consequences, however, misses the mark – at least if applied to theatre. He argues that 'the "musicalization" of the phonetic layer of language, which leads to its autonomization, definitively destroys the aspect of linguistic meaning'.[13] Is this really a case of 'either-or'?

On the one hand I would agree: since music is an abstract, mostly non-referential 'language', it is to be expected that musicalization in theatre will also result in changes in the audience's traditional expectations of theatrical communication. When, for example, Marthaler abandons structuring systems like narrative, story or character development in his devised productions[14] and replaces them with a dramaturgy of (musical) numbers or actions, the audience is encouraged to ask different questions about content and form, compared to what they are habituated to. The necessity for a certain scene or action may well be predominantly musical and a concern about its psychological motivation would be misleading for both the performers and the audience.

On the other hand, theatre is never as purely abstract and self-referential as music *can* be. Convention will always make us approach a theatre space with a different set of expectations of causality, coherence and narrativity than those with which we approach a concert hall. Musicalization (of language, but also in general) on the theatrical stage questions and plays with those expectations,

---

[11]   Catherine Bouko, 'Jazz Musicality in Postdramatic Theatre and the Opacity of Auditory Signs', *Studies in Musical Theatre*, 4/1 (2010), pp. 75–87, p. 78.

[12]   Elmar Budde, 'Zum Verhältnis von Sprache, Sprachlaut und Komposition in der neueren Musik', in Rudolf Stephan (ed.), *Über Musik und Sprache* (Mainz, 1974), pp. 9–19, p. 18.

[13]   Budde, 'Zum Verhältnis von Sprache', p. 19.

[14]   For example: *Murx* (Berlin, 1993), *Stunde Null* (Hamburg, 1995), *The Unanswered Question* (Basel, 1997), *Die Spezialisten* (Hamburg, 1999), *20th Century Blues* (Basel, 2000), or *O.T.* (Zurich, 2004).

offering new cohesive strategies and elements: the investigation of voices, the musical development of a visual or acoustic motif, the experience of time, or the sonority of space, for example. At first sight, the inclination of a theatrical or linguistic event towards the self-referentiality and self-reflexivity of music liberates from the semiotic compulsion; from the obligation to search for the primarily semiotic function (as the Prague School would call it) of everything on stage. And potentially, by worrying less about 'what it means', the audience can focus their attention on 'what it is' and thus challenge, widen and reflect on their own modes of perception and observation. Elevator Repair Service's artistic director, John Collins, describes this succinctly in reflecting on his experience of watching the Wooster Group:

> I realised that I could watch and listen to that show the way I looked at abstract art. I didn't have to make sense according to familiar rules of narrative or spoken or written language. This was a great thing to come to understand because this show was making sense to me in a way that I hadn't experienced before. It was a piece of theater making sense musically.[15]

At the same time, musicalization in the theatre will always deal with concrete spaces, bodies, texts and para-texts that, despite all its attempts to aspire to the abstract qualities of music will, almost inevitably, suggest elements of meaning. Discursive meaning and non-musical forms of coherence can thus be reintroduced by making use of the *connotative* referential potential of music and the interaction of musical coherence with textual, visual, kinetic or spatial coherence.

Let me give two examples: In Marthaler's *Stunde Null* [*Zero Hour*] (Hamburg 1995), a production based on the difficulties of commemorating the fiftieth anniversary of the end of WWII, Graham F. Valentine launches into a long speech that is collaged from decrees of the Allies in English, French, Russian and German with sound poetry by Kurt Schwitters thrown in for good measure. As his speech becomes more and more nonsensical, turning towards gibberish and pure vocal sound, it actually makes more and more 'sense', shifting from bureaucratic jargon, meaningless in its edited form, to a vocal evocation of the war's soundscape (through the onslaught of Schwitters's syllables: trucks, machine-guns, bombs, crackling radio reception, etc.), which becomes easily comprehensible as an eerie echo with a 50-year delay.[16]

In Einar Schleef's *Verratenes Volk* (Berlin 2000) the rhythmitized choral delivery of passages from Alfred Döblin's novel *November 1918*, on which the production is based, makes it deliberately difficult to follow the text in a discursive way. However, the friction between the revolutionary impetus of the choir (the military tone of multiplied and rhythmically organized voices) and its rhythmic

---

[15]   John Collins in Jen Harvie/Andy Lavender (eds.), *Making Contemporary Theatre. International Rehearsal Processes* (Manchester, 2010), p. 87.

[16]   For a more detailed analysis of this scene see Roesner, *Theater als Musik*, pp. 80–89.

shape (the increasing rhythmical stumbling, the often counter-semantic phrasing, the uneven metric accentuation) prompts the audience to read the text against the grain and suggests that the ostentatious self-confidence of the revolutionary masses is in fact quite questionable.[17]

Musicality, then, is often embraced by theatre-makers as a provider of a different kind of coherence (in the sense of structuring, connecting, attuning scenic material) that may at times replace, but often accompanies or counterpoints linguistic and narrative coherence and challenges their dominant position. Musicality thus also becomes part of the concerns and new developments in postdramatic dramaturgies.[18]

Musical Dramaturgies

In assessing the rehearsal and development processes of leading contemporary theatre companies, Harvie and Lavender speak of the turn from 'narrativity to thematicity'.[19] Hand in hand with this, I would argue, goes a renewed interest in form: while dramatic text and narratives provide clear structures that have implications for duration, rhythm, hierarchies, décor, etc., 'themes' or 'stimuli' are much more in search of form and dramaturgy:

> To the degree that productions are no longer following a dramatic text, the idea of dramaturgy changes profoundly. The theatre of images, the physical and dance theatre, the object- and music-theatre and not least the emphasis on the performative dimension of theatre itself require establishing a new dramaturgical logic. [...] Dramaturgy thus deals with internal logic and contingencies, with de-hierarchized systems and individual premises. The regulatory instance in theatre is no longer necessarily a narrative. For the dramaturgy it can now equally be a discursive field or a particular rhythm which organizes the interplay of heterogeneous materials.[20]

Recent strategies and solutions include the use of lecture performances, promenade theatre, interactive and/or immersive settings, game play and rules, improvisation, forms derived from spaces, sites or architecture and of course musical forms,

---

[17]   Also for this scene I provide a more detailed analysis in *Theater als Musik*, pp. 215–16.

[18]   With dramaturgy I refer to its continental European understanding as the thematic organization, aesthetic composition, interpretive strategies and core conceptual backbone of a theatrical event – whether it is text-based or not – and not merely the playwright's arc of narrative or character development. See also Mary Luckhurst, *Dramaturgy: A Revolution in Theatre* (Cambridge, 2006) and Cathy Turner/Synne K. Behrndt, *Dramaturgy and Performance* (Basingstoke/New York, 2007) on this distinction.

[19]   Harvie/Lavender, *Making Contemporary Theatre*, p. 14.

[20]   Christel Weiler, 'Dramaturgie', in Erika Fischer-Lichte/Doris Kolesch/Matthias Warstat (eds.), *Metzler Lexikon Theatertheorie* (Stuttgart, 2005), pp. 80–83, pp. 81–2.

dramaturgies and performance conventions. Director Rufus Norris, for example, who recently collaborated with composer Adam Cork for the verbatim musical *London Road* (NT London, 2011), in which compositions were based closely on the inherent musicality of 'the melodic speech patterns captured on Alecky Blythe's recorded interviews with the people of Ipswich'[21] after a series of murders in their community, understands musicality 'as an architecture that influences [his] approach to text and collaboration with actors'.[22] Similarly, Sara Jane Bailes reflects on Elevator Repair Service's collaborations, particularly between John Collins and Steve Bodow, by describing the role of the latter as 'a fine dramaturgical complement to Collins's directorial position. Together, Collins and Bodow always explore musical impulses in the rehearsal room, allowing "pacing, rhythm, dynamics, moods and instrumentations" to organise material'.[23] Another example of such an intensive dramaturgical collaboration is Ariane Mnouchkine's working relationship with musician Jean-Jacques Lemêtre.[24]

Scores / Polyphony / Hierarchy
One strategy which we have already seen in previous chapters[25] is the use of scores (or proto-scores[26]) modelled on musical practices: at times this is more an analogy, a way of thinking, but at other times this amounts to creative uses of musical notation, influencing devising processes and performance aesthetics.[27] Christoph Marthaler is an example of the former, as Stefanie Carp, his dramaturg in many of his productions, explains:

> Christoph Marthaler as a director works like a composer. The form of his production is always a particular composition. Whether he directs a play or a collage of texts and music, he submits his material of language, gestures, actions, music and procedures to a quite specific musical theme. He turns the material in a rhythmical and sonic score, which accompanies the entire

---

[21]   http://www.nationaltheatre.org.uk/londonroad [24.07.2012].

[22]   Rufus Norris in Sara Jane Bailes, 'Between People. Rufus Norris interviewed by Sara Jane Bailes', *Performing Arts Journal*, 81 (2005), pp. 62–73, p. 62.

[23]   Bailes in Lavender/Harvie, *Making Contemporary Theatre*, p. 88.

[24]   See David Williams (ed.), *Collaborative Theatre: The Théâtre du Soleil Sourcebook* (London, 1999).

[25]   See for example Chapter 1 on Appia.

[26]   See the section on 'thinking in and working with scores' in my chapter '"It is not about labelling, it's about understanding what we do" – Composed theatre as discourse', in Matthias Rebstock/David Roesner (eds.), *Composed Theatre. Aesthetics, Practices, Processes* (Bristol, 2012), pp. 319–62, pp. 331–6.

[27]   A current research project, *The Didascalic Imagination*, at the Research Centre for Visual Poetics (University of Antwerp) (2013–2017) is investigating these aspects – amongst other forms and developments of the *Regiebuch* in contemporary theatre and the digital age further. See http://www.visualpoetics.be/?action=project&id=35 [13.06.2013].

performance as a subtext. This score, often more than the text, thematizes the unavailing longing of the characters.[28]

In Marthaler's case, this 'score' usually does not manifest itself in the form of musical notation but emerges more or less consciously from a collaborative process. If we look at Robert Wilson's 'storyboard' drawings (see Figure 6.1), however – which often precede almost everything else in the process of creating a show for him and his collaborators – and remind ourselves that he regularly attributes precise timings to each sequence of the series of images, we already have a proto-score.[29] Wilson himself insists:

> My texts are not meant to tell a story, they are constructed like actual musical scores. All the gestures of the characters are numbered, all the rhythms of the lights and of the actions are calculated to the second, as in a score in which light, sound, and action converge.[30]

Other practitioners (such as the Lose Combo in Berlin, for example) use actual musical scores and 'transpose' them for the 'orchestra' of theatrical means: gestures, images, lighting, words.[31] They also, conversely, use various methods of deconstruction to transform the pixels of a photographic image into musical instructions for an instrumentalist in a multi-media installation.[32] The notion of the score is also present in the recording technologies that led to thinking in 'track': the possibility of recording, manipulating and mixing individual layers of voices, instruments or sound; a technology that is now ubiquitous and literally at people's

---

[28]   Stefanie Carp, 'Langsames Leben ist lang. Zum Theater von Christoph Marthaler', *Theaterschrift*, 12 *Zeit/Temps/Tijd/Time* (1997), pp. 64–77, p. 66.

[29]   See for example Holm Keller's description of the genesis of Wilson's *Einstein on the Beach* (Avignon 1976): 'Wilson's work on a new piece starts with fixing its structure: a performance is, for example, meant to take four hours and 45 minutes and consist of four acts. The first act is divided in parts A1 and B1, the second in C1 and A2, the third in B2 and C2, while the fourth actor is made of parts A3, B3 and C3. Same letters refer to similar sections. Both between the four acts and at the beginning and end of the piece there are transitional sections, so-called "knee plays." Those are called K1, K2, K3, K4 and K5. Wilson allocated each of these 14 section a fixed duration: K1 will be 8 minutes, A1 21 minutes, B1 27 minutes, K2 6 minutes and so on' (Holm Keller, *Robert Wilson* [Frankfurt am Main, 1997], p. 17).

[30]   Wilson in Franco Quadri/Franco Bertoni/Robert Stearns, *Robert Wilson* (New York, 1998), p. 36.

[31]   See http://www.lose-combo.de/de/archiv/projekt/16 [26.07.2012] for a description of the project.

[32]   See Jörg Laue's chapter '… To Gather Together What Exists in a Dispersed State …', in Rebstock/Roesner, *Composed Theatre*, pp. 133–54. See also William Fetterman, *John Cage's Theatre Pieces: Notations and Performances* (Amsterdam, 1996) for a range of further techniques and strategies of using a wide range of visual objects as 'scores'.

fingertips in software such as GarageBand on the iPad. For some theatre-makers, this introduced the possibility of developing their work to a pre-existing timeline: The Wooster Group, Christoph Schlingensief (*Hamlet*, Zurich 2001) and Goat Island (*The Lastmaker*, Zagreb 2007) have each used sound-tracks from films as an organizing principle.

Robert Wilson found even more extensive and particularly interesting ways of translating the principle of tracks into his performance practice. Like a recording technician, who will treat the tracks for an album as separate units that can be individually cut, manipulated and moved around, Wilson often treats elements like text, gesture and lighting in a similar way. He says about the creation process for *The Golden Windows* (New York City 1985):

> The visual book was written with no regard to the text. The text was written with no regard to the visual. And then they were put together. You can find relationships between the two, but the visual does not necessarily decorate the text. I made the gestures without thinking about what the text was saying.[33]

In addition to this practice of 'letting each contributing art form be guided by its own inherent grammar',[34] the notion of trackwork is also a spatial principle in Wilson's work. As one can see from his conceptual drawings (see Figure 6.1), Wilson divides the stage into

> successive, horizontal playing zones ('tracks', Wilson calls them), in each of which activities take place singly or simultaneously. The activity in one zone is continually juxtaposed with the activities in other zones, and the eye must move constantly to take them all in.[35]

Wilson comments on this practice:

> [...] in each of the zones there's a different 'reality' – a different activity defining the space so that from the audience's point of view one sees through these different layers, and as each occurs it appears as if there's no realization that anything other than itself is happening outside that particularly designated area.[36]

---

[33] Wilson in Susan L. Cole, 'Robert Wilson directs *The Golden Windows* and *Hamletmaschine*', in Susan L. Cole (ed.), *Directors in Rehearsal: A Hidden World* (New York/London, 1992), pp. 144–69, p. 156.

[34] Keller, *Robert Wilson*, p. 22.

[35] Calvin Tomkins, 'Time to think', in John Rockwell (ed.), *Robert Wilson: The Theater of Images* (New York, 1984), pp. 54–95, pp. 74–5.

[36] Robert Wilson, 'From Speech introducing *Freud*', in Drain, *Twentieth Century Theatre*, p. 59–60.

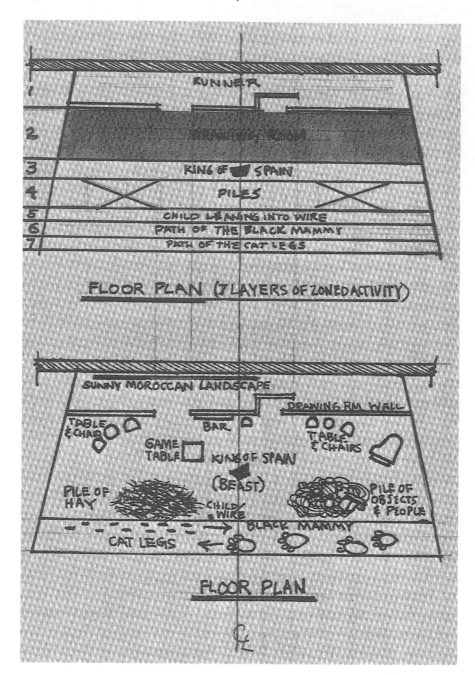

Figure 6.1   Floor Plan for Robert Wilson's *King of Spain* (Byrd Hoffman School of Byrds 1969)

This independence and autonomy is, however, ultimately quite organized, like in a polyphonic piece of music. Wilson's decisions on the precise interplay of all the elements and tracks, however separately they may have been developed and however unconnected semantically they may appear, are ultimately based on his artistic intuition about when it feels 'right'. It is the *rhythmical* relationship between them that he is most concerned about:

> So, in the beginning it may seem quite arbitrary, this placement of two things together that are happening on simultaneous, parallel tracks. But it's very important, you see, for me the way they either align, or are slightly out of phase, or are very much out of phase.[37]

Despite all the claims for separation and independence of tracks, there are many examples where discrete elements are also clearly compositionally intertwined – most obviously in the recurring 'mickey-mousing'[38] routines that many of Wilson's productions feature. What the idea of a score provides for Wilson (and other contemporary theatre-makers such as Heiner Goebbels) is to think of the theatre as a multitude of discrete 'voices', whose simultaneity needs formal organization, but whose *semantic* relations they seek to liberate from those production conventions and reception habits that they feel to be dominated by established hierarchies of means, redundancy of meaning, linearity and a singular expressive vision.

The musical *dispositif* and in particular the notions of polyphonic scores and tracks renegotiate the interdependence of the theatrical means of expression of a production as well as the relationship between the 'internal and external communications system'[39] of theatre. Christoph Marthaler and Heiner Goebbels in particular make use of the idea and characteristics of musical polyphony. As a musical principle, 'polyphony' is based on the relative rhythmic and melodic independence and autonomy of simultaneous voices, which nonetheless create a whole; harmonious, but full of tensions and counter-movements.[40] They afford the listener the privilege of choosing between following individual voices or trying to concentrate on the whole, fully aware that they won't be able to fully grasp the individuality and complexity in the ephemeral act of listening. For Goebbels, Marthaler, Wilson or Stemann, however, polyphony is more than a compositional principle; it is also – in the wake of Brecht – an ideological stance. As early as 1948 Brecht says in one of his key theoretical essays entitled *A Short Organum of the Theatre*:

---

[37]   Robert Wilson, 'The Space in the Text: An Interview with Robert Wilson', in Sigrid Bauschinger/Susan Cocalis (eds.), *Vom Wort zum Bild. Das neue Theater in Deutschland und in den USA* (Bern, 1992), pp. 245–56, pp. 251–2.

[38]   Based on principles of tightly associating the movements of animated Disney characters with a tailored score, I use 'mickey-mousing' to refer to the synchronization of acousmatic sound with an actor's gestures and movements, often to comic effect.

[39]   Manfred Pfister, *The Theory and Analysis of Drama* (Cambridge, 1991), p. 40.

[40]   See also Chapter 4.

So let us invite all the sister arts of the drama, not in order to create an 'integrated work of art' [*Gesamtkunstwerk*] in which they all offer themselves up and are lost, but so that together with the art of acting they may further the common task in their different ways; and their relations with one another consist in this: that they lead to mutual alienation.[41]

This dialectic idea of polyphony is indeed applied and extended by many of today's theatre-makers: in Marthaler's theatre this is particularly salient in the musical and textual material he collocates, as well as in the organization of his 'choric ensemble'[42] in the space and time of the performance. The different materials and eclectic sources of his devised projects, as well as the personnel on stage, are used polyphonically in the sense that they maintain their autonomy and individual specific weight, but at the same time form a perfectly attuned collective. This allows the audience to let their attention oscillate between being absorbed by minute detail (like Bruno Cathomas's drooling in *Murx*, Berlin 1993) versus watching with what Anton Ehrenzweig calls 'dedifferentiation'[43] – a kind of unconscious scanning (for instance in order to capture the spatially and temporally widespread rhythm of the collapsing beds in *Stunde Null*, Hamburg 1995). This process, however, has often been described as quite taxing in Marthaler's theatre and comes with a heightened awareness of the audience regarding its own act of spectatorship.

Heiner Goebbels takes this idea of theatrical polyphony even further by extending the musical process of de-hierarchization to virtually all constituent elements of the theatre, including lighting, sound design and video. He also reflects on this approach more explicitly as an attempt to elicit critical awareness, maturity and self-determination in the audience. The strategies of separation and de-hierarchization, to which Goebbels is committed in his collaborative devising processes as well as in treatment of his material(s), are intended to spill over to the reception process:

> All hierarchization [...] is in its essence totalitarian, art being no exception. The totalitarian in theatre doesn't stop at the audience. It frontally jumps down from the apron stage in order to overwhelm the audience, to patronize it. [...] There is no room for an individual experience.[44]

---

[41]   Brecht in George W. Brandt (ed.), *Modern Theories of Drama: A Selection of Writings on Drama and Theatre 1850–1990* (Oxford, 1998), p. 246.

[42]   See Detlev Baur, 'Der Chor auf der Bühne des 20. Jahrhunderts', in Peter Riemer/Bernhard Zimmermann (eds.), *Der Chor im antiken und modernen Drama* (Stuttgart, 1999), pp. 227–46, p. 227.

[43]   Anton Ehrenzweig, *The Hidden Order of Art: A Study in the Psychology of Artistic Imagination* (London, 1967), p. 123.

[44]   Goebbels, 'Gegen das Gesamtkunstwerk', p. 135. See also his collection of essays *Ästhetik der Abwesenheit* (Berlin, 2012), which will published translated into English by Routledge in 2014.

Goebbels argues against the dissolution of the individual arts and 'voices' in a total work of art, and for a kind of interplay that allows them to assert themselves in 'a presence that is held in a constant state of suspense'.[45] This, according to Goebbels, then allows for a theatre of experience, ideally resulting in a shared responsibility of artists and audience. The idea of the musical score and the principles of polyphony allow Marthaler, Goebbels and Wilson to offer their theatrical material in new ways that are less logocentric or character-driven. Wilson, for example, says about his production *Edison* (New York 1979): '*Edison* was not conceived from a story, but from a structure [...]. The show is above all an attempt to push as far as possible the discrepancy between image and hearing, and thus between light and sound.'[46]

Rhythm / Duration / Repetition
The (re-)discovery of theatre as a durational art form, as a 'waiting room' (*Wartesaal*) or 'institute for the annihilation of time' (*Zeitvernichtungsanstalt*)[47] and as an increasingly slow and outdated medium (compared to the general acceleration of communication and arts production, which Paul Virillo has most vocally outlined[48]), has led to a more and more conscious and experimental engagement with the temporality and rhythmicity of theatre.[49]

Inspired by the musical experiments on silence, duration, repetition (Cage, Glass, Stockhausen, Reich), contemporary theatre-makers have used unconventional concepts of time and rhythm both in their creation processes and in their resulting aesthetics. They have explored the performative effects of extremely long or short rehearsals, have used repetition in training (from repetition of forms in psychophysical training influenced by Asian and/or Buddhist practices to Sanford Meisner's repetition exercises) and have set themselves performative tasks, which – by means of their durational design – are intended to take them into states of exhaustion, loss of control and towards intuitive and immediate performances.

In the performances, then, directors like Marthaler and Schleef (but also Howard Barker, Frank Castorf, Robert Lepage, René Pollesch, Michael Thalheimer and companies including Elevator Repair Service and Forced Entertainment) introduce elements of repetition, extreme tempi and tempo changes (retardation/acceleration), pauses and silences, overall duration or explicit rhythmicality into

---

[45] Goebbels, 'Gegen das Gesamtkunstwerk', p. 136.

[46] Wilson in Quadri et al., *Robert Wilson*, p. 36.

[47] Guido Hiß, 'Marthalers Musiktheater', in Hans-Peter Bayerdörfer (ed.), *Musiktheater als Herausforderung* (Tübingen, 1999), pp. 210–24, p. 213.

[48] For example in *Polar Inertia* (London, 1999).

[49] Two publications which focus on this development are *Theaterschrift*, 12 *Zeit/Temps/Tijd/Time* (1997) and Dramaturgische Gesellschaft (ed.), *Zeitworte. Dokumentation des Symposions Geteilte Zeit* (2008), at http://www.dramaturgische-gesellschaft.de/dramaturg/index.php [25.07.2012].

their work beyond what could be justified by narrative or characterization of the dramatic personae (where these exist).

Klaus Dermutz's seminal edited volume on Christoph Marthaler from 2000 bears the title *Die langsamen Menschen sind die besseren Menschen* [*The Slow People Are the Better People*]. I would argue that the political or moral attribution given to a particular tempo – as in this title – is by no means coincidental. Marthaler's work has repeatedly employed slowness both as an aesthetic feature *and* a reflection of a conscious resistance to a society in which speed and acceleration have become major aims and achievements. In an interview[50] he observed that more and more people seem to be pushed aside by the centrifugal powers of our time and tend to fall off the fast-spinning carousel, and that it was precisely these people he took an interest in, watching and studying them and putting them on stage as figures in his theatrical inventions.

Marthaler and others reinstate timing and rhythm as autonomous, self-sufficient, non-representational factors of theatre, just like Michael Thalheimer or René Pollesch do at the faster end of the scale. In the rhythmic over- or undercoding that these techniques of musicalization result in, there is also a fundamental critique of the teleology and causality that are suggested in most areas of life. In a theatre where repetition, pauses, silence, lack of focus, multiple characters and a circular sense of time predominate, the audience finds itself confronted with fragmentation, contingency and a necessity to endure what probably corresponds more aptly to their individual experiences of daily life than does the latest well-made play or telenovela. A seemingly abstract use of musical principles thus transforms into a highly accurate reflection on and questioning of the concrete ways in which we experience our environment.

Space

In questioning the paradigm of representation, the proscenium arch stage has also come under scrutiny and a wide range of contemporary theatre practices has explored and redefined notions of space, site and stage and built the dramaturgy of their pieces to a great extent on that exploration. Quite often acoustic and musical aspects of space become an important part of this interrogation. While proscenium arch theatre follows a set of normative rules about rendering the human voice as audible as possible while seeking to suppress all 'interfering' sounds, performances in the outdoors, in derelict industrial buildings, in moving vehicles, in total darkness or in sound installations require a different, namely a musical disposition in the creative process which embraces and creatively uses the material and architectural challenges and their impact on the theatrical sonosphere.

The British company Sound and Fury, for example, chose to stage the story of their one-man show *Going Dark* (2011), about an astronomer and single parent who is afflicted by a condition which renders him increasingly blind, in the round

---

[50] In Renate Härtl, *Verweile doch, du bist so schön. Christoph Marthaler inszeniert Goethes Faust √1+2*, TV-Documentary by Renate Härtl for ZDF, 1994.

using very low lighting and periods of complete blackout. Paired with an elaborate surround-sound score with music, voice-overs and ambient noises, the audience – alongside the main character – increasingly had to rely on their sense of hearing rather than seeing in order to follow the unfolding narrative.

Intermusicality

Another strong theme that begins to pervade the practices and discourses of the musicality *dispositif* is what I would call intermusicality, with reference to intertextuality:

> Intertextuality refers to the characteristic particularly of literary texts to be related to other texts. [...] Kristeva explicitly invoked Bakhtin when coining the term intertextuality in order to describe the dialogic relation of all texts amongst each other. According to Kristeva every text builds itself as a 'mosaic of citations with every text being an absorption and transformation of another text'.[51]

Similar to how Kristeva defines intertextuality and following Ingrid Monson's[52] definition of the term in the jazz context, intermusicality in theatre forms a web of references, of allusions, quotations, citations and evocations that allocate an important role to the audience's individual and collective knowledge of the origins, contexts and layers of meanings that certain musical materials, principles or styles bring with them. The actual web of references can vary significantly, however, as some examples will show.

As Diedrich Diedrichsen has described perhaps most vocally,[53] the pop or rock song has become a hugely important ingredient in contemporary theatre. Some directors have been known to bring their extensive collection of LPs to rehearsals (Jürgen Kruse), others pick a selection of iconic songs as an atmospheric through-line through their performances (Nübling/Wittershagen), yet others (as we will see in more detail below) actually claim that theatre *itself* should ideally be like a good pop song (Thalheimer). Pop songs and their musical characteristics become

---

[51]   Richard Aczel in Ansgar Nünning (ed.), *Metzler Lexikon Literatur- und Kulturtheorie* (Stuttgart/Weimar, 1998), p. 241.

[52]   Ingrid Monson defines intermusicality as 'a way to begin thinking about the particular ways in which music and, more generally, sound itself can refer to the past and offer social commentary' (*Saying Something: Jazz Improvisation and Interaction* [Chicago/London, 1996], p. 97). Monson is thus exploring 'how music functions in a relational or discursive rather than an absolute manner [...]. The topic of interest here is the musical quotation or allusion, which embodies the conflict between innovation and tradition in jazz performance as well as the larger question of how instrumental music conveys cultural meaning' (ibid.).

[53]   See for example his article 'Fülle des Wohllauts. Ein guter Popsong bleibt auch im Theater immer er selbst – von der Rolle der Musik bei Thalheimer, Christoph Marthaler, Alain Platel, Frank Castorf und manch anderem', *Theater heute*, 10 (2003), pp. 18–25.

strong and persuasive 'containers' of a current or past *zeitgeist*, an evocation of intersubjective emotions, style, fashion or ideological identification. The musical *dispositif* that contemporary theatre taps into and reiterates, as well as interrogates, is the 'soundtrack of your life' paradigm. With radio, Walkmen, and now MP3 players, music has become the potentially ubiquitous and increasingly personalized accompaniment to our lives. Music is no longer most strongly associated with the moment of its production (playing music or attending a concert), but with travel, friends, personal or historic events, exercise, television programmes, etc.

Sampling

One technology that has become particularly influential not just in music production but also as a 'Kulturtechnik' [cultural technique][54] and 'Aufschreibesystem' [notational system],[55] is the sampler. This device is an expression of intermusicality on the technological and popular side of things and, given theatre's keen interest in popular culture in the post-modern era, it has proven a vital metaphor and model of praxis.[56] The fundamental principles of sampling have already been introduced by modernism in the form of collage (in the fine arts), or montage (in film), but the sampler as a digital technology, developed and launched for *music* production in the early Eighties, adds to these techniques a great amount of flexibility in editing and manipulating the sampled material (a recording of voice, sound, music) and putting it at composers' and musicians' fingertips in real time. A sample is thus not merely a citation, a clipping put in a new context, but is the transformation of a citation into composable material: any of the musical parameters (tempo, duration, pitch, timbre, volume) can be altered and samples can be combined, repeated, varied or fragmented. By making the sample accessible through 'conventional' instruments by means of MIDI (music instrument digital interface) technology, the sample can be 'played with' through a keyboard, guitar, drum or woodwind instrument, allowing the composer or performer to use their musical physicality and body memory while engaging with material that may be entirely alien to the instrument of their choice.

Sampling is a *dispositif*, which marks perhaps the opposite end on a scale of compositional practices and ideologies of 'musicality' in theatre in relation to

---

[54]   Jochen Bonz, 'Sampling. Eine postmoderne Kulturtechnik', in Christoph Jacke/Eva Kimminich/Siegfried J. Schmidt (eds.), *Kulturschutt. Über das Recycling von Theorien und Kulturen* (Bielefeld, 2006), pp. 333–53.

[55]   Friedrich Kittler, *Aufschreibesysteme 1800–1900* (München, 1995 [1985]). The book title has been translated into *Discourse Networks* (Stanford, 1990); 'notation systems' is the literal translation of Aufschreibesysteme.

[56]   Adriano Shaplin of The Riot Group, for example, refers to his adaption of *King Lear* entitled *Victory at the Dirt Palace* (Edinburgh 2002, see http://www.theriotgroup.com/works/victory-at-the-dirt-palace [07.08.2012]) as a 'totally hip hop approach to sampling. I'm not trying to sample the most obscure parts of *King Lear*, I'm trying to sample the most obvious parts, that everyone might know' (in Duška Radosavljević, *The Contemporary Ensemble. Interviews with Theatre-Makers* [London/New York, 2013], p. 142.

Wagner's *Gesamtkunstwerk*. Where the latter seeks to amalgamate and harmonize the interplay of the arts and celebrate individual creative genius, sampling exposes the composite nature of the art work, the heterogeneous provenance of its parts, its cracks and fissures, its materiality and the collaborative nature of creativity. It is founded in a 'lack of faith towards originality'[57] in a romantic sense and produces a welcome amount of 'Reibungshitze' [frictional heat][58] that Bonz feels to be characteristic of quotation as a cultural technique.

It is, therefore, not surprising that Heiner Goebbels has always shown an attraction to the *idea* of the sampler. He clarifies: 'I am not interested in the technical aspect of the sampler, not the instrument itself, but the use of the sample as an attitude [Haltung].'[59] Sampling allows for and suggests that anything can become material of an artistic process (echoing Adorno's concept of material[60]) and shares, as an attitude and approach, significant territory with some of the discourses and practices of devising theatre.[61] A key aspect of sampling, as Balme reminds us, is that 'the original context clings to the selected pieces music'[62] and that one could thus describe the 'dramaturgy of sampling as a possibility of allowing alterity to be also sensually experienced, to actually present it and not just re-present it in its irreducible otherness'.[63]

The Archaic and Indigenous in Music

In a perhaps slightly bold move I would compare another recent development with this cultural technique of citation and acculturation – in contrast to sampling and its interest in technical innovation, however, this demonstrates an interest in the ancient and archaic. I am referring to the rediscovery of myth and of folk traditions both local and exotic, often closely associated with historical musical styles and practices. We find examples of this in the work and processes of practitioners such as the Théâtre du Soleil, Sidi Larbi Cherkaoui[64] or the Polish theatre ensembles Song of the Goat and Gardzienice, both of which have been heavily influenced by Jerzy Grotowski.[65] The relevance of this work in the context of this book on

---

[57]   Bonz, 'Sampling', p. 335.

[58]   Bonz, 'Sampling', p. 336.

[59]   Goebbels in Christopher Balme, 'Heiner Goebbels: Zur Dramaturgie des Samplings', in Stefan Tigges (ed.), *Dramatische Transformationen. Zu gegenwärtigen Schreib- und Aufführungsstrategien im deutschsprachigen Theater* (Bielefeld, 2008), pp. 225–36, p. 225. Balme has quite rightly remarked on the Brechtian nature of this approach.

[60]   See for example Monika Wagner, *'Das' Material der Kunst: Eine andere Geschichte der Moderne* (München, 2001).

[61]   See Heddon/Milling, *Devising Performance*.

[62]   Balme, 'Heiner Goebbels', p. 235.

[63]   Balme, 'Heiner Goebbels', p. 235.

[64]   See http://www.sadlerswells.com/show/Myth [01.08.2012].

[65]   Ben Spatz describes the relationship of songs, training and performance in Gardzienice's work in detail and compares it to the work of Grotowski's Workcenter (Ben Spatz, 'To Open a Person: Song and Encounter at Gardzienice and the Workcenter', *Theatre*

musicality is two-fold: firstly there is an explicit and extensive use of often archaic and/or indigenous music, which becomes a focal point of the ensemble training and pathway to unlocking the expressive potential of the individual. Secondly there is, as Claude Lévi-Strauss has suggested, a deep structural relationship between myth and music, the 'two sisters begotten by language'.[66] Both myth and music are renditions, actualizations and variations of underlying themes. They are also both not linear: 'exactly as in a musical score, it is impossible to understand a myth as a continuous sequence. [...] That is, we have to read not only from left to right, but at the same time vertically, from top to bottom.'[67] According to Demetris Zavros, Lévi-Strauss thus 'creates binary categories that expose myth as a system structurally comparable to music since both of them are structured simultaneously on vertical (harmonic, synchronic) and horizontal (melodic, diachronic) axes'.[68] Lévi-Strauss points out two other axes, which are relevant for our context:

> Like a musical work, myth operates on the basis of a twofold continuum: one part of it is external and is composed in the one instance of historical, or supposedly historical, events forming a theoretically infinite series from which each society extracts a limited number of relevant incidents with which to create its myths; and in the other instance, the equally infinite series of physically producible sounds, from which each musical system selects its scale.[69]

Particularly in the work of Polish theatre company Gardzienice there is a strong sense of working with this understanding of musicality as something which connects, organizes and vitalizes the vertical and the horizontal and also draws on songs and folk tunes[70] as myths: 'unfinalizable'[71] (to use Bakhtin's term once more) series of performances with strong historical and personal resonances.

Topics, 18/2 [2008], pp. 205–22, p. 210) and Mario Frendo elaborates: 'Grotowski's work in the theatre was intrinsically linked with musical activity. Grotowski's was a musicality which transcended the idea of sounds in space audibly experienced by an audience. Flaszen underlines this when he claims that "simple audibility was not the issue" (Flaszen 2010: 175). It was a musicality that fed on the quintessential energy created by the sound-silence dynamic. [...] this energy informs the work of the actor as the source of action. What generated action in Grotowski's theatre was the body-voice dynamic, a dynamic which was musically organized through song and movement' (Frendo, 'Embodied Musicality', p. 214; the quotation is from Ludwik Flaszen, *Grotowski and Company* [Holstebro/Malta/Wroclaw, 2010]).

[66]   Claude Lévi-Strauss, *Myth and Meaning* (London, 2001 [1978]), p. 47.
[67]   Lévi-Strauss, *Myth and Meaning*, p. 39.
[68]   Demetris Zavros, 'Composing Theatre on a Diagonal: Metaxi ALogon, a Music-centric Performance', in Rebstock/Roesner, *Composed Theatre*, pp. 201–19, p. 205.
[69]   Claude Lévi-Strauss, *The Raw and the Cooked* (London, 1970), p. 16.
[70]   'Folk tunes provide a base from which the training develops' (Paul Allain, *Gardzienice: Polish Theatre in Transition* [Amsterdam, 1997], p. 61.)
[71]   Mikhail Bakhtin, *Problems of Dostoevsky's Poetics* (Minneapolis, MN, 1984), p. 61.

Gardzienice
Gardzienice is probably the ensemble with the most outspoken and most profound
relationship with musicality in this context:

> European theatre was born perhaps twice: in the ancient times and in the Middle
> Ages, both times from the spirit of music. And both times its true background
> was folk song. In Gardzienice Theatre, we witness how a Mystery Play is born,
> yet again, out of the spirit of music.[72]

First and foremost, musicality is a cornerstone of the training method of
the company:

> Staniewski's emphasis on music and musicality in training is the key to the
> company's rigorous performance technique. It is through Gardzienice's advanced
> application of musicality that the central themes of ecology, indigeneity, the
> archaic, and reciprocity coalesce.[73]

In calling it an 'advanced application of musicality',[74] Alison Hodge seems to
almost suggest that there is an established method or technique of that name that
comes in different levels of difficulty or intensity. While it is certainly true that
Gardzienice engage with the musicality *dispositif* more fully and holistically than
others (such as, on average, drama schools in Europe), it is important, in my view,
to think of 'musicalities' rather than presuming *one* way of training or performing
with this term.

The thrust of Gardzienice's notion of musicality is quite distinct: they aim
at a wholeness of the training and performing experience and a universality of
their theatrical language. Musicality is a vehicle to connect body, voice and
consciousness,[75] as well as to attune the performers to each other.[76] It is also

---

[72] Leszek Kolankiewicz in Alison Hodge, 'Włodzimierz Staniewski: Gardzienice and
the Naturalised Actor', in Alison Hodge (ed.), *Actor Training* (London, 2010), pp. 268–87,
p. 270.

[73] Hodge, 'Włodzimierz Staniewski', p. 271.

[74] Hodge, 'Włodzimierz Staniewski', p. 271.

[75] 'The actors [...] try to find their own organic rhythmic sounds and gestures that
express state of body/consciousness. These are rehearsed repetitively with the precise
momentum of a musical phrase. The actors are concerned with contacting their inner
musicality – finding a personal melody which can lead their work' (Hodge, 'Włodzimierz
Staniewski', p. 274). See also Konstantinos Thomaidis, 'Singing from Stones.
Physiovocality and Gardzienice's Theatre of Musicality', in Dominic Symonds/Millie
Taylor (eds.), *Gestures of Music Theater: The Performativity of Song and Dance* (Oxford:
Oxford University Press, 2014), pp. 242–58.

[76] 'Above all, the distinguishing characteristic of the songs [used in Gardzienice's
training, DR] is that they are ensemble songs, group songs, choral songs. Where solo parts
exist, these are almost always in relation to the group: rising out of it, responding to it, leading

integrated rather than separated in their notion of theatre, as Paul Allain attests: 'Gardzienice do not instigate "voice warm-ups" as a separate unit in training, as is familiar in many British acting schools, but sing as part of the total creative process.'[77] Hodge confirms and extends this description:

> The actors learn a particular way of seeing which engages the whole body [...]. The training is extended through exploring vocal phenomena such as breathing patterns, an actor's personal sounds (sighs, cries and shouts), rhythmic exercises based on laughter and ritualistic vocal traditions such as lamentation. The actors explore harmony, polyphony, antiphony and dissonance, rhythm and counterpoint.[78]

For Gardzienice the boundaries between training and performance, explorations and dramaturgy are fluid: 'The vocal and musical score defines the physical shape of a performance. [...] Music provides the base from which all action unfolds.'[79] Gardzienice's artistic director Włodzimierz Staniewski lists the different aspects of musicality separately here, but these do not remain distinct in Gardzienice's practice:

> There are three aspects to my process: one is concerned with the expansion of our system of perception; the second with how to find ways to absorb and introduce musicality into our practice; and the third with how to frame it within a performance.[80]

This fluidity between training, rehearsal and performance is also characteristic of a practice we have in principle already encountered with Chaikin's Open Theatre – there, however, it is based on quite different musical models and ideologies. Let us look a bit more closely on the specific notion of 'musicality' put forward by Staniewski:[81]

> Staniewski defines the term 'musicality' as a specific feeling for music which corresponds with the Pythagorean concept of the *harmonia mundi*: 'I am utterly convinced that the Earth is musical, that it has musicality and that every part of nature can be musical' [...]. He regards musicality as the vital source for

---

it, challenging it, and eventually returning to it. Different kinds of song require different kinds of group coordination, such as harmonic resonance, rhythmic synchronization, or call-and-response, but "tuning" in a broad sense is always essential' (Spatz, 'To Open a Person', p. 210).

[77] Allain, *Gardzienice*, p. 61.
[78] Hodge, 'Włodzimierz Staniewski', p. 275.
[79] Allain, *Gardzienice*, p. 62.
[80] Hodge, 'Włodzimierz Staniewski', p. 271.
[81] See also Thomaidis, 'Singing from Stones'.

his theatre: 'everything in our theatre practice comes from musicality and ends in musicality' […]. It is Staniewski's belief that musicality has a spiritual significance, that the original power of life originated in sound, and that consequently sound and spirit are very closely connected.[82]

A few things stand out here: compared to other *dispositifs* we have encountered, the spiritual dimension is particularly strong and explicit for Gardzienice: 'We have to do something with the training of our senses, our memory, so that musicality can still be part of our way of communicating with the world, and with "holiness."'[83] It is a pantheistic sense of spirituality that underpins this 'sense of musical and rhythmical harmony and understanding'.[84] Hodge quite rightly thus calls it a 'musicality of the natural environment'[85] and it is this primary idea rather than a refined concept of Western art music that lies at the heart of Gardzienice's practice. Staniewski:

> Music as it is sometimes understood, is an aesthetic term, having historical connotations. It is related to a codified system operating in terms of notation. Musicality, on the other hand, is for me very close to the spirit. Musicality exists everywhere. I believe that the earth itself is musical.[86]

Consequently, he sees the relationship with music as an art form, academic and high-brow, as inverted: Western art music is not the superior development of a more primitive *harmonia mundi*, but musicality is precisely what breaks the mould, what challenges the accepted systems: 'Everything which sounds beyond the "edges" of the codified system is musicality.'[87] He thus compares musicality to a rough diamond, 'properly framed by the gold of the codified music'.[88] Where Goethe, Kleist or Appia saw music's virtue in the pure, refined and artistically sublime of highly developed sounds and structures, Staniewski promoted an altogether more 'chtonic' notion of musicality, in which a sense of the 'authentic' or 'organic' of certain musical practices (however problematic one might find this idea) features. In the quest for this kind of musicality a strong interest in historical musical practices is equally present as an intercultural sense of discovery: Gardzienice displays conscious efforts to tap into musical cultures from times and places foreign to the theatre-maker of today. While not referring to Gardzienice specifically, Marcus Tan describes the resulting aesthetics very well: 'Music, sound

---

[82] Hodge, 'Włodzimierz Staniewski', p. 274.
[83] Staniewski in Hodge, 'Włodzimierz Staniewski', p. 271.
[84] Allain, *Gardzienice*, p. 63.
[85] Hodge, 'Włodzimierz Staniewski', p. 274.
[86] Włodzimierz Staniewski/Alison Hodge, *Hidden Territories: The Theatre of Gardzienice* (London/New York, 2004), p. 63.
[87] Staniewski/Hodge, *Hidden Territories*, p. 64.
[88] Staniewski/Hodge, *Hidden Territories*, p. 65.

and song in intercultural performances are consequently integral performative texts, actants that assist in the construction of the culturally kaleidoscopic *mise en scène*.'[89]

New Acting Ideals – New Forms of Rehearsal

As we have seen in previous chapters, the musically informed dramaturgies and new paradigms with respect to mimesis and representational aesthetics both require and bring forth a different generation of actors and a different understanding of the actor's task. Given the complexity of theatrical languages and the eclecticism of styles, approaches, training backgrounds of the creative teams, it is unsurprising that the palette of skills required by the actor is particularly colourful and varied. The notion that there should be one 'method' which would apply to the full range of acting opportunities an actor might come across in their career, one key to unlock all theatrical challenges, has become increasingly implausible. Kurzenberger describes the transition from August Wilhelm Iffland's much-quoted notion of the actor as 'Menschendarsteller' [people representer[90]] to a 'contemporary "Spielemacher" [playmaker] with a multiplicity of functions and divergent methods of performance'.[91] Roselt and Weiler – in their edited volume on 'Acting Today'[92] – make the increasing dissolution of boundaries between theatre and other arts (which I will come back to) partly responsible for the increasing proliferation of acting styles and approaches:

> Contemporary theatre is characterized by a wide range of acting styles. The boundary crossing between theatre, performance, dance, visual arts and working with new media seems to have become common. [...] Acting thus becomes recognizable as a process of permanent self-generation and invention of what's new in front of an audience, which coins the aesthetics of contemporary theatre profoundly.[93]

Interestingly, Roselt and Weiler do not mention music in their list of bordering art forms; however, I would contest it should definitely be considered in this context given that music and notions of musicality play a particularly vital part

---

[89] Marcus Cheng Chye Tan, *Acoustic Interculturalism: Listening to Performance* (Houndmills, 2012), p. 22.

[90] Iffland's seminal essay 'Fragmente über Menschendarstellung' ['Fragments over people representation'] was published 1785 (Gotha).

[91] Hajo Kurzenberger, 'Multiperspektivität des Darstellens. Zum Paradigmenwechsel des Schauspielens', in Anton Rey/Hajo Kurzenberger/Stephan Müller (eds.), *Wirkungsmaschine Schauspieler – Vom Menschendarsteller zum multifunktionalen Spielemacher* (Berlin/Köln, 2011), pp. 74–84, p. 76.

[92] Roselt/Weiler, *Schauspielen heute*.

[93] Roselt/Weiler, *Schauspielen heute*, back cover.

in the redesign of our understanding of what actors (and also directors) do (or should do) today. Being able to sing, play instruments, be musically literate, conversant in styles both classical and popular and, importantly, being able to draw upon and translate this musical literacy to working with texts, ensemble work, physical scores, gestural codes are all certainly part of the job description of the contemporary actor.[94] For the actor in an adaptation of a classical play or a piece of new writing, musicality becomes a vital component of their 'toolkit'; for the 'task performer', as one could call the actors in Heiner Goebbels's demanding devised pieces of theatre (following Gerald Siegmund[95]), musicality becomes an indispensable strategy of dealing with the genre-defying range of demands and actions whose one common denominator is that none of them strives for 'as if' realism.

Theatre director and educator at NYU's Tisch School of the Arts, Fritz Ertl, consequently also lists 'musicality' as one of the requirements for the interdisciplinary training of the contemporary actor:[96]

> If space requires students to consider the visual picture, controlling everything that is seen in a theatrical production, musicality requires students to master everything that is heard – what I call the aural track. Because we live in a culture that is so obsessively visual, we sometimes forget how important and ubiquitous is sound.[97]

I fully agree with Ertl, but would not restrict the relevance of 'musicality' to the acoustic sphere of the theatrical event, as I have outlined variously in this book. In fact, in Appia's writings we already saw that musicality became instrumental in describing qualities of movement and the visual properties of space design as much as textual delivery or music and sound effects (see Chapter 1). Along with the developments in acting, the role of the director has inevitably changed as well, as Alison Oddey outlines:

---

[94] Recent years have also seen the advent of a new category called 'actor-musician' or 'actor/muso' and Rose Bruford College (UK), for example, already offers a BA specifically dedicated to this hybrid between an actor and an instrumentalist. Actor-musicians have featured in musical productions by John Doyle (e.g. *Sweeney Todd*, Broadway 2005; *Company*, Broadway 2006) or Horwood and Travis (*Sunset Boulevard*, West End 2009), in which the actors accompany themselves and each other and are, so to speak, the acting ensemble as well as the orchestra. In a less commercial way this practice can also be observed in companies such as Filter (see below), Kneehigh or Propeller.

[95] See Gerald Siegmund, 'Task Performance als Choreographie. Die Aufgabe des Schauspielers', in Sandner, *Heiner Goebbels. Komposition als Inszenierung*, pp. 127–31.

[96] Fritz Ertl, 'Interdisciplinary Training. Directing for Actors', in Arthur Bartow (ed.), *Training of the American Actor* (New York, 2006), pp. 251–68.

[97] Ertl, 'Interdisciplinary Training', p. 251.

The changing role and shift of directorial practice comes with the interest in the musicality of text and composition, so that the director is composing in collaboration with others, transposing video, lighting, sound or animation, which is then edited and notated as a score in the process of rehearsal. The shift is seen in the director's compositional skills, in the creating, composing and editing of a textual score, in a musical theatricality to be conducted, in a role of director that might be described as being a *conductor-composer-collaborator*.[98]

Oddey gives a range of examples, such as the work of director Simon McBurney (of British theatre company Complicité), who has been described as 'more like a conductor than a director sometimes' and who, according to Oddey, 'thinks of theatre as a musical activity'.[99] Or, emphasizing the notion of transfer of musical principles to 'non-musical' aspects of theatre, she points us to Graeme Miller, 'a theatre-maker, theatre director, sound artist and composer of "many things that may include music"'.[100]

'Musicality', consequently, not only impacts on the actor and director's work, but on the rehearsal process itself. Christoph Marthaler or Ruedi Häusermann do not begin their rehearsals with read-throughs at a table, but learning and singing songs at the piano. These may or may not find their way into the devised performance, but have become an established starting point and part of the ensemble building process.[101] 'Rehearsals', as Annemarie Matzke puts it, 'are always also performative situations, which constitute a specific working context'.[102] New rehearsal and devising strategies may derive from a specific space, as Matzke exemplifies, but also, as I would add, from a specific sense of musicality, which forms a basic structure, a leaping off point, a roadmap and emotional landscape, etc. for the rehearsal process and its slow gestation process in an actual production. Echoing what we have already observed about new dramaturgies in contemporary theatre, Matzke writes:

> The difference of theatre forms in postdramatic theatre is that here the logic of the production [Inszenierung] is only generated in and through the rehearsals rather than being prescribed by dramatists […], and can thus also always be profoundly questioned (by the actors, the creative team etc.).[103]

---

[98]   Alison Oddey, *Re-Framing the Theatrical. Interdisciplinary Landscapes for Performance* (Houndmills, 2007), pp. 23–4.

[99]   Oddey, *Re-Framing the Theatrical*, p. 40. At the time of writing, Complicité also advertised a workshop on 'Sound-led Processes', for example, at CSSD in January 2013.

[100]   Oddey, *Re-Framing the Theatrical*, p. 164. The quotation is by Miller himself.

[101]   In the context of psycho-physical theatre, Eilon Morris finds accordingly that 'rhythm is a primary mechanism for achieving commonality, connectivity, and dialogue across a group of performers and between individual artists' (Eilon Morris, 'Collaborating in Time. The formation of Ensemble through Rhythm', in John Britton [ed.], *Encountering Ensemble* [London, 2013]: pp. 363–6).

[102]   Annemarie Matzke, 'Konzepte proben – Probenprozesse in postdramatischen Theaterformen', in Rey/Kurzenberger/Müller, *Wirkungsmaschine Schauspieler*, p. 44.

[103]   Matzke, 'Konzepte proben', p. 51.

But even in more 'traditional' processes based on a dramatic text, music can become a transformative part of the rehearsal process. Director Andreas Kriegenburg, for example, describes how he uses music as early as during read-throughs at the table, influencing the quality of the reading and the discussions around the play, as well as channeling the actor's imagination in certain directions.[104] He adds an interesting aspect by referring to what he calls the protective function of music:

> Often music has the purpose of filling the air, of avoiding silence. It offers a possibility to make the dishonesty more bearable for the actor, to actually offer them protection.[105]

His colleague Sebastian Nübling, in tandem with his musician Lars Wittershagen, also introduces music early on in the process and also uses it to a great extent for the benefit of the actor rather than subsequently the audience, who may only get to hear a small part of the music used in rehearsal. After an initial phase in which Nübling and Wittershagen decide on a specific musical cosmos that could connect with the play in question (e.g. music by Sarah Kane's favourite band *Tindersticks* for Nübling's production of *Crave*, Theater Basel, 2000), Wittershagen adapts, rearranges and recomposes this music into different tracks and samples with a distinct atmospheric and rhythmic character. This material is often played back during rehearsal, sometimes acting as a jump-start in eliciting a particular mood, sometimes as a source of friction that the actors have to go against and stand their ground. It also introduces a new time order that dictates the pacing of the scene, and serves as a stage direction and tempo indication, on the basis of which Nübling develops the rhythmically precise and versatile physical interaction of his actors that has become his trademark. The playlist of songs or samples that Wittershagen assembles and constantly modifies on his computer in preparation for rehearsals serves as the dramaturgical, emotional and rhythmic backbone of the production. It becomes a kind of co-director in this process and an omnipresent additional collaborator on stage. In the end, while much of the music may not be played back during the performances, it has become a kind of sub-text (or 'sub-music') that lives on in the minds of the actors as a shared internalized reference point. This use of music during the rehearsal process is at least partly responsible, I would argue, for the concentrated and precisely channelled performative energy of Nübling's productions. Nübling uses the resistance of (popular) music and its almost uncontrollable richness in connotations prior to the performance as a rehearsal technique that ultimately heightens the actors' awareness, presence and communication on stage.

Musicality then has become one of the core strategies not only of postdramatic or devised forms of theatre, but also of what has becomes known

---

[104] See Kriegenburg in Ortrud Gutjahr (ed.), *Regietheater!* (Würzburg, 2008), pp. 142–3.

[105] Kriegenburg in Gutjahr, *Regietheater!*, pp. 142–3.

as *Regietheater*[106] – a theatre aesthetic in which a director or creative team rigorously and often radically reinterpret, reimagine and adapt texts from the dramatic canon.[107] In Gronemeyer and Stegemann's recently edited book on directing, director Jette Steckel lists musicality prominently when asked about the competencies a director should bring to their job: 'Musicality, a certain technical ability and most of all knowledge of human nature, a heightened sensitivity towards people are the most important.'[108] A similar discourse has, unsurprisingly, developed in opera and music-theatre alongside the advent of *Regietheater* on the dramatic stage. In opera, notions of *Bebilderung* (merely supplying images to go alongside the music) and *Werktreue* (utmost faithfulness to the score) have given way to new directorial languages. The sacrosanct status of the score is slowly and occasionally being replaced by the advent of adaptations, radical new readings and director-auteurs, such as Peter Konwitschny, Hans Neuenfels, David Marton, Christoph Schlingensief, Sebastian Baumgarten,[109] Richard Jones, Peter Sellars, in institutions such as the Neuköllner Oper or Opera North, to name but a few.

Sven Friedrich, director of the Richard Wagner Museum in Bayreuth, reflects on this development and argues for a directorial practice 'from the spirit of music'. He refers to Meyerhold's verdict that the director had to be a musician in the first place[110] and to Appia's suggestion that 'music should command all the elements'[111] and that 'the theatre should achieve such malleability that it would comply with the musical demands without grumbling'.[112]

Musicality and the Ensemble

Another aspect how the musicality *dispositif* has contributed to reshaping the contemporary landscape of theatre-making is its role in ensemble formation. In her recent book on *The Contemporary Ensemble* (2013), Duška Radosavljević

---

[106] This is often wrongly translated as 'director's theatre', shifting the focus from the activity (Regie = directing, *mise en scène,* staging) to the person (director).

[107] For more detail on the often controversial debate about *Regietheater*, see for example Gutjahr, *Regietheater!*; Gerhard R. Koch et al. (eds.), *Wagnerspektrum 2/2005: Schwerpunkt / focussing on Regietheater* (Würzburg, 2005); Jürgen Schläder, *OperMachtTheaterBilder: Neue Wirklichkeiten des Regietheaters* (Berlin, 2006) or the guest-edited issue (by Gundula Kreuzer and Clemens Risi) of *The Opera Quarterly*, 27/2–3 (2011).

[108] In Nicole Gronemeyer/Bernd Stegemann (eds.), *Lektionen: Regie* (Berlin, 2009), p. 166.

[109] See for example the cover of *Theater der Zeit* (3/2012) which translates into 'David Marton and Sebastian Baumgarten. The Other Opera. Expeditions into the Future of Music Theatre'.

[110] See Chapter 2.

[111] Appia in Sven Friedrich, 'Um die "Geburt aus dem Geiste der Musik" bittend. Überlegungen zum "Regietheater" auf der Opernbühne', in Koch, *Wagnerspektrum 2/2005*, pp. 31–55, p. 47.

[112] Appia in Friedrich, 'Um die "Geburt"', p. 47.

provides many examples in her extensive range of interviews for theatre-makers who draw heavily on musicality and/or a notion of 'chorus' as core cohesive elements in their ensemble practice and identity.[113] This can apply both to aesthetics and working principles. Radosavljević notes that 'Barker, Adassinsky and Shaplin tend to use musical analogies when discussing their creative process'[114] and argues that 'the organising structure of the ensemble implies that the actor's contribution is closer to that of a musician – which is also where the term "ensemble" is more frequently found'.[115]

Let's look at some of the ways in which these theatre-makers reflect on the role of musicality for their theatre in a bit more detail. Ian Morgan, performer with Song of the Goat (Teatr Pieśń Kozła) who, like Teatr Zar or Kneehigh, have been directly influenced by Gardzienice, reflects on the principles of the company's rehearsal process: there is usually an 'initial stage of gathering inspirations around the territory, narrative, theme, texture, etc. Then we might explore these elements – often starting by learning and tasting music and song in the space, then possibly combined with elements of text'.[116] The materials, texts and actions that emerge from this process are later organized in montage by director Grzegorz Bral 'not based on narrative logic but on energy and musicality'.[117]

Emma Rice, artistic director of Kneehigh, emphasizes a different aspect of the influence of musicality and Gardzienice's take on it. For her, it is about learning a way of making music and theatre distinct from classical training, which she describes as a different way of 'owning' music[118] and of feeling 'cracked open' as a performer 'in a way that three years at Drama School hadn't touched me!'[119] It is not only a way of generating, assembling and organizing material, but is about changing one's craft. As with Gardzienice, making music is also an important part of the communal experience: life and work get inseparably intertwined as the ensemble sleeps, eats, runs, sings and creates theatre together.[120]

In other forms of ensemble that are based, for example, on a strong presence of a writer (Adriano Shaplin, Howard Barker), musicality becomes a currency in the artistic exchange: the writers/directors know the performative abilities of their ensemble very well, have internalized the 'sound' of the individual performers and now tailor the writing like commissioned composers would write their arias or concertos for specific

---

[113] See also Eilon Morris, *Via Rythmós. An Investigation of Rhythm in Psychophysical Actor Training* (PhD Thesis, University of Huddersfield, 2012), which investigates the role of rhythm in ensemble building in great detail.

[114] Radosavljević, *The Contemporary Ensemble*, p. 16.

[115] Radosavljević, *The Contemporary Ensemble*, p. 3.

[116] Morgan in Radosavljević, *The Contemporary Ensemble*, p. 123.

[117] Morgan in Radosavljević, *The Contemporary Ensemble*, p. 112.

[118] See Rice in Radosavljević, *The Contemporary Ensemble*, p. 106.

[119] Rice in Radosavljević, *The Contemporary Ensemble*, p. 106.

[120] See Radosavljević's interview with Joanna Holden in *The Contemporary Ensemble*, pp. 109–15.

musicians playing off their strengths. Shaplin, whose ensemble The Riot Group Radosavljević describes as a 'musical "intersubjective unit"', says:

> I don't think about creating a character so that the actor has to transform themselves to embody it. I think of the role much more like a tailor – I'm building a suit for the actor that has to fit them right, I'm building a part for their voice, for the sound of their voice and their morphology. [...] I do think of actors as instruments. Like a cello, or a bass guitar. I think that I have their lung capacities inscribed in my wrist. When I'm writing, I now know how big Stephanie's lungs are. In my muscle memory, I know where Stephanie is gonna take a breath versus where Drew is gonna take a breath.[121]

He also emphasizes the importance of listening to how the actors speak his lines, which is why he tends to only finish plays during and not before rehearsals:

> The closest formula is that if I'm working on page six it means that I have heard the pages one through five aloud already, because now I have the idea about the next place to go. I'm constantly adjusting the script based on how it sounds and how it feels to try and do it with my actors.[122]

Shaplin summarizes that he thinks of playwriting as 'writing music for instruments'[123] and has titled a playwriting class he teaches 'This Playwriting Class is a Music Class'.[124]

There is, I would argue, an additional and distinct strand in continental European ensemble theatre, which comes more out of the tradition of Weimar cabaret and Dada performances, epitomized most clearly by Swiss theatre-maker Christoph Marthaler. The much-quoted 'Marthaler family' of actors, musicians, dramaturgs, designers, etc., is characterized, perhaps above all, by the practice of communal singing and a strong sense of collage, montage and musical structure combined with rhythmical audacity (the infamous slowness) in shaping performances.[125] For the actors, argues Andreas Müry, this very different way of working is 'a kind of therapy. It relieves them of the paroxysm of psychology, from the dictates of "as-if"-realism'.[126]

---

[121] Shaplin in Radosavljević, *The Contemporary Ensemble*, p. 141.
[122] Shaplin in Radosavljević, *The Contemporary Ensemble*, p. 141.
[123] Shaplin in Radosavljević, *The Contemporary Ensemble*, p. 146.
[124] Shaplin in Radosavljević, *The Contemporary Ensemble*, p. 146.
[125] On his rehearsal process see, for example, Patricia Bennecke, 'Wir wollen eine geniale Idee nur noch einmal überprüfen', *Theater heute, Jahrbuch* (1998), pp. 128–35; Christoph Marthaler/Anna Viebrock, 'Die Gesprächsprobe. Über künstlerische und andere Gärprozesse', *Theater heute, Jahrbuch* (1997), pp. 9–24; or Klaus Dermutz (ed.), *Christoph Marthaler* (Salzburg, 2000).
[126] Andreas Müry, 'Dada in Zeitlupe. Christoph Marthaler', *du*, 9 (1993), pp. 16–17, p. 16.

In the tradition of Dada or Merz, however, this development is not only a departure from the realist paradigm of theatre, but also a (re)discovery of the complex interplay between the arts, a celebration of interrogating and dissolving boundaries between artistic disciplines and media. I have in this chapter increasingly referred to theatre-makers who may perhaps better be described as choreographers, composers, music-theatre directors, etc.: this is not an oversight on my part, but a symptom of the fact that today's theatre continues and expands on the tendency towards interart practices that we have found to be a characteristic of many practitioners mentioned in this book.[127] While I have tried to focus on theatre-makers and the influence of a musical *dispositif* on dramatic theatre, it has proven to be often problematic to draw a clear line distinguishing this phenomenon against similar developments in dance, music-theatre, opera or concert practices. I would argue that this proclivity towards interart[128] and hybrid genres has intensified in contemporary theatre practices and that musicality has become one of the strong catalysts in these processes.

To explain my metaphoric use of the term 'catalyst', it may suffice to define it as an entity that facilitates two other entities' interaction with each other more easily. In this, the catalyst produces something that enables interaction without itself being consumed. The musicality *dispositif* thus reduces the activation energy needed for the interaction and interplay between music and theatre (as well as other contributing arts and media). The catalyst also determines to a great extent *how* theatre and music interact and react with each other; for example, whether they merge or remain distinct, whether they act as two very similar or dissimilar elements. The mutual reactions can manifest themselves in subtle changes as well as evaporate in a big bang; at times they produce energy (in chemistry this is called 'exothermic'; in the theatre, perhaps, 'insight, fascination, experience'), on other occasions energy is absorbed (the so-called 'endothermic' reaction, which in theatre may translate to 'boredom, predictability or redundancy').

In the following four case studies, I will analyze such reactions, but will for the purpose of keeping the argument of the book coherent actually focus on practices which would still be considered 'theatre' even though each of them pushes against certain conventions in theatrical modes of production or reception, for which musicality, as we will see, plays a vital part. The four productions include staging new writing, adaptations of classical texts, multimedia adaptations of novels and devised theatre in order to cover a relevant range. In each case I was able to interview

---

[127] I have recently co-investigated this tendency under the heading of 'Composed Theatre' (Rebstock/Roesner, *Composed Theatre*), seeking to describe a practice situated somewhere between established performative genres, which is characterized by an explicitly compositional approach to the theatre and all of its expressive components.

[128] See the Introduction for more detail on the notion of interart.

a member of each creative team and thus gain insight on how they each made sense of their notion of musicality and its impact on the work and working process.[129]

Case Studies

Michael Thalheimer – Theatre as a Good Pop-song

Michael Thalheimer is currently one of the most successful directors in the German-speaking theatre circuit; he is invited to all the major theatres and is director in residence at the Deutsches Theater Berlin.[130] He almost exclusively directs dramatic texts from the canon: Büchner, Lessing, Goethe, Shakespeare, Chekhov. He has also on occasion directed operas. Thalheimer is one of those directors who – like Robert Wilson, Einar Schleef or Frank Castorf – have a strong signature: his productions are instantly recognizable, partly due to his unique essentialist approach to text, the strict gestural score of his actors and his continuous collaboration with stage designer Olaf Altman (see for example Figure 6.2) and composer Bert Wrede.

With regard to musicality it becomes evident in talking to Thalheimer that two leading metaphors guide his work and the way he describes his process and aesthetic ambitions. On the one hand he compares theatre to a 'good pop song'[131] and the production to a score.[132] The first metaphor describes a *dispositif* of music reception, an effect on the audience he would like to achieve: a pop song, he says, is 'timeless' and 'expresses an emotional world-view and a sense of time'.[133] Ideally, he would want to seduce his audience to feel as if they are sitting at home listening to a good song. A good pop song appeals to 'your mind and your heart'[134] and it 'needs no further explanation, is self-sufficient [genügt sich selbst]'. It seems to me that Thalheimer is interested in the capacity of pop songs to compress narratives and emotional landscapes into a very short form, to cut to the bone.[135]

---

[129] I would like to thank Gareth Fry, Jörg Gollasch, Sean Holmes and Michael Thalheimer very much for their generous contribution by engaging with the questions of this book project in the interviews they gave me.

[130] See a short portrait and indicative list of productions on the website of the Goethe Institute at http://www.goethe.de/kue/the/reg/reg/sz/tha/enindex.htm [12.08.2012]. See also Peter M. Boenisch, 'Exposing The Classics: Michael Thalheimer's Regie beyond the Text', *Contemporary Theatre Review*, 18:1 (2008), pp. 30–43.

[131] Michael Thalheimer, 'Director Michael Thalheimer interviewed by David Roesner' (Phone conversation, 20.06.2012). Thalheimer means pop in the wide sense of the word (popular) and not as a specific genre to be distinguished, for example, from rock, R&B, folk, etc.

[132] Thalheimer, 'Director Michael Thalheimer'.

[133] Thalheimer, 'Director Michael Thalheimer'.

[134] Thalheimer, 'Director Michael Thalheimer'.

[135] See Simon Frith, 'Towards an Aesthetic of Popular Music', in Simon Frith (ed.), *Taking Popular Music Seriously. Selected Essays* (Aldershot, 2007), pp. 257–74.

Figure 6.2   Michael Thalheimer's *Die Wildente* (Deutsches Theater
Berlin 2008)

Good pop songs[136] capture an essence and offer it to be experienced rather than
merely received as a message: this is the model of engagement Thalheimer seeks
to emulate with his productions. Gestures becomes recognizable 'riffs', structure
is characterized by clarity and repetition and while some of his productions have
been described as calculated and cold, those which do connect with the audience
do so at very high levels of emotional intensity (ranging from bliss to outrage).[137]
What Thalheimer seems to capture in this notion is the attempt to shift the
audience's disposition through the use of musicality towards a less interpretative
mode of watching, allowing them to experience theatre with an immediacy and
directness that pop music can at times achieve.

Thalheimer further extends the pop analogy to the production process by
comparing the ensemble explicitly with a band, in which individuals play
different instruments, but try to create one coherent sound.[138] He or his actors
sometimes also describe dramatic characters as particular instruments, using

---

[136] Thalheimer mentions Bob Dylan, Neil Young and Tindersticks as examples but is
not set on a certain style ('Director Michael Thalheimer').

[137] See dramaturg Sonja Anders's analysis of the audiences' reactions in 'Mitte – Rampe
– Vorn: Jedem sein Regietheater. Zuschauerreaktionen auf Thalheimer-Inszenierungen', in
Gutjahr, *Regietheater!*, pp. 115–24.

[138] Thalheimer, 'Director Michael Thalheimer'.

the respective qualities and characteristics of these instruments and their roles, timbres, functionalities as a way of accessing traits of the *dramatis personae*. This is also where the metaphor of the score, which we have encountered on several occasions in this book already, comes in: 'Theater is a kind of score and rehearsals are, besides many other things, the development of a very particular score, which eventually gets presented to an audience.'[139] For Thalheimer, as for Meyerhold or others, the score represents the idea that theatre is multi-voiced and unfolds in time; it is shorthand for a dramaturgy that is acutely aware of the rhythmic and formal qualities of theatre. In contrast to opera, Thalheimer says, echoing Meyerhold, the director in theatre ought to be 'more musical':[140] here, he needs to create and develop the score for the performance, while in an opera this job has largely been taken care of by the composer.

Thalheimer, in contrast to Wilson, for example, does not start with form, structure, rhythm; the score emerges slowly and towards the end of the rehearsal process after an intense engagement with the *semantic* layers of the text in question. Thalheimer spends a lot of time with his actors discussing and analyzing the text in great detail and depth.[141] The (musical) structure that eventually arises, he says, needs to come naturally out of the shared process between him and the actors of taking ownership of the text and its layers of meaning and emotion. It is about discovering the 'distinctive core'[142] of the play, and tackling the question of 'what story do we actually want to tell'.[143] The development of the score entails a close investigation of the musical qualities of the text, based on questions such as 'where are thematic repetitions in the text […], where are the silences, what kind of rhythm does the performance with the actors as a whole develop, where is the tempo and the aggression, where are slowness and retarding moments, where are the fermatas'.[144] However, while the analytical confrontation with the dramatic text's form and content is discursive, cerebral and conscious, the musicality of giving it shape as sound, gesture, rhythm, or in other words the gradual devising of the performance's score, is more intuitive,[145] embodied and unconscious.[146]

---

[139] Thalheimer, 'Director Michael Thalheimer'.

[140] Thalheimer, 'Director Michael Thalheimer'.

[141] See Michael Thalheimer, '"… diese Arbeit am pulsierenden Zentrum der Stücke". Ein Interview mit Ortrud Gutjahr', in Gutjahr, *Regietheater!*, pp. 189–202.

[142] Thalheimer, '… diese Arbeit', p. 189.

[143] Thalheimer, 'Director Michael Thalheimer'.

[144] Thalheimer, 'Director Michael Thalheimer'.

[145] Dramaturg John von Düffel, who has worked with Thalheimer, confirms this in his chapter 'Michael Thalheimer – das Bauchsystem' (in Melanie Hinz/Jens Roselt [eds.], *Chaos und Konzept: Proben und Probieren im Theater* [Berlin, 2011], pp. 51–70). In his experience, he says, Thalheimer is someone 'who – considering the clarity and strictness of his productions – acts on a gut level surprisingly often' (ibid., p. 51).

[146] It is Thalheimer's background as a drummer that comes to the fore here, and which provides him with a form of knowing I have referred to in Chapter 4 as 'an embodied,

Where there are explicitly 'musical' instructions, Thalheimer describes, they always follow an analysis of content: only after clarifying *what* is being said does the *how* (in the sense of tempo, pause, timbres, etc.) enter the decision, and it only works, according to Thalheimer, if the actor – through listening and trying out – internalizes these instructions as something embodied and felt, something that has become 'natural and organic'.[147] Not only does this prevent the production from feeling contrived, but it also ensures a certain 'durability' of it:

> My production of *Emilia Galotti*, for example has been performed now for seven years.[148] The ensemble of the Deutsches Theater still manages on every night to play this 'score' highly emotionally, as if for the first time. This only happens, because the score was developed together and not imposed by me.[149]

There is, however, as his dramaturg John von Düffel describes, a period of fine-tuning and editing towards the end of this process of devising, where Thalheimer does take charge of the final shape of the score, and it is the production's rhythm that is at the centre at this stage:

> The inventions, ideas, playful moments, which are created in rehearsal, produce a kind of form, and this form remains unfinished; it becomes finalized only at the end of the rehearsal process as something that crystallizes from the material. And this is where finally the drummer Michael Thalheimer comes into play: [...] there is something in the end which is so characteristic for his performances: the rhythmitization by the director. In the phase of structuring in the dress rehearsals, where the performance is put together, Michael Thalheimer is all drummer-director, and the drummer makes the pulse more precise and drives on the beat. And this is, next to the radical reduction to an essence, part of the signature of Michael Thalheimer: the sophisticated musicality of his productions. One often feels it is a song playing and this is because at the end of the process – not at its beginning! – there is a systematic rhythm, which clocks our perception and organizes the scenic narrative.[150]

---

tacit and contextualized phenomenon, varied and subjective: a verb rather than a noun' (Ian Sutherland/Sophie Krzys Acord, 'Thinking with Art: From Situated Knowledge to Experiential Knowing', *Journal of Visual Art Practice*, 6/2 [2007], pp. 125–40, p. 126).

[147] Thalheimer, 'Director Michael Thalheimer'.

[148] *Emilia Galotti* premiered in 2001 at the Deutsches Theater Berlin and was performed for an exceptional period of eight years – the interview with Ortrud Gutjahr dates from 2008. For an English review see Neil Martin Blackadder, 'Emilia Galotti (review)', *Theatre Journal*, 58/2 (2006), pp. 350–51.

[149] Thalheimer, '... diese Arbeit', p. 196.

[150] von Düffel, 'Michael Thalheimer', pp. 66–7.

Musicality, for Thalheimer, is less a premeditated dramaturgical concept or an approach to training[151] and more an instinctive (on a personal level) and emergent (on the ensemble level) phenomenon. He describes musicality as relatively unintentional, but as something that 'happens to him'[152] in the encounter with the text when spoken by the actors.[153] Starting with the early rehearsals at the table when hearing the actors speak their lines he begins to detect a score in what he hears. To his mind musicality in theatre only makes sense as a lived ('gelebt') and embodied part of one's artistic identity; only then can it become an organic and spirited experience ('erlebbar'), creating a sensuality of theatre as opposed to an 'empty' formalism, or something that is too cerebral ('ausgedacht').[154]

Filter – Theatre as Concert

Aesthetically, the British ensemble Filter could not be more different to Michael Thalheimer. Whereas his theatrical language is often perceived as cool, slick, stylized and poignant, Filter deliberately embrace an aesthetic that is messy, anarchic, seemingly chaotic and often decidedly silly.

The company was formed in 2003 by actors Ollie Dimsdale and Ferdy Roberts and musician Tim Phillips. It works with a pool of regular collaborators – actors, musicians and directors – and has produced adaptations of classical texts (Shakespeare, Chekhov, Brecht) as well as devised projects. Music and sound play a central role, both in the creation process as well as the actual performance, thus the notion of the theatre ensemble as a band[155] that we have come across a number of times so far is perhaps most fully realized and at its most literal in their work. Their productions, while ultimately rehearsed and crafted, have the appeal of a spontaneous live concert, the music being a wild mix of jazz, '70s rock, Balkan, tango, ska, reggae and much more: 'Filter is an experimental company famed for its sonic virtuosity',[156] as the *Guardian* critic Michael Billington put it.

For Filter, sound and music are very much a starting point (in contrast to Thalheimer, as we have seen): 'The idea begins musically and then everyone

---

[151] Thalheimer told me he was perfectly happy with the level of 'conventional' drama school training that his actors brought with them and did not engage in any particular exercises during the rehearsal process either: the musicality arose, he claims, from the work on the text itself (Thalheimer, 'Director Michael Thalheimer').

[152] Thalheimer, 'Director Michael Thalheimer'.

[153] See the similarities to Michel Leloup's reflections in the case study on Bred in the Bone in Chapter 5.

[154] Thalheimer, 'Director Michael Thalheimer'.

[155] Holmes says about Filter's production of *Twelfth Night* that it was 'like a band doing the play' (Sean Holmes, 'Director Sean Holmes interviewed by David Roesner' [Phone conversation, 20.06.2012]).

[156] http://www.filtertheatre.com/page/Press/ [14.08.2012].

[...] is thinking in those terms.'[157] This serves as a 'release of creative energy', setting the tone for a different kind of rehearsal practice, but also as a fresh way into the material. In the case of their Shakespeare productions, director Sean Holmes, who directed several of Filter's shows, speaks of music and sound as a way to 'release the play' or to 'unleash the spirit' of Shakespeare.[158] Musicality, in part, is meant to give Filter license to 'free [themselves] from the tyranny of received ideas about Shakespeare',[159] but there is also a more directly practical side to this understanding.

Musicality as Problem-Solving

In reflecting on the role of music and sound in the creation process of Filter, Holmes emphasizes the often quite pragmatic and tangible benefits of thinking and working musically. For Filter it offered a 'quick and dirty' approach to Shakespeare on a small budget. *Twelfth Night*,[160] for example, was originally devised in two and a half weeks, *A Midsummer Night's Dream* in only 10 days.[161] Key to this was that the actors knew their lines and that the musicians were in the rehearsal room from day one. The effect of this close collaboration with the musicians, and actually their leadership in rehearsal, as Holmes describes it, is this:

> When you work with musicians [...] in twenty seconds they can up with something that the equivalent in rehearsal would take you two weeks, because of their technical ability and their shared language. [...] So what is exciting is the swiftness with which they achieve something quite complete compared to acting which means that they can lead because they can change something and the actor can then respond to what they are doing.[162]

He thus describes his role as a director for Filter as 'letting the group of actors, often led by the instincts of the musicians'[163] develop the initial ideas. It also allowed the group not to get bogged down by philological scruples too much, but to move quickly through the play. Again, Holmes credits musicality with this:

---

[157] Holmes, 'Director Sean Holmes'.

[158] Holmes, 'Director Sean Holmes'. Holmes reminds us that Shakespeare as a writer was 'very aware of sound' and that *Twelfth Night* in particular is 'drenched with the idea of musicality'.

[159] Holmes, 'Director Sean Holmes'.

[160] The spoof documentary *What you Will* (dir. by Guy de Beaujeu and Simon Reade, 2012) gives insight into the production and its reception.

[161] Holmes, 'Director Sean Holmes'.

[162] Holmes, 'Director Sean Holmes'.

[163] Holmes, 'Director Sean Holmes'.

You think differently when you are making music. You use different parts of your brain,[164] almost different parts of your body and that is very, very useful if you are thinking like that and feeling like that. It means you make different decisions when you meet the text.[165]

Outside eye Annette Vieusseux confirms this in her rehearsal diary of Filter's *The Caucasian Chalk Circle* (2006): 'A frequently asked question is "can we do that sonically?" Devising with sound initiates bold staging decisions.'[166] Sound and music turn from being an ingredient – often in the mode of illustration – to a way of working, a way of thinking.

'Can we do it sonically' is thus both an aesthetic credo of Filter ('sonic' being their preferred term to describe 'the interplay of music and sound and the fact that all of it is created live on stage'[167]) and also the question of choice to solve narrative or theatrical problems in rehearsal. Holmes gives a few examples: for *Midsummer Night's Dream* there were not enough actors in the cast to cover the fairies, so they paired up actors with musicians and sent them away to come up with an idea of how to do the fairies, arriving at a scrap-book of ideas. Eventually practically all of the magic of the wood of Athens was created through sound, creating an interesting balance between the 'ridiculous and then incredibly atmospheric and powerful'.[168] To me, the simplicity and transparency of creating the 'magical' soundscapes was at the same time funny and ironic, but also quite effective and captivating, particularly by transforming and composing very 'modest' sound events into complex and layered soundscapes. At one point, for example, an actor visibly records a small croaking sound by a frog-shaped guiro (a percussion instrument common in South America and Asia), which is then sampled and looped into the ambience of a nocturnal forest.

Holmes also comments on musicality in relation to the emotional score of a dramatic text: 'Good writing can go very quickly from one mood or emotion to another and music can support this in production immensely.'[169] He elaborates:

What the best writers understand is how jagged and odd and contradictory we are as humans, and what a lot of the music in those shows is doing is working in that way; the way it is contrapuntal, the way it slides from one thing to another is very strong.[170]

---

[164] See the section on Bred in the Bone's work in Chapter 5 as well.

[165] Holmes, 'Director Sean Holmes'.

[166] Annette Vieusseux, 'Rehearsal Diary of Filter's *The Caucasian Chalk Circle*, National Theatre' (2006), http://www.stagework.org.uk/webdav/harmonise@Page%252F@ id=6016&Section%252F@id=1605.html [08.08.2012]. I thank Sarah McCourt for pointing me to this valuable source.

[167] Holmes, 'Director Sean Holmes'.

[168] Holmes, 'Director Sean Holmes'.

[169] Holmes, 'Director Sean Holmes'.

[170] Holmes, 'Director Sean Holmes'.

In summary, for a lot of the questions that all theatre ensembles, particularly those with limited budgets, ask themselves, Filter have made it a habit to look for answers through musical means first. The sonic becomes a main creative driver of production processes. Filter taps into the tempo and the non-verbal simultaneity with which music, particularly improvised music, can be created and they use the imaginative powers of music and sound to create and evoke images, movement, memories, spaces and emotions with comparatively few means. This has inevitably meant that the traditional roles of actors, directors and musicians are put up for discussion.

Redefining Actors and Musicians

The crucial decision, it seems to me, is – as we have seen with Bred in the Bone or Theater T1 (see Chapter 5) – that musicians and actors are equally present at all rehearsals and that there is no strict separation as to who can speak to what aspect of the process.[171] Vieusseux confirms that 'Filter's methodology explicitly attempts to counter divisions between musicians and actors, so the creation of the music occurs collaboratively during the rehearsal period'.[172] Likewise, the musicians are integrated into the acting ensemble and make suggestions regarding the staging of the narrative.

The respective differences in ability are not ignored, however, but used productively, embracing and working with the aesthetics of an actor's untrained singing voice, for example, or working with instruments and musical technologies that the actors can quickly learn to handle playing[173] with the charm of a certain 'punk' approach to music, mixed with the proficiency and virtuosity of the musicians. Vice versa, Holmes found that casting the musicians as the mechanicals in *A Midsummer Night's Dream* 'worked brilliantly'[174] as it allowed him to make use of 'the actual awkwardness'[175] and amateurism that are characteristic for Peter Quince and his troupe.

In addition the musicians challenge their tried and tested musicianship by expanding the range of instruments: in the case of the *Caucasian Chalk Circle* Vieusseux describes that it 'reflects the eclecticism that's defining this production

---

[171] Vieusseux: 'From the beginning of their process, the musicians went through the play act by act, thinking about the rhythms and textures of each one and interacting with what was occurring in the rehearsal room' (Vieusseux, 'Rehearsal Diary').

[172] Vieusseux, 'Rehearsal Diary'.

[173] Vieusseux describes that for *Caucasian Chalk Circle* 'the composers have also created electronic banks of sound samples that are triggered by midi keyboards (with colour-coded keys so that this music can be played easily by the actors)' (Vieusseux, 'Rehearsal Diary').

[174] Holmes, 'Director Sean Holmes'.

[175] Holmes, 'Director Sean Holmes'.

so far: the most frequently used instruments are a glockenspiel, an accordion, a toy piano, a melodica and a cocktail drum kit'.[176]

In this collaborative and interdisciplinary process, director Sean Holmes felt his own role change. In contrast to his days at the RSC, for example, he says he saw a transformation of seeing the director as 'one more skill in the room, rather than the leader of all the ideas'.[177] The differences in the working process and the understanding of everyone's roles have a tangible impact on the aesthetics of the ensemble's productions.

The Live Concert Aesthetics

It is no accident, I would argue, that a significant portion of Philip Auslander's book *Liveness* deals with music performance, more specifically with rock culture.[178] Popular music has seen the most intense debate about the relationship and the ethics of live performance versus the use of pre-recorded material, playback, lip-syncing, etc., in performance with the suggestion that – in some genres more than others – not to play live amounts to an ethical betrayal and an artistic sell-out.[179]

Filter not only adopt the pragmatics of keeping things 'live' – avoiding the logistics of recording and cueing endless sound effects – but also cater for the craving for liveness of a pop-culturally conversant audience. By ostensibly creating sound and music live in performance, they remind us also of *theatre's* liveness, and celebrate its ephemerality and momentousness.[180] There is also, however, an element of playfulness and irony in this (compared, for example, to the way in which Katie Mitchell uses Foley sound, as we will see later). Here is a description from *Caucasian Chalk Circle* again:

> All of the sounds are generated onstage so the audience can see it being created. Random props from the rehearsal room continue to be used for effects in this show's 'language' – plastic bags scrunched into microphones to create the sounds of soldiers footsteps on snow, and the amplified metal 'sonic bin' has myriad effects, from door knocks to bridge creaks. Bells, cymbals and lengths of chain are also used. Bongo drum tubes create the dripping sounds of snow melting, and Sean brings to rehearsal his young son's 'moo' toy to add to the sounds of the farm-yard. Sound effects are usually performed (mostly with microphones) rather than pre-recorded – the most consistent example being the

---

[176] Vieusseux, 'Rehearsal Diary'.

[177] Holmes, 'Director Sean Holmes'.

[178] See Philip Auslander, *Liveness: Performance in a Mediatized Culture* (London/ New York, 1999), pp. 61–111.

[179] See Auslander's case study of the 'Milli Vanilli scandal' (*Liveness*, pp. 61–2) which illustrates this point.

[180] They also do this by strategically planting episodes of audience interaction, such as inviting spectators to get involved in games of throwing balls or food at the stage, or eat pizza, which gets delivered at some point in the performance.

breathing, giggling and crying sounds of the child using a small Marshall amp and a microphone. Sound design is also important for communicating place (such as wind for some of the exterior scenes) and off-stage action (Cath [cast member Cath Whitefield, DR] can excellently mimic an air raid siren, which scores the coup in Act One).[181]

Filter use musicality in this context also as a set of expectations that we have built in relation to the use of sound and music in theatre (often guided, however, by television and film) and employ intermusicality (or intersonicality) in the sense of a continuous and often humorous play with conventions. In many genres of theatre, sound is used as a semiotic prompter and modifier for the audience to subconsciously judge the mood, the movement, the intention, the impact, etc., of actions and spaces on stage. Like a bat uses sound to map the space around it, adjusting its position by the speed and direction of returning soundwaves, audiences use sound to navigate the meaning-making process in theatrical performance, aligning and balancing what they see with what they hear. Filter use this process extensively, but point us very directly to these conventions, exposing them and drawing comedic effect from them.

In *A Midsummer Night's Dream*, for example, all the magic is aural, not visual: Cupid's flower, which Puck delivers to Oberon and with which he creates all the love confusion, is invisible, but audible. The actors mime to a flurrying sound effect, controlled live by one of the musicians, and their movements (picking up the flower, squeezing its juice on prospective lovers) are synchronized with the sound. When first receiving the flower from Puck, however, Oberon seems to be unable to catch it. His attempts to pluck it from the air are in vain, the sound continues and the mere theatrical device of the flower's invisibility becomes an actual problem for the character who chases the sound around the room. Puck, however, with some impatience over his master's ineptitude, eventually simply points resolutely into the air and following his clue, Oberon finally catches the flower and the sound stops.

Filter manage, however, not to let musicality be reduced to an ironic subversion: the emphasis on live created sound is both a celebration of self-reflexivity – reminding us that we are in a theatre, watching a performance, pointing to the history of theatre sound technology, its media and its powers – and it also shamelessly exploits the strong *immersive* and emotive qualities that music and sound design possess.[182]

In contrast to other artists who also place sound production and sonic experiment at the heart of their performances (e.g. Carola Bauckholt's *hellhörig*, Munich 2008), Filter use their musicality in pursuit of finding interesting ways to

---

[181] Vieusseux, 'Rehearsal Diary'.

[182] See Lynne Kendrick/David Roesner (eds.), *Theatre Noise. The Sound of Performance* (Newcastle upon Tyne, 2011), in which several authors (Jeanne Bovet, Ross Brown, Misha Myers, Gareth White) discuss the connection between sound and immersiveness in theatre.

deliver the narrative at hand, while ensuring that 'the music is leading the action of the play, not the other way round':[183]

> Music is integral to the storytelling in *The Caucasian Chalk Circle* – Frank McGuinness (who has written this version) commented early in rehearsals that the music is 'like a character in its own right'. [...] So long as the music supports and enhances the clarity of the story-telling, there's plenty of room for playing around with the musical elements of the show, 'extemporising, like a band does'.[184]

Filter (and other ensembles like Kneehigh or Theatre Alibi) do expose their characters as constructed, based on an agreement with the audience rather than a magical transformation of the actor[185] and they also point to the nuts and bolts – sometimes the creaking joints – of story-telling, but they do still ultimately see theatre as a place to unfold a narrative. Music becomes a particularly potent ally in this aim, at times, as Frank McGuinness put it, another character in the room. There is, however, at least one more function of Filter's particular musical *dispositif* (and this could also be said of the other ensembles I have just mentioned) – a way in which a particular musicality becomes part of the 'brand' of a company, beyond its actual narrative, theatrical or performance contribution.

The Meta-Musical Appeal

Musicality for Filter also means buying into a certain twenty-first-century *zeitgeist*, using music that quickly cites a wide range of styles, some contemporary, some deliberately retro, and uses the appeal of familiarity and recognition this has on audiences. The musicality of Filter and others is an interpersonal point of reference, an extra-theatrical point of entry, and an important part of the appearance and impression of the product – the brand identity, if we put it in socio-economic terms. Their musicality embraces what Claudia Bullerjahn – with reference to film music – calls the 'metafunction'[186] of music:

> The individually desired target audience specificity manifests itself in certain stylistic requirements towards the music, which initially have no connection to the actual film in question, but are solely designed to select the circle of adressees.[187]

---

[183]   Holmes, 'Director Sean Holmes'.

[184]   Vieusseux, 'Rehearsal Diary'.

[185]   Multi-roling, casting against type, stepping out of character, etc., are some of the strategies to ensure this.

[186]   Claudia Bullerjahn, 'Ein begriffliches Babylon: Von den Schwierigkeiten einer einheitlichen Filmmusik-Nomenklatur' (1999), http://www.sign-lang.uni-hamburg. de/Medienzentrum/zmm-news/zmmNewsA/archiv/Sommer99%20%C4/Sommer99/ Bullerjahn.htm [02/07/2007].

[187]   Bullerjahn, 'Ein begriffliches Babylon', p. 10.

The liveness, the eclectic and quirky but always recognizable style, the improvised feel of the music (even if it actually is quite set in the end) – all these are part of a way of attracting audiences, and particularly audiences which may not normally choose to see a more traditional play.[188]

Karin Beier – The Theatricality and Materiality of Music

As for Thalheimer and Filter, Shakespeare has been an important figure in Karin Beier's remarkable career. Starting off by directing a small independent theatre company in Cologne called 'Countercheck Quarrelsome' in the late Eighties devoted exclusively to innovative stagings of Shakespeare's plays, she was then invited to direct *Romeo and Juliet* (1993) and *A Midsummer Night's Dream* (1994) for the Schauspielhaus Düsseldorf, both of which became an instant success with critics and audiences alike. In 2007 Beier became the artistic director at the Schauspiel Köln, voted 'best theatre' in 2010 and 2011 by German-speaking critics.[189]

More recently, she has tried her hand at what could be seen to fall under the bracket of the postdramatic, particularly by discovering Austrian Elfriede Jelinek (see also Chapter 4) for herself and engaging in devising projects not based on any dramatic template. Two recent projects in particular are of interest in the context of my study: *Demokratie in Abendstunden. Eine Kakophonie* [*Democracy in the Evening Hours. A Cacophony*[190]] based on texts by Joseph Beuys, John Cage, Rainald Goetz and others in a double-bill with Jelinek's *Kein Licht* [*No Light*] (Schauspiel Köln, 2011) and a triple bill of three Jelinek texts *Das Werk/Im Bus/Ein Sturz* [*The Works/In the Bus/A Fall*[191]] (Schauspiel Köln, 2010). Both projects were developed together with composer and

---

[188] This effect can be seen elsewhere as well, for example in Robert Wilson's collaborations with Tom Waits or Lou Reed, who – as musicians and song-writers – have a devout following, many of whom may have originally been unfamiliar with Wilson's theatre. Theatre as concert, I might add, has proliferated in range of forms recently, employing different styles, musical and theatrical languages and aesthetic aims. Nikolaus Stemann, Christoph Marthaler, Nico and the Navigators, Simon Rattle/Peter Sellars or Heiner Goebbels, to name but a few, have played with the concert as a performative setting, as a way of coping with postdramatic writing (Stemann's Jelinek production *Die Kontrakte des Kaufmanns*, see Figure 4.1), as an ironic and bitter-sweet homage to romanticism (Marthaler's *Schöne Müllerin*, based on Schubert's Liederzyklus) or as an experiential space in which to encounter and explore sounds, images, voices (Goebbels's *Eraritjaritjaka*, based on twentieth-century string quartet music and writings by Elias Canetti). In contrast to Filter's approach, music and the culturally encoded modus of the concert are here less of a narrative vehicle than a site and time of contemplation for Goebbels and a rich set of traditions and conventions for Marthaler, which can be exploited for both melancholic and satirical effect.

[189] See also http://www.goethe.de/kue/the/reg/reg/ag/bei/enindex.htm [25.10.2012].

[190] Translation at http://www.goethe.de/kue/the/reg/reg/ag/bei/enindex.htm [25.10.2012].

[191] Translation at http://www.goethe.de/kue/the/reg/reg/ag/bei/enindex.htm [25.10.2012].

theatre musician Jörg Gollasch[192] and have been influenced strongly by his compositional approach to theatre and voice. Characteristically he integrates chorus work, experimental musicianship and soundscapes into dense tapestries which interweave the sonic and visual materialities of theatre, the performativity of music and the musical qualities of text into epic theatrical productions (see Figures 6.3 and 6.4).[193]

Beier's and Gollasch's musicality is explicitly influenced by concepts of John Cage such as his interest in the musicality of noise or practices of working in time brackets, etc., and Mauricio Kagel who also widened the idea of what materials were 'composable' and theatricalized the act of making music, often using satirizing musical microcosms for social commentary.[194]

This is particularly evident in the first devised part of *Demokratie in Abendstunden*, which is actually based on the idea of an orchestra rehearsal that is increasingly fraught with conflict and dissent, but ideas of 'instrumental theatre' have also strongly influenced their collaborations on *King Lear* (2009), *Das Werk* (2010), and *Die Troerinnen* (2013) and are thus not limited to postdramatic or devised practices.

As Gollasch explains, the working process in these productions could be described as 'a collaborative compositional process',[195] not only using music 'as an atmosphere, but also a principle of development and creation'.[196] In order to facilitate this, Gollasch gets involved in Beier's productions as early as at the stage of casting, where they discuss what actors and musicians to involve based not least on emerging ideas for the *musical* dramaturgy of the piece. Choosing 'instrumentation', both literally but also figuratively, as a set of vocal and physical qualities that the actors and musicians bring to the rehearsal stage, becomes an important conceptual and dramaturgical decision. Musicality manifests itself at this stage as a move towards a potential soundscape, a focus on certain sonic qualities provided by a mixture of instruments and sounding

---

[192] Critic Alexander Haas endorses this collaboration in his review of *Demokratie*: 'As in her last Jelinek-world-premiere *Das Werk. Im Bus. Ein Sturz*, Beier works together with composer Jörg Gollasch. Even more than last year this is a congenial cooperation. Even more consequently Beier relies on Gollasch to musically and rhythmically work through the scenes (in: *taz*, 14.10.2011 [25.10.2012]).

[193] Andreas Wilink, for example, describes *Das Werk/Im Bus/Ein Sturz* as follows: 'masses of text collapse over you, litanies bury you, draw you in like a maelstrom, take your breath' (in http://www.nachtkritik.de, 29.10.2010 [25.10.2012]), and Stefan Bläske considers it 'staged congenially and powerfully, with a chorus before and choreography after the interval, with a large contingency of 60 singers and with earth and water having it off with each other' (in http://www.nachtkritik.de, 06.05.2011 [25.10.2012]).

[194] I interviewed Jörg Gollasch in Cologne in May 2012, who spoke of his and Beier's interest in Cage and Kagel's practices and philosophies.

[195] Jörg Gollasch, 'Theatre musician and composer Jörg Gollasch interviewed by David Roesner' (Cologne, Germany, 25.05.2012).

[196] Gollasch, 'Theatre musician and composer'.

Figure 6.3   Karin Beier's *Demokratie in Abendstunden* (Schauspiel Köln 2011)

materials underpinned by a tendency of Beier and Gollasch (and their main stage designer Johannes Schütz) to treat instruments *also* as props or material and to treat props and materials also as instruments. Beier and Gollasch have thus established a mode of working in which they quite often start with a musical idea, an improvisation with the actors and musicians, a musical soundscape, before starting to think about adding text.

Musicality, however, also comes into play with respect to rhythm and structure: adapting and managing Jelinek's rhizomatic prose for *Das Werk*, for example, required them to actually come up with and assert a structure in the editing process, which, as Gollasch reports, often followed musical rather than narrative considerations. The ensuing structure and dramaturgy is often based on a principle of 'building blocks' (*Bausteinprinzip*)[197] or a 'modular way of working'[198] which allows them to work on individual and discrete units – whether these are predominantly musical, choreographed or text-based. These units are developed and rehearsed and can later be assembled, recombined, edited, layered and juxtaposed. This approach complements both Beier's interest in 'cuts' and quick shifts in rhythm or 'temperature' of scenes and Gollasch's compositional disposition towards layered rhythmical patterns, often based on uneven time signatures, and their overlapping, repetition and displacement against each other.

---

[197] Gollasch, 'Theatre musician and composer'.
[198] Gollasch, 'Theatre musician and composer'.

Figure 6.4   Karin Beier's *Demokratie in Abendstunden* (Schauspiel Köln
               2011). Photograph by Klaus Lefebvre

An important part of this 'monadic'[199] approach to the rhythm and dramaturgy
of the piece is for Beier and Gollasch to embrace 'blank spaces' (*Leerstellen,*[200] not
dissimilar to *temps mort* in film) as part of the texture: Gollasch uses this term to
describe sections in which 'only' music happens, where the theatre temporarily
becomes a concert and the lack of action, text or narrative creates an 'empty
moment' against the theatrical context and horizon of expectation.

Like Filter, Beier mixes musicians and actors in her ensembles without keeping
their roles entirely separate; the effect is, however, somewhat different: where Filter
playfully juxtaposes virtuosity and comedic amateurism, Beier investigates theatrical
presence by asking her performers to move in and out of their respective training
backgrounds and 'comfort zones', leaving the safe ground of their professional
skills, whether that means singing for a cellist, playing percussion for an actor or
reciting text for a harp player. In one production, musicians were contractually
asked to train a fellow actor in their instrument during the rehearsal process, while
on the other hand feeding off the actors' instinctive ability to lend theatrical presence
and energy to the act of making music. Borders of competence are deliberately
crossed and the restrictions on each side are then explored for their theatrical and
musical potential: what effects and affects can be gained from pushing against
professional limits? Gollasch describes how, in particular, they became interested

---

[199]   Gollasch, 'Theatre musician and composer'.
[200]   Gollasch, 'Theatre musician and composer'.

in the immediacy and vulnerability of performers who are not guarding themselves with a thick layer of protective professionalism. They chose, for example, not to work with a professional opera chorus for the long choric passage in *Das Werk*, but got an amateur men's chorus from Cologne involved. Gollasch felt it was much more engaging 'to see these people on stage with their vests and bellies, standing there with no stage persona and representing the "worker's chorus" [...] much more aptly than the professional ensembles we looked at'.[201]

For the directing process itself, this means a few shifts of emphasis. Interpreting the text is no longer the primary concern, even though text remains a core material of the production. The scenic material often emerges out of the theatricality of making music, particularly when the music in question itself plays with conventions and expectations, for example by using unusual instruments, spatial settings, playing techniques, sounds, etc. Directing becomes an act of composing with the stage, in the sense of assembling and organizing material and adjusting parameters such as volume, timbre or tempo. It also becomes more concerned with layering expressive means – in Beier's case this is, however, never abstract, but always conscious of the associative potential of the music, rhythms, gestures, set design, etc. The soundscapes, mud baths, textual onslaughts are never pure exercises in sound, vision and form, but opportunities for memories, personal and interpersonal connotations and layers of meaning.

Katie Mitchell – A Filmic Musicality

In contrast to all of the above, British director Katie Mitchell's work is originally much more indebted to a British tradition of dramatic realism and naturalistic acting methods and aesthetics.[202] Since the ground-breaking production of *Waves* at the National Theatre in London in 2006,[203] however, Mitchell has developed a trademark for her productions which combines naturalist performances with complex and defamiliarizing layers of mediatization. Many of her productions[204] now consist of producing a film live on stage, including elaborate camera work, simple but intricate lighting, handmade visual effects and a live sound-track, including score, voice-over and Foley sound.[205]

---

[201] Gollasch, 'Theatre musician and composer'.

[202] Her book *The Director's Craft* (London, 2008) also demonstrates this approach and context very clearly.

[203] See Katie Mitchell, *Waves* (London, 2008).

[204] For example *... some trace of her* (NT, 2008), *Wunschkonzert* (Schauspiel Köln, 2009), *Al Gran Sole Carico D'Amore* (Salzburg Festival, 2009), *Miss Julie* (Schaubühne, Berlin, 2010), *Die Ringe des Saturn* (Avignon Festival, 2012).

[205] Jack Foley inaugurated the art of creating everyday sound effects for Universal Studios in 1927, which is interesting in that, right at the dawn of the 'talkies', i.e. sound film, the art of creating sound effects artificially rather than recording them in real life began its ascent.

Her musicality (and that of her actors and collaborators, such as video artist Leo Warner and sound-designer Gareth Fry) is three-fold, I would argue: firstly, music and sound play a crucial part in the process of development and rehearsal of her intermedial production[206] so that the sonic becomes an important dramaturgical and creative driver. Secondly, a rhythmical and polyphonic (and sometimes also homophonic) approach to the interplay of complex layers of theatrical performance and theatrical media organizes the overall spectacle and creates dynamically changing hierarchies of performance tasks, expressive means and perceptive attention. And thirdly, musicality becomes a modus of performance, not just with respect to acting, but to the overall coordination and timing of the very complex web of activities on stage, which one critic called 'a fascinatingly precise chorcography of the production of filmic illusion'.[207]

An Early Presence of Sound and Music

In my interview with Gareth Fry[208] he highlighted the fact that, unlike in most other theatre productions, in Katie Mitchell's work he is involved in the rehearsal process from very early on. Leaving the complex visual score to one side for a moment, the productions are already quite complex sonically and the development of the overall soundscape is instrumental for the direction of the piece as a whole. One layer is the musical score, written by Paul Clarke, who will provide 'a CD or two worth of music before rehearsals begin'[209] based on some agreed ideas about musical style and idiom. This musical layout (which in the end is often performed live or at least partially live) provides the rehearsals with 'a palette of music to experiment with',[210] but by not being written for a specific scene, transition or moment, the music at this stage only sets the *tone* in advance of the rehearsals and is only later tailored rhythmically to the performances the actors have created. Music and performance engage in an iterative process, developing together, rather than one being strictly modelled on the other.

A second sonic layer consists of the use of subtle, low-level sounds and drones, which Mitchell and Fry utilize dramaturgically, exploiting the emotional, atmospheric and structuring functions of these sounds:

> We spend an awful lot of time working on what we call tonal sounds, darker,
> semi-musical sounds; sounds that have an emotional impact on the audience,

---

[206] See also David Roesner, '"An entirely new art form" – Katie Mitchells intermediale Bühnen-Experimente', *Forum Modernes Theater*, 24/2 (2009), pp. 101–19.

[207] Anonymous, 'Die Nacht brodelt vor elf Sternen', at http://www.kulturraum verdichtung.de/katie-mitchell-inszeniert-kroetz-wunschkonzert-in-koeln.html (12/2008) [18.10.2012].

[208] Gareth Fry, 'Sound designer Gareth Fry interviewed by David Roesner' (Phone conversation, 18.06.2012).

[209] Fry, 'Sound designer Gareth Fry'.

[210] Fry, 'Sound designer Gareth Fry'.

but you are not able to establish what they are, you can't work out what created them. And they tend to be drones and high sounds […] and they form quite a musical score that we tie in very closely to what the performers are doing. Katie has this system of events and intentions […] and the sound gets tied in very heavily with the performers' shifts, the dramaturgical shifts […] the emotional gear shifts in the show.[211]

Fry stresses that these sounds are more than the quite ubiquitous 'Hollywood style'[212] attempts to manipulate the audience's emotional experience: 'What we try to do is more a sort of punctuation of moments rather than trying to direct the audience how to feel.'[213] Even though being designed for the audience, the sonic score also provides an important reference point for the performers, supporting the development of their score of activities and its repetition in performance. As the acting is very different from a naturalistic stage production, in that actors continuously change roles, from camera acting, to operating cameras, handling props, focusing lights, creating live sound effects or visual effects, the sonic score may well also provide an aid for stepping in and out of character, not unlike the way early silent film production discovered the use of off-screen music to support the actor's presence and emotional engagement, by evoking atmosphere and masking the noise of the technical machinery of film production.

Polyphonic Strategies

Musicality in Mitchell's production is, however, not confined to the soundscape (to which I should add the use of live voice-over and the already mentioned visibly produced Foley effects). The visible and audible simultaneity of many layers of film-making (which normally tend to be separated out in time and space) and their synthesis in the projected filmic image (see Figure 6.5) create an audio-visual polyphony, which both suggest a coherent representation of a world and deconstructs it at the same time by exposing the incongruence between the (theatrical) means of production and their effect on the film screen. The sound of rain is created by wrinkling a plastic bag; the ghostly appearance of a character before another character's inner eye is a simple play with light angles and a sheet of Plexiglas. In contrast to Goebbels's separation of different theatrical layers which leaves gaps and contradictions for the audience to fill or bridge, all elements of Mitchell's production can actually be subsumed under an overarching fictional narrative, but the dissection and exposition of each contributing part nonetheless creates what critic Lyn Gardner called a 'curious and disconcerting split sensation'.[214]

---

[211] Fry, 'Sound designer Gareth Fry'.

[212] Fry, 'Sound designer Gareth Fry'.

[213] Fry, 'Sound designer Gareth Fry'.

[214] Lyn Gardner, 'Waves Sets a High-water Mark for Multimedia Theatre', http://www.guardian.co.uk/stage/theatreblog/2006/dec/04/wavessetsahighwatermarkfo? (04.12.2006) [17.10.2012].

Figure 6.5   Katie Mitchell's *Waves* (National Theatre London 2006)

We could call it a *narrative* homophony created by a *theatrical* polyphony, and this is made possible by the joined-up creation process, as Fry describes it:

> It very much develops synchronously. [...] We tend to have all the elements in rehearsals, video cameras, projection screens, Foley objects, microphones, speakers, sound engineers, often a one to one representation of the set, so that we can get a very good sense in rehearsals of what we are creating. [...] The rehearsal process tends to be like a very long technical rehearsal.[215]

Where in conventional rehearsal processes technical rehearsals are limited to a few days at the end of the process, often merely adding sound and light, etc. to an already largely finished product, mostly emphasizing, illustrating and amplifying what is already being expressed in text, gesture or voice, here the development is integrated. Musicality not only manifests itself as a strong awareness of the simultaneity of a wealth of elements on stage and the need to organize them, but also a factor that significantly changes the way of working and does so far beyond the inner circle of director and actors, but creatively connects *all* contributors of the final production.

---

[215] Fry, 'Sound designer Gareth Fry'.

A Musical Dual Consciousness

I have mentioned earlier that musicality can become part of what actors call their 'dual consciousness',[216] the simultaneous attention to the character's fictional world and the theatrical reality of its performance. Normally this 'twofoldness' (as a cognitive scientist might call it[217]) relates to the duality of 'being the character' while also being fully aware of technical aspects of acting. Musicality in this context could be an awareness of rhythmical or formal aspects of a speech while delivering it, or sensitivity to a co-actor's gestural timing, or vocal timbre and melody while also relating to them emotionally as a character. In Mitchell's production, there is yet another level to this, as the actors are so strongly involved in the mechanics of the stage and switch from tasks related to the character and their fictional world to others, which are focused on its very construction, but are framed by the production as very much part of the performance. To give this multi-tasking form, timing, presence and a certain grace, musicality is applied to *all* aspects of performance. In order to create and maintain this awareness, Mitchell works with a method of rehearsal she calls 'dancing through'[218] the show – here, the actors go through the whole show leaving all the equipment temporarily aside, but instead 'going through their notation and reminding themselves of the flow of one thing to another […]. A lot of the rehearsals are about the musicality of the flow of the show, the movements from one place to another to achieve the shots'.[219] This musical sense of the overall connection between acting and stage logistics is also manifest in the notation systems Mitchell and her actors had to develop to keep track of and facilitate such complexity and precision.

As is the case with many of the directors in this book, Mitchell is, perhaps unsurprisingly, also an opera director and seems to be able to translate ideas and methods from one genre to the other and to extend this integrative approach to even further media and genres such as the novel or the film noir. What Dolja Dragasevic says about Meyerhold in this context thus rings true for directors such as Thalheimer or Mitchell, even though the times, technologies and aesthetics have changed:

> Meyerhold employed operatic devices to extend the vocabulary of the dramatic theatre and to affirm the heightened form of performance. In turn he used his experience in the dramatic theatre to enrich and dramatise the language of opera. In both cases it was music that guided his theatre practice.[220]

---

[216] See Bella Merlin, *Acting – The Basics* (London/New York, 2010), p. 27.

[217] See for example Bence Nanay, 'Musical Twofoldness', *The Monist*, 95/4 (2012), pp. 606–23.

[218] Fry, 'Sound designer Gareth Fry'.

[219] Fry, 'Sound designer Gareth Fry'.

[220] Dolja Dragasevic, *Meyerhold, Director of Opera. Cultural Change and Artistic Genres* (PhD Dissertation, Goldsmith College, 2005), p. 347.

But as I have also sought to demonstrate, this mutual influence, this idea of the operatic always being the flipside of the 'musicality in the theatre' coin, is only one of the pathways in this field. Others include, as I have mentioned, 'Neue Musik' [New Music] and its interest in widening the material of composition, popular/comedic performances from *commedia* to slapstick, from Dario Fo to Monty Python and their expertise in rhythm and timing, or developments in the visual arts towards sound installations and soundscapes and their sensitivity to the interplay of sounds, objects, spaces and audiences. It certainly seems that the already heterogeneous nature of musicality in theatre has further increased in diversity in recent years, resulting in a wide range of processes and aesthetics, connected, however, by a shared aim to address a discontent with existing practices, and to reform and innovate the theatre as an art form.

Conclusion
Paradoxes of Musicality

When I started this project, my expectation was to find musicality to be a key driver for theatrical training and creation in a rather selective range of practices and perhaps in relation to quite peculiar aesthetics. The findings of this book, however, demonstrate that musicality was, and continues to be, a central, influential, transformative and multi-faceted *dispositif* with significant impact on the theatrical landscape of the last 150 years and more. Even though the list of theatre-makers and practices mentioned in this book is long, it is still, as I am quite aware, by no means exhaustive. Rather than trying to catalogue all instances of musicality in the theatre, the ambition of this book is to create a context for further enquiries and analyses within theatre studies, opera studies and musicology (while also challenging their disciplinary boundaries).

Musicality, I have argued, has proven to be a term prone to a wide range of attributions and appropriations rather than a stable singular notion. In this sense, "musicality in theatre" does not offer a unifying theory, an instrument of cohesion binding together a range of quite different theatrical visions, practices and aesthetics, but instead offers itself as a point of entry to discover and compare important aspects of these visions and practices. Musicality's interplay with(in) theatre has given rise to a number of different and at times even contradictory practices and aesthetics – it has, for example, been connected both with movements to (re-)theatricalize theatre in pursuit of an ontological uniqueness of the medium, but also with ambitions to redefine theatre as an interdisciplinary art form with blurring boundaries between different media and modes of (re-)presentation. I have also sought to demonstrate how the different facets of the musicality discourse frequently become visible through the prisms of key metaphors or analogies such as the director as conductor, the actor as instrument and/or instrumentalist, and the playtext or performance as score.

Quite often the musicality *dispositif*, as I have described it, is characterized by polarities and paradoxes: while Appia promotes musicality as a pathway to the 'inner essence' of the dramatic work, Meyerhold and others use it to highlight theatre as artifice and to create distance. While Appia and Meyerhold use musicality not least to discipline actors, Chaikin, for example, employs it to liberate them. Likewise, musicality seems at times to guarantee immediacy, at others to encourage self-reflexivity. Dahlhaus describes this paradoxical understanding of music as the language of emotions and sensations and – going back to its descriptions in antiquity – as a kind of "sounding mathematics" as the

'the central problem [of] music aesthetics of the 18th and early 19th century'.[1] In other words, the musicality *dispositif* is characterized by conflicting notions of music as either a 'structuring or emotive power'[2] between 'sensitive-intuitive and conceptual-rational perception'.[3]

Musicality is not only influential on the level of aesthetic effect, transforming ways of staging, addressing text or serving as a catalyst or organizing principle between the different arts and media on the theatrical stage. I found that it is also seen and utilized to provide a shift in the cognitive processes involved in making theatre, offering a different and often pre-linguistic form of coherence, a distinct way of thinking and perceiving. With Levitin we could speak of a different 'process of feature extraction, followed by another process of feature integration':[4] in relation to music this means that our brain processes the sonic information that reaches our ears at a basic level, 'decomposing the signal into information about pitch, timbre, spatial location, loudness, reverberant environment, tone durations and the onset times for different notes'[5] and then at a higher level combines all the 'low-level elements into an integrated representation', coming to 'an understanding of form and content'.[6] The assertion we have encountered frequently in this book is that it is possible to transfer or extend this kind of cognitive activity to the theatre as a whole, rather than just its musical components. With this idea, practitioners sometimes target the creative process and sometimes the audience, but generally describe it as a vehicle to complement or even replace more logocentric cognitive processes; i.e. meaning-making processes based predominantly on language, semiosis and narrative.

As we have seen, the notion of 'musicality' changes significantly through its different manifestations in the discourse, and there is also a diverse range of *functions* that this term is employed to provide, based on the theatrical strategies of the individual theatre-maker or ensemble. They use music or musicality alternatively as an analogy for theatre, as a set of formal models, a template of working methods, as a simile or metaphor, as an embodied practice, a habitus or way of thinking – but the common denominator remains that the musicality *dispositif* is credited with a *transformative* potential; the power to bring about change in a theatrical environment that is seen to need changing.

---

[1]   Carl Dahlhaus, 'Kleists Wort über den Generalbass', in Joachim Kreutzer (ed.), *Kleist-Jahrbuch, 1984* (Berlin, 1984), pp. 13–24, p. 17.

[2]   See Lisbeth Bloemsaat-Voerknecht, *Thomas Bernhard und die Musik* (Würzburg, 2006), p. 30.

[3]   Schopenhauer in Bloemsaat-Voerknecht, *Thomas Bernhard und die Musik*.

[4]   Daniel J. Levitin, *This Is Your Brain On Music* (London 2008), p. 103.

[5]   Levitin, *This Is Your Brain On Music*.

[6]   Levitin, *This Is Your Brain On Music*.

Musicality and Theatricality

In Chapter 2 I have already suggested that musicality is a term strongly connected to 'theatricality': both terms are employed to identify an ontological essence of their art form – even if one is fully aware how historically and culturally contingent this is – while at the same time aiming at being transferable to other life events altogether. 'Theatricality', for example, set out on the one hand to identify what pertains uniquely to theatre as an art form or more broadly as a particular aesthetic communicative setting;[7] on the other, it enabled the application or investigation of some of these qualities to events and situations such as the Duke and Duchess of Cambridge's Royal Wedding, the opening ceremony of the 2012 Olympics or the assassination of Saddam Hussein, to quote some recent examples. I suggest using 'musicality' in a quite similar fashion: as a term to shed light on what may be considered key qualities of 'music' in a given context, and also on how some of these qualities (of perception, of cognition, of composition, of creation, etc.) may apply to 'non-musical' scenarios. Before I turn to these I want to briefly reflect on how this idea of musicality in the theatre may enrich our understanding of genres where it might seem redundant to even consider it: opera, music-theatre and musical theatre.

A Musicality of Opera and Other Music-Led Genres

I have pointed out in the introduction that while this book explicitly focuses on theatre, opera (and later also music-theatre and the musical) has proven to be a continuous silent (or not so silent) partner, counterpart and sometimes anti-model in the development of the musicality *dispositif* for theatre. At first sight, it may well seem redundant to discuss the musicality of opera, of course, given that music is the 'element that makes opera opera'.[8] I would, however, suggest, that the term, as I have sought to develop it here, can add to the discourse of opera, music-theatre and musical studies. In the case of opera, we know that its study is still characterized by the disciplinary divide in particular between musicology and theatre studies, both of which have demonstrated quite selective interests and competences, fragmenting and limiting their approach to 'opera' (notable exceptions not withstanding[9]). Nicholas Till asserts that opera has been

---

7   See, for example, Burns (Harlow, 1972); Lehmann (1986); Kotte (1998); Münz (Berlin, 1998); Feral (2002); Davis (Cambridge, 2003).

8   Roberta Montemorra Marvin/Downing A. Thomas (eds.), *Operatic Migrations. Transforming Works and Crossing Boundaries* (Farnham, 2006), p. 6.

9   See for example Levin (Stanford, 1993; Chicago, 2007); Abbate (Princeton, N.J./ Oxford, 2002); Koch et. al. (Würzburg, 2005); Marvin/Thomas (Farnham, 2006); Schläder (Berlin, 2006; Berlin, 2009); Mungen (Würzburg, 2011); Till (Cambridge, 2012).

'marginalized by both musicology and theatre studies'[10] and Christopher Morris asks: 'wasn't opera repeatedly overlooked by musicology's sister disciplines for its indulgence of music at the expense of literature, dance, and theater?'[11] Likewise one could ask whether an understanding of opera *as performance* has not remained under-reflected due to an overreliance on libretto and score as the assumed 'original work', which performance could only dilute or distract from?[12] As Till puts it, opera studies needs to concern itself with 'the materiality of performance practices and events, and with the institutions and cultural discourses that sustain them. To study opera we have to study more than operas.'[13]

The discourse on opera in performance, whether it is in academic analyses or reviews, still works strongly with an assumed separation of the 'work' and its 'interpretation' (sometimes even just its 'illustration' or 'Bebilderung') in a stage production.[14] The musicality *dispositif*, I would argue, offers *one* opportunity to question this separation and to highlight instead the multi-layered interweaving of music and theatre. For opera as a performed practice, musicality is still a quality that needs to be discussed rather than taken for granted. To put it provocatively, I would say that not all opera (nor music-theatre or musical theatre) in performance is 'musical' – at times the musicality remains confined to the musical score and its execution but does not significantly affect the theatrical performance – which is exactly what Appia already admonished more than 100 years ago. What Philip Auslander has convincingly proposed for music performance ('music is, what musicians *do*'[15]), I would apply to the music-theatrical genres as well: opera/

---

[10]   Nicholas Till (ed.), *The Cambridge Companion to Opera Studies* (Cambridge, 2012), p. 3.

[11]   Christopher Morris, 'Operatic Migrations: Transforming Works and Crossing Boundaries (review)', *The Opera Quarterly*, 23/1, Winter 2007 (2007), pp. 120–26, p. 120.

[12]   David Levin points out: 'Academic writing on opera has not ignored questions of performance. But for the most part, these questions have been historical. But what we do not possess – what musicologists and non-musicologists alike have tended to shy away from – is a sense of how stage performance can shape and even alter our understanding of opera' (David J. Levin, *Unsettling Opera: Staging Mozart, Verdi, Wagner and Zemlinsky* [Chicago: University of Chicago Press, 2007], p. 6).

[13]   Till, *The Cambridge Companion*, p. 2. Similar arguments could of course be made for the study of musicals, which also falls between disciplines and discourses.

[14]   A recent new study on performance analysis of opera performances, still talks about libretto, music and 'their concretisation on stage' (http://www.theaterforschung.de/annotation.php4?ID=3851 [16.06.2013]). (See Stephanie Großmann, *Inszenierungsanalyse von Opern: eine interdisziplinäre Methodik* [Würzburg: Königshausen & Neumann, 2013]). David Levin's book *Unsettling Opera*, on the other hand, addresses this very problem and offers a series of analyses that interrogate and problematize the status of 'work', suggesting instead to look at opera in performance as 'polylogism' of 'multiple, sometimes conflicting expressive registers' (Levin, *Unsettling Opera*, p. 12).

[15]   This is how he put it in his keynote at the 11th Congress of the Gesellschaft für Theaterwissenschaft (German Society for Theatre Studies) 'Sound and Performance' (4–7

music-theatre/musicals are what singers, directors, conductors and designers, etc., *do*. Carolyn Abbate echoes this when asking what it means 'to write about [...] about an opera live and unfolding in time and not an operatic work?'[16] The kind of musicality I have sought to outline in this book is arguably to be found more in the 'drastic' rather than the 'gnostic' approach, if we follow her (and Vladimir Jankélévitch's) influential distinction, which seeks to emphasize the live, material, even carnal aspects of music(-theatre) *performance* over the conceptual, hermeneutic and theoretical features of *works*.[17] (Levin rightly points out that the drastic and the gnostic are, of course, not mutually exclusive but often enter a very dynamic interplay.[18]) The musicality *dispositif* in opera and other music-theatrical genres describes this wider field of activity, process and discourse, *including* but not limited to, the musical characteristics of the score.

Concentrating on the realm of theatre in this book has allowed me to pinpoint more clearly what I have sought to define as the musicality *dispositif* – this plurality of vectors, discourses, institutions and practices based on contextualized notion of 'music'. The metaphorical and transformative powers of this term are more tangible here, but they certainly also apply to opera, music theatre, ballet, Tanztheater, the musical or composed theatre, where musicality can equally be a quality and attunement in the process of training, staging or perceiving. What is 'musical' in this context, then, potentially extends to all aspects of opera- and music-theatre-making and is not necessarily determined exclusively by the composer.

If we then look at the many contemporary attempts to dissolve, redefine or critically interrogate opera, different musicality *dispositifs* could be analyzed which characterize new forms and genres from 'New Singing Theatre',[19] 'New Music Theatre'[20] and 'Experimental Music-Theatre'[21] to 'Composed Theatre'.[22] Here it is often specifically the turn towards applying musical or even compositional thinking to the theatre *as a whole* that carries forth and articulates the *dispositif* in this new range of forms, which are seen to be situated across or between traditional understandings of 'dramatic theatre' and 'opera', etc. What this suggests is a stretching of the idea of what, for example, opera *is*: Can 'opera' also be a musical approach to dramatic

---

October 2012, University of Bayreuth, Germany). See also his article 'Performance Analysis and Popular Music: A Manifesto', *Contemporary Theatre Review*, 14/1 (2004), pp. 1–13.

[16] Carolyn Abbate, 'Music – Drastic or Gnostic', *Critical Inquiry*, 30/Spring (2004), pp. 505–36, p. 505.

[17] See Abbate, 'Music – Drastic or Gnostic'.

[18] Levin, *Unsettling Opera*, p. 9.

[19] Michael Bawtree, *The New Singing Theatre. A Charter for the Music Theatre Movement* (New York/Bristol, 1991).

[20] Eric Salzman/Thomas Desi, *The New Music Theatre* (Oxford, 2008).

[21] Frieder Reininghaus/Katja Schneider (eds.), *Experimentelles Musik- und Tanztheater* (Laaber, 2004).

[22] Matthias Rebstock/David Roesner (eds.), *Composed Theatre. Aesthetics, Practices, Processes* (Bristol, 2012).

theatre, characterized by a particular attention to form, to a lyricism of text, to sung qualities of voice? 'Musicality' can help distinguish, compare and productively relate phenomena on a wide spectrum between 'opera to everyday performance'.[23] In a final brief outlook, I want to take this idea even further, beyond the realm of the arts and into the wider context of humanities and life sciences.

The Musicality *dispositif* in the Humanities and Life Sciences

Aesthetic *dispositifs* can be understood as epistemological models for complex systems and interactions. Musicality as *one* such *dispositif* captures an attunement of the senses, of the body and of cognition modelled on different modes of musical production and reception in pursuit of creative, aesthetic or ideological aims. I have developed this notion in relation to theatre, but musicality can also be described in other art forms, such as in film (e.g. for Walter Ruttmann or Dziga Vertov) or in visual art (e.g. Paul Klee or Wassily Kandinsky), to name but a few.

Following Jacobus Leodiensis's dictum 'musica ad omni extendere se videtur'[24] and thus branching out from the arts into the wider circle of humanities and life sciences, it becomes evident that musicality could also highlight and differentiate the wide range of analogies, metaphors and strategies in place. The discourse around leadership and management, for example, frequently draws upon the relationship of conductor and orchestra, or the interactional model of an improvising jazz combo to distinguish and promote styles of interpersonal relations and personal development.[25] At times, however, these analogies amount to not much more than "jazzing up" relatively established theories, therefore a more contextualized and closer look at the musical specifics could add rigour and insight.

In the area of sports and medical sciences, technologies for measuring performance or supporting diagnosis provide acoustic feedback.[26] In sports, these

---

[23]   Anno Mungen (ed.), *Mitten im Leben. Musiktheater von der Oper bis zur Everyday-Performance mit Musik* (Würzburg, 2011).

[24]   'Music extends onto all aspects of life', in Christian Kaden/Volker Kalisch, 'Musik', in Karl-Heinz Brack (ed.), *Ästhetische Grundbegriffe. Historisches Wörterbuch in sieben Bänden* (Stuttgart/Weimar, 2005), pp. 256–308, p. 257.

[25]   See for example Max Depree, *Leadership Jazz* (New York, 1992); Anette Prehn/Kjeld Frendes, *Play your Brain. Adopt a Musical Mindset and Change Your Life and Career* (London, 2011); Itay Talgam, 'Lead Like the Great Conductors. Talk at TEDGlobal July 2009 in Oxford (UK)' (2009), http://www.ted.com/talks/itay_talgam_lead_like_the_great_conductors.html [20.05.2012]; Deniz Ucbasaran/Andy Lockett/Michael Humphreys, 'Leading Entrepreneurial Teams: Insights from Jazz' (NY), http://www.isbe.org.uk/content/assets/I._Creative_Industries_Entrepreneurship-_Deniz_Ucbasaran.pdf [11.12.2012].

[26]   A good example from the world of amateur sports is the connection of Nike's running monitor chip with Apple's iPod/iPhones controlling your musical playlist according to running performance, while also recording your training and making it public on social

can be used to monitor or increase performance while in medicine the sonification of technology as well as the sounds and rhythms of the body itself (breathing, heartbeat, voice, etc.) require musical sensitivity of doctors and nurses to detect, distinguish and interpret these acoustic signals towards diagnosis and treatment. Equally, a wide range of *therapeutic* methods contains musical and rhythmical stimuli to support recovery,[27] and in sport, music is used to affect the motivation and organization of physical performance. As I have mentioned in the Introduction, Tia deNora, who has investigated this in relation to fitness classes, even speaks of music as a 'prosthetic technology of the body',[28] which both impacts very directly on the vital functions of the body, and also influences the psychosomatic composure of the person in training.

Beyond the realm of sports and medicine, deNora highlights the significance of music (and I would add: of musicality) in a psychological and sociological sense for both individual constructions of self and social interactions. She goes further than merely pointing us to the obvious role of music as representation or symbolic reference of an individual and their social identity but assigns an active and constitutive role to music for creating and modifying what she calls 'musically composed identities'.[29]

In pedagogy, to give a final example, there is an increasing interest in the musical-rhythmical design of processes of teaching and learning.[30] Language acquisition accompanied by music, rhythmization of contents, musically structured forms of learning, which operate with patterns of repetition, variation, differences in tempo, modulation, changes of timbre or counterpoint, all represent applications for the transfer of the musicality *dispositif* to pedagogical strategies.

Musicality has the potential of being recognized as a versatile tool in the arts and humanities: as an epistemological model, a mode of creativity and production, an organizing principle, a unique perceptive sensitivity and a form of cognitive engagement and meaning-making. Author Wallace Stevens puts this more poetically: 'The principle of music would be an addition to humanity if it were not humanity itself, in other than human form.'[31] Musicality is thus certainly not the privilege of a few talented individuals but an omnipresent foundation of our lives.

---

media, thus adding two layers of competition. See http://www.apple.com/de/ipod/nike/run. html [21.05.2012].

[27] Oliver Sacks's study *Musicophilia: Tales of Music and the Brain* (New York, 2007) gives a range of fascinating case studies in the area of neurology and musicality.

[28] Tia DeNora, *Music in Everyday Life* (Cambridge, 2000), p. 102.

[29] DeNora, *Music in Everyday Life*.

[30] See for example Stephen Malloch/Colwyn Trevarthen (eds.), *Communicative Musicality: Exploring the Basis of Human Companionship* (Oxford/New York, 2009) and Kate E. Gfeller, *Multidisciplinary Perspectives on Musicality: Essays from the Seashore Symposium* (Iowa, 2006).

[31] Wallace Stevens in Tim Armstrong, 'Player Piano. Poetry and Sonic Modernity', *Modernism/Modernity*, 14/1 (2007), pp. 1–19, p. 14.

Bibliography

Abbate, Carolyn, *In Search of Opera* (Princeton, NJ/Oxford: Princeton University Press, 2002).

———, 'Music – Drastic or Gnostic', *Critical Inquiry*, 30 (2004): 505–36.

Ackerley, Chris J./Gontarski, Stanley E., *The Grove Companion to Samuel Beckett. A Reader's Guide to His Works, Life and Thought* (New York: Grove Press, 2004).

Agamben, Giorgio, *Che cos'è un dispositivo?* (Roma: Nottetempo, 2006).

———, 'Notes on Gesture (1978)', in Giorgio Agamben (ed.), *Infancy and History: The Destruction of Experience* (London/New York: Verso, 2007): 155–67.

Agud, Ana, 'Musikalische und sprachliche Zeit', in Albrecht Riethmüller (ed.), *Sprache und Musik. Perspektiven einer Beziehung* (Laaber: Laaber, 1999): 67–86.

Albert, Claudia, 'Dirigenten und Oberkellner: Eislers Kritik der musikalischen Verhältnisse', in Albrecht Riethmüller (ed.), *Brecht und seine Komponisten* (Laaber: Laaber, 2000): 133–54.

Albright, Daniel, *Untwisting the Serpent: Modernism in Music, Literature, and Other Arts* (Chicago, IL/London: University of Chicago Press, 2000).

———, *Beckett and Aesthetics* (Cambridge: Cambridge University Press, 2003).

Alerby, Eva/Ferm, Cecilia, 'Learning Music. Embodied Experience in the Life-World', *Philosophy of Music Education Review*, 13/2 (2005): 177–85.

Allain, Paul, *Gardzienice: Polish Theatre in Transition* (Amsterdam: Harwood Academic, 1997).

Allain, Paul/Harvie, Jen, *The Routledge Companion to Theatre and Performance* (London: Routledge, 2006).

Antohin, Anatoly, 'Meyerhold Biomechanics' (2005), http://biomechanics. vtheatre.net/meyer.html [17.08.2011].

Appia, Adolphe, *Die Musik und die Inscenierung* (München: F. Bruckmann, 1899).

———, 'Actor, Space, Light, Painting (1919)', in Richard C. Beacham (ed.), *Texts on Theatre* (London/New York: Routledge, 1993): 114–15.

———, 'Music and the Art of the Theatre (1899) [Excerpts]', in Richard C. Beacham (ed.), *Texts on Theatre* (London/New York: Routledge, 1993): 29–58.

———, *Music and the Art of the Theatre*, translated by Robert W. Corrigan and Mary Douglas Dirks (Coral Gables, FL: University of Miami Press, 1962).

———, 'Theatrical Experiences and Personal Investigations (1921)', in Richard C. Beacham (ed.), *Texts on Theatre* (London/New York: Routledge, 1993): 22–8 and 161–6.

———, 'Theatrical Production and its Prospects for the Future (1921)', in Richard C. Beacham (ed.), *Texts on Theatre* (London/New York: Routledge, 1993): 124–34.

————, 'The Work of Living Art (1919)', in Richard C. Beacham (ed.), *Texts on Theatre* (London/New York: Routledge, 1993): 167–78.

Arnold, Paul, 'The Artaud Experiment', *The Tulane Drama Review*, 8/2 (1963): 15–29.

Aronson, Arnold, *American Avant-garde Theatre: A History* (London/New York: Routledge, 2000).

Artaud, Antonin, *The Theatre and its Double. Translated by Victor Corti* (London: Calder Publications, 1970).

————, *Selected Writings. Edited by Susan Sontag* (Berkeley/Los Angeles, CA: University of California Press, 1988).

Asmus, W.D., 'Practical aspects of theatre, radio and television. Rehearsal notes for the German premiere of Beckett's *That Time* and *Footfalls* at the Schiller-Theater Werkstatt, Berlin (1.9.76)', *Journal of Beckett Studies*, 2 [Online] (1977), http://www.english.fsu.edu/jobs/num02/Num2WalterAsmus.htm [28.02.2012].

Aston, Elaine, 'On Collaboration: "Not Ordinary, Not Safe"', in Elaine Aston/Elin Diamond (eds.), *The Cambridge Companion to Caryl Churchill* (Cambridge: Cambridge University Press, 2009): 144–62.

Aston, Elaine/Diamond, Elin (eds.), *The Cambridge Companion to Caryl Churchill* (Cambridge: Cambridge University Press, 2009).

Augoyard, Jean-François/Torgue, Henry, *Sonic Experience: A Guide to Everyday Sounds* (Montreal: McGill Queens University Press, 2005).

Auslander, Philip, *From Acting to Performance: Essays in Modernism and Postmodernism* (London: Routledge, 1997).

————, *Liveness: Performance in a Mediatized Culture* (London/New York: Routledge, 1999).

————, 'Performance Analysis and Popular Music: A Manifesto', *Contemporary Theatre Review*, 14/1 (2004): 1–13.

————, 'Musical Personae', *TDR*, 50/1 (2006): 100–119.

Austerlitz, Paul, *Jazz Consciousness: Music, Race, and Humanity* (Middletown, CT: Wesleyan University Press, 2005).

Bablet, Denis/Bablet, Marie-Louise, *Adolphe Appia 1882–1928. Actor – Space – Light* (London/New York: Calder/Riverrun Press, 1982).

Bailes, Sara Jane, 'Between People. Rufus Norris interviewed by Sara Jane Bailes', *Performing Arts Journal*, 81 (2005): 62–73.

Bailey, Derek, *Improvisation. Its Nature and Practice in Music* (Ashbourne, Derbyshire: Moorland Publishing, 1980).

Bakhtin, Mikhail, *The Dialogic Imagination: Four Essays* (Austin: University of Texas Press, 1981).

————, *Problems of Dostoevsky's Poetics* (Minneapolis, MN: University of Minnesota Press, 1984).

Balkin, Sarah, 'Regenerating Drama in Stein's *Doctor Faustus Lights the Lights* and Woolf's *Between the Acts*', *Modern Drama*, 51/4 (2008): 433–57.

Balme, Christopher (ed.), *Das Theater von Morgen. Texte zur deutschen Theaterreform* (Würzburg: Königshausen und Neumann, 1988).

———, 'Intermediality: Rethinking the Relationship between Theatre and Media' (2004) [Online], http://epub.ub.uni-muenchen.de/13098/1/Balme_13098.pdf [11.06.2013].

———, 'Heiner Goebbels: Zur Dramaturgie des Samplings', in Stefan Tigges (ed.), *Dramatische Transformationen. Zu gegenwärtigen Schreib- und Aufführungsstrategien im deutschsprachigen Theater* (Bielefeld: transcript, 2008): 225–36.

Barber, Stephen, *The Screaming Body* (London: Creation Books, 1999).

Barker, Clive, *Theatre Jazz. Workshop held at Warwick University, Spring 2003* (DVD documentation, Exeter Digital Archives, Drama Department, University of Exeter).

Barker, Howard, *Arguments for a Theatre* (London: John Calder, 1989).

Barnett, David, 'Christoph Marthaler. The Musicality, Theatricality and Politics of Postdramatic Direction', in Maria M. Delgado/Dan Rebellato (eds.), *Contemporary European Theatre Directors* (London/New York: Routledge, 2010): 185–203.

Barthes, Roland, 'The Grain of the Voice', in Roland Barthes, *Image-Music-Text* (New York: Hill and Wang, 1977): 179–89.

Basting, Barbara, 'Drastische Töne. Die Komponistin Olga Neuwirth und ihre Zusammenarbeit mit Elfriede Jelinek: unerhörte musikalische Sprachen', *du*, 700/10 *Elfriede Jelinek. Schreiben. Fremd bleiben* (1999): 22–5.

Baur, Detlev, 'Der Chor auf der Bühne des 20. Jahrhunderts', in Peter Riemer/Bernhard Zimmermann (eds.), *Der Chor im antiken und modernen Drama* (Stuttgart: Metzler, 1999): 227–46.

Bawtree, Michael, *The New Singing Theatre. A Charter for the Music Theatre Movement* (New York/Bristol: Oxford University Press/The Bristol Press, 1991).

Bayerdörfer, Hans-Peter (ed.), *Musiktheater als Herausforderung: interdisziplinäre Facetten von Theater- und Musikwissenschaft* (Tübingen: Niemeyer, 1999).

Beacham, Richard C., *Adolphe Appia: Texts on Theatre* (London/New York: Routledge, 1993).

———, *Adolphe Appia. Artist and Visionary of the Modern Theatre* (Reading: Harwood 1994).

Beacham, Richard C./Volbach, Walther R., *Adolphe Appia. Essays, Scenarios, and Designs* (Ann Arbor: UMI Research Press, 1989).

Beckett, Samuel, *Play; And Two Short Pieces for Radio* (London: Faber and Faber, 1964).

Behrendt, Joachim-Ernst, *Das Jazzbuch* (Frankfurt am Main: Wolfgang Krüger, 1989).

Belgrad, Daniel, *The Culture of Spontaneity. Improvisation and the Arts in Postwar America* (Chicago/London: Chicago University Press, 1998).

Benguerel, André-Pierre/D'Arcy, Janet, 'Time-warping and the perception of rhythm in speech', *Journal of Phonetics*, 14 (1986): 231–46.

Bennecke, Patricia, '"Wir wollen eine geniale Idee nur noch einmal überprüfen"', *Theater heute Jahrbuch* (1998): 128–35.

Benson, Stephen, 'For Want of a Better Term? Polyphony and the Value of Music in Bakhtin and Kundera', *Narrative*, 11/3 (2003): 292–311.

Benveniste, Émile, 'Der Begriff des "Rythmus" und sein sprachlicher Ausdruck', in Émile Benveniste (ed.), *Probleme der allgemeinen Sprachwissenschaft* (München: List Verlag, 1974): 363–74.

Berghaus, Günter, *Theatre, Performance and the Historical Avant-Garde* (Basingstoke: Palgrave, 2009).

Bergson, Henri, *Laughter. An Essay on the Meaning of the Comic* (Rockville, MD: Arc Manor, 2008 [1900]).

Berliner, Paul F., *Thinking in Jazz. The Infinite Art of Improvisation* (Chicago/ London: Chicago University Press [Kindle Edition], 1994).

Bermbach, Udo/Borchmeyer, Dieter/Danuser, Hermann/Friedrich, Sven/ Kienzle, Ulrike/Vaget, Hans, 'Schwerpunkt/focusing on: Regietheater', *Wagnerspektrum*, 2 (2005).

Bernhard, Thomas, *The President & Eve of Retirement* (New York: Performing Arts Journal Publications, 1982).

——, 'Minetti', in Thomas Bernhard, *Stücke 2. Der Präsident, Die Berühmten, Minetti, Immanuel Kant* (Frankfurt am Main: Suhrkamp, 1988): 245–6.

Berry, Cicely, *Voice and the Actor* (New York: Wiley, 1973).

Bertha, Csilla, 'Music and Words in Brian Friel's *Performances*', in Donald E. Morse/Csilla Bertha/Mària Kurdi (eds.) *Brian Friel's Dramatic Artistry: The Work Has Value* (Dublin: Carysfort Press, 2006).

Bethman, Brenda L., '"My Characters Only Live Insofar as They Speak": Interview with Elfriede Jelinek', *Women in Germany Yearbook* (Lincoln: University of Nebraska Press, 2000): 61–72.

Binns, Michael, 'Music, Theatre and Silence', *Gambit. International Theatre Review*, 38/Theatre and Music Issue (1981): 6–16.

Bjerstedt, Sven, *Att agera musikaliskt. Musikalitet som norm och utbildningsmål i västerländsk talteater* [*Musicality in Acting: Musicality as a Standard and an Educational Goal for Western Spoken Theatre*] (Master Thesis, Lunds Universitet. Musikhögskolan i Malmö, 2010).

Blackadder, Neil Martin, 'Emilia Galotti (review)', *Theatre Journal*, 58/2 (2006): 350–51.

Blacking, John, *How Musical is Man?* (Seattle: University of Washington Press, 1973).

Bloemsaat-Voerknecht, Lisbeth, *Thomas Bernhard und die Musik* (Würzburg: Königshausen & Neumann, 2006).

Blumenthal, Eileen, *Joseph Chaikin: Exploring at the Boundaries of Theater* (Cambridge: Cambridge University Press, 1984).

Boenisch, Peter M., 'Exposing The Classics: Michael Thalheimer's Regie beyond the Text', *Contemporary Theatre Review, Special issue 'German Theatre Beyond the Text'*, 18:1 (2008), pp. 30–43.

Bonz, Jochen, 'Sampling. Eine postmoderne Kulturtechnik', in Christoph Jacke/ Eva Kimminich/Siegfried J. Schmidt (eds.), *Kulturschutt. Über das Recycling von Theorien und Kulturen* (Bielefeld: transcript, 2006): 333–53.

Borchmeyer, Dieter, 'Saat von Göthe gesäet ... Die "Regeln für Schauspieler" – ein theatergeschichtliches Gerücht', in Wolfgang F. Bender (ed.), *Schauspielkunst im 18. Jahrhundert. Grundlagen, Praxis, Autoren* (Stuttgart: Franz Steiner Verlag, 1992): 261–87.

Bormann, Hans-Friedrich/Brandstetter, Gabriele/Matzke, Annemarie (eds.), *Improvisieren. Paradoxien des Unvorhersehbaren. Kunst – Medien – Praxis* (Bielefeld: transcript, 2010).

Bottoms, Stephen James, 'Towards a Rhythm Method: Exploring "Psychological Realism" in Sam Shepard's *Buried Child*', *Studies in Theatre Production*, 10 (1994): 4–19.

———, *The Theatre of Sam Shepard: States of Crisis* (Cambridge: Cambridge University Press, 1998).

Bouko, Catherine, 'Jazz Musicality in Postdramatic Theatre and the Opacity of Auditory Signs', *Studies in Musical Theatre*, 4/1 (2010): 75–87.

Bourdieu, Pierre, *Outline of a Theory of Practice* (Cambridge: Cambridge University Press, 1977).

Bowman, Wayne D., *Philosophical Perspectives on Music* (Oxford: Oxford University Press, 1998).

Brandstetter, Gabriele/Finter, Helga/Weßendorf, Markus (eds.), *Grenzgänge. Das Theater und die anderen Künste* (Tübingen: Gunter Narr, 1998).

Brandstetter, Gabriele/Wiens, Birgit (eds.), *Theater ohne Fluchtpunkt: Das Erbe Adolphe Appias: Szenographie und Choreographie im zeitgenössischen Theater* (Berlin: Alexander Verlag, 2010).

Brandt, George W. (ed.), *Modern Theories of Drama: A Selection of Writings on Drama and Theatre 1850–1990* (Oxford: Clarendon Press, 1998).

Branigan, Kevin, *Radio Beckett. Musicality in the Radio Plays of Samuel Beckett* (Oxford: Peter Lang, 2008).

Braun, Edward, *Meyerhold. A Revolution in Theatre* (London: Methuen, 1979).

———, *The Director and the Stage: From Naturalism to Grotowski* (London: Methuen, 1982).

Brauneck, Manfred, *Die Welt als Bühne. Geschichte des europäischen Theaters* (Stuttgart/Weimar: Metzler, 1993).

———, *Theater im 20. Jahrhundert. Programmschriften, Stilperioden, Reformmodelle* (Reinbeck bei Hamburg: Rowohlt, 1998 [1982]).

Brecht, Bertolt, 'Über gestische Musik', in Bertolt Brecht, *Gesammelte Werke, Band 17: Schriften zum Theater 3* (Frankfurt am Main: Suhrkamp, 1967): 482–5.

Brougher, Kerry/Strick, Jeremy/Wiseman, Ari/Zilczer, Judith, *Visual Music: Synaesthesia in Art and Music Since 1900* (London: Thames & Hudson, 2005).

Brown, Calvin S., 'Theoretische Grundlagen zum Studium der Wechselverhältnisse zwischen Literatur und Musik', in Steven Paul Scher (ed.), *Literatur und Musik. Ein Handbuch zur Theorie und Praxis eines komparatistischen Grenzgebietes* (Berlin: Erich Schmidt Verlag, 1984): 28–39.

Brown, Ross, *Sound: A Reader in Theatre Practice* (Basingtoke: Palgrave, 2010).

Bruhn, Siglind, 'A Concert of Paintings: "Musical Ekphrasis" in the Twentieth Century', *Poetics Today*, 22/3 (Fall 2001): 551–605.

Brüstle, Christa/Ghattas, Nadia/ Risi, Clemens/Schouten, Sabine (eds.), *Aus dem Takt. Rhythmus in Kunst, Kultur und Natur* (Bielefeld: transcript, 2005).

Bryden, Mary (ed.), *Samuel Beckett and Music* (Oxford: Clarendon Press, 1998).

Budde, Elmar, 'Zum Verhältnis von Sprache, Sprachlaut und Komposition in der neueren Musik', in Rudolf Stephan (ed.), *Über Musik und Sprache* (Mainz: Schotts Söhne, 1974): 9–19.

Bullerjahn, Claudia, 'Ein begriffliches Babylon: Von den Schwierigkeiten einer einheitlichen Filmmusik-Nomenklatur' (1999), http://www.sign-lang.uni-hamburg.de/Medienzentrum/zmm-news/zmmNewsA/archiv/Sommer99%20%C4/Sommer99/Bullerjahn.htm [02/07/2007].

Bunz, Melanie, 'Instabil. Musik und Digitalität als Momente der Verschiebung', in Christoph Jacke/Eva Kimminich/Siegfried J. Schmidt (eds.), *Kulturschutt. Über das Recycling von Theorien und Kulturen* (Bielefeld: transcript, 2006): 271–81.

Bürger, Peter, *Theory of the Avant-Garde* (Minneapolis: University of Minnesota Press, 1984).

Bürgers, Irmelin, '"Es ist immer die Musik, die mich rettet …". Thomas Bernhards Sprachpartituren', in Hans Werner Henze (ed.), *Musik und Sprache. Neue Aspekte der musikalischen Ästhetik IV* (Frankfurt am Main: Fischer, 1990): 173–91.

Burns, Elizabeth, *Theatricality: A Study of Convention in the Theatre and in Social Life* (Harlow: Longman, 1972).

Bussolini, Jeffrey, 'What is a Dispositive?', *Foucault Studies*, 10 (2010): 85–107.

Cadullo, Bert/Knopf, Robert, *Theater of the Avant-garde, 1890–1950: A Critical Anthology* (New Haven/London: Yale University Press, 2001).

Campbell, Patricia Shehan, 'How Musical We Are: John Blacking on Music, Education, and Cultural Understanding', *Journal of Research in Music Education*, 48/4 (2000): 336–59.

Carlson, Marvin, *Theories of the Theatre: A Historical and Critical Survey, From the Greeks to the Present. Expanded Edition* (Ithaca, NY/London: Cornell University Press, 1993).

Carnegy, Patrick, *Wagner and the Art of the Theatre* (New Haven/London: Yale University Press, 2006).

Carp, Stefanie, 'Langsames Leben ist lang. Zum Theater von Christoph Marthaler', *Theaterschrift*, 12 *Zeit/Temps/Tijd/Time* (1997): 64–77.

Castellucci, Claudia/Castellucci, Romeo/Guidi, Chiara/Kelleher, Joe/Ridout, Nicholas, *The Theatre of Socìetas Raffaello Sanzio* (London: Routledge, 2007).

Cecchetto, David/Cuthbert, Nancy/Lassonde, Julie/Robinson, Dylan, *Collision: Interarts Practice and Research* (Newcastle upon Tyne: Cambridge Scholars Publishing, 2008).

Cesare, T. Nikki, "'Like a chained man's bruise": The Mediated Body in Eight Songs for a Mad King and Anatomy Theater', *Theatre Journal*, 58 (2006): 437–57.

Chagas, Paulo C., 'Polyphony and Embodiment: A Critical Approach to the Theory of Autopoiesis', *TRANS. Revista Transcultural de Música*, 9 [Online] (2005), http://www.sibetrans.com/trans/a179/polyphony-and-embodiment-a-critical-approach-to-the-theory-of-autopoiesis [16.08.2011].

Chaikin, Joseph, *The Presence of the Actor* (New York: Theatre Communications Group, 1972).

——, 'Joseph Chaikin: Continuing Work. An Interview with Peter Hulton, Paris 1981', *Theatre Papers: The Fourth Series (1983–84)*, 4/1 (1983): 1–40.

Chansky, Dorothy, 'Drama', in David J. Nordloh (ed.), *American Literary Scholarship: An Annual, 2006* (Durham and London: Duke University Press, 2008): 421–51.

Chapple, Freda/Kattenbelt, Chiel (eds.), *Intermediality in Theatre and Performance* (Amsterdam/New York: Rodopi, 2006).

Chekhov, Michael, *To the Actor. On the Technique of Acting* (London: Routledge, 2002 [1953]).

Chion, Michel, *Audio-Vision. Sounds on Screen* (New York: Columbia University Press, 1994).

Christ, William/Delone, Richard/Kliewer, Vernon/Rowell, Lewis/Thomson, William, *Materials and Structure of Music. Third Edition* (Englewood Cliffs, NJ: Prentice-Hall, 1980).

Churchill, Caryl, *The Skriker* (London: Nick Hern, 1994).

——, *Plays: 4* (London: Methuen Drama, 2009).

Cole, Susan L., 'Robert Wilson directs *The Golden Windows* and *Hamletmaschine*', in Susan L. Cole (ed.), *Directors in Rehearsal: A Hidden World* (New York/London: Routledge, 1992): 144–69.

Cole, Toby (ed.), *Playwrights on Playwriting. From Ibsen to Ionesco* (New York: Cooper Square Press, 2001 [1960]).

Cole, Toby/Chinoy, Helen Krich (eds.), *Actors on Acting. The Theories, Techniques, and Practices of the World's Great Actors, Told in Their Own Words* (New York: Crown, 1970).

Collins, John, 'Performing Sound / Sounding Space', in Lynne Kendrick/David Roesner (eds.), *Theatre Noise. The Sound of Performance* (Bristol: Intellect, 2011): 23–32.

Collison, David, *The Sound of Theatre: a History* (Eastbourne: PLASA, 2008).

Cook, Nicholas, *Analysing Musical Multimedia* (Oxford: Clarendon Press, 1998).

——, *Music. A Very Short Introduction* (Oxford: Oxford University Press, 1998).

——, 'Between Process and Product: Music and/as Performance', *Music Theory Online*, 7 (2001), http://www.societymusictheory.org/mto/issues/mto.01.7.2/mto.01.7.2.cook.html#FN8: 1–21 [13.09.2006].

————, 'Theorizing Musical Meaning', *Music Theory Spectrum*, 23/2 (2001): 170–95.

Cooper, Grosvenor W./Meyer, Leonard B., *The Rhythmic Structure of Music* (Chicago/London: University of Chicago Press, 1960).

Craig, Edward Gordon, *On the Art of Theatre* (London: Routledge, 2009 [1911]).

Crimp, Martin, *The Treatment* (London: Nick Hern Books, 1993).

————, *Attempts on Her Life* (London: Faber and Faber, 1997).

Crook, Tim, *Radio Drama: Theory and Practice* (London: Routledge, 1999).

Cross, Ian, 'Musicality and the human capacity for culture' [preprint], published in: *Musicae Scientiae, Special Issue: Narrative in music and interaction* (2008): 147–67, http://www.mus.cam.ac.uk/~ic108/PDF/IRMC_MS07_2. pdf [29.12.2009].

Curtin, Adrian, 'Cruel Vibrations: Sounding Out Antonin Artaud's Production of *Les Cenci*', *Theatre Research International*, 35/3 (2010): 250–62.

————, 'The Art *Music* of Theatre: Howard Barker as Sound Designer', *Studies in Theatre and Performance*, 32/3 (2012): 269–84.

————, *Avant-Garde Theatre Sound: Staging Sonic Modernity* (New York: Palgrave Macmillan, 2014).

D'haen, Theo, 'Frames and Boundaries', *Poetics Today*, 10/2 (1989): 429–37.

Dahlhaus, Carl, 'Kleists Wort über den Generalbass', in Joachim Kreutzer (ed.), *Kleist-Jahrbuch, 1984* (Berlin: Erich Schmidt Verlag, 1984): 13–24.

Daniels, Barry (ed.), *Joseph Chaikin & Sam Shepard: Letters and Texts 1972–1984* (New York: Theatre Communications Group, 1994).

Davies, David, *Philosophies of the Performing Arts* (Malden, MA/Oxford: Wiley & Blackwell, 2011).

Davis, Rocío G./Fischer-Hornung, Dorothea/Kardoux, Johanna C. (eds.), *Aesthetic Practices and Politics in Media, Music, and Art* (New York: Routledge, 2011).

Davis, Tracy C./Postlewait, Thomas (eds.), *Theatricality* (Cambridge: Cambridge University Press, 2003).

De La Motte, Diether (ed.), *Zeit in der Musik – Musik in der Zeit* (Frankfurt am Main: Peter Lang, 1997).

De La Motte-Haber, Helga/Reinecke, Hans-Peter, *Ein Beitrag zur Klassifikation musikalischer Rhythmen. Experimentalpsychologische Untersuchungen* (Köln: Arno Volk Verlag, 1968).

Deeken, Alfons, *Process and Permanence in Ethics: Max Scheler's Moral Philosophy* (New York: Paulist Press, 1974).

Delalande, Francois, 'Sense and Intersensoriality', *Leonardo* 36/4 (2003): 313–16.

Deleuze, Gilles/Guattari, Felix, *A Thousand Plateaus* (Minneapolis: University of Minnesota Press, 1987).

Delgado, Maria M./Svich, Caridad, *Theatre in Crisis?: Performance Manifestos for a New Century* (Manchester: Manchester University Press, 2002).

Dennen, James, 'On Reception of Improvised Music', *TDR*, 53/4 (2009): 139–49.

DeNora, Tia, *Music in Everyday Life* (Cambridge: Cambridge University Press, 2000).

Dermutz, Klaus (ed.), *Christoph Marthaler. Die einsamen Menschen sind die besonderen Menschen* (Salzburg: Residenz, 2000).

DeRose, David J., 'Sam Shepard as musical experimenter', in Matthew Roudané (ed.), *The Cambridge Companion to Sam Shepard* (Cambridge: Cambridge University Press, 2002): 227–46.

Derrida, Jacques/Thévenin, Paule, *The Secret Art of Antonin Artaud* (Cambridge, MA/London: The MIT Press, 1998).

Derrida, Jacques, *Writing and Difference* (London/New York: Routledge, 1978 [1967]).

Diederichsen, Diederich, 'Fülle des Wohllauts. Ein guter Popsong bleibt auch im Theater immer er selbst – von der Rolle der Musik bei Thalheimer, Christoph Marthaler, Alain Platel, Frank Castorf und manch anderem', *Theater heute*, 10 (2003): 18–25.

Dragasevic, Dolja, *Meyerhold, Director of Opera. Cultural Change and Artistic Genres* (PhD Thesis, Goldsmith College, 2005).

Drain, Richard (ed.), *Twentieth-Century Theatre: A Sourcebook* (London/New York: Routledge, 1994).

Dramaturgische Gesellschaft (ed.), *Zeitworte. Dokumentation des Symposions Geteilte Zeit. Theater zwischen Entschleunigungsoase & Produktionsmaschine* (2008), http://www.dramaturgische-gesellschaft.de/dramaturg/index.php [12.07.2012].

Drever, John Levack, 'Sound effect – object – event. Endemic and exogenous electro-acoustic sound practices in theatre', in Ross Brown (ed.), *Sound: A Reader in Theatre Practice* (Basingstoke: Palgrave, 2010): 188–205.

Dreysse Passos De Carvalho, Miriam, *Die Szene vor dem Palast: Zur Theatralisierung des Chors bei Einar Schleef* (Frankfurt am Main: Peter Lang, 1999).

Düffel, John von, 'Michael Thalheimer – das Bauchsystem', in Melanie Hinz/Jens Roselt (eds.), *Chaos und Konzept: Proben und Probieren im Theater* (Berlin: Alexander Verlag, 2011): 51–70.

Dukore, Bernard F. (ed.), *Dramatic Theory and Criticism: Greeks to Grotowski* (Boston, MA: Thomson Heinle, 1974).

Dunbar, Zachary, 'Melodic Intentions: Speaking Text in Postdramatic Dance Theatre', in Lynne Kendrick/David Roesner (eds.), *Theatre Noise. The Sound of Performance* (Newcastle upon Tyne: Cambridge Scholars Publishing, 2011): 164–73.

Ehrenzweig, Anton, *The Hidden Order of Art: A Study in the Psychology of Artistic Imagination* (London: Weidenfeld & Nicolson, 1967).

Elfferding, Wieland, 'Thomas Bernhards Musik', *Der Freitag*, 09.02.2001.

Emons, Hans, *Für Auge und Ohr: Musik als Film – oder die Verwandlung von Kompositionen in Licht-Spiel* (Berlin: Frank & Timme, 2005).

Engelhardt, Jürgen/Dahlhaus, Carl/Stephan, Rudolf, *Gestus und Verfremdung. Studien zum Musiktheater bei Strawinsky und Brecht/Weill* (München/Salzburg: Emil Katzbichler, 1984).

Epstein, David S., *Shaping Time. Music, the Brain, and Performance* (New York: Schirmer Books, 1995).

Ertl, Fritz, 'Interdisciplinary Training. Directing for Actors', in Arthur Bartow (ed.), *Training of the American Actor* (New York: Theatre Communications Group, 2006): 251–68.

Esslin, Martin, *Antonin Artaud. The Man and His Work* (London: Calder, 1976).

Esterhammer, Angela (ed.), *Romantic Poetry, Vol. 7* (Amsterdam: John Benjamins Publishing Company, 2002).

Evans, Benjamin, 'Five Problems for Interdisciplinary Art', in David Cecchetto et al. (eds.), *Collision: Interarts Practice and Research* (Cambridge: Cambridge Scholars, 2008): 19–33.

Evans, Mark, *Jacques Copeau* (London: Routledge, 2006).

Fatone, Gina Andrea, 'Gamelan, Techno-primitivism and the San Francisco Rave Scene', in Graham St John (ed.), *Rave Culture and Religion* (London: Routledge, 2004): 196–208.

Feldman, Peter, 'The Sound and Movement Exercise as Developed by the Open Theatre. An Interview with Peter Hulton', *Theatre Papers*, 1/1 (1977): 1–14.

Féral, Josette, 'Theatricality: The Specificity of Theatrical Language', *SubStance*, 31/2/98 and 31/3/99 (2002): 94–108.

———, 'Introduction: Towards a Genetic Study of Performance – Take 2', *Theatre Research International*, 33/3 (2008): 223–33.

Fetterman, William, *John Cage's Theatre Pieces: Notations and Performances* (Amsterdam: Harwood Academic Publishers, 1996).

Fiebach, Joachim (ed.), *Manifeste europäischen Theaters. 1960–2000 von Grotowski bis Schleef* (Berlin: Theater der Zeit, 2002).

Finter, Helga, 'Die Theatralisierung der Stimme im Experimentaltheater', in Klaus Oehler (ed.), *Zeichen und Realität, Bd. 3* (Tübingen: Stauffenburg Verlag, 1984): 1007–21.

———, *Der subjektive Raum. Band 2: Antonin Artaud und die Utopie des Theaters* (Tübingen: Gunter Narr, 1990).

———, 'Antonin Artaud and the Impossible Theatre: The Legacy of the Theatre of Cruelty', *TDR*, 41/4 (1997): 15–40.

Fischer-Lichte, Erika, *Semiotik des Theaters. Band 1: Das System der theatralischen Zeichen* (Tübingen: Narr, 1994 [1983]).

———, *Theaterwissenschaft* (Tübingen: Franck, 2010).

Fischer-Lichte, Erika/Hasselmann, Kristiane/Rautzenberg, Markus (eds.), *Ausweitung der Kunstzone. Interart Studies – Neue Perspektiven der Kunstwissenschaften* (Bielefeld: transcript, 2010).

Fischlin, David/Heble, Ajay, *The Other Side of Nowhere. Jazz, Improvisation, and Communities in Dialogue* (Middletown, CT: Wesleyan University Press, 2004).

Flaszen, Ludwik, *Grotowski and Company* (Holstebro/Malta/Wroclaw: Icarus Publishing Enterprise, 2010).

Flusser, Vilém, *Gesten* (Bensheim/Düsseldorf: Bollmann, 1991).

Fowler, Kenneth, *Received Truths: Bertolt Brecht and the Problem of Gestus and Musical Meaning* (New York: AMS, 1991).

Frank, Johanna, 'Resonating Bodies and the Poetics of Aurality; Or, Gertrude Stein's Theatre', *Modern Drama*, 51/4 (2008): 501–27.

Frendo, Mario, 'Embodied Musicality: Nietzsche, Grotowski, and Musicalized Processes in Theatre Making', *Studies in Musical Theatre*, 7/2 (2013): 207–19.

Friedrich, Sven, 'Um die "Geburt aus dem Geiste der Musik" bittend. Überlegungen zum "Regietheater" auf der Opernbühne', in Gerhard Koch et al. (eds.), *Wagnerspektrum 2/2005: Schwerpunkt/focussing on Regietheater* (Würzburg: Königshausen & Neumann, 2005): 31–55.

Frith, Simon, 'Towards an Aesthetic of Popular Music', in Simon Frith (ed.), *Taking Popular Music Seriously. Selected Essays* (Farnham: Ashgate, 2007): 257–74.

Frost, Anthony/Yarrow, Ralph, *Improvisation in Drama* (London: Macmillan, 1990).

Fry, Gareth, 'Sound Designer Gareth Fry Interviewed by David Roesner' (Phone conversation, 18.06.2012).

Fryer, Paul, 'Subject: Bred In The Bone, "Unreal City", 19th and 20th April' (e-mail to the SCUDD mailing list) [17.04.2012].

Fuchs, Georg, *Die Schaubühne der Zukunft* (Berlin/Leipzig: Schuster & Loeffler, 1905).

Gabbard, Krin (ed.), *Jazz Among the Discourses* (Durham/London: Duke University Press, 1995).

——— (ed.), *Representing Jazz* (Durham/London: Duke University Press, 1995).

Gale, Maggie B./Deeney, John F. (eds.), *Routledge Drama Anthology and Sourcebook: From Modernism to Contemporary Performance* (London/New York: Routledge, 2010).

Gardner, Lyn, 'Waves Sets a High-water Mark for Multimedia Theatre' (2006), http://www.guardian.co.uk/stage/theatreblog/2006/dec/04/wavessetsa highwatermarkfo? [14.03.2009].

Georgiades, Thrasybulos, *Musik und Rhythmus bei den Griechen. Zum Ursprung der abendländischen Musik* (Hamburg: Rowohlt, 1958).

Gfeller, Kate E. (ed.), *Multidisciplinary Perspectives on Musicality: Essays from the Seashore Symposium* (Iowa City: University of Iowa, College of Liberal Arts & Sciences, School of Music, 2006).

Giannachi, Gabriella/Kaye, Nick/Shanks, Michael, *Archaeologies of Presence. Art, Performance, and the Insistence of Being* (London: Routledge, 2012).

Giddins, Gary/Deveaux, Scott, *Jazz* (New York: W.W. Norton, 2009).

Gitlin, Todd, *The Whole World Is Watching: Mass Media in the Making and Unmaking of the New Left* (Berkeley/Los Angeles, CA/London: University of California Press, 1980).

Gladkov, Aleksandr, *Meyerhold speaks. Meyerhold rehearses* (London/New York: Routledge, 1997).

Goebbels, Heiner, 'Das Hören und Sehen organisieren', in Nicole Gronemeyer/Bernd Stegemann (eds.), *Lektionen: Regie* (Berlin: Theater der Zeit, 2009): 58–66.

————, 'Wenn ich möchte, dass ein Schauspieler weint, geb' ich ihm eine Zwiebel', in Anton Rey/Hajo Kurzenberger/Stephan Müller (eds.), *Wirkungsmaschine Schauspieler – Vom Menschendarsteller zum multifunktionalen Spielemacher* (Berlin/Köln: Alexander Verlag, 2011): 64–70.

————, *Ästhetik der Abwesenheit: Texte zum Theater* (Berlin: Theater der Zeit, 2012).

————, '"It's all part of one concern": A "Keynote" to Composition as Staging', in Matthias Rebstock/David Roesner (eds.), *Composed Theatre. Aesthetics, Practices, Processes* (Bristol: Intellect, 2012): 111–20.

————, *Aesthetic of Absence* (London: Routledge, 2014) (forthcoming).

Goehr, Lydia, *The Quest for Voice: On Music, Politics, and the Limits of Philosophy* (Oxford: Oxford University Press, 1998).

Goethe, Johann Wolfgang, 'Simple Imitation of Nature, Manner, Style', in John Gage (ed.), *Goethe on Art* (London: Scholar Press, 1980 [1788]): 21–4.

Goffman, Erving, *Frame Analysis: An Essay on the Organization of Experience* (London: Harper and Row, 1974).

Gollasch, Jörg, 'Theatre Musician and Composer Jörg Gollasch Interviewed by David Roesner' (Cologne, Germany, 25.05.2012).

Gordon, Robert, *The Purpose of Playing: Modern Acting Theories in Perspective* (Ann Arbor: University of Michigan Press, 2006).

Göttert, Karl-Heinz, *Geschichte der Stimme* (München: Fink, 1998).

Gottlieb, Vera, 'Vakhtangov's Musicality: Reassessing Yevgeny Vakhtangov (1883–1922)', *Contemporary Theatre Review*, 15/2 (2005): 259–68.

Govan, Emma/Nicholson, Helen/Normington, Katie, *Making a Performance: Devising Histories and Contemporary Practices* (London/New York: Routledge, 2007).

Graham, Gordon, *Philosophy of the Arts: An Introduction to Aesthetics* (London/ New York: Routledge, 2005).

Graham-Jones, Jean, 'Editorial comment: hearing theatre', *Theatre Journal*, 58/3 (2006): ix–xii.

Greenberg, Clement, 'Towards a Newer Laocoon', in Clement Greenberg, *The Collected Essays and Criticism, Vol. 1* (Chicago: University of Chicago Press, 1986–1993 [1940]): 23–38.

Greenblatt, Stephen, 'The Interart Moment', in Ulla Britta Lagerroth/Hans Lund/ Erik Hedling (eds.), *Interart Poetics: Essays on the Interrelations of the Arts and Media* (Amsterdam: Rodopi, 1997): 13–15.

Greene, Naomi, 'Antonin Artaud: Metaphysical Revolutionary', *Yale French Studies*, 39 (1967): 188–97.

Grillparzer, Franz, *Grillparzers sämtliche Werke in zwanzig Bänden. Volume 15* (Tübingen: J. G. Cotta, 1892).

Gronemeyer, Nicole/Stegemann, Bernd (eds.), *Lektionen: Regie* (Berlin: Theater der Zeit, 2009).

Großmann, Stephanie, *Inszenierungsanalyse von Opern: eine interdisziplinäre Methodik* (Würzburg: Königshausen & Neumann, 2013).

Grund, Uta, *Zwischen den Künsten. Edward Gordon Craig und das Bildertheater um 1900* (Berlin: Akademie Verlag, 2002).

Gumbrecht, Hans Ulrich, 'Rhythmus und Sinn', in Hans Ulrich Gumbrecht/K. Ludwig Pfeiffer (eds.), *Materialität der Kommunikation* (Frankfurt am Main: Suhrkamp, 1988): 714–29.

Gutjahr, Ortrud (ed.), *Regietheater!* (Würzburg: Königshausen & Neumann, 2008).

Haas, Alexander, 'Wutbürgerthesen und Aufstandsparolen', *taz*, 04.10.2011.

Härtl, Renate, *Verweile doch, du bist so schön. Christoph Marthaler inszeniert Goethes Faust √1+2* (TV-Documentary by Renate Härtl for ZDF, 1994).

Harvie, Jen/Lavender, Andy (eds.), *Making Contemporary Theatre. International Rehearsal Processes* (Manchester: Manchester University Press, 2010).

Hauber, Annette/Jost, Ekkehard/Wolbert, Klaus (eds.), *That's Jazz: Der Sound des 20. Jahrhunderts* (Darmstadt: Institut Mathildenhöhe Darmstadt, 1988).

Heddon, Deirdre/Milling, Jane, *Devising Performance. A Critical History* (Basingstoke: Palgrave Macmillan, 2006).

Hegarty, Paul, *Noise/Music: A History* (London: Continuum International Publishing Group, 2007).

Helbling, Hanno, *Rhythmus. Ein Versuch* (Frankfurt am Main: Suhrkamp, 1999).

Hempfer, Klaus W./Volbers, Jörg (eds.), *Theorien des Performativen. Sprache – Wissen – Praxis. Eine kritische Bestandsaufnahme* (Bielefeld: transcript, 2011).

Hinz, Melanie/Roselt, Jens (eds.), *Chaos und Konzept: Proben und Probieren im Theater* (Berlin: Alexander Verlag, 2011).

Hiß, Guido, *Der theatralische Blick. Einführung in die Aufführungsanalyse* (Berlin: Reimer, 1993).

———, 'Marthalers Musiktheater', in Hans-Peter Bayerdörfer (ed.), *Musiktheater als Herausforderung. Interdisziplinäre Facetten von Theater- und Musikwissenschaft* (Tübingen: Niemeyer, 1999): 210–24.

———, *Synthetische Visionen: Theater als Gesamtkunstwerk von 1800 bis 2000* (München: Epodium, 2005).

Hodge, Alison (ed.), *Twentieth Century Actor Training* (London: Routledge, 2000).

———, 'Włodzimierz Staniewski: Gardzienice and the Naturalised Actor', in Alison Hodge (ed.), *Actor Training* (London: Routledge, 2010): 268–87.

——— (ed.), *Actor Training* (London: Routledge, 2010).

Hofmannsthal, Hugo von, *The Lord Chandos Letter and Other Writings* (New York: New York Review Books, 2005).

Hölker, Mareike, *Vom Sinn zur Sinnlichkeit: eine empirische Untersuchung der Abkehr von traditionellen Stimm- und Sprechidealen in zeitgenössischen Theaterinszenierungen* (MA Thesis, University of Hildesheim, 2005).

Hollier, Denis, 'The Death of Paper, Part Two: Artaud's Sound System', in Edward Scheer (ed.), *Antonin Artaud. A Critical Reader* (London: Routledge, 2004): 159–68.

Holmberg, Arthur/Innes, Christopher, *The Theatre of Robert Wilson* (Cambridge: Cambridge University Press, 1996).

Holmes, Sean, 'Director Sean Holmes Interviewed by David Roesner' (Phone conversation, 20.06.2012).

Honegger, Gitta, 'Fools on the Hill: Thomas Bernhard's Mise-en-Scène', *Performing Arts Journal*, 19/3 (1997): 34–48.

Honing, Henkjan, *Musical Cognition: A Science of Listening* (Piscataway, NJ: Transaction, 2009).

Horst, Jörg van der, 'Theaterdeponien. Eine Polemik', in Christoph Jacke/Eva Kimminich/Siegfried J. Schmidt (eds.), *Kulturschutt. Über das Recycling von Theorien und Kulturen* (Bielefeld: transcript, 2006): 282–306.

Houghton, Norris, *Moscow Rehearsals. An Account of Methods of Production in the Soviet Theatre* (London: George Allen & Unwin, 1938).

Hulton, Dorinda, 'Joseph Chaikin and Aspects of Actor Training: Possibilities Rendered Present', in Alison Hodge (ed.), *Actor Training* (London: Routledge, 2010): 164–83.

———, 'Joseph Chaikin: The Presence of the Actor', *Studies in Theatre and Performance*, 30/2 (2010): 219–24.

Husserl, Edmund, *On the Phenomenology of the Consciousness of Internal Time (1893–1917)* (Dordrecht: Kluwer, 1990).

Innes, Christopher, *Avant Garde Theatre. 1892–1992* (London: Routledge, 1993).

———, *Edward Gordon Craig: A Vision of Theater* (London: Routledge, 2004 [1998]).

Jacoby, Heinrich, *Jenseits von 'Musikalisch' und 'Unmusikalisch': die Befreiung der schöpferischen Kräfte dargestellt am Beispiele der Musik* (Hamburg: Christians, 1984).

Jäger, Siegfried, 'Theoretische und methodische Aspekte einer Kritischen Diskurs- und Dispositivanalyse' (2000), http://www.diss-duisburg.de/Internetbibliothek/ Artikel/Aspekte_einer_Kritischen_Diskursanalyse.htm [08.07.2011].

Jakobson, Roman, 'Closing Statements: Linguistics and Poetics', in Thomas A. Sebeok (ed.), *Style in Language* (Cambridge, MA: MIT Press, 1960): 350–77.

Jarzina, Asja, *Gestische Musik und musikalische Gesten. Dieter Schnebel's Visible Music* (Berlin: Weidler, 2005).

Jelinek, Elfriede, 'Ich möchte seicht sein', in Christa Gürtler (ed.), *Gegen den schönen Schein. Texte zu Elfriede Jelinek* (Frankfurt am Main: Neue Kritik, 1990 [1983]): 157–61.

———, 'I Want to Be Shallow. Translated by Jorn Bramann' (1997 [1983]), www. elfriedejelinek.com [Follow link 'Zum Theater'] [09.03.2012].

———, *Ein Sportstück* (Reinbeck bei Hamburg: Rowohlt, 1999).

———, *Sports Play. Translated by Penny Black* (London: Oberon, 2013).

Jestrovic, Silvija, 'Theatricality as Estrangement of Art and Life In the Russian Avant-garde', in *Histories and Theories of Intermedia (Blog)* [Online], Blog entry on 28.01.2008, http://umintermediai501.blogspot.co.uk/search?q=Theat ricality+as+Estrangement [04.11.2011].

Johnstone, Keith, *Impro: Improvisation and the Theatre* (London: Methuen Drama, 1981).

Jurgensen, Manfred (ed.), *Bernhard. Annäherungen* (Bern/München: Francke, 1981).

———, 'Die Sprachpartituren des Thomas Bernhard', in Manfred Jurgensen (ed.), *Bernhard. Annäherungen* (Bern/München: Francke, 1981): 99–122.

Jurs-Munby, Karen, 'The Resistant Text in Postdramatic Theatre: Performing Elfriede Jelinek's Sprachflächen', *Performance Research*, 14/1 (2009): 46–56.

Kaden, Christian/Kalisch, Volker, 'Musik', in Karl-Heinz Brack (ed.), *Ästhetische Grundbegriffe. Historisches Wörterbuch in sieben Bänden* (Stuttgart/Weimar: Metzler, 2005): 256–308.

Kaempf, Simone, 'Thorsten Lensing, Jan Hein (Theater T1): Portrait' (2012), http://www.goethe.de/kue/the/pur/tuj/enindex.htm [30.05.2012].

Kahn, Douglas, *Noise Water Meat. A History of Sound in the Arts* (Cambridge, MA: The MIT Press, 1999).

Kamin, Dan, *Charlie Chaplin, One-man Show* (London: Scarecrow Press, 1984).

Kane, Sarah, *Complete Plays* (London: Methuen, 2001).

Kanzog, Klaus/Kreutzer, Hans Joachim (eds.), *Werke Kleists auf dem modernen Musiktheater* (Berlin: Erich Schmidt Verlag, 1977).

Kartomir, Margaret J./Mendonça, Maria, 'Gamelan', in Stanley Sadie (ed.), *New Grove Dictionary of Music and Musicians, 2nd edition, Vol. 9* (London: Macmillan, 2001): 497–507.

Keller, Holm, *Robert Wilson* (Frankfurt am Main: Fischer, 1997).

Kendrick, Lynne/Roesner, David (eds.), *Theatre Noise. The Sound of Performance* (Newcastle upon Tyne: Cambridge Scholars Publishing, 2011).

Kerkhoven, Marianne van/Schlüter, Björn Dirk (eds.), *Theaterschrift: Theater und Musik (Band 9)* (Bruxelles: Kaaitheater, 1995).

Kesting, Marianne, 'Musikalisierung des Theaters – Theatralisierung der Musik', *Melos - Zeitschrift für neue Musik*, 3 (1969): 101–9.

Kielholz, Jürg, *Wilhelm Heinrich Wackenroder. Schriften über die Musik. Musik- und literaturgeschichtlicher Urprung und Bedeutung in der romantischen Literatur* (Frankfurt am Main: Peter Lang, 1972).

Kirby, Michael, 'On Acting and Not-Acting ', *TDR*, 16/1 (1972): 3–15.

Kittler, Friedrich, *Aufschreibesysteme 1800–1900* (München: Wilhelm Fink, 1995 [1985]).

Kleb, William, 'Sam Shepard's Inacoma at the Magic Theatre', *Theater*, 9/1 (1974): 59–64.

Kleist, Heinrich von, 'Brief an Marie von Kleist', in Heinrich von Kleist, *Werke und Briefe in vier Bänden, Bd. 4 Briefe* (Berlin: Aufbau Verlag, 1995 [1811]): 481.

Klug, Christian, *Thomas Bernhards Theaterstücke* (Stuttgart: Metzler, 1991).

Knopf, Robert (ed.), *Theatre and Film. A Comparative Anthology* (New Haven/ London: Yale University Press, 2005).

Knowlson, James, *Damned to Fame: The Life of Samuel Beckett* (New York: Simon & Schuster, 1996).

Koch, Gerhard R./Bermbach, Udo/Borchmeyer, Dieter/Danuser Hermann (eds.), *Wagnerspektrum 2/2005: Schwerpunkt/focussing on Regietheater* (Würzburg: Königshausen & Neumann, 2005).

Kolesch, Doris/Schrödel, Jenny (eds.), *Kunst-Stimmen* (Berlin: Theater der Zeit, 2004).

Kolleritsch, Otto (ed.), *Die Musik, das Leben und der Irrtum: Thomas Bernhard und die Musik* (Wien: Universal-Edition, 2000).

Kordes, Barbara, *Musikalische Lesarten: Heiner Goebbels und Heiner Müller* (Göttingen: V & R Unipress, 2009).

Kostelanetz, Richard, *American imaginations: Charles Ives, Gertrude Stein, John Cage, Merce Cunningham, Robert Wilson* (Berlin: Merve Verlag, 1983).

Koszarski, Richard, *An Evening's Entertainment. The Age of the Silent Feature Picture, 1915–1928* (New York: Charles Scribner's Sons, 1990).

Kotte, Andreas, 'Theatralität: Ein Begriff sucht seinen Gegenstand', *Forum Modernes Theater*, 13/2 (1998): 117–33.

———, *Theaterwissenschaft* (Köln/Weimar/Berlin: Böhlau, 2005).

Kramer, Jonathan D., *The Time of Music. New Meanings, New Temporalities, New Listening Strategies* (London: Schirmer Books, 1988).

Kreutzer, Hans-Joachim, *Obertöne: Literatur und Musik: Neun Abhandlungen über das Zusammenspiel der Künste* (Würzburg: Königshausen und Neumann, 1994).

Kronegger, Marlies, *The Orchestration of the Arts: A Creative Symbiosis of Existential Powers; the Vibrating Interplay of Sound, Color, Image, Gesture, Movement, Rhythm, Fragrance, Word, Touch* (Dordrecht/Boston/London: Kluwer Academic Publ.: 2000).

Kuba, Alexander, 'Geste/Gestus', in Erika Fischer-Lichte/Doris Kolesch/ Matthias Warstat (eds.), *Metzler Lexikon Theatertheorie* (Stuttgart: Metzler, 2005): 129–36.

Kühn, Clemens, *Musiklehre. Grundlagen und Erscheinungsformen der abendländischen Musik* (Laaber: Laaber, 1981).

Kuhn, Gudrun, *'Ein philosophisch-musikalisch geschulter Sänger'. Musikästhetische Überlegungen zur Prosa Thomas Bernhards* (Würzburg: Königshausen & Neumann, 1996).

Kuhn, Thomas, *The Essential Tension* (Chicago: University of Chicago Press, 1977).

Kühn, Ulrich, *Sprech-Ton-Kunst. Musikalisches Sprechen und Formen des Melodrams im Schauspiel- und Musiktheater (1770–1933)* (Tübingen: Niemeyer, 2001).

Kulezic-Wilson, Danijela, 'From Musicalisation of Theatre to Musicality of Film: Beckett's *Play* on Stage and on Screen', in Lynne Kendrick/David Roesner (eds.), *Theatre Noise. The Sound of Performance* (Newcastle upon Tyne: Cambridge Scholars Publishing, 2011): 33–43.

Kunz, Henriette, *'Ich komme von der Sprache her' – Das Neue Theater der Elfriede Jelinek und seine Konfrontation mit dem herrschenden Code* (München/ Ravensburg: Grin Verlag, 2005).

Kurt, Ronald, 'Komposition und Improvisation als Grundbegriffe einer allgemeinen Handlungstheorie', in Ronald Kurt/Klaus Näumann (eds.), *Menschliches Handeln als Improvisation* (Bielefeld: transcript, 2008): 17–46.

Kurzenberger, Hajo, *Der kollektive Prozess des Theaters: Chorkörper – Probengemeinschaften – theatrale Kreativität* (Bielefeld: transcript, 2009).

———, 'Multiperspektivität des Darstellens. Zum Paradigmenwechsel des Schauspielens', in Anton Rey/Hajo Kurzenberger/Stephan Müller (eds.), *Wirkungsmaschine Schauspieler – Vom Menschendarsteller zum multifunktionalen Spielemacher* (Berlin/Köln: Alexander Verlag, 2011): 74–84.

Lagaay, Alice, 'Towards a (Negative) Philosophy of Voice', in Lynne Kendrick/ David Roesner (eds.), *Theatre Noise. The Sound of Performance* (Newcastle upon Tyne: Cambridge Scholars Publishing, 2011): 57–69.

Lagerroth, Ulla Britta/Lund, Hans/Hedling, Erik (eds.), *Interart Poetics: Essays on the Interrelations of the Arts and Media* (Amsterdam: Rodopi, 1997).

Lamb, Charles, *The Theatre of Howard Barker* (London: Routledge, 2005).

Langer, Susanne, *Feeling and Form* (New York: Charles Scribner's Sons, 1953).

Larrue, Jean-Marc, 'Sound Reproduction Techniques in Theatre: A Case of Mediatic Resistance', in Lynne Kendrick/David Roesner (eds.), *Theatre Noise. The Sound of Performance* (Newcastle upon Tyne: Cambridge Scholars Publishing, 2011): 14–22.

Laske, Otto, 'A search for a theory of musicality', *Languages of Design*, 1/3 (1993): 209–28.

Law, Alma/Gordon, Mel, *Meyerhold, Eisenstein and Biomechanics. Actor Training in Revolutionary Russia* (Jefferson, NC/London: McFarland, 1996).

Laws, Catherine, 'The Music of Beckett's Theatre', in Danièle De Ruyter-Tognotti et al. (eds.), *Three Dialogues Revisited (Samuel Beckett Today)* (Amsterdam: Rodopi, 2008): 121–33.

Leach, Robert, *Vsevolod Meyerhold* (Cambridge: Cambridge University Press, 1989).

———, 'Meyerhold and Biomechanics', in Alison Hodge (ed.), *Twentieth Century Actor Training* (London: Routledge, 2000): 37–54.

Lehmann, Hans-Thies, 'Theatralität', in Manfred Brauneck/Burghard König (eds.), *Theaterlexikon. Begriffe und Epochen, Bühnen und Ensembles* (Reinbeck bei Hamburg: Rowohlt, 1986): 1032.

———, *Postdramatic Theatre* (London/New York: Routledge, 2006).

Leiter, Samuel L., *From Stanislavsky to Barrault. Representative Directors of the European Stage* (New York: Greenwood Press, 1991).

Leloup, Matthieu, 'Director Matthieu Leloup Interviewed by David Roesner' (Rose Bruford College, London, 20.04.2012).

Lensing, Thorsten, 'Director Thorsten Lensing Interviewed by David Roesner' (Phone conversation, 07.05.2012).

Lévi-Strauss, Claude, *The Raw and the Cooked* (London: Cape, 1970).

———, *Myth and Meaning* (London: Routledge, 2001 [1978]).

Levin, David J. (ed.), *Opera Through Other Eyes* (Stanford: Stanford University Press, 1993).

Levinson, Jerrold, 'Hybrid Art Forms', *Journal of Aesthetic Education*, 18 (1984): 5–13.

———, 'Musical Thinking', *JMM – Journal of Music and Meaning*, 1 [Online] (2003), http://www.musicandmeaning.net/issues/showArticle.php?artID=1.2 [18.01.10].

Levitin, Daniel J., *This Is Your Brain On Music: Understanding a Human Obsession* (London: Atlantic, 2008).

Ley, Graham, *The Theatricality of Greek Tragedy: Playing Space and Chorus* (Chicago: Chicago University Press, 2007).

Lid, Tore Vagn, *Gegenseitige Verfremdungen: Theater als kritischer Erfahrungsraum im Stoffwechsel zwischen Bühne und Musik* (Frankfurt am Main: Peter Lang, 2011).

Liebau, Eckart/Zirfas, Jörg (eds., *Die Sinne und die Künste: Perspektiven ästhetischer Bildung* (Bielefeld: transcript, 2008).

Linklater, Kristin, *Freeing the Natural Voice* (London: Nick Hern Books, 2006).

Lippmann, Edward A., *Musical Aesthetics: A Historical Reader. Vol. III. The Twentieth Century* (Stuyvesant, NY: Pendragon Press, 1986).

Lock, Graham/Murray, David (eds.), *Thriving on a Riff: Jazz and Blues Influences in African American Literature and Film* (Oxford/New York: Oxford University Press, 2009).

Lubkoll, Christine, *Mythos Musik. Poetische Entwürfe des Musikalischen in der Literatur um 1800* (Freiburg: Rombach, 1995).

Lucaciu, Mihai, '"This scream I've thrown out is a dream": Corporeal Transformation Through Sound, an Artaudian Experiment', *Studies in Musical Theatre*, 4/1 (2010): 67–74.

Luckhurst, Mary, *Dramaturgy: A Revolution in Theatre* (Cambridge: Cambridge University Press, 2006).

Lyotard, Jean-François, *The Post-Modern Condition: A Report on Knowledge* (Manchester: Manchester University Press, 1984).

Macdonald, Ian, *The New Shostakovich* (London: Fourth estate, 1990).

Maconie, Robin, *The Concept of Music* (Oxford: Clarendon Press, 1990).

Magee, Bryan, *The Philosophy of Schopenhauer* (Oxford: Clarendon Press, 1997).

Mahnkopf, Claus-Steffen, 'Vermag Musik die Zeit vergessen zu machen? Überlegungen zur Künstlichkeit der Zeit', in Nikolaus Müller-Schöll/Saskia Reither (eds.), *Aisthesis. Zur Erfahrung von Zeit, Raum, Text und Kunst* (Schliengen: Edition Argus, 2005): 163–71.

Malaev-Babel, Andrei, *The Vakhtangov Sourcebook* (London: Routledge, 2011).

Malloch, Stephen. 'Musicality: The Art of Human Gesture', in Catherine Stevens et al. (eds.), *Proceedings of the 7th International Conference on Music Perception and Cognition* (Sydney, Australia: Causal Productions, 2002).

Malloch, Stephen/Trevarthen, Colwyn (eds.), *Communicative Musicality: Exploring the Basis of Human Companionship* (Oxford/New York: Oxford University Press, 2009).

Manning, Eric, *Politics of Touch. Sense, Movement, Sovereignty* (Minneapolis, MN: University of Minnesota Press, 2007).

Marranca, Bonnie (ed.), *American Dreams: The Imagination of Sam Shepard* (New York: Performing Arts Journal Publications, 1981).

Marthaler, Christoph/Viebrock, Anna, 'Die Gesprächsprobe. Ein Theater heute-Gespräch mit Christoph Marthaler und Anna Viebrock über künstlerische und andere Gärprozesse', *Theater heute, Jahrbuch* (1997): 9–24.

Marvin, Roberta Montemorra/Thomas, Downing A. (eds.), *Operatic Migrations. Transforming Works and Crossing Boundaries* (Farnham: Ashgate, 2006).

Massow, Albrecht von, 'Absolute Musik', in Hans Heinrich Eggebrecht (ed.), *Handwörterbuch der musikalischen Terminologie, Bd. 1* (Stuttgart: Franz Steiner Verlag, 1992): 1–17.

Matthews, John, *Training for Performance: A Meta-disciplinary Account* (London: Methuen Drama, 2011).

Matzke, Annemarie, 'Der unmögliche Schauspieler: Theater-Improvisieren', in Hans-Friedrich Bormann/Gabriele Brandstetter/Annemarie Matzke (eds.), *Improvisieren. Paradoxien des Unvorhersehbaren. Kunst – Medien – Praxis* (Bielefeld: transcript, 2010): 161–82.

———, 'Konzepte proben – Probenprozesse in postdramatischen Theaterformen', in Anton Rey/Hajo Kurzenberger/Stephan Müller (eds.), *Wirkungsmaschine Schauspieler – Vom Menschendarsteller zum multifunktionalen Spielemacher* (Berlin/Köln: Alexander Verlag, 2011): 42–52.

———, 'Versuchsballons und Testreihen. Wie auf Theaterproben Wissen hervorgebracht und standardisiert wird', in Melanie Hinz/Jens Roselt (eds.), *Chaos und Konzept: Proben und Probieren im Theater* (Berlin: Alexander Verlag, 2011): 132–49.

———, *Arbeit am Theater: Eine Diskursgeschichte der Probe* (Bielefeld: transcript, 2012).

McAuley, Gay, 'Not Magic but Work: Rehearsal and the Production of Meaning', *Theatre Research International*, 33/3 (2008): 276–88.

———, *Not Magic But Work: An Ethnographic Account of a Rehearsal Process* (Manchester: Manchester University Press, 2012).

McCullough, Christopher (ed.), *Theatre Praxis: Teaching Drama Through Practice* (London: Palgrave Macmillan, 1998).

Mckinney, Joslin/Butterworth, Philip, *The Cambridge Introduction to Scenography* (Cambridge: Cambridge University Press, 2009).

Meier, Hedwig, *Die Schaubühne als musikalische Anstalt: Studien zur Geschichte und Theorie der Schauspielmusik* (Bielefeld: Aisthesis, 1999).

Melchinger, Siegfried, *Die Welt als Tragödie. Bd. 1: Aischylos, Sophokles* (München: Beck, 1979).

Melson, Kelli Jeanine, *The Practice and Pedagogy of Vsevolod Meyerhold's Living Legacy of Actor Training: Theatrical Biomechanics* (PhD Thesis, Exeter, 2009).

Merlin, Bella, *Acting – The Basics* (London/New York: Routledge, 2010).

Meyer, Karl-A., *Improvisation als flüchtige Kunst und die Folgen für die Theaterpädagogik* (PhD Thesis, Universität der Künste Berlin, 2005).

Meyer, Petra Maria, *Intermedialität des Theaters. Entwurf einer Semiotik der Überraschung* (Düsseldorf: Parerga Verlag, 2001).

———, (ed.), *Acoustic turn* (Tübingen: Fink, 2008).

———, '"Happy new Ears": Creating Hearing and the Hearable', in Matthias Rebstock/David Roesner (eds.), *Composed Theatre. Aesthetics, Practices, Processes* (Bristol: Intellect, 2012): 81–108.

Meyerhold, Vsevolod, 'From "On the Theatre". Translated by Nora Beeson', *The Tulane Drama Review*, 4/4 (May 1960): 134–48.

———, *Vsevolod Meyerhold: Theaterarbeit 1917–1930. Edited by Rosemarie Tietze* (München: Carl Hanser, 1974).

———, *Meyerhold on Theatre. Translated and edited with a critical commentary by Edward Braun* (London: Methuen, 1998).

Milling, Jane/Ley, Graham, *Modern Theories of Performance. From Stanislavski to Boal* (Basingstoke: Palgrave, 2001).

Mitchell, Katie, *The Director's Craft: A Handbook for the Theatre* (New York: Routledge, 2008).

———, *Waves: A Record of the Multimedia Work Devised by Katie Mitchell and the Company from the Text of Virginia Woolf's Novel The Waves* (London: Oberon Books, 2008).

Mittermayer, Manfred, *Thomas Bernhard* (Stuttgart/Weimar: J. B. Metzler, 1995).

Moldoveanu, Mihail, *Komposition, Licht und Farbe in Robert Wilsons neuem Theater. Mit dem Körper denken* (Stuttgart: Daco, 2001).

Molinari, Cesare, *La Commedia dell'Arte* (Milano: Mondadori, 1985).

Monson, Ingrid, *Saying Something: Jazz Improvisation and Interaction* (Chicago/London: University of Chicago Press, 1996).

Morris, Christopher, 'Operatic Migrations: Transforming Works and Crossing Boundaries (review)', *The Opera Quarterly*, 23/1 (2007): 120–26.

Morris, Eilon, *Via Rythmós. An Investigation of Rhythm in Psychophysical Actor Training* (PhD Thesis, University of Huddersfield, 2012).

———, 'Collaborating in Time. The Formation of Ensemble through Rhythm', in John Britton (ed.), *Encountering Ensemble* (London: Bloomsbury, 2013): 363–6.

Mücke, Panja, *Musikalischer Film – Musikalisches Theater. Medienwechsel und szenische Collage bei Kurt Weill* (Münster: Waxmann, 2011).

Müller, Jürgen E., 'Intermedialität als poetologisches und medientheoretisches Konzept', in Jörg Helbig (ed.), *Intermedialität. Theorie und Praxis eines interdisziplinären Forschungsgebiets* (Berlin: Erich Schmidt Verlag, 1998): 31–40.

Müller-Henning, Detlef, 'Vom Musikalischen in Kleists Prosa', in Klaus Kanzog/Hans Joachim Kreutzer (eds.), *Werke Kleists auf dem modernen Musiktheater* (Berlin: Erich Schmidt Verlag, 1977): 45–59.

Müller-Schöll, Nikolaus, 'Theatre of Potentiality. Communicability and the Political in Contemporary Performance Practice', *Theatre Research International*, 29/1 (2004): 42–56.

Mundi, Thorsten, *Benno, fieps Dich rein! Die Probensprache des Theaters als Medium der Bedeutungsproduktion* (München: m press, 2005).

Mungen, Anno (ed.), *Mitten im Leben. Musiktheater von der Oper bis zur Everyday-Performance mit Musik* (Würzburg: Königshausen & Neumann, 2011).

Murray, David/Lock, Graham (eds.), *Thriving on a Riff: Jazz and Blues Influences in African American Literature and Film* (Oxford/New York: Oxford University Press, 2009).

Müry, Andreas, 'Dada in Zeitlupe. Christoph Marthaler', *du*, 9 (1993): 16–17.

Nanay, Bence, 'Musical Twofoldness', *The Monist*, 95/4 (2012): 606–23.

Naumann, Barbara (ed.), *Die Sehnsucht der Sprache nach der Musik. Texte zur musikalischen Poetik um 1800* (Stuttgart/Weimar: Metzler, 1994).

Näumann, Klaus, 'Improvisation: Über ihren Gebrauch und ihre Funktion in der Geschichte des Jazz', in Ronald Kurt/Klaus Näumann (eds.), *Menschliches Handeln als Improvisation* (Bielefeld: transcript, 2008): 133–58.

Nehring, Elisabeth, *Im Spannungsfeld der Moderne. Theatertheorien zwischen Sprachkrise und 'Versinnlichung'* (Tübingen: Gunter Narr, 2004).

Nettl, Bruno, '"Musical Thinking" and "Thinking about Music" in Ethnomusicology: An Essay of Personal Interpretation', *The Journal of Aesthetics and Art Criticism*, 52/1, *The Philosophy of Music* (1994): 139–48.

Nettl, Bruno, et al., 'Improvisation', in Stanley Sadie (ed.), *New Grove Dictionary of Music and Musicians, 2nd edition, Vol. 12* (London: Macmillan, 2001): 94–133.

Niccolini, Elisabetta, *Der Spaziergang des Schriftstellers: 'Lenz' von Georg Büchner, 'Der Spaziergang' von Robert Walser, 'Gehen' von Thomas Bernhard* (Stuttgart/Weimar: Metzler, 2000).

Nietzsche, Friedrich, *Die Geburt der Tragödie aus dem Geiste der Musik* (Stuttgart: Reclam, 1993 [1871]).

Noszlopy, Laura/Cohen, Matthew Isaac (eds.), *Contemporary Southeast Asian Performance: Transnational Perspectives* (Newcastle upon Tyne: Cambridge Scholars Publishing, 2010).

Novarina, Valère, 'Letter to the Actors. Translated by Allen S. Weiss', *TDR*, 37/2 (1993 [1979]): 95–104.

Nünning, Ansgar (ed.), *Metzler Lexikon Literatur- und Kulturtheorie* (Stuttgart/Weimar: Metzler, 1998).

Oddey, Alison, *Re-Framing the Theatrical. Interdisciplinary Landscapes for Performance* (Basingstoke: Palgrave, 2007).

Oppenheim, Lois, *Directing Beckett* (Ann Arbor: University of Michigan Press, 1997).

Otto-Bernstein, Katharina, *Absolute Wilson: The Biography* (New York: Prestel, 2006).

Ovadija, Mladen, *Dramaturgy of Sound in Futurist Performance* (PhD Thesis, University of Toronto, 2009).

————, *Dramaturgy of Sound in the Avant-Garde and Postdramatic Theatre* (Montreal: McGill-Queen's University Press, 2013).

Pasolli, Robert, *A Book on the Open Theatre* (New York: Bobbs-Merrill, 1970).

Pater, Walter, *The Renaissance. Studies in Art and Poetry* (Oxford/New York: Oxford University Press, 1986 [1873]).

Paulin, Scott D., 'Chaplin and the Sandblaster: Edmund Wilson's Avant-Garde Noise Abatement', *American Music* (2010): 265–96.

Pavis, Patrice, 'Der zeitgenössische Schauspieler: Von der Rolle zur Partitur und Subpartitur', in Sigrid Gareis/Tillmann Broszat/Christopher Balme/Markus Moniger (eds.), *Global Player/Local Hero. Positionen des Schauspielers im zeitgenössischen Theater* (München: ePodium Verlag, 2000): 38–45.

Pelinski, Ramón, 'Embodiment and Musical Experience', *TRANS. Revista Transcultural de Música*, 9 [Online] (2005), http://redalyc.uaemex.mx/pdf/822/82200914.pdf [16.08.2011].

Peters, Jens, 'Crowd or Chorus? Howard Barker's Mise-en-scène and the Tradition of the Chorus in the European Theatre of the 20th Century', *Studies in Theatre and Performance*, 32/3 (2012): 305–16.

————, *Narration and Dialogue in Contemporary British and German-language Drama (Texts – Translations – Mise-en-scène)* (PhD Thesis, University of Exeter, 2013), http://hdl.handle.net/10871/14393 [25.02.2014].

Pfister, Manfred, *Das Drama. Theorie und Analyse* (München: UTB, 1988 [1982]).

————, *The Theory and Analysis of Drama* (Cambridge: Cambridge University Press, 1991).

Picon-Vallin, Béatrice, 'Meyerhold's Laboratories', in Mirella Schino (ed.), *Alchemists of the Stage. Theatre Laboratories in Europe* (Holstebro/Malta/Wroclaw: Icarus, 2009): 119–39.

————, 'Vsevolod Meyerhold und sein Poet-Schauspieler. Annäherungen an den Meyerholdschen Schauspieler' (2010), http://www.athanor.de/dateien/VsevolodMeyerhold-undseinPoet-Schauspieler.pdf [07.11.11].

Pierson, Stephen, 'Cognitive Science and the Comparative Arts: Implications for Theory and Pedagogy' (2001), http://www.cognitivecircle.org/ct&lit/CogCircleResearch/CogLit_Pedag.html [10.01.10].

Pilz, Dirk, 'Jazz mich, und ich liebe dich. *Der Lauf zum Meer* – Thorsten Lensing und Jan Hein verwandeln William C. Williams in Jazz' (2009), http://www.nachtkritik.de/index.php?option=com_content&task=view&id=2331 [06.05.2012].

Pitches, Jonathan, *Vsevolod Meyerhold* (London: Routledge, 2003).

Porombka, Stephan/Schneider, Wolfgang/Wortmann, Volker (eds.), *Kollektive Kreativität. Jahrbuch für Kulturwissenschaften und ästhetische Praxis* (Tübingen: Francke, 2006).

Poschmann, Gerda, *Der nicht mehr dramatische Theatertext. Aktuelle Bühnenstücke und ihre dramatische Analyse* (Tübingen: Max Niermeyer, 1997).

Posner, Roland/Robering Klaus/Sebeok, Thomas Albert (eds.), *Semiotik: ein Handbuch zu den zeichentheoretischen Grundlagen von Natur und Kultur, Volume 3* (Berlin/New York: de Gruyter, 2003).

Powell, Larson/Bethman, Brenda, '"One must have tradition in oneself, to hate it properly": Elfriede Jelinek's Musicality', *Journal of Modern Literature*, 32/1 (2008): 163–83.

Prehn, Anette/Frendes, Kjeld, *Play Your Brain. Adopt a Musical Mindset and Change Your Life and Career* (London: Marshall Cavendish, 2011).

Prieto, Eric, *Listening in: Music, Mind, and the Modernist Narrative* (Lincoln/ London: University of Nebraska Press, 2002).

Primavesi, Patrick, 'Geräusch, Apparat, Landschaft: Die Stimme auf der Bühne als theatraler Prozeß', *Forum Modernes Theater*, 14/2 (1999): 144–72.

Pütz, Peter, *Die Zeit im Drama. Zur Technik dramatischer Spannung* (Göttingen: Vandenhoeck und Ruprecht, 1977 [1970]).

Quadri, Franco/Bertoni, Franco/Stearns, Robert, *Robert Wilson* (New York: Rizzoli, 1998).

Radosavljević, Duška, *The Contemporary Ensemble. Interviews with Theatre-Makers* (London/New York: Routledge, 2013).

Rahmer, Sigismund, *Heinrich von Kleist als Mensch und Dichter. Nach neuen Quellenforschungen* (Berlin: Reimer, 1909).

Rajewsky, Irina, *Intermedialität* (Tübingen/Basel: UTB, 2002).

Rambo-Hood, Markee, 'Postdramatic Musicality in The Black Rider', *Networking Knowledge: Journal of the MeCCSA Postgraduate Network*, 3/2 (2010): 1–11.

Reason, Dana, '"Navigable Structures and Transforming Mirrors". Improvisation and Interactivity', in David Fischlin/Ajay Heble (eds.), *The Other Side of Nowhere. Jazz, Improvisation, and Communities in Dialogue* (Middletown, CT: Wesleyan University Press, 2004): 71–83.

Rebstock, Matthias, 'Composed Theatre: Mapping the Field', in Matthias Rebstock/David Roesner (eds.), *Composed Theatre. Aesthetics, Practices & Processes* (Bristol: Intellect, 2012): 17–51.

Rebstock, Matthias/Roesner, David (eds.), *Composed Theatre. Aesthetics, Practices, Processes* (Bristol: Intellect, 2012).

Reininghaus, Frieder/Schneider, Katja (eds.), *Experimentelles Musik- und Tanztheater* (Laaber: Laaber, 2004).

Remshardt, Ralf Erik, 'The Skriker by Caryl Churchill', *Theatre Journal*, 47/1 (1995): 121–3.

Ridout, Nicholas, 'On the Work of Things: Musical Production, Theatrical Labor, and the "General Intellect"', *Theatre Journal*, 64/3 (2012): 389–408.

Riemann, Hugo, *System der musikalischen Rhythmik und Metrik* (Schaan, Liechtenstein: Sändig Reprint, 1981 [Leipzig, 1903]).

Riethmüller, Albrecht (ed.), *Brecht und seine Komponisten* (Laaber: Laaber, 2000).

Robinson, Harlow, 'Love for Three Operas: The Collaboration of Vsevolod Meyerhold and Sergei Prokofiev', *The Russian Review*, 45/3 (1986): 287–304.

Rockwell, John (ed.), *Robert Wilson: The Theater of Images* (New York: Contemporary Arts Center, Byrd Hoffman Foundation, 1984).

Rodenburg, Patsy, *The Actor Speaks: Voice and the Performer* (London: Methuen Drama, 1997).

Roesner, David, *Theater als Musik. Verfahren der Musikalisierung in chorischen Theaterformen bei Christoph Marthaler, Einar Schleef und Robert Wilson* (Tübingen: Gunter Narr, 2003).

———, 'The Politics of the Polyphony of Performance: Musicalization in Contemporary German Theatre', *Contemporary Theatre Review*, 18/1 (2008): 44–55.

———, '"An entirely new art form" – Katie Mitchells intermediale Bühnen-Experimente', *Forum Modernes Theater*, 24/2 (2009): 101–19.

———, 'Musicking as *Mise en scène*', *Studies in Musical Theatre*, 4/1 (2010): 89–102.

———, 'Musicality as a paradigm for the theatre – a kind of manifesto', *Studies in Musical Theatre*, 4/3 (2010): 293–306.

———, 'Musikalisches Theater – Szenische Musik', in Anno Mungen (ed.), *Mitten im Leben. Musiktheater von der Oper bis zur Everyday-Performance mit Musik* (Würzburg: Königshausen & Neumann, 2011): 193–211.

———, '"It is not about labelling, it's about understanding what we do" – Composed theatre as discourse', in Matthias Rebstock/David Roesner (eds.), *Composed Theatre. Aesthetics, Practices, Processes* (Bristol: Intellect, 2012): 319–62.

———, 'Musikalität als ästhetisches Dispositiv: Analogien und Transfers', in Jörg Huber/Roberto Nigro/Elke Bippus (eds.), *Ästhetik x Dispositiv. Die Erprobung von Erfahrungsfeldern* (Zürich/Wien/New York: Edition Voldemeer, 2012): 195–206.

Roselt, Jens, *Seelen mit Methode. Schauspieltheorien von Barock- bis zum postdramatischen Theater* (Berlin: Alexander Verlag, 2005).

———, 'Vom Diener zum Despoten. Zur Vorgeschichte der modernen Theaterregie im 19. Jahrhundert', in Nicole Gronemeyer/Bernd Stegemann (eds.), *Lektionen: Regie* (Berlin: Theater der Zeit, 2009): 23–37.

———, 'Menschendarstellung – was denn sonst?', in Anton Rey/Hajo Kurzenberger/Stephan Müller (eds.), *Wirkungsmaschine Schauspieler – Vom Menschendarsteller zum multifunktionalen Spielemacher* (Berlin/Köln: Alexander Verlag, 2011): 20–28.

Roselt, Jens/Weiler, Christel (eds.), *Schauspielen heute. Die Bildung des Menschen in den performativen Künsten* (Bielefeld: transcript, 2011).

Roudané, Matthew, *The Cambridge Companion to Sam Shepard* (Cambridge: Cambridge University Press, 2002).

Rudlin, John, 'Jacques Copeau: The Quest for Sincerity', in Alison Hodge (ed.), *Twentieth Century Actor Training* (London: Routledge, 2000): 43–62.

Rudnitsky, Konstantin, *Meyerhold the Director* (Ann Arbor: Ardis, 1981).

Sacher, Reinhard Josef, *Musik als Theater. Tendenzen zur Grenzüberschreitung in der Musik von 1958–1968* (Regensburg: Bosse, 1985).

Sacks, Oliver, *Musicophilia: Tales of Music and the Brain* (New York: Knopf, 2007).

Safir, Margery Arent, *Robert Wilson from Within* (London: Sylph Editions, 2011).

St John, Graham (ed.), *Rave Culture and Religion* (London: Routledge, 2004).

Salzman, Eric/Desi, Thomas, *The New Music Theatre* (Oxford: Oxford University Press, 2008).

Sandner, Wolfgang (ed.), *Heiner Goebbels. Komposition als Inszenierung* (Berlin: Henschel, 2002).

Saussure, Ferdinand de, *Cours de linguistique générale* (Paris: Payot, 1922).

Savarese, Nicola, '1931 Antonin Artaud Sees Balinese Theatre at the Paris Colonial Exposition', *TDR*, 45/3 (2001): 51–77.

Savran, David, 'The Search for America's Soul: Theatre in the Jazz Age', *Theatre Journal*, 58/3 (2006): 459–76.

———, *Highbrow/Lowdown: Theater, Jazz, and the Making of the New Middle Class* (Ann Arbor: University of Michigan Press, 2009).

Sawyer, R. Keith, *Group Creativity. Music, Theater, Collaboration* (Mahwah, NJ/ London: Lawrence Erlbaum [Kindle Edition], 2007 [2003]).

Schaeffer, Pierre, *Traité des objets musicaux: Essai interdisciplines* (Paris: Éditions du Seuil, 1966).

Schafer, R. Murray, *The Soundscape: Our Sonic Environment and the Tuning of the World* (Rochester, VT: Destiny Books, 1994).

Scheer, Edward (ed.), *Antonin Artaud. A Critical Reader* (London: Routledge, 2004).

Scher, Steven Paul (ed.), *Literatur und Musik. Ein Handbuch zur Theorie und Praxis eines komparatistischen Grenzgebietes* (Berlin: Erich Schmidt Verlag, 1984).

——— (ed.), *Music and Text: Critical Inquiries* (Cambridge: Cambridge University Press, 1992).

Schläder, Jürgen, *Oper Macht Theater Bilder: Neue Wirklichkeiten des Regietheaters* (Berlin: Henschel, 2006).

——— (ed.), *Das Experiment der Grenze. Ästhetische Entwürfe im Neuesten Musiktheater* (Berlin: Henschel, 2009).

Schmidt, Beate A./Altenburg, Detlef (eds.), *Musik und Theater um 1800* (Sinzig/ Rhein: Studio Verlag, 2012).

Schmidt, Christina, *Tragödie als Bühnenform: Einar Schleefs Chor-Theater* (Bielefeld: transcript, 2010).

Schmidt, Paul (ed.), *Meyerhold at Work* (Manchester: Carcanet New Press, 1981).

Schnebel, Dieter, 'Sprache als Musik in der Musik', in Steven Paul Scher (ed.), *Literatur und Musik* (Berlin: Erich Schmidt Verlag, 1984): 209–20.

Schnell, Ralf, 'Einleitung', *Die Zeitschrift für Literaturwissenschaft und Linguistik (Lili): Thema: Musikalität*, 141/1 [Online] (2006), http://www.uni-siegen.de/ lili/ausgaben/2006/lili141.html?lang=de [11.07.2011].

Schnitzler, Günter/Spaude, Edelgard (eds.), *Intermedialität. Studien zur Wechselwirkung zwischen den Künsten* (Freiburg im Breisgau: Rombach Verlag: 2004).

Schoenmakers, Henri/Bläske, Stefan/Kirchmann, Kay/Ruchatz, Jens (eds.), *Theater und Medien. Grundlagen – Analysen – Perspektiven* (Bielefeld: transcript, 2008).

290 *Musicality in Theatre*

Schramm, Helmar, *Karneval des Denkens. Theatralität im Spiegel philosophischer Texte des 16. und 17. Jahrhunderts* (Berlin: Akademie Verlag, 1996).

Schröter, Jens, 'Intermedialität', http://www.theorie-der-medien.de/text_detail. php?nr=12 [20.02.2006].

Schwarz, Monika, *Musikanaloge Ideen und Struktur im französischen Theater: Untersuchungen zu Jean Tardieu und Eugene Ionesco* (München: W. Fink, 1981).

Seibt, Oliver, *Der Sinn des Augenblicks. Überlegungen zu einer Musikwissenschaft im Alltäglichen* (Bielefeld: transcript, 2010).

Seidel, Wilhelm, *Über Rhythmustheorien der Neuzeit* (Bern/München: Francke, 1975).

———, *Rhythmus – eine Begriffsbestimmung* (Darmstadt: Wissenschaftliche Buchgesellschaft, 1976).

———, 'Absolute Musik', in Ludwig Finscher (ed.), *Die Musik in Geschichte und Gegenwart. Sachteil Band 1* (Kassel: Bärenreiter/Metzler, 1994): 15–23.

Serafine, Mary Louise, *Music as Cognition. The Development of Thought in Sound* (New York: Columbia University Press, 1988).

Shepard, Sam, *Four two-act plays* (London: Faber, 1981).

———, *Hawk Moon: A Book of Short Stories, Poems, and Monologues* (New York: Performing Arts Journal Publications, 1981).

Shevtsova, Maria, *Robert Wilson* (London/New York: Routledge, 2007).

Shryane, Jennifer, 'Sprich zu mir in Seuchensprache/Speak to Me in Plague Language (Vanadium-i-ching, 1983): An Analysis of Einstürzende Neubauten as Artaudian Artists', *Studies in Theatre and Performance*, 30/3 (2010): 323–40.

Siegmund, Gerald, 'Task Performance als Choreographie. Die Aufgabe des Schauspielers', in Wolfgang Sandner (ed.), *Heiner Goebbels. Komposition als Inszenierung* (Berlin: Henschel, 2002): 127–31.

Sierz, Aleks, *The Theatre of Martin Crimp* (London: Methuen Drama, 2006).

Simhandl, Peter, *Bildertheater. Bildende Künstler des 20. Jahrhunderts als Theaterreformer* (Berlin: Gadegast, 1993).

Simonov, Ruben Nikolaevich, *Stanislavsky's Protégé: Eugene Vakhtangov* (New York: Drama Book Specialists, 1969).

Sloboda, John A., *The Musical Mind. The Cognitive Psychology of Music* (Oxford: Oxford University Press, 1985).

Small, Christopher, *Music. Society. Education* (London: John Calder, 1980).

———, *Musicking: The Meanings of Performing and Listening* (Hanover: University Press of New England, 1998).

Smart, Jacqueline/Mermikides, Alex, 2009 (eds.), *Devising in Process* (London: Palgrave/Macmillan, 2009).

Smith, Bruce R., *The Acoustic World of Early Modern England* (Chicago: University of Chicago Press, 1999).

Smith, Matthew Wilson, *The Total Work of Art* (London/New York: Routledge, 2007).

Sollich, Robert/Risi, Clemens/Reus, Sebastian/Jöris, Stephan (eds.), *Angst vor der Zerstörung: Der Meister Künste zwischen Archiv und Erneuerung* (Berlin: Theater der Zeit, 2008).

Souksengphet-Dachlauer, Anna, *Text als Klangmaterial. Heiner Müllers Texte in Heiner Goebbels' Hörstücken* (Bielefeld: transcript, 2010).

Soules, Marshall, 'Improvising Character: Jazz, the Actor, and Protocols of Improvisation', in Daniel Fischlin/Ajay Heble (eds.), *The Other Side of Nowhere: Jazz, Improvisation, and Communities in Dialogue* (Middletown, CT: Wesleyan University Press, 2004): 268–97.

Spatz, Ben, 'To Open a Person: Song and Encounter at Gardzienice and the Workcenter', *Theatre Topics*, 18/2 (2008): 205–22.

———, 'Citing Musicality: Performance Knowledge in the Gardzienice Archive', *Studies in Musical Theatre*, 7/2 (2013): 221–35.

Spolin, Viola, *Improvisation for the Theater. Third Edition* (Evanston, IL: Northwestern University Press 1999 [1963]).

Staniewski, Włodzimierz/Hodge, Alison, *Hidden Territories: The Theatre of Gardzienice* (London/New York: Routledge, 2004).

Stein, Gertrude, *Lectures in America* (Boston: Beacon Press, 1935).

———, *Last Operas and Plays. With an Introduction by Bonnie Marranca* (Baltimore/London: Johns Hopkins University Press, 1995).

Stein, Philipp, *Goethe als Theaterleiter* (Berlin/Leipzig: Schuster & Loeffler, 1904).

Stein, Susan Alyson, 'Kandinsky and Abstract Stage Composition: Practice and Theory, 1909–12', *Art Journal*, 43/1 (1983): 61–6.

Steiner, Christiane, *Text und Theatralität in Frank Castorfs König-Lear-Inszenierung* (MA Thesis, FU Berlin, 1996).

Stemann, Nicolas, 'Nicolas Stemann im Gespräch mit Nicole Gronemeyer und Bernd Stegemann', in Nicole Gronemeyer/Bernd Stegemann (eds.), *Lektionen: Regie* (Berlin: Theater der Zeit, 2009): 169–77.

Stephan, Rudolf (ed.), *Über Musik und Sprache* (Mainz: Schotts Söhne, 1974).

Stourac, Richard/McCreery, Kathleen, *Theatre As a Weapon: Workers' Theatre in the Soviet Union, Germany and Britain, 1917–1934* (London: Taylor & Francis, 1986).

Sutherland, Ian/Acord, Sophie Krzys, 'Thinking with Art: From Situated Knowledge to Experiential Knowing', *Journal of Visual Art Practice*, 6/2 (2007): 125–40.

Sutton, R. Anderson, 'South-east Asia', in Stanley Sadie (ed.), *New Grove Dictionary of Music and Musicians, 2nd edition, Vol. 24* (London: Macmillan, 2001): 94–107.

Switzky, Lawrence, 'Hearing Double: "Accousmatic" Authority and the Rise of the Theatre Director', *Modern Drama*, 54/2 (2011): 216–43.

Symonds, Dominic 'The Corporeality of Musical Expression: "The Grain of the Voice" and the Actor-musician', *Studies in Musical Theatre*, 1/2 (2007): 167–82.

Symonds, Dominic/Taylor, Millie (eds.), *Gestures of Music Theater: The Performativity of Song and Dance* (Oxford: Oxford University Press, 2014).

Tairov, Alexander, *Notes of a Director, trans. William Kuhlke* (Coral Gables, FL: University of Miami Press, 1969).

————, *Das entfesselte Theater: Aufzeichnungen eines Regisseurs* (Berlin: Alexander-Verlag, 1989 [1923]).

Tan, Marcus Cheng Chye, *Acoustic Interculturalism: Listening to Performance* (Basingstoke: Palgrave Macmillan, 2012).

Tardieu, Jean, *Théâtre de chambre* (Paris: Gallimard, 1966).

————, *La Sonate et les trois messieurs ou Comment parler musique* (Paris: Gallimard, 2003 [1956]).

Taylor, Millie, *Music in Theatre: Towards a Methodology for Examining the Interaction of Music and Drama in Theatre Works of the Twentieth Century.*' (PhD Thesis, Exeter, 2000).

Taylor-Batty, Mark/Taylor-Batty, Juliette, *Samuel Beckett's Waiting for Godot* (London/New York: Continuum, 2008).

Terwen, Jan Willem, *Gamelan in the 19th Century Netherlands: An Encounter Between East and West* (Utrecht: Koninklijke VNM, Koninklijke Vereniging voor Nederlandse Muziekgeschiedenis, 2009).

Thalheimer, Michael, 'Director Michael Thalheimer Interviewed by David Roesner' (Phone conversation, 20.06.2012).

Thomaidis, Konstantinos, 'Singing from Stones. Physiovocality and Gardzienice's Theatre of Musicality', in Dominic Symonds/Millie Taylor (eds.), *Gestures of Music Theater: The Performativity of Song and Dance* (Oxford: Oxford University Press, 2014), pp. 242–58.

Thomas, Ed, 'Flowers of the Dead Red Sea', in Brian Mitchell (ed.), *Ed Thomas: Three Plays* (Bridgend: Seren, 1994): 101–66.

Thomas, Troy, 'Interart Analogy: Practice and Theory in Comparing the Arts', *Journal of Aesthetic Education*, 25/2 (1991): 17–36.

Thomson, Peter/Sacks, Glendyr (eds.), *The Cambridge Companion to Brecht. 2nd Edition* (Cambridge: Cambridge University Press, 2006).

Tigges, Stefan (ed.), *Dramatische Transformationen. Zu gegenwärtigen Schreib- und Aufführungsstrategien im deutschsprachigen Theater* (Bielefeld: transcript, 2008).

Till, Nicholas, '"I don't mind if something's operatic, just as long it's not opera". A Critical Practice for New Opera and Music Theatre', *Contemporary Theatre Review*, 14/1 (2004): 15–24.

————, 'Investigating the Entrails: Post-operatic Music Theatre in Europe', in Nicholas Ridout/Joe Kelleher (eds.), *Contemporary Theatres in Europe. A Critical Companion* (London/New York: Routledge, 2006): 34–46.

————, *Cambridge Companion to Opera Studies* (Cambridge: Cambridge University Press, 2012).

————, 'Stefano Gervasoni's "Pas Si": Staging a Music Theatre Work Based On a Text by Samuel Beckett', *Contemporary Theatre Review*, 23/2 (2013): 220–32.

Tobias, James, 'Cinema, Scored. Toward a Comparative Methodology for Music in Media', *Film Quarterly*, 57/2 (2003): 26–36.

Tomkin, Calvin, 'Time to think', in John Rockwell (ed.), *Robert Wilson: The Theater of Images* (New York: Contemporary Arts Center, Byrd Hoffman Foundation, 1984): 54–95.

Totzeva, Sophia, *Das theatrale Potential des dramatischen Textes: ein Beitrag zur Theorie von Drama und Dramenübersetzung* (Tübingen: Gunter Narr Verlag, 1995).

Trehub, Susan E., 'The Developmental Origins of Musicality', *Nature Neuroscience*, 6/7 (2003): 669–73.

Truax, Barry, *Handbook for Acoustic Ecology* (Vancouver: Cambridge Street Publishing, 1999).

Turk, Horst (ed.), *Theater und Drama: theoretische Konzepte von Corneille bis Dürrenmatt* (Tübingen: Gunter Narr, 1992).

Turner, Cathy/Behrndt, Synne K. *Dramaturgy and Performance* (Basingstoke/New York: Palgrave Macmillan, 2007).

Turner, J. Clifford, *Voice & Speech in the Theatre* (London: A&C Black, 1993 [1950]).

Vieusseux, Annette, 'Rehearsal Diary of Filter's *The Caucasian Chalk Circle*, National Theatre' (2006), http://www.stagework.org.uk/webdav/harmonise@ Page%252F@id=6016&Section%252F@id=1605.html [08.08.2012].

Voegelin, Salomé, *Listening to Noise and Silence. Towards a Philosophy of Sound Art* (New York/London: Continuum, 2010).

Volbach, Walther R., *Adolphe Appia. Prophet of the Modern Theatre. A Profile* (Middletown, CT: Wesleyan University Press, 1968).

Vourloumis, Hypatia, '"My Dog Girl": Cok Sawitri's Agrammaticality, Affect and Balinese Feminist Performance', in Laura Noszlopy/Matthew Isaac Cohen (eds.), *Contemporary Southeast Asian Performance: Transnational Perspectives* (Newcastle upon Tyne: Cambridge Scholars Publishing, 2010): 107–31.

Wachtangow, Jewgeni B., *Schriften* (Berlin: Henschel Verlag, 1982).

Wagner, Monika, *'Das' Material der Kunst: Eine andere Geschichte der Moderne* (München: Beck, 2001).

Walsh, Enda, *Disco Pigs. Sucking Dublin. Two plays* (London: Nick Hern Books, 1997).

———, *Bedbound & Misterman. Two Plays by Enda Walsh* (London: Nick Hern Books, 2001).

Walton, J. Michael (ed.), *Craig on Theatre* (London: Methuen, 1999).

Walwei-Wiegelmann, Hedwig (ed.), *Goethes Gedanken über Musik. Eine Sammlung aus seinen Werken, Briefen, Gesprächen und Tagebüchern* (Frankfurt am Main: Insel Verlag, 1985).

Weber-Lucks, Theda, *Körperstimmen. Vokale Performancekunst als neue musikalische Gattung* (PhD Thesis, TU Berlin 2005).

Weiler, Christel, 'Dramaturgie', in Erika Fischer-Lichte/Doris Kolesch/Matthias Warstat (eds.), *Metzler Lexikon Theatertheorie* (Stuttgart: Metzler, 2005): 80–83.

Weiss, Allen S., 'Mouths of Disquietude: Valère Novarina between the Theatre of Cruelty and Écrits Bruts', *TDR*, 37/2 (1993): 80–94.

Wellbery, David E., *Lessing's Laocoon: Semiotics and Aesthetics in the Age of Reason* (Cambridge: Cambridge University Press, 2009).

Welsch, Wolfgang, 'Auf dem Weg zu einer Kultur des Hörens?', in Arnica-Verena Langenmaier (ed.), *Der Klang der Dinge. Akustik – eine Aufgabe des Design* (München: Silke Schreiber, 1993): 86–111.

Welton, Martin, *Feeling Theatre* (Basingstoke: Palgrave Macmillan 2011).

Whitelaw, Billie, *Billie Whitelaw ... Who He?* (London: Hodder & Stoughton, 1995).

Wild, Katharina, *Schönheit. Die Schauspieltheorie Edward Gordon Craigs* (Berlin: Theater der Zeit, 2011).

Williams, David (ed.), *Collaborative Theatre: The Théâtre du Soleil Sourcebook* (London: Routledge, 1999).

Wilson, Robert, 'Production Notes on the *King of Spain*, a Play Presented by the Byrd Hoffmann School of Byrds', in William M. Hoffman (ed.), *New American Plays, vol. III* (New York: Hill & Wang, 1970): 245–72.

———, 'The Space in the Text: An Interview with Robert Wilson. Moderator: Andrzej Wirth', in Sigrid Bauschinger/Susan Cocalis (eds.), *Vom Wort zum Bild. Das neue Theater in Deutschland und in den USA* (Bern: Francke, 1992 [1988]): 245–56.

Windrich, Friedrich J., *TechnoTheater: Dramaturgie und Philosophie bei Rainald Goetz und Thomas Bernhard* (München: Fink, 2007).

Wolf, Werner, *The Musicalization of Fiction. A Study in the Theory and History of Intermediality* (Amsterdam: Rodopi, 1999).

Worrall, Nick, *Modernism to Realism on the Soviet Stage. Tairov — Vakhtangov — Okhlopkov* (Cambridge: Cambridge University Press, 1989).

Worth, Libby, 'On Text and Dance: New Questions and New Forms', in Elaine Aston/Elin Diamond (eds.), *The Cambridge Companion to Caryl Churchill* (Cambridge: Cambridge University Press, 2009): 71–87.

Wulf, Christoph/Fischer-Lichte, Erika (eds.), *Gesten. Inszenierung, Aufführung, Praxis* (München: Fink, 2010).

Yacobi, Tamar, 'Interart Narrative: (Un)Reliability and Ekphrasis', *Poetics Today*, 21/4 (2000): 711–49.

Yob, Iris M., 'Why is Music a Language of Spirituality?', *Philosophy of Music Education Review*, 18/2 (2010): 145–51.

Zarrilli, Phillip, *Acting (Re)considered: A Theoretical and Practical Guide* (London/New York: Routledge, 2002).

Zavros, Demetris, 'Composing Theatre on a Diagonal: Metaxi ALogon, a Music-centric Performance', in Matthias Rebstock/David Roesner (eds.), *Composed Theatre. Aesthetics, Practices, Processes* (Bristol: Intellect, 2012): 201–19.

Zimmermann, Bernhard (ed.), *Antike Dramentheorien und ihre Rezeption* (Stuttgart: M & P, 1992).

Index